SHREK

From the Swamp to the Screen

John Hopkins

HARRY N. ABRAMS, INC., PUBLISHERS

Foreword
Mike Myers 7

Part 1
A Big, Green Ogre Is Born 9

Part 2
We're Definitely Not
in the Swamp Anymore 51

Part 3
So Close, Yet So Far Far Away 91

Part 4
Warts and All 117

Part 5
Happily Ever After 155

Credits 168

Acknowledgments 175

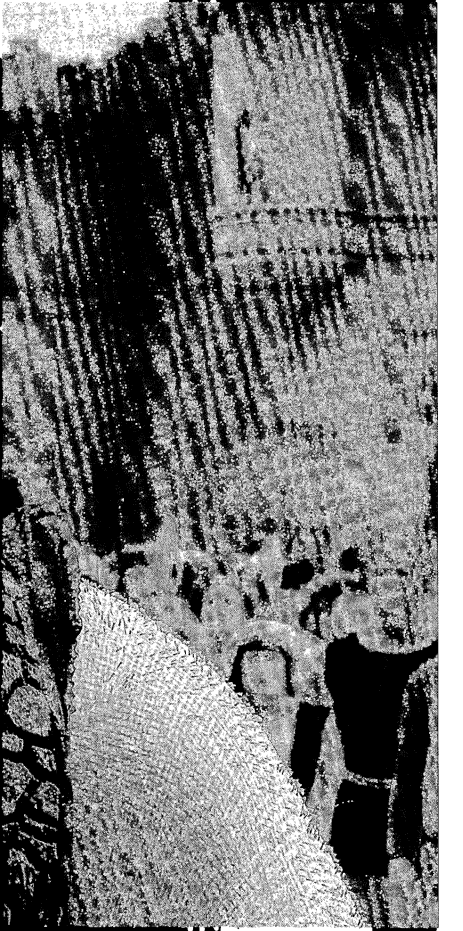

Foreword

Shrek is the first animated character I've ever voiced, so it took me a while to get to know him. At first, I did Shrek as a Canadian, and everybody was happy with how it turned out, but I knew I could give it more. I finally made a connection. I had good friends growing up in Canada who had Scottish fathers. What always struck me about their fathers was that they were incredibly passionate and could go from "I love you" to "Get out of my house!" in a matter of seconds. Of course, none of them were, in fact, ogres, but the fit was undeniable. I put the voice to the test, and everyone agreed that I had found Shrek.

Shrek 2 gave me a chance to explore Shrek's character even further. I had to relate to another identity crisis of Shrek's as he is thrust into the possibility of not being accepted by his in-laws. In the end, he *is* accepted, but not without a tremendous amount of effort on his part. I think the movie proves that you can't wait for your "happily ever after" to come to you; you have to pursue it with unwavering dedication and, yes, passion.

That same brand of passion (without the "Get out of my house!" volatility, of course) is a metaphor for everything I've experienced during the making of these two films. On the first film, I immediately knew I was dealing with a group of people who not only had the talent to potentially make something wonderful but who had the fervor to make it so. Director Andrew Adamson, Executive Producer Jeffrey Katzenberg, Producers Aron Warner and David Lipman, and the teams at DreamWorks and PDI have taken fairy tales, turned them on their head, and breathed new life into a much needed and much loved genre. And I, along with the millions of viewers who love these films, can't thank them enough for it.

To me, the people of DreamWorks and PDI are simply magicians. However, you have in your hands a book that tells the secrets of how these guys have done their tricks. I hope you enjoy it.

Mike Myers

Part 1
A Big, Green Ogre Is Born

n 1994, Laurie MacDonald, co-head of DreamWorks Motion Pictures, handed DreamWorks co-founder Jeffrey Katzenberg a copy of the children's book *Shrek!*, which John Williams had brought to her attention.

So Katzenberg took a look at the book by William Steig . . . a long look, and discovered a most unusual tale. In it, there were no handsome princes or virtuous damsels in distress, no dancing bears or singing mermaids. Instead, there was an ogre who was so ugly "any snake dumb enough to bite him instantly got convulsions and died." He ventured forth (after being kicked out by his loathsome parents), seeking neither fame nor fortune. Far from it. He wandered about rather aimlessly, and nothing delighted him more than repulsing every living creature that populated the countryside. And his smell! The less said about that the better.

So what did Katzenberg (and countless children around the world) see in this special but very peculiar tale? "Irreverence, humor, and a wonderful heart," says Katzenberg. His idea was to meld the story potential of *Shrek!* with what was then state-of-the-art computer-generated (CG) animation. And so, somehow, Dream-Works in association with Pacific Data Images (PDI) would have to take this very unusual fairy tale and expand it into a full-length animated feature.

Once upon a time there was a lovely princess

She was locked away in a castle guarded by a terrible fire-breathing dragon

"Let's be honest people— without that book none of us would be here. **"**

— Shrek

> *"I think I feel a little differently than other people do. For some reason I've never felt grown up."*
>
> —William Steig, the author of *Shrek!*

Caldecott Award–winning author and illustrator William Steig was an artist impossible to categorize. His career as a cartoonist for the *New Yorker*, which spanned more than six decades, often involved brutally funny insights into the romantic foibles of men and women. Yet, he was also the author of more than twenty-five children's books, among them *Shrek!* Lee Lorenz, Steig's biographer and cartoon editor at the *New Yorker* for years, said, "He's like Thurber: He doesn't have any offspring."

Born and raised in New York, he graduated from high school at fifteen and supported his family during the Depression by selling his drawings. (His unusual education involved City College, the National Academy of Design, and five days at Yale, prompting his admission that he had a "defective education.") Among Steig's most popular characters were irreverent kids fearlessly speaking their minds. A famous cartoon of the time showed a small boy at the dinner table announcing to his parents, "I say it's spinach and I say the hell with it."

As early as 1936 he was blazing new, highly creative paths. Besides wood carvings (displayed at the Downtown Gallery), he embarked on a series of personal "symbolic drawings" that showed people in the grip of powerful human emotions, such as shame or embarrassment. The *New Yorker* rejected them as too idiosyncratic for the magazine, but when issued as a series of books in the late 1930s and '40s (*About People*, *The Lonely Ones*, and *All Embarrassed*) they drew enthusiastic praise from anthropologist Margaret Mead and psychoanalysts such as A. A. Brill.

Steig was married four times, and in the 1950s penned a series of mordant drawings of men and women trapped in the pit of romantic illusion and despair. A famous image from the book *The Rejected Lovers* shows a little man being squashed under the sole of a woman's shoe, yet rapturously clinging to her high heel. The caption reads: "What a woman!" In appraising these painful drawings, Steig commented, "I think it should be obvious that I like women."

Yet another creative tributary opened for Steig in 1968 with a famous series of children's books, such as *CDB!* (as in "see the bee") and *Roland the Minstrel Pig*. He extended this foray into the world of childhood with children's novels, such as *Dominic*, about a dog, and *Abel's Island*, about a mouse. It seems paradoxical that a man so penetrating and rueful about romantic relationships would also have the theme of family running throughout his work. But it's this tension of tenderness and shocking honesty that gives Steig's creations, including *Shrek!*, such power.

Among the early renderings of the Shrek character is this version, which is closely aligned to Steig's original ogre.

But how exactly would Katzenberg and others build upon this slender, but very funny, volume? For *Shrek* director Andrew Adamson (who would go on to direct *Shrek 2* as well) a starting point was the moment in the book when "Shrek has a nightmare with butterflies and children skipping around with flowers. That's an inversion of the expected. It's kind of like turning what we think is beautiful on its ear. And so to me, as an extension of that, it was finding in every aspect of the story—'How can we take this and from Shrek's point of view make it not what you expect?'"

Yet, the book has few actual events. *Shrek* director Vicky Jenson notes, "It's a small book, but it does set a tone. . . . The main characters are there. A basic progression of what happens is there. But it's a twenty-page storybook. Turning it into a movie requires a little more than just adaptation. It needed more plot. But what's at the heart of it is much the same as far as attitude goes."

Certainly, the unique irreverence of the book would have to be preserved. At the same time, however, Shrek as a character does not exactly grow or develop in a way capable of sustaining an entire feature-length motion picture. It was obvious the creators would have to delve within the character of the ogre himself and discover the very human hopes, fears, conflicts, and dreams of a classic movie hero. As Adamson put it, it was a task of "deconstructing traditional fairy tales and reconstructing a new fairy tale."

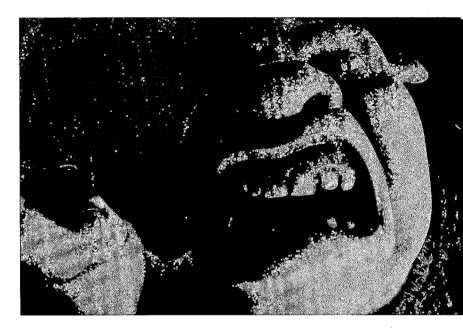

"Man, that first Shrek was one nasty dude! Cool but nasty! He had this flame thing shooting out of his mouth, turning knights in armor red-hot like a lobster. It was wild! And his face . . . Ewwwww! Man! You think Shrek's ugly now!"

— Donkey

The other part of Katzenberg's idea was equally challenging: using CG technology to transform *Shrek* from the static world of the page into a highly realistic 3-D world that only computer-generated animation was capable of producing. "The story itself was sort of a fractured fairy tale," says Katzenberg. "And I thought the animation technique should be as different as the story and the sensibility of the movie. In other words, visually it needed to be different. And that would help define it as being different."

Yet, as impressive as CG animation was at the time, it was still a relatively new art form. It had significant limitations, including a rather sterile "CG look" to settings and backgrounds, as well as human characters of limited mobility or expressiveness. Pixar's *Toy Story*, considered by many at PDI/DreamWorks to be the *Snow White* of CG animation, exploited these limitations brilliantly, with its relatively simple toy characters set against a visually striking, but bleak, suburban environment. PDI/DreamWorks's *Antz* marked a significant advance in CG animation, with its groundbreaking use of proprietary facial- and fluid-animation technology.

But if *Shrek*, both as a character and as a world, was to have the emotional depth and dimension its creators wanted, the state of the art would have to advance considerably. As *Shrek 2* director Kelly Asbury recalls, "The original thought was, there's never been much success with organic characters with good facial animation. And that was Jeffrey's initial call, to do a CG animation film that really had an organic quality to it."

Story development proved equally challenging. After Chris Farley worked for a year as the first voice of Shrek, his untimely death threw the production into one of its most difficult stages. Much of the film had been built around Farley's comedic persona, and, as Adamson recalls, "There was a period of time when we were trying to re-find the movie without Chris, and we ended up making a movie . . . that was just too conservative, too traditional."

A major turning point was when Mike Myers agreed to take on the role of Shrek. Suddenly, a fresh perspective was brought to the role that the creators could start building upon. "It really is impossible to give Mike Myers too much credit for the contributions he has made," says Katzenberg, "not only in *Shrek* but once again in *Shrek 2*. He had an

extraordinary impact on the movie." It was during this phase that the story developed in several crucial ways: the idea of populating Shrek's world with a multitude of fairy-tale characters took root, along with Shrek's cynicism about being stuck in a fairy-tale world.

Shrek 2 producer Aron Warner (who also produced *Shrek*) points out several other concurrent developments: "One of them was starting the movie in an outhouse. That was a really big turning point. For some reason you suddenly had this idea of, 'Oh, that's who Shrek is. He's reading this fairy tale, he thinks it's crap, we love it but we also think it has been hackneyed and overused.' This appeals to our sensibility as viewers, and it's true to the character. This development really had a kind of subtle ripple effect throughout everything."

"Aye . . . some of my best ideas come from inside the outhouse."
— Shrek

"You know you should sweep me off my feet, out yonder window, and down a rope onto your valiant steed!"

But there was something deeper to Shrek as a character that the creators were still struggling with. Recalls Katzenberg, "I think the hardest part was, 'How do you make a big, green, stinky ogre somebody an audience can fall in love with.' In the end, these movies, if they work, connect with audiences because they're allegories. The challenge here was to create a character who had enough dimension and complexity, so that we recognize that Shrek's journey is, in fact, all of our journeys . . . I'm fond of saying there's a little ogre in all of us, whether we want to admit it or not."

It was perhaps here that Mike Myers's contribution was most keenly felt. Katzenberg believes Myers, "probing to understand the character of Shrek, drove us to have to answer these questions about, 'Who is this character? And what is it that he's in search of? And what is his journey about?' And Mike is the one who really pushed us hard . . . asking the questions as well as answering them. For example, this is a character who had to come to love himself. To let go of his self-loathing. He could never receive love until he could feel good about himself. Mike really, really helped define and author that about the character."

Aron Warner points to a specific moment in the evolving story that clarified for him this essential element. "There was something that Joe Stillman, one of the writers, really cracked for us," says Warner, "which is the moment when Shrek overhears Fiona and Donkey talking in the mill. And there was something about that moment that spoke to his delicate vulnerability as a character. Everyone related to it, and you had immediate compassion for him."

Through this intricate process of trial and error a story was slowly taking shape that would provide the narrative backbone to the final *Shrek*.

By Christmas of 1999, an entire rough, storyboarded version of *Shrek* was shown for the first time. After years of struggle and setback, Adamson remembered gazing up at the screen and thinking *"that's the movie we're making. It wasn't exactly there yet, it was more of a sketch. It was like a first draft of a script."* But the core of *Shrek* as a story was finally established.

"How could anyone love an ogre? I still don't understand it.**"**

— Farquaad

TECHNICAL CHALLENGES: ACHIEVING "HYPER-REALITY"

As the story world of *Shrek* expanded and deepened, the technical challenges increased proportionally. Ironically, at the earliest stages of production, it was hoped that CG technology would provide a relatively fast, simple, and efficient way of animating *Shrek*. But as the scope and ambition of *Shrek* expanded, it was obvious the creators would demand the maximum that CG animation could offer—and then considerably more.

Shrek the movie was morphing into a visual epic, requiring a huge number of locations with diverse looks and moods. (Ultimately, there were thirty-six unique locations, more than any other CG-animated film of the time.) There were multitudes of creatures (over one thousand would end up in Shrek's swamp alone) set in an alternate world that would need to be imbued with an organic look of unprecedented detail and richness. It would fall to *Shrek* production designer James Hegedus to establish and refine an overall look and feeling for the nacent world of the film. The goal was not exact reality but, as Katzenberg puts it, a "kind of hyper-reality." Among Hegedus's strongest influences would be the works of American Realist painters Grant Wood and N. C. Wyeth, as well as the Impressionists, with their subtle color palette, warm lighting, cool shadows, and extensive use of complementary colors.

To set this "hyper-real" world in motion, the so-called Holy Grails of CG animation would have to be advanced. There would need to be "virtual forests" with billions of leaves, and clothing that wrinkles and reacts to light like real fabric. Subtle atmosphere—from the delicate early morning mist of a forest to the steaming cauldron of a volcanic lair—would need to be reproduced. Convincing lighting, a notoriously difficult task for CG animation, would have to be advanced and refined. Aron Warner recalls, "Andrew Adamson's original plan was to make the film with live-action minature sets and backgrounds and animate all the characters in CG. Our job at PDI was to convince Andrew that we could do the entire film in CG and still achieve the naturalistic lighting that at the time could only be achieved in live action."

But lighting was only part of the puzzle. The creators would also have to master other elements of nature—fire, wind, rain, and various flowing liquids—whether for an outrageous scene of Shrek showering in mud or a shot as "simple" as the pouring of a glass of milk (which, like most visual effects, requires huge computational power). Even cinematic effects such as lens flare, dolly shots that don't quite keep perfect pace with the characters, and the shaking of a handheld camera would be re-created for film-savvy audiences.

This was an intense, creative process that involved the simultaneous collaboration of every artist at PDI/Dreamworks. As *Shrek 2* producer David Lipman (who was co-executive producer on *Shrek*) describes it, there are more than "three hundred people having to

Vivid examples of PDI/DreamWorks's technical innovation in computer animation. Some of the same fluid-simulation programs used for Shrek's mud shower were also utilized for the bubbling lava surrounding the Dragon's lair.

"Shrek and Donkey, two stalwart friends,
off on a whirlwind, big city adventure."

think alike and work alike, and yet they all have different pieces that they are contributing, and it all adds up to one single thing."

Yet none of this effort would be wasted on the dubious notion of technology for the sake of technology. Instead, its sole purpose was quite simple: to so overwhelm the audience with the sense of a convincing alternate reality that they would suspend their disbelief, and thus allow the story itself to have maximum impact. Vicky Jenson says, "Everything that has been done has been done because that's what our story needed. *Nothing* gets in the way of the story. It's not like something will jump out at you and say, 'Oh my God, that's the most amazing chrome I've ever seen.' Nothing is just there for the sake of its own glory. It's all there to support the story and keep you in that world." Adds Adamson, "Just having wind blowing in the trees and things like that—it's one of those things you don't notice, but you expect it, and if it's not there you notice its absence, and that's when you lose the suspension of disbelief."

And, of course, one of the most difficult aspects of the grail would also be the most important: convincing human and humanlike characters, expressing the most delicate and fleeting of emotions. Aron Warner remembers, "The thing that was scary about *Shrek* [from a technical point of view] was the human animation, or near-human animation. And not just the look of the characters but more about, 'Could we get the performances with the subtlety that we really wanted?'" In short, "How do you get emotion from this big green guy?" Ultimately, the answer was not to be found purely in the pursuit of extreme realism. "What we're not doing is photorealism," says Katzenberg. "We're doing animation." This, then, would require a

Donkey's Top Five Favorite Bedding Materials

1. Flame-retardant hay
2. Shredded phone books
3. Hot-air popcorn
4. Green anti-static packing peanuts
5. Dux bed with innovative inner-spring system

careful, artistic blending of both the real and the unreal. The scientifically observed, as well as the broadly imagined.

All this and more would have to somehow be achieved using a technology that, if not exactly in its infancy, was still in its early stages of development. *Shrek* visual effects supervisor Ken Bielenberg explains: "Everything's a case of trial and error. For instance, we had shots of Donkey—it was actually somebody's first day in production, and they made one change which they thought was an innocent change and the next day we got renderings from about half a dozen shots with donkey looking like a Chia pet. It's just so adorable we've saved those [shots] and look back on them every once in a while for a good laugh."

A simple animator error temporarily transformed Donkey into something resembling a Chia pet.

"Adorable!? Adorable!!?? Man all I can say is — their error was my trial. It was ridiculous! Struttin' around all day, looking like Lassie with her tail plugged into a light socket! "

— Donkey

Life in the Swamp

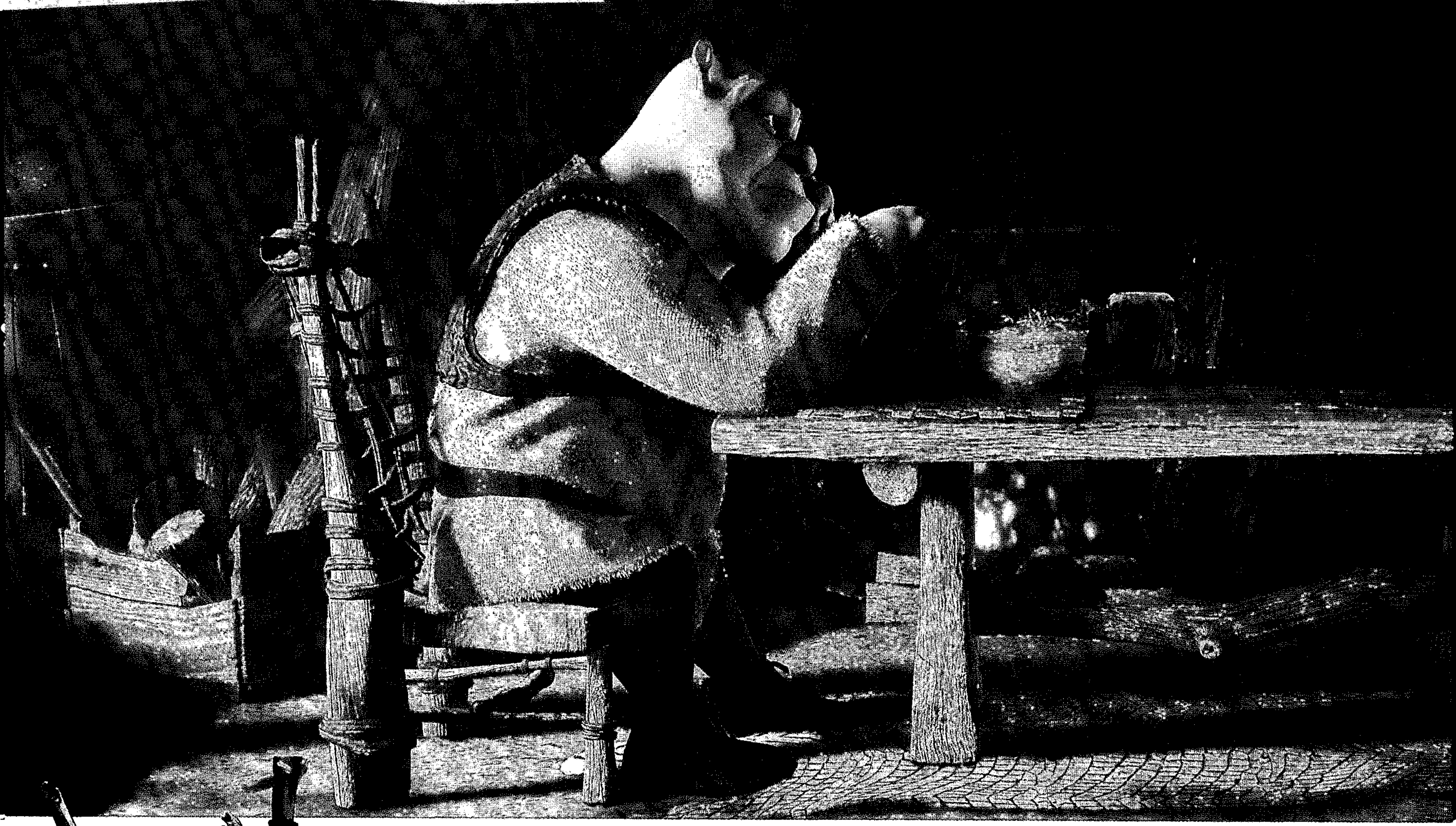

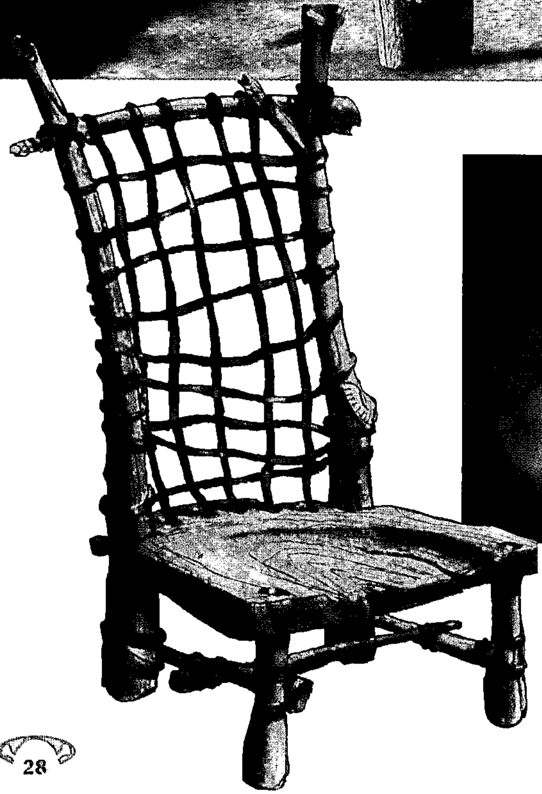

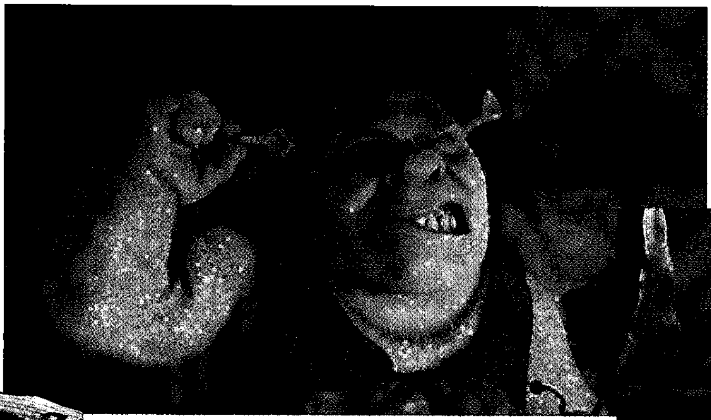

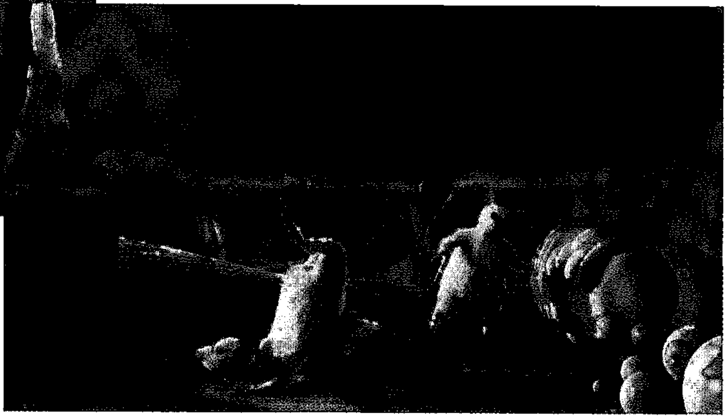

Recipe For The Perfect Swamp Martini

"One martini is not enough. Two martinis is two much. Three martinis is not enough."

Ingredients

4 ounces of super-premium swamp essence (using fresh botanicals and aromatics for distillation, creating a rare marriage of softness, clarity of taste, and appearance)

0–1 ounce of dry . . . whatever.
(It's best if skipped, anyway.)

ice

eyeball

1. Chill martini glasses* in the freezer, or simply fill with ice cubes and water, and let rest for 1 minute.
   (Shrek uses an ice-cold stream.)

2. Fill a martini shaker or any large tumbler with ice. Add swamp essence and stir for fifteen seconds.
   (Shrek prefers his martini stirred instead of shaken, so as not to "bruise" the essence.)

3. Strain liquid into martini glass and garnish with eyeball.

4. Repeat entire procedure as necessary.

Bottoms up!

*For those striving for the ultimate in authenticity, Shrek's glass consists of a corked, inverted glass funnel with a bundled twig stem and base.

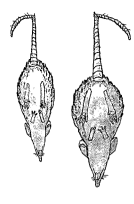

Every detail in Shrek's rustic swamp abode contributes to our understanding of his comfortable, but lonely, bachelor existence. Here, prop renderings highlight Shrek's table setting—complete with an ear-wax candle—for a quiet dinner of eels and soup. His solitude is interrupted by the Three Blind Mice, who knock over a jar of eyeballs used to garnish martinis.

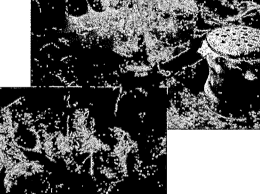

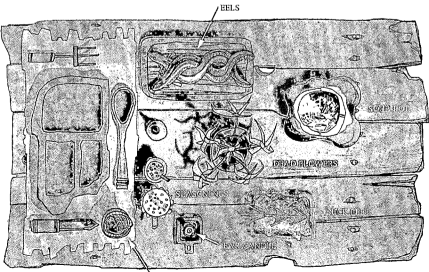

EELS

SOUP

DEAD FLOWERS

SEASONING

DUCK DATE

EAR CANDLE

NAPKIN IN CUP

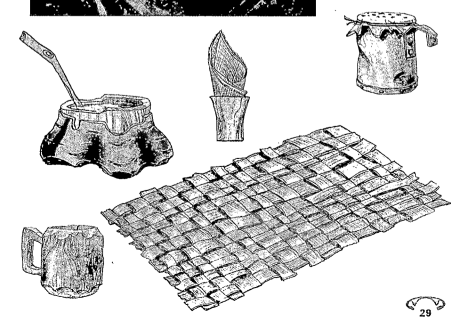

SHREK TAKES THE WORLD BY STORM

As the production of *Shrek* was nearing an end, a kind of nervous confidence began to take hold. *Shrek 2* director Conrad Vernon remembers showing the then-unreleased film at Leonard Maltin's film class at USC: "They wanted us to go there and speak and tell them how we did it . . . and I thought, 'Oh God, it's a *college* audience. These guys are *film students*. They're going to just scrutinize *everything*.' So I sat there in the back, and I was really nervous, and as soon as the opening credit sequence was finished there was applause. I mean, they all just started cheering and clapping. I was like, 'this is amazing!'"

Another prerelease screening took place when *Shrek* was invited to the Cannes film festival. For the first time in eighteen years, an animated feature was in competition. Aron Warner recalls, "I couldn't believe it. The first twenty minutes of that movie I was sunk in my seat so low, because—you've got this audience in tuxedos and gowns, and it's silence as Shrek jumps in the pond and farts. And I'm going, 'Oh my God.' . . . And then they start laughing. And then they started laughing more. And then more. And then the rest was, 'Okay, they get it.' It was harrowing and hilarious at the same time."

But this is the movie business. And despite six years of effort involving the hopes, dreams, and careers of hundreds of artists and technicians . . . despite all of the advertising and advance word of mouth . . . despite all the undeniable brilliance of *Shrek* . . . despite *everything* . . . you cannot create a hit. You can only make the best movie you and hundreds of other fellow artists are capable of making. And then, you hope for the best.

In its first weekend in release, *Shrek* had the best nonsequel opening for an animated feature ever, and for DreamWorks its best opening up to that time. To put that in perspective, *Shrek's* opening even outpaced DreamWorks' own *Gladiator*, which for an animated film was truly remarkable. In a way, what was even more astounding was its broad appeal. Audiences were split evenly among family and nonfamily. It was obvious that adults as well as children appreciated the sophisticated (and not so sophisticated) humor of *Shrek*.

Just a few of the one-sheet posters from the fifty-one countries in which *Shrek* was released

And the news got even better. In the second weekend, the film's grosses actually went up. *Shrek* went on to be the top-grossing film of 2001, with a worldwide box office of $479.2 million.

Critics were equally enthusiastic. From small local papers to *The New Yorker*, the universal appeal of *Shrek* came shining through. Said Roger Ebert, "*Shrek* is jolly and wicked, filled with sly in-jokes and yet somehow possessing a heart." Peter Rainer of *New York* magazine praised the writers Ted Elliot, Terry Rossio, Joe Stillman, and Roger S. H. Schulman for *Shrek*'s "marvelous slapstick irreverence," and was especially taken with Mike Myers's Shrek and Eddie Murphy's Donkey, "who is so funny and so gloriously an emanation of the actor that, afterwards, you might make the mistake that Murphy was actually in the movie, braying at full comic throttle."

The following year *Shrek* won the first Academy Award® exclusively for feature-length animation, and against some very tough competition. But the biggest thrill for fans was when Shrek and Donkey made a very rare public appearance on the awards show. The "big green guy" had come a long way.

It was clear that pretty much everyone who saw *Shrek* connected with its universal themes. As Jeffrey Katzenberg put it, "Each of our characters comes to understand that there's something wonderful—warts and all—about who they are. I think that's true for all of us—that the people who ultimately come to know us and love us see the strengths inside us. Whether you're a princess, a donkey, or even a big, green, stinky ogre, you can find love and happiness."

THE CHATTER BOX

Overheard Backstage at the Oscars

Donkey: I don't like these AMA awards.

Shrek: This is the Oscars, Donkey.

Donkey: Don't get me wrong, Dick Clark's an okay fella, but enough with the award shows, ya know?

Shrek: Dick Clark is not here! This is the Oscars.

Donkey: Yeah, right, every time I turn around it's like, Dick Clark! Dick Clark! Oh, hi Dick, what are you up to? You're putting on another award show? Bless you! I'll go rent a tux right away . . .

Shrek: See you later.

Donkey: . . . Speaking of tuxes, mine's really starting to ride up on me. . . . How old is Dick Clark anyhow? . . . Shrek?

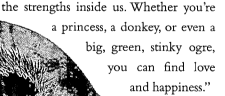

❝Love means never having to say you're smelly . . .❞

— Shrek

Shrek Character Development

Using William Steig's storybook Shrek as a point of departure, various artists conceptualized the character before Shrek arrived at his final CG form.

As with Shrek, early versions of Donkey were more stylized and cartoonlike. Although Donkey's final design is more realistic, it displays an exuberance that goes beyond the nature of an actual donkey. Anatomical modifications, such as binocular eye placement and doglike body movements, allow Donkey to convincingly interact with human characters.

Puss In Boots Character Development

"Now ye ogre, pray for mercy from Puss In Boots!"

Character sketches need to convey the entire range of physical and emotional qualities that the character will express in the story. For Puss In Boots, the task was to express feline prowess with a softer, more appealing look by blending anatomical realism and fanciful imagination.

Shrek 4-D

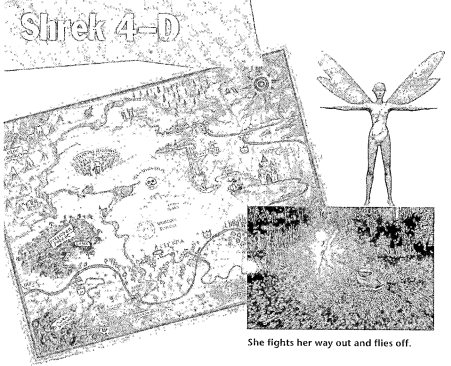

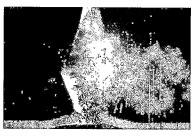

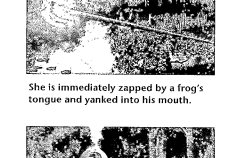

As the curtain opens, Tinkerbell appears, waves her wand, and reveals a lush storybook landscape.

She is immediately zapped by a frog's tongue and yanked into his mouth.

She fights her way out and flies off.

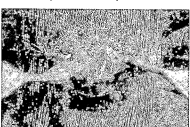

Clinging to her with its tongue, the frog is dragged along for a wild ride. Finally, she rockets through a tree—which the frog hits head-on.

Donkey: Oh, come on, Shrek, who needs a map when you got animal instinct?

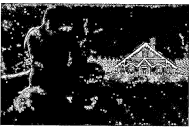

She hits Donkey in the nose, showering him with pixie dust.

Suddenly, Thelonius—on orders from the late Lord Farquaad—bolts out of the forest on horseback, leaps over Shrek and Donkey, and heads for Fiona, who has been waiting in the onion carriage.

Fiona uses her best martial-arts skills to fight him off, but Thelonius catches her. They gallop away.

Shrek: Cut to the chase, Donkey!

Thelonius, with Fiona struggling and screaming, comes upon Gingerbread Man putting the finishing touches on his house. He leaps onto and over the roof.

Shrek and Donkey, however, smash right through the front door and burst out the back of the house covered in candy.

Shrek 4-D

An essential part of the *Shrek* saga can be found in *Shrek 4-D*, a multimedia attraction featured at the Universal theme parks in Hollywood, California, Orlando, Florida, and Osaka, Japan. Picking up where *Shrek* left off, Shrek, Fiona, and Donkey are heading off for a honeymoon when they are accosted by the jealous ghost of Lord Farquaad.

Once again, the voice talents of Mike Myers, Eddie Murphy, Cameron Diaz, and John Lithgow are featured, and the project brought together much of the same team that created *Shrek* and *Shrek 2*. David Lipman, co-executive producer of *Shrek* and a producer of *Shrek 2*, wrote and produced the attraction, and *Shrek* head of layout, Simon Smith, directed. Harry Gregson-Williams, one of the composers on *Shrek*, wrote the music.

From the outset, the creators vowed to avoid what Lipman terms "a generic ride where a bunch of stuff gets busted up." Instead, they wanted an

Far ahead, Thelonius leaps through the gates of a foggy cemetery.

Shrek and Donkey hit a bump and tumble out of the carriage, which magically turns back into an onion.

Donkey: I can do this. I'm a noble steed . . . It's just a park . . . with no children and no playground.

Suddenly, Farquaad's ghost materializes from his crypt.

The stone dragon roars to life and lumbers after Shrek and Donkey on foot.

Out of nowhere, the real dragon scoops up Shrek and Donkey and takes off, with the stone dragon in hot pursuit.

The real dragon then plunges into a deep ravine, the stone dragon on her tail.

A dragon dogfight ensues.

Donkey: Like I always say, behind every successful donkey is a fire-breathing dragon!

Dragon lets loose a fireball and smashes a hole at the end of the gorge, but the stone dragon can't make it through without shearing its wings off.

attraction "that's enjoyable and entertaining, but also its own unique little adventure. It was important that it have a real narrative to it." Because *Shrek 4-D* serves as a narrative link between the two movies, it was particularly important to make sure that something established in the ride would not conflict with *Shrek 2*. "We had to keep things clean," says Lipman, "and not step on anything that was happening in *Shrek 2*."

The ride utilizes four high-resolution digital projectors. Wearing special OrgreVision glasses, audience members experience true 3-D effects such

as an aerial dogfight with a fire-breathing dragon and a plunge down a 1,000-foot waterfall. But the effects are not just visual. The audience seats are capable of both vertical and horizontal motion and have built-in tactile transducers, pneumatic air propulsion, and water-spray nodules.

Shrek 4-D is the logical extension of 3-D computer animation and represents an intriguing glimpse into its possible future. The special effects quite literally place the audience inside the action, which is simultaneously hilarious and hair-raising.

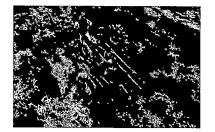

Meanwhile, at the top of
Fairytale Falls . . .

The raft begins to drift toward the falls
with Thelonius still on it. Fiona breaks
free and delivers a wicked left-right
combo to his head.

He tumbles off the raft, gets
caught in the strong current,
and disappears over the edge
with a scream.

Donkey: We'll save you!

They jump onto the raft.

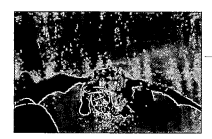

The raft hits a rock and smashes to bits, sending Shrek, Fiona,
and Donkey flying over the falls.

Fiona is plucked from her doom by
Thelonius, who hangs on by a slim
branch. Fiona grabs Shrek, who in turn
grabs Donkey. But the branch breaks.

Shrek: I love you.
Fiona: I love you too.
Donkey: My short furry life is flashing
before my eyes.

The second before impact, Dragon
swoops down and saves them.

Unaware of Dragon's rescue, Farquaad's
ghost gloats as Fiona appears to rise
above the edge of the falls.

Shrek: We've got a loaded dragon here . . .
Fiona: And we're not afraid to use it!

Dragon shoots a fireball at
Farquaad, who explodes in the sky.

Dragon deposits Shrek and Fiona at the honeymoon suite of the Fairytale Falls Hotel.

Shrek: Let the honeymoon begin!

An Unofficial
CG Animation Timeline

The development of computer-generated (CG) animation involved a host of technological innovations that span much of the twentieth century. Its close cousin, computer-generated images (CGI), also played an integral role, along with key advances in computer-game technology.

1950 Oscilloscope wave patterns are photographed and displayed as art.

1951 The first computer-graphic display is presented to the public.

1952 Mr. Potato Head is invented, later to star in Pixar's *Toy Story*.

1956 Scientists at Lawrence Livermore National Laboratory connect a graphic display to an IBM 704 computer.

1958 Saul Bass creates CGI-influenced titles for Alfred Hitchcock's *Vertigo*.

1960 The term *computer graphics* is first coined by William Fetter of Boeing for highly sophisticated "human factor" cockpit drawings.

1963 The computer mouse, an essential tool in computer animation, is invented.

1963 The first computer-generated film is created by Edward Zajac of Bell Labs.

1965 The first American exhibition of computer art takes place at Howard Wise Gallery in New York City.

1966 The first CG consumer product, Odyssey (a computer game), is introduced.

1967 The world's first 3-D computer-animated human is created for a Boeing cockpit simulator.

1970 Minicomputers become this decade's tool of choice for 3-D computer animation.

1972 The video game Pong is developed.

1973 Moore's Law (that the number of transistors on a microchip will double every year and a half) is first posited by Intel's chairman Gordon Moore. This exponential increase in computer power will make advanced CG animation possible.

1974 3-D computer-generated imagery (CGI) takes a stunning leap forward when Peter Fonda's head is digitized and rendered in *Futureworld*.

1976 Steve Wozniak and Steve Jobs start Apple Computer.

1978 Bump mapping, a technique that simulates wrinkled surfaces, is first introduced. Years later, Shrek's highly detailed (if slightly unsettling) green skin will depend on such technology.

1980 Pacific Data Images (PDI) is founded.

1980 The video game Donkey Kong is introduced. According to Donkey, "it was a proud day for donkeys everywhere."

1981 The film *Looker* features Cindy, the first virtual character (played by Susan Dey).

1982 Disney's *Tron* is the first live-action film with more than twenty minutes of computer-generated animation.

1982 The "Genesis effect" for *Star Trek II*, created by George Lucas's Industrial Light and Magic (ILM), is the first all computer-animated visual-effects film shot.

1984 *Still Life Etude*, created at Hiroshima University is an early simulation of light, fog, rain, and skies (several of the so-called Holy Grails of CG animation).

1984 Pixar is founded.

1985 *The Black Cauldron* is the first animated feature film from Disney to use computer-generated animation.

1986 Pixar is purchased from Lucasfilm by Steve Jobs.

1988 *Locomotion*, a PDI short, is an early, successful example of "squash-and-stretch" computer animation.

1988 Pixar wins the Academy Award for the short *Tin Toy*, a precursor to *Toy Story*.

1989 *The Abyss* includes the first convincing 3-D CG character animation.

1991 *Terminator II* is the first blockbuster movie with multiple morphing effects and simulated natural human motion.

1992 *Aladdin* features Disney's first use of 3-D organic surfaces and a fully computer-animated character.

1992 "Facetracker," an early facial-motion capture system, was developed by Simm-

Graphics to animate the Super Mario video-game character.

1993 *Jurassic Park* sets new standards for computer-generated characters and effects.

1995 Pixar's landmark *Toy Story* is the first fully 3-D computer-animated feature. It is an unprecedented creative and commercial success.

1995 The Sony Playstation is introduced.

1996 DreamWorks acquires a stake in PDI.

1998 Disney/Pixar's *A Bug's Life* and PDI/DreamWorks's *Antz* are released.

2001 The Academy of Motion Pictures Arts and Sciences approves a new Oscar category for Best Animated Feature Film. *Shrek* wins the award.

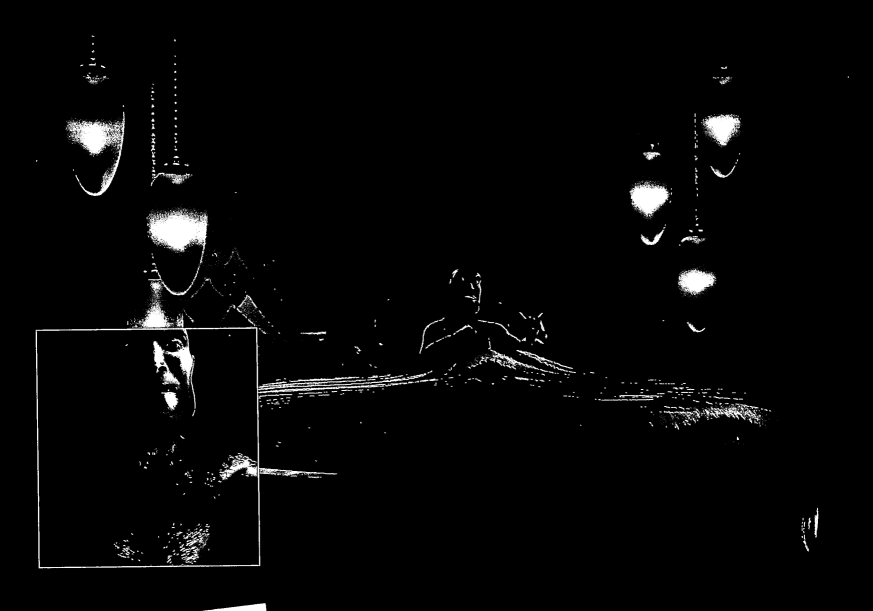

A Brief History of PDI

In 1980, at the dawn of the personal computer revolution, a young electrical engineer named Carl Rosendahl started a computer-animation company called Pacific Data Images (PDI), in Sunnyvale, California. It was an audacious move, especially considering that there was no real computer-animation industry to speak of at the time. With the addition of Richard Chuang and Glen Entis, fledgling PDI got its start doing broadcast graphics for Brazilian broadcaster Globo-TV. Allied with computer-graphics pioneer Harry Marks, its first big break came in 1983 with the opening graphics for the TV show *Entertainment Tonight.*

What is now rather mundane—so-called flying graphics—was then a striking visual innovation. Says Rosendahl, "Once that got on the air, the whole world opened up for us. The broadcast-graphics people were aggressive about trying to do something new and different that no one had seen before." PDI was soon providing broadcast graphics for ABC, CBS, ESPN, MTV, and many others. *Antz* producer Brad Lewis, who was then executive producer of commercials for PDI, recalls, "It got to the point where if you were watching a ball game on TV, within ten minutes you'd see something PDI had done, either because we did broadcast graphics during a show opening or because we did a car or beer spot."

Early on, Rosendahl and others at PDI dreamed of eventually making computer-animated feature films. But this was a vastly more complicated creative and technological puzzle that would literally require years to solve. A

In stark contrast to Shrek's humble dwelling, Lord Farquaad's "bachelor pad" is opulently decadent. Detailed settings such as this one play an important role in helping define characters.

Behind-the-Screen Politics

Good chemistry among actors is essential to any production, and CG characters are no different. Near the beginning of filming SHREK, there were some bumpy moments to overcome.

Shrek: Uh, yeah, I don't know if those nerds at PDI/Dreamworks were either working too hard or too little, but whoever designed Farquaad must have put in the wrong combination of ones and zeros, 'cause that guy was a real pain in the HAGGIS!

Farquaad: Yes, I admit that perhaps I may have come across as a bit "demanding" on set, but a college-educated thespian of my caliber is used to a certain number of required and essential amenities.

Donkey: Oh, man! That Farquaad dude was a major prima donna. He had to have his own private trailer lined in Peruvian velvet! And he'd only drink bottled water imported from the Himalayas! I drank from the toilet, and I had to share my trailer with the mice and Pinocchio, and let me tell you, three blind rodents and a wooden boy can muster up quite a stink!

Fiona: Yeah, at first Farquaad did cause tensions to rise quite a bit on set. I thought Shrek was gonna give him the ol' ogre wallop on top of his prissy, needy skull, and if he wasn't, I would! Luckily the geniuses at PDI/DreamWorks took care of the problem and put Farquaad in his place.

Peace returned to the set when the animators lowered Farquaad an inch.

series of company-financed, award-winning shorts helped break new technical ground that would prove essential in the development of CG animation. *Burning Love*, in 1998, introduced a more natural, painterly style to the typical hard-edged look of computer graphics, and the 1990–91 shorts *Locomotion* and *Gas Planet* advanced PDI's early capabilities in character animation.

Equally important was the establishment of PDI's highly collaborative, yet focused, working environment (so essential to the success of *Shrek*). Director Roger Gould says, "Even back then, there was always a goal to tell stories and create characters. . . . Everyone there had this crazy, mixed passion for creating imagery and using computer graphics." Echoing PDI's dictum of technology serving the needs of the story, he remembers that it was always "not about how you do it, it's what the picture is on the screen."

PDI's breakthrough effects on *Terminator 2*, *Batman*, *Lethal Weapon 3*, and countless other live-action movies finally got the undivided attention of Hollywood. Even so, says Rosendahl, "we pitched a number of projects for years before it finally clicked. Jeffrey Katzenberg was one of the few people in L.A. who actually got it. . . . . There are people who recognize things ahead of their time and take risks and go for it. Jeffrey is one of those guys in animation."

While at Disney, Katzenberg was instrumental in the renaissance of the traditional, animated feature. Another piece of the puzzle fell into place when DreamWorks, founded by Katzenberg, Steven Spielberg, and David Geffen, acquired a stake in PDI in 1996. At last, the traditions of classical animation and storytelling were combined with visionary, state-of-the-art CG technology. With the release of *Antz* in 1998, Carl Rosendahl's dream of creating a pure, computer-animated feature was finally realized.

Part 2
We're Definitely Not in the
Swamp Anymore

The decision to go ahead with *Shrek 2* was made before the first film was even finished. For Katzenberg, the decision hinged on a series of unanswered character and story questions from the first movie: "I think the story we had to tell actually has four parts to it. I felt we had only told a part of the story. I felt it was incomplete. I was obviously enthusiastic about the first movie and thought it would be successful, but I also felt that organically there were so many questions that I would love to have answered. Why was she in that tower? And who put her there? And what was the reason for that? And who is prince charming? Was somebody else meant to rescue her?"

But it was a not a decision made lightly. *Shrek 2* producer Aron Warner observes that successful sequels are "a very rare thing to be able to pull off, and *Shrek*—by design accident, divine grace, whatever—managed to tell a story that was just really basic, classic emotion. It was something that almost everybody who saw it could relate to at some level. You hope you can keep doing that over and over again, but how many movies actually do that?" Katzenberg concurs, noting, "I think the biggest single challenge of *Shrek 2* is trying to meet people's expectations."

This was a daunting challenge, and for *Shrek 2* director Conrad Vernon (and countless others at PDI/DreamWorks) the most important thing was "to make sure we stuck with the original film's heart and soul and intent and sincerity and not go off onto some other tangent." However, surprise and unpredictability would have to figure into the story. According to Vernon, it was essential to "give the audience something they're not expecting that's good. *Shrek* surprised everyone, and now we've got to surprise them again."

"*Donkey Story*, now that would have been a sequel! Man, it had everything—action, romance, fancy catering. Sort of like *Doctor Zhivago*. Only instead of Omar, it's me—a donkey with an attitude."

— Donkey

At all costs, the creators wanted to avoid succumbing to the dreaded sequel syndrome of "bigger is better." This strategy can distract the audience from a basic lack of story and character involvement. As Vernon ruefully notes, "I've seen it a million times where these big, huge, beautiful computer-animated effects come on, and, if there's no story to support it, it only holds your attention for about ten minutes."

The creators felt confident they could deal with all these considerations. There was, however, one issue to which they kept coming back. *Shrek 2* director Andrew Adamson puts it this way: "We got them married at the end of the first film and that kind of left us with a bit of a dilemma on what to do next. And so it really was a challenge to say, 'Okay, how do we progress them beyond that,' because they're supposed to be living happily ever after."

The next step in the *Shrek* saga wasn't exactly easy or obvious. However, the ending of the first *Shrek* did provide a clue. As Shrek and Fiona fade into the distance, glowing in marital bliss, who in the audience doesn't feel at least a slight twinge of doubt as to how things will *really* work out?

Approaching the story outline, Adamson kept these basic but crucial questions in mind. He says, "I wanted to make it about, 'You don't just marry the spouse, you marry the whole family.' And I wanted to make it about the nature of 'happily ever after.' At one point I toyed with the idea of Shrek's parents coming to stay with them and how Fiona deals with it." Still, a certain story catalyst was missing, and Adamson knew it.

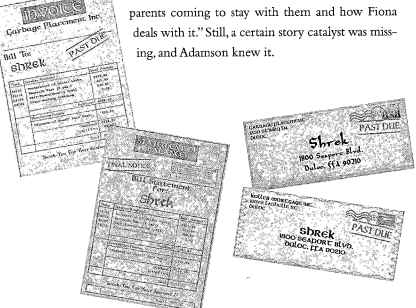

THE CHATTER BOX

To Do the Sequel or Not?

SHREK: Of course, I had my reservations. I'm an actor. Do I really want to play the same guy again? I visited that territory. I'm always looking for a fresh challenge. When I decided to take on the role of an ogre in the first picture, I didn't take it lightly. Sure, technically, I already was an ogre, but in order to become "Shrek" it took months of tedious preparation. I was a vegan before I started the project. Once I became that character, it's been hard to come back. I still find myself drifting toward him, late at night. It's scary sometimes. So, when the studio approached me to do SHREK 2, I was a little wary. I don't want to be known around town as the "Shrek" guy, but I have to say, the story was great and I wanted in.

Piled-up mail from when Shrek was away on his honeymoon

Honeymoon Bliss

A romantic moment

Hansel's
Honeymoon
Hideaway

*Hansel's
Honeymoon
Hideaway*

Our honeymoon cottage

Handsome Devil

A mermaid crashed our picnic, but I threw her back!

A honeymoon scrapbook of
movie stills and development art

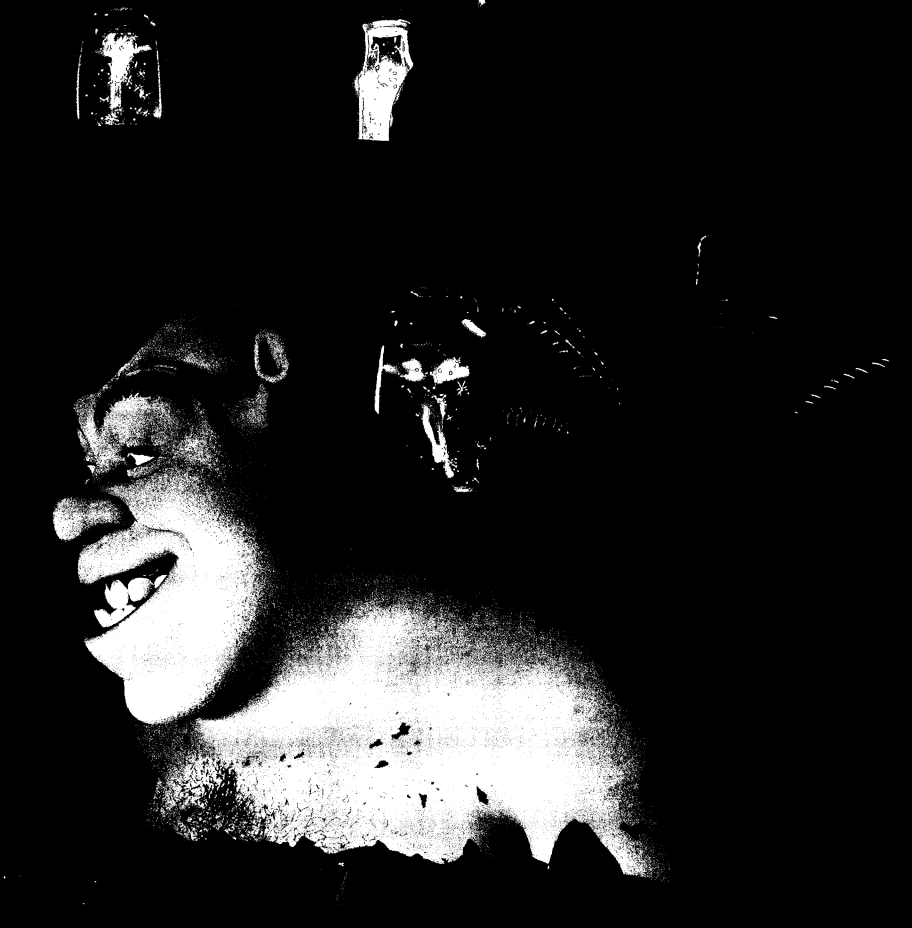

The importance of this outline was compounded by the decision to go directly from outline to storyboard, bypassing, at least initially, a completed screenplay. The reasons to move quickly ahead were compelling: because of the huge popularity of *Shrek*, and the enormous lead in time required in animation, it was essential to hit the ground running. Besides, the *Shrek* team was (for the most part) still intact, well seasoned, and ready to go. On top of this, much of Shrek's world had already been invented and was well understood by the creators.

Of course, writing would still be central to the creation of *Shrek 2*, but it would have to mesh with the unique production requirements of a highly complex CG movie. *Shrek 2* producer David Lipman elaborates: "Andrew Adamson is constantly writing and rewriting pages. Sequences are given out to the board artists, and they get rewritten, and when we go to record the actors, the actors make the lines their own." In short, the writing of *Shrek 2* would be a nonstop affair from beginning to end.

There was another good reason to take the plunge: at heart, animation is a storyboard-driven process. For Adamson, "the ability to storyboard a movie is an expensive writing tool and a really inexpensive production tool, because you get to watch the movie before you make it." As an example, he points out the story dictum that you can't have your biggest action sequence in the middle of the second act; it will kill the film. Yet, this is precisely what the creators did with the Dragon's keep sequence in the first *Shrek*. "Because this process allows you to be experimental and instinctual, you can just say, 'I feel this should work.' You can try it and see if it works without spending the time to shoot it or animate it." But before any of this could happen, Adamson had to first finish the outline.

Inspiration arrived in the form of a movie, specifically, *Guess Who's Coming to Dinner.* It was, said Adamson, "a movie I hadn't seen for years. It's just a great setup. You're dealing with bigotry, expectations, realistic stereotypes in a fairy-tale world." In it, Adamson recognized the familiar Shrekian theme of inverted expectations, only here it was the theme of *family* expectations that struck him the most. He realized the concept could be sharpened even further if Shrek and Fiona were to visit Fiona's parents, instead of Shrek's parents visiting them.

Suddenly, Adamson's odyssey came to a swift conclusion. Within a week, he had an outline, and, although it was only a few pages long (and subject to myriad changes), it would ultimately form the spine for *Shrek 2.*

The outline describes a reluctant Shrek and Fiona (along with Donkey) traveling to the Kingdom of Far Far Away to meet Fiona's parents, the King and Queen. Of course, the royal couple are shocked at Fiona's choice of husband, and after a disastrous "getting to know you" dinner, a distraught Fiona is visited by a Fairy Godmother, who offers to find her a "prince charming." Fiona refuses, but the Fairy Godmother, whose son is none other than the *real* Prince Charming, presses her agenda with the King by referring enigmatically to a certain "deal" between them. She insists that Shrek be "removed" from the picture so her son can marry Fiona.

The reluctant King hires the services of an assassin to put a hit on Shrek, the assassin being none other than the dreaded Puss In Boots (a swashbuckling, debonair Spanish house cat). Puss ambushes Shrek, getting the better of him, until he's suddenly stricken with an acute hairball attack. Moved by Shrek's kindness in not taking advantage of him during his moment of

These examples of development art, one a view inside the onion carriage and the other a sweeping panorama, are just two of many such images made for the journey to Far Far Away scene.

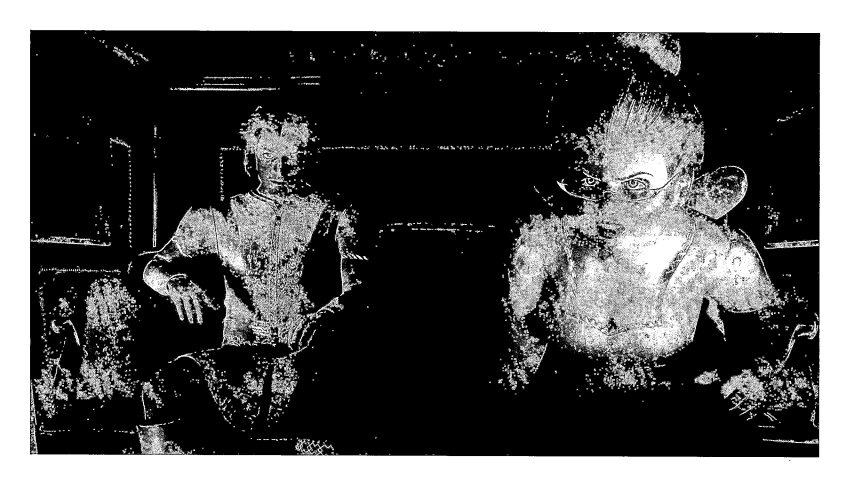

weakness, Puss pledges his eternal loyalty and confesses to the nefarious plot. Thrown into despair, Shrek seeks the services of the very same Fairy Godmother so he can transform himself into the handsome prince charming he thinks Fiona desires. And from there, the misunderstandings continue to escalate.

On the one hand, this is a natural extension of the first *Shrek*. Says Warner, "They'd just gotten married, and people accepted their kind of unusual relationship in their small world in the swamp. But take them out to their peers and the rest of the world and the public. Then they have to face the fact that they aren't people who would normally fit in. How do they deal with that?"

Yet, in many ways, *Shrek 2* is quite different in tone and content. Warner terms it "a more complex, almost French farce and comedy of manners where there is a joy in unraveling the little bits and pieces" of an intricate plot. And, as in any good farce, there is a strong element of romantic misunderstanding. This convention allowed the creators to explore and deepen Shrek's character, for it is through this kind of painful mishap that Shrek faces his innermost demons of identity and insecurity.

"This is Fairy Godmother. I'm either away from my desk or with a client. But if you come by the office, we'll be glad to make you a personal appointment. Have a happy ever after."

Directors Vernon and Asbury point to an interesting contradiction in Shrek's character. When it comes to physical bravery, he's like James Bond: fearless. Says Vernon, "He's a big strong ogre and so he has lots of confidence." But when it comes to the more delicate task of dealing with emotions, he's far less assured. Asbury illuminates this with another movie archetype: Ernest Borgnine's Marty. Like Shrek, "he's a great guy in many ways," says Asbury, " but you can tell he's not necessarily had the happiest life in the world. It's not been that easy, he hasn't always been just cheerful and happy."

The formidable villainess in *Shrek 2* is the Fairy Godmother. The creators had always loved the idea of a corrupt, dangerous version of this beloved fairy-tale character, but had not found a way of using her in the first *Shrek*. However, in the affluent, superficial world of Far Far Away, she seemed a perfect fit. This became more apparent once she was viewed in a distinctly contemporary light.

This "kindly old lady" runs a thriving business empire by preying on people's fears and insecurities, then selling them the appropriate potion. As Adamson puts it, she embodies the phenomenon of a public figure "that propagates a certain image for how you're meant to live, then charges you for it." And once she discovers Shrek's deepest emotional vulnerability, his insecurity with Fiona, she ruthlessly exploits it for her own selfish ends. In a very direct, emotional, and moral way, she is the perfect opponent for Shrek.

The Fairy Godmother billboard in downtown Far Far Away (missing the animated arm that waves back and forth in the movie)

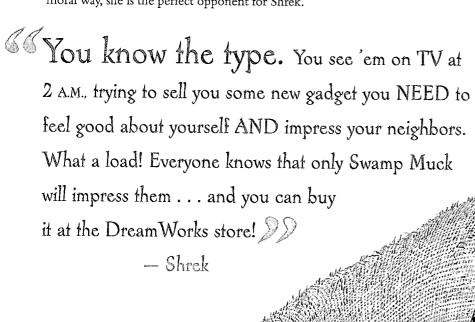

"You know the type. You see 'em on TV at 2 A.M., trying to sell you some new gadget you NEED to feel good about yourself AND impress your neighbors. What a load! Everyone knows that only Swamp Muck will impress them . . . and you can buy it at the DreamWorks store!"

— Shrek

"I think that's our little girl."

COSTUME DESIGN

Costume designer Isis Mussenden was first approached about designing costumes for *Shrek* by Aron Warner. She came to the task a highly accomplished costume designer, with an extensive background in live-action films. Among her first tasks were making actual patterns and "swatching" fabrics. "It's good for the animators to touch the fabrics and get a sense of them," explains Mussenden, "and to see the color saturation and how the light shines on them." As always, technical considerations were important: highly complex fabrics or textures may not be practical to animate.

For *Shrek 2*, the wardrobes of Shrek and Fiona were altered and expanded considerably. The "ogre" Shrek still has his trademark tunic and snakeskin vest. But his transformation into Handsome Shrek required some new thinking. "We needed a Prada version of the Shrek outfit," says Mussenden, "like he was shopping on Rodeo Drive."

Fiona's needs were a little more complicated. In the first film, she wore a relatively simple, green dress. But for *Shrek 2,* she needed something fresh. Ultimately, Mussenden settled on three basic costumes. The first was a simple lilac dress, designed to reflect the casual comfort of swamp living. The second dress was more formal and weightier, suitable for life inside her parent's castle. Finally, for the grand ball at the end of the movie, Mussenden created a beautiful, sequined gown. Her inspiration came in part from an old photograph of a classic Chanel dress.

These are just a few of the many costume design sketches that were generated for *Shrek* and *Shrek 2.* In general, about fifteen different sketches were made for each main character. In the second film, Shrek's trademark outfit had to be modified to suit his "handsome" persona, while Fiona's simple green dress was augmented with more formal attire.

CONCEPTUAL ART:
LOOKING AT THE BIG PICTURE

As soon as the outline was completed, a small advance team dove right into preproduction on the film. Production designer Guillaume Aretos explains, "During the preproduction phase, there is a very limited team that includes the directors, producers, production designer, art director, and writers." At this earliest stage of working on the film, according to Aretos, he and art director Steve Pilcher "focus on conceptual painting, and on creating the main characters, by sculpting them and starting to digitize them."

One of the purposes of the conceptual or development art is to help focus and inspire the entire production, and a good example of this involved the creation of the setting for Far Far Away. A central location for much of *Shrek 2*, Far Far Away was conceived as a medieval version of a Beverly Hills–type community where famous fairy-tale characters go to retire. Loaded with money, these "stars" commission extravagant mansions on the hill, protected by wrought-iron gates crowned with their illustrious names.

When Jeffrey Katzenberg was reviewing the early concept drawings for Far Far Away, he loved the Beverly Hills overtones and wanted more. Aretos remembers Katzenberg

asking, "You know what? Why don't we do Rodeo Drive right under the castle?" It was a stroke of inspiration.

To understand and absorb its unique ambience, Aretos visited Beverly Hills and took hundreds of photos, documenting the city's architectural icons, design motifs, and streetscapes. As the concept renderings progressed, Far Far Away came to resemble more and more the familiar mecca of conspicuous consumption we all know and love: broad, immaculate streets lined with palm trees, star-map stands, carriage limos, and oversized shop windows crammed with every conceivable luxury.

However, this was more than just clever visual satire. The perception of Beverly Hills—its emphasis on glamour and glitter, appearance over reality—was perfect for intensifying the Shrekian themes of identity and self-doubt. After all, it is the Fairy Godmother who dominates this land of milk and honey, and it is her insidious influence that can be found on every street corner and store sign. It is in this world of image and unreality that Shrek, as an ogre and an outcast, must struggle to survive and ultimately triumph.

> **"What do you mean, 'No ogres in Beverly Hills?'** If you ask me, they're roaming all over . . . they're just disguised in designer clothes."
>
> — Shrek

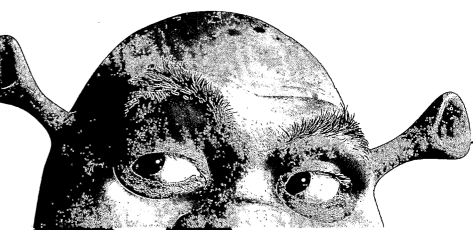

As Shrek, Fiona, and Donkey arrive in Far Far Away, they pass mansions of famous fairy-tale characters such as Cinderella and Jack (with his beanstalk in the front yard). Vanity plates, stretch carriage limos, and tabloid vending machines are just a few of the clues that signal they are definitely not in the swamp anymore. These concept drawings, prop renderings, and the color key on the opposite page exemplify the extraordinary level of detail that goes into constructing each setting.

The art department carefully studied the unique ambience of Beverly Hills and its shopping mecca, Rodeo Drive, as inspiration for Far Far Away. But they also needed to make sure it fit into the medieval world they created. These development sketches, prop drawings, and movie stills demonstrate how everything from shopping bags to storefronts to fanciful architecture became part of the atmosphere.

"*Wow! It's going to be champagne wishes and caviar dreams from now on.*"

SETTING THE SCENE

Developing a visual idea for a setting is just the first stage. Conceptual art also serves to define and sharpen key scenes. An example is the scene in the forest where Shrek and Donkey first meet Puss In Boots. For *Shrek 2* art director Steve Pilcher it was a process of first understanding the narrative thrust of the scene: Shrek and Donkey wander down a path to meet the King, unaware they are being stalked by the dreaded ogre-hunter Puss In Boots, with whom they will soon tangle.

Working within this mini-story, Pilcher strives to "respect the storyboards and get in sync with the directors and storyboard artists." At the same time, he has to "think of the environment 'globally.'" For Pilcher, this involves asking a series of basic character blocking questions: "First of all, you need a stage for the characters to act and fight. Where do they spend most of their time? Then you have to get them from point A to B, B being where they end up. So how far into the forest do you begin the scene?" Blocking also involves designing various objects and visual features within the scene. In this case, the environment cannot-be-too-crowded with rocks and tress or it will inhibit he action. Yet, if the environment is too empty, it will not look like a real forest.

As Pilcher and others progressed in their conceptualizing, they began manipulating the various visual elements to intensify the mood and buildup within the scene. The lighting design is particularly important; it defines much of the look and feeling of the scene, as well as serving as a guidepost for artists later in the production process. "The set says a thousand different things according to how you light it," says Aretos. "The great thing in our job is we don't have a DP [director of photography], so the DP is us."

Although the actual CG lighting process will happen much later in production, it is first laid out conceptually in the art department's early renderings. Within these renderings all the light sources must be clearly specified. For example, in a daytime interior, it might be a window, an open door, or a crack in a wall. Or perhaps all three. At night, it might be any number of things: torches, a fire in a hearth, or the moon. Both the location of the light and its color temperature ("warm" sunlight or "cold" moonlight, for example) are especially important.

This series of renderings establishes the visual foundation for the scene and serves as a guide for all the creative departments.

However, successful lighting is more than just a static, overall look or feeling, no matter how accurate or expressive. It is also a dynamic element as the scene unfolds. "Just as a story will have a peak and resolution," says Pilcher, "how do we 'ramp it up' with lighting and the way it's set dressed and staged?"

In the forest scene with Shrek and Puss, Pilcher did something a little different with the lighting design. Usually, as characters proceed into a forest, gently dappled sunlight gives way to a darker, more mysterious look. Pilcher, however, reversed this timeworn approach; as the scene progresses, it actually gets brighter. Because the scene ends in a burst of comedy and reconciliation between Shrek and Puss, this seemingly contradictory lighting strategy better suits the needs of the scene.

It was important, however, to create a variety and richness in the overall look of the forest, and to not, as Pilcher puts it, "make it too predictable, visually." As Shrek and Donkey wind their way down the path, the trees change from pines to oak. Concurrently, there is less and less exposed earth, and more and more moss. All these visual elements culminate in a rather idyllic (as opposed to scary) setting for the climactic action.

It is at this point in the scene where a striking visual element emerges: a massive, ancient oak. Says Pilcher, "We needed something iconic to help anchor the scene visually." In this case, the oak helps create a sense of place for the final action and provides a strong compositional element. Moreover, its subtle but powerful presence underlines the momentous significance of the scene: Puss's introduction into the world of *Shrek*.

In later stages, the entire environment will be extensively decorated with pine needles, acorns, fallen branches, rocks, and pebbles, along with richly varied moss. (Achieving, says Pilcher, "a visual richness that the audience can no longer predict. They take the forest for granted, and just feel it and enjoy it.") But before any of this finishing or "surfacing" takes place, the visual foundations of composition, mood, lighting, and blocking are first established with conceptual art.

"And there's that bush shaped like Shirley Bassey."

" *I need to have someone taken care of.* "

NEW CHARACTERS JOIN THE CAST

At the same time as the conceptual renderings were progressing, the art department was also charged with creating the new characters: Puss In Boots, Fairy Godmother, Prince Charming, and the King and Queen, along with Handsome Shrek and Noble Steed (Shrek and Donkey transformed by the magic potion). This was a real challenge, in part because the number of leads had doubled from the first movie.

Character designer and sculptor Tom Hester and his staff at Hester Studios were brought into this process early on, and played a crucial role in visually defining these characters. Having been instrumental in designing many of the original characters in *Shrek*, including Shrek himself, Hester was well prepared for the task. Working from a basic description in the synopsis, as well as detailed input from the directors and producers, Hester got to work tackling all the major characters.

His approach is somewhat unconventional: instead of the more typical method of starting with conceptual sketches, Hester tends to dive right into what he calls "clay sketches," or actual sculptures. This allows the directors and producers to gain a complete perspective of the new characters right away. (For a more detailed explanation of how this works, please see "The Art of Character Design" on pages 84–85.)

Concurrently, the art department was progressing along the same lines, but with the more traditional approach of using sketches. These initial renderings serve the same purpose as the conceptual paintings for settings: they help the creators to explore and eventually define the final version of the character.

In the case of Puss In Boots, the earliest sketches depict quite a different cat from the final character. Comments Aretos, "We were heading toward a more 'heavy cat.' A big strong cat, a bit badly behaved, weak and at the same time arrogant." A particular inspiration was the famous nineteenth-century version of Puss In Boots by French illustrator Gustave Doré. His feline sported a belt with dead mice hanging by their tails, along with a necklace of beaks and feathers. Says Aretos, "He was a very mean–looking cat, as soon as he jumped into his boots."

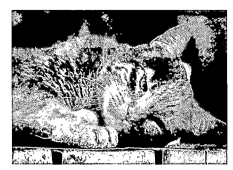
Director Andrew Adamson's cat, Joshua, provided a source of inspiration for Puss In Boots.

For Aretos, this classical approach "was interesting, but as we evolve the character there is new information always coming in. And with any creative process there is a self-definition of the creation happening in front of your eyes that you don't really control." A key example of this was when actor Antonio Banderas agreed to play Puss. "That led us into a somewhat different direction," says Aretos. "The cat became a little bit skinnier, a little bit nicer, because Antonio Banderas is a very charming guy."

What was especially influential was Banderas's portrayal of the character Zorro. "We studied the way he looks at the camera, the way he plays with the camera, cocking an eye to the audience, the shadow under the brim of his hat, that type of thing." In other words, "the charming Zorro. We tried to put that in the cat." (For more on the contribution actors make in defining and developing the characters, please see Part 4.)

A turning point came when Aretos saw director Conrad Vernon pitching his storyboards of Shrek and Puss in the forest. Aretos remembers, "It was hilarious from the get go," and was particularly struck with Vernon's success in visualizing Puss in action. "That defined the character even more," says Aretos. From these dynamic storyboards, Aretos deduced that Puss "had to be able to be a very cute little cat, and yet at the same time a fierce feline."

Once Puss In Boots was clearly established, at least on paper, it was time for the next step: creating a model or *maquette,* and digitizing him for the CG world he would soon inhabit. Like so many aspects of 3-D animation, the tremendous realism that CG technology is capable of achieving comes with a price: in this case, the need to create a laboriously detailed yet expressive maquette.

It was at this stage that Tom Hester got directly involved. Using the finalized sketches from the art department, Hester sculpted an initial model. The results were anatomically impressive, but perhaps *too* realistic for where the character was going. In addition, Puss had other curious anatomical requirements. For example, he would have to walk and stand (effortlessly) on two legs. Another issue: to achieve convincing emotions, Puss would need to use his eyebrows. Problem: cats don't have eyebrows. So, in a sense, Aretos, Hester, and others were not just studying and mastering the anatomy of an existing animal, they were also having to radically, but subtly, alter this anatomy for their own purposes.

Working with Chris Aguirre, Hester managed to "merge the softer, 'plush-toy' approach [of the sketches] with the more realistic anatomical elements of the original sculpture to give Puss a believably solid structure." Two additional influences affected the final version of Puss In Boots: Hester's pet cat Sultana and Andrew Adamson's cat Joshua.

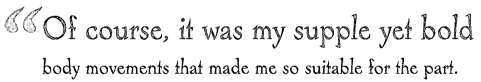

"Of course, it was my supple yet bold body movements that made me so suitable for the part. That, and my native intelligence. Oh, yes! And of course . . . my well-regarded modesty! "

— Puss In Boots

("Since this *is* Hollywood," quips Hester, "Andrew's cat also wanted a piece of the action.")

Once the maquette was completed, it had to be digitized, and here an entirely new set of challenges opened up. Says Aretos, "Any time you digitize in 3-D to make a character, even if it's digitized perfectly, it never looks like the sculpture." Instead, it becomes a highly technical yet creative process of making the model details work in the computer world of 3-D animation. During this stage the character is further refined, and Pilcher recalls long meetings where department heads would sit around the table deciding "the exact size, by millimeter, of pupils," having to factor in "that a daytime pupil is, of course, smaller than a nighttime, dilated pupil."

Yet, as impressive as all this is, an obvious question presents itself: How do you actually get these characters to move inside the computer? The answer involves a highly technical process of *setting up* the characters, and requires the close collaboration of character designers, technical directors (TDs), animators, directors, and producers. Essentially, TDs provide the tools animators need to effectively (and efficiently) animate the characters. Explains *Shrek 2* supervising character TD Larry Cutler, "We're responsible for making the characters move. It seems simple, but these characters are incredibly complex. Ultimately, we're providing a very complex piece of software that animators use to make the characters act and perform . . . to create the feeling that they're actually thinking and doing things."

This high-tech alchemy would require the construction of "virtual" bodies consisting of bone, joints, flesh, fat, and layers of skin (not to mention clothes and hair), along with controls to manipulate everything—from the powerful arms of Shrek to a single whisker on Puss In Boots's face. Ultimately, it would take a year to concurrently set up all of the characters. (For more detailed descriptions of the processes of *modeling* and *character setup,* see pages 86–87 and 88–89). Once setup was completed, Puss and his fellow characters became fully realized creations, ready for action and embued with all the expressive attributes of living, thinking, feeling beings.

THE CHATTER BOX

Prime-Time Exclusive!

Interviewer: With no professional history in the field, you must be pretty happy to be a part of such a successful franchise.

PUSS: Oh, you have no idea. Before SHREK 2 I was living on a small farm in the countryside of Spain. All of my fourteen brothers and sisters and my thirty-seven half-brothers and sisters were getting on my nerves. Now that I am living in the lap of luxury in Hollywood, California, I have yet to contact any of them.

As far as my professional experience is concerned, it is true . . . I had none. However, when I auditioned for the roll of Puss In Boots, I felt very confident I would land the part. You see—I am a very, very attractive young cat, and many of the women working in casting thought so as well. I dated many of them until my part in SHREK 2 was secure. I have yet to contact any of them.

Interviewer: Shrek, Donkey—did you feel the addition of Puss In Boots was necessary to the sequel?

SHREK: It wasn't ever an issue for me. I was going to get paid either way. However, I have to say that when I first met Puss on set . . . he was adorable. I'm not really a cat guy, but he was adorable.

DONKEY: No way, man! When I first heard that a Puss In Boots was gettin' involved, I called the producers. I yelled! I stomped! I clomped! They told me to calm down, and just read the script, and that everything was going to be okay.

When I read the script, and got to Puss In Boots as the ogre killer, it caught my interest. Shrek was going to be knocked off? Hallelujah to the heavens! I was going to carry the rest of the film! (Not that I already didn't. Kids love me 'cause I'm cute and sassy! Shrek don't have any of that!) But Puss In Boots becomes the third friend? More like a third wheel of a broken-down pickup truck! But I never let on any animosity towards the little fella, and I gave him a warm Hollywood welcome. Now we're the best of friends—we cruise around, go clubbing, all that good stuff!

PUSS: Yes, a true Hollywood friendship. I have yet to contact him.

"Bon appetit!"

"Excuse me!"

"An ogre from a swamp. How original."

"Not that there's anything wrong with that. Right, Harold?"

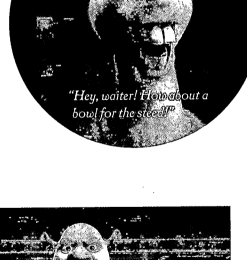

"Hey, waiter! How about a bowl for the steed!"

"No! Of course not. That's assuming you don't eat your young."

"Oh, no, we usually prefer the ones who've been locked away in a tower."

This intricate scene is a textbook example of the seamless integration of character design, set design, lighting, and animation.

"Better out than in, I always say, eh, Fiona?"

The Art of Character Design

Alfred Hitchcock once said that to make a successful movie, all you had to do was put Cary Grant in front of the camera; such is the power of stardom. But more often than not, stars are made, and when it came time for PDI/DreamWorks to make a star out of Shrek, they faced a daunting task. Forget for a moment the world-famous ogre, loved and adored by millions of movie fans. In the beginning, Shrek existed only as a sketchy (albeit striking) character in a children's book. To ensure his successful transition from book to film, one of the first people PDI/DreamWorks called on was character-designer Tom Hester.

Having worked as a designer/supervisor/sculptor on films such as *An American Werewolf in London* and *Cocoon*, Hester had a history of turning story ideas and character concepts into seemingly real, flesh-and-blood creations. He describes his job in ths way: "I create characters, *by their very form*, that convey their personalities and traits, and that are also able to carry the story."

Hester's involvement with *Shrek* began early on, starting in 1996. Up to that point, most of the character-design work consisted of sketches (although sculptor Loren Sorman had made an early bust of Shrek).

Storyboard artists Mike Ploog and Ken Harsha, along with numerous development artists and designers such as Paul Shardlow, Carter Goodrich and Nicola Marlet generated a huge number of portraits. While these early renderings were valuable, Hester approached the design of Shrek quite differently.

Along with colleagues Dennis Gordon, Tim Lawrence, and Charles Rivera, Hester generally eschews the traditional character sketch and, instead jumps directly into what he terms *clay sketches*. These conceptual clay sculptures allow directors and producers to see the character in the round and gain a far more accurate idea of where Hester is going with the overall design. "Instead of looking at multiple drawings, which are one angle each," says Hester, "you can see the entire form in front of you." In the course of creating Shrek, more than 100 of these clay sketches were made.

As the directors and producers gravitated toward a more humanized and vulnerable Shrek on the story level, so too did Hester with his clay sculptures. Early versions of Shrek, says Hester, were "very fleshy, with an extreme level of caricature. He was top heavy, with very thin legs for comedic effect." But over time a more "normalized" anatomy began to take hold. An important turning point was when Mike Myers was cast for the voice of Shrek. "We incorporated some aspects of Mike's eyes and eyebrows," says Hester. Once Shrek lost his hair (becoming totally bald), the final version of the character was close at hand.

Hester shares PDI/DreamWorks's obsession with making CG characters as expressive and lifelike as possible. "The features of the characters' faces should always be readable," says Hester, adding, "understanding visually what a character is thinking is critical to the story." Yet, at the same time, the ultimate objective is to go beyond pure reality without losing a sense of the real. Hester touches on this elusive balance when he comments, "I tend to prefer an exaggeration of features and proportions, but at the same time a realistic logic to the movement."

Nowhere does this elusive balance apply more aptly than with the creation of Donkey. On the one hand, Hester's character design reflects a bouncy exuberance far beyond the actual physicality of a real donkey. Yet, at the same time, Donkey has to convincingly interact with a world full of humans. Part of Hester's solution was anatomical: by giving Donkey binocular eye placement, for example, his entire physical presence was made more humanlike and believable.

But it goes deeper than that. For Hester, the key was designing "an animal that evoked Eddie Murphy." This hidden realism is part of what Hester calls "an audience identification with the character. They should be faintly familiar in a way that sparks recognition on some level." Another aspect of this balance was modeling Donkey in part on a very familiar creature, the dog. Says Hester, "He is a donkey, but he had to act more like a faithful dog to work." Thus, Donkey's movements, while often wild and exaggerated, are rooted in this most common and identifiable of creatures.

For Shrek 2, there were a number of interesting character additions, including Handsome Shrek and Noble Steed (Shrek and Donkey transformed after ingesting a magic potion). In designing Handsome Shrek, Hester was faced with a simple but difficult task: how to turn an ogre into a hunk, without losing the ogre. "He had to be handsome," says Hester, "with an athletic physique, yet still be recognizable as Shrek. I used toned-down aspects of his ogre features like his squared-off nose and underbite, and gave him the body of a football player—big, strong, and developed, but with a softening layer of body fat."

Noble Steed was also an example of bringing out the signature features of Donkey within a radically different body. He was pretty much given the body of a show horse," says Hester, "and his head, after a lot of experimentation, was given the dopey smile and binocular eye placement of Donkey." The result is a character utterly different from before, yet totally recognizable as Donkey.

One of Hester's favorite characters in Shrek 2 is the King. To zero in on the King's defining characteristics, Hester had HesterStudios team member Dennis Gordon create an entire series of sculptures. Hester felt strongly that an essential quality to get across was the King's uneasy and secretive nature, and he used actor Peter Lorre as one of his inspirations. "I eventually strengthened his jawline," comments Hester, "and changed a lot of the facial proportions, but left the uneasy look in his eyes. I like that he has a big secret to hide, but you'll have to see the film to find out what that secret is!"

The Process of Modeling

To achieve a convincing 3-D character in CG animation, clay models known as maquettes are sometimes created. *Shrek 2* production designer Guillaume Aretos explains, "Because we have to create our actors in 3-D, we jump on that immediately. Setting up those actors is a very complex technological process." It is because of this complexity that models are usually reserved for the main characters, such as Shrek or Puss In Boots.

First, the artist or designer sketches out a multitude of character versions. These early renderings visually describe the character both statically (in terms of shape and details) and dynamically (how the character leaps or laughs). They are refined into style sheets that become the character "blueprint" that will guide everyone from directors to writers to animators.

More importantly, they must capture the character's "essence" in all its complexity, hence the wide spectrum of emotions that are portrayed in the renderings. In the case of Puss In Boots, these early versions reveal both a charming cad and a somewhat fearsome feline. They show playfulness to be sure, but Puss does have a rather grim task to accomplish when he first confronts Shrek, and the sketches have to reflect this ambiguity.

Usually, PDI/DreamWorks sculpts two kinds of maquettes: the first one is gestural, for capturing the elusive feel and emotion of the character. This type of maquette could be a stand-alone sculpture, its look is so lifelike and energized. The other is a static, anatomical maquette that will be digitized for the computer.

Shrek 2 modeling supervisor Jeff Hayes and his crew digitize the maquettes and work with the producers, the directors, and the art

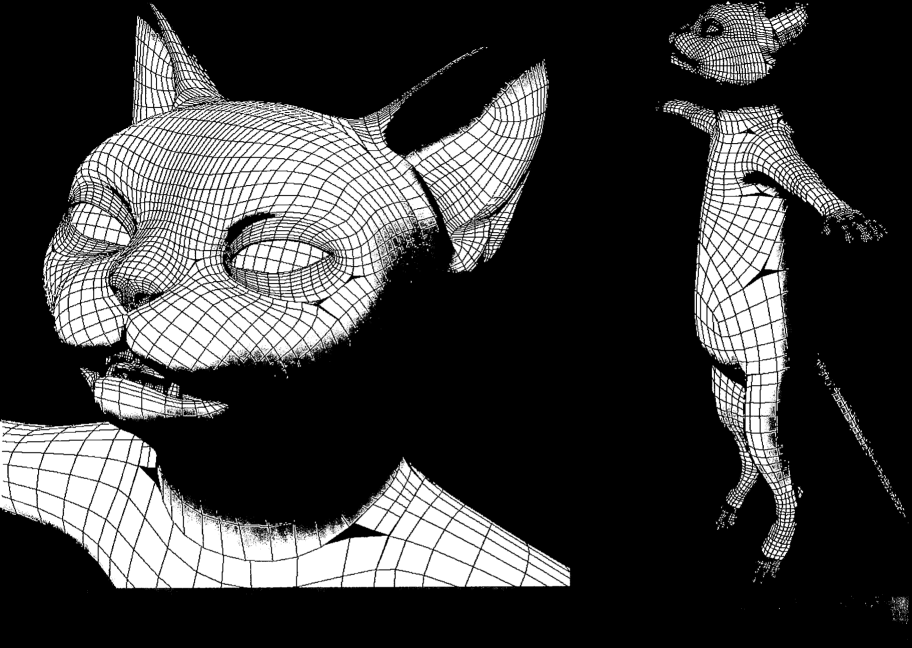

department to further refine the now-CG models in the computer. Unlike the 2-D characters in traditional animation, these 3-D characters will be viewed from an infinite number of angles, so the completed maquette must be as perfect a representation as possible.

To digitize a maquette, the modeler draws a grid over its entire surface. Where the lines cross are points, or vertices. Using a special mechanical arm, the modeler pinpoints each of these vertices, and in turn these coordinates are mapped in the "virtual space" of the computer (again, defined numerically by the three axes). From here, the computer can stretch a "skin" over the coordinates, achieving a kind of geodesic, multifaceted form of the actual object.

The process of scanning the maquette is quite straightforward and can be done in a day. The real work begins when the modeler has to infuse this relatively simple, gridlike form with the myriad subtleties

and details of the finished character. The challenge is both technical and artistic.

For example, in the case of Fiona in the first *Shrek,* her initial digital scan yielded decidedly mixed results. Her cute, upturned lip looked puffy, and her large, catlike eyes acquired a rather spooky and unnerving look. Says Hayes, "The sculpture looked good, but once we got her into the computer, it began to look freaky." In all, it took a year of experimentation to get her look exactly right.

Every detail, no matter how small, says something about the character. According to Aretos, "There is a lot of very fine tweaking on eyelids, on the size of eyeballs, and so forth," for all the characters. (Many of the surface details, however, such as fur or hair, are created much later.) The net result of this elaborate process is a character ready to be "set up" and then placed inside the virtual 3-D world of *Shrek 2.*

The Process of Character Setup

Once digitized successfully, a character continues through the so-called pipeline to the character setup department, where a team of fifteen technical directors (TDs) use PDI's proprietary software to *set up* the 3-D model. This is the intermediate step between modeling and animation, and without it the character would be nothing but an inert, rigid sculpture. It is, says *Shrek 2* production designer Guillaume Aretos, "a very complex technological process to put in all the virtual 'cables and wires' and systems, and to make them move nicely for animation." In addition, a lot of the final character design happens during this phase.

To ensure the successful transition from a clay maquette to a "living, breathing character," Beth Hofer, director of character development at PDI, and her character TD crew work with the digitized models to build the underlying musculature system and animation controls that will ultimately drive the character's performance. Like in a living being, joints move bones, bones in turn move muscles, and muscles move skin. Installing all these anatomical elements and making them move convincingly is extremely complicated, but it will give the animators the tools they need to achieve subtle, realistic action. Comments supervising animator Tim Cheung, "For computer animation, setup is so important. At PDI I think

we have one of the best setup teams in the industry. These are the tools we use to make the characters move. And when we have a really good setup it makes the animation a lot easier."

High-level or *mega controls* allow animators to readily manipulate several primary controls at once. For example, if the animator chooses to turn Shrek's head, wrinkles will automatically form on the back of his fat neck. Grins, scowls, even breathing movements can all be easily achieved using these high-level controls. Lead character TD Dick Walsh describes it this way: "When you decide you want to smile you don't think, 'I'm going to make my cheeks puff, I'm going to expose my teeth,' you just smile and stuff happens. That's the way our system works. We define the muscles a smile will activate, and from that point on everything happens." These high-level controls are essential tools for animators; otherwise, they would have to individually manipulate each muscle, and the time (and expense) required would be outrageously prohibitive.

Part of the TD's job is to define the movement of character joints in ways unique to each character. Thus, Shrek's amble consists of one set of motion parameters, whereas Puss's are quite different. Donkey is incapable of Fiona's grace, while Fairy Godmother possesses an entirely different set of motion attributes. To help create these natural and

convincing character movements, TDs, along with animators such as Raman Hui and Tim Cheung, study anatomy in great detail. Photographic stop-motion breakdowns of humans and animals are particularly useful. Says supervising character TD Larry Cutler, "we have lots of anatomy books lying around. We'll use any reference we can get our hands on." And, if references are lacking, Cutler and others will create their own motion studies. For *Shrek 2*, for example, Cutler videotaped people in full body armor swinging swords to better understand the complications and constraints of armor on human motion.

Primary characters have about 585 animation controls and more than 300 joints in their bodies, but there are exceptions. In the case of Puss In Boots, the controls were far more numerous and varied. Character TD supervisor Lucia Modesto explains: "Puss has the same setup as a normal character plus a tail, plus a belt, plus a sword, hat, feathers, and whiskers. The number of controls in Puss corresponds to about four characters' worth of controls." Puss's tail alone features more than fifty joints that had to be carefully delineated. Even his individual whiskers have controls.

Secondary characters, such as gnomes and dwarfs, are created from generic models (male, female, child) and body types (fat, medium build, skinny, etc.). Along with generic animation controls and parameters, defining attributes such as skin color, hairstyle, and clothing, allow "virtual crowds" of thousands (with convincing variety) to be created with relative ease. "On average," says Modesto, "we have about eight facial variations per generic character. So if you multiply faces times body types, that is a huge amount of variation."

Setting up a character also involves controls for lip sync, that is, manipulating the character's mouth in conjunction with the voice track to make it seem that the character is talking. This involves breaking down language into critical sounds called *phonemes* and creating a corresponding lip movement. For example, the sound of "mmmmm" requires the lips to be pressed together. These *poses* (keyed off a wide variety of phonemes) are saved in a software "toolbox" to be used as needed. An extensive library of poses is created and saved for each major character. PDI's advanced facial animation system, which permits the animators exquisite control of a character's facial expressiveness, is worthy of a discussion in its own right.

Part 3
So Close,
Yet So Far Far Away

As the initial story outline for *Shrek 2* was nearing completion, the creators were ready to assign individual sequences to the story artists. It is the job of the story artist to visualize the sequences on a series of panels, similar in form to a comic strip but with far greater detail. These panels not only need to convey the basic story points of the sequence, they must also provide a precise moment-to-moment depiction of composition, movement, humor, as well as character emotion and expression. (Further down the road, these depicted emotions will also serve as important "acting indicators" for the animators.)

In short, storyboard artists are storytellers employing a multitude of skills. According to *Shrek 2* director Kelly Asbury, "They're writers, they're actors, they're cameramen, they're designers, they're cartoonists, they're illustrators, they're voice talent. You have to have all of these abilities" to create a successful storyboard and ultimately attain what Asbury terms "a visually drafted script."

Moreover, this "boarding" process becomes a means of creative discovery. "We don't have a set with actors," says *Shrek 2* director Conrad Vernon, "so storyboarding is our 'take one, take two, take three.' You try many different things." Storyboards are also revised constantly to encompass new story developments. Once approved, these boarded sequences are scanned to a story reel, where scratch dialogue, sound effects, and temporary music are added. The sequences are then extensively edited and revised, and only eventually linked with other sequences to form an entire storyboarded movie.

One of the most important roles of directors and producers is to supervise the overall boarding process, and thus effectively shape and guide the story itself. A sequence is initiated or *launched* when the directors and producers huddle with the story artist and describe in detail a particular sequence. They convey what the given sequence has to achieve on many different levels, including plot, humor, character, and tone.

Chris Miller, head of story on *Shrek 2*, serves as a liaison between the story artists and the directors, and is himself a story artist. As Miller describes it, he and the other story artists (ranging in number from five to seven during the course of production) are given "the role to support the directors' and producers' vision. You're always working toward what they want." At the same time, however, "you're given first crack at where the camera is going, what the characters are saying, and what they are doing." Miller adds, "In a way, you're wearing every hat and are given great latitude. There's a lot of trust toward the board artists to come up with material."

A good example of how this all works in practice is the scene in *Shrek 2* when Shrek and Donkey first encounter Puss In Boots. Within this single sequence, the story artist has to introduce a major character, provide critical revelations for Shrek to respond to, and at the same time be very, very funny.

In addition to all his other duties as director, Vernon was given the task of storyboarding this sequence. "A lot of directors I've worked with don't draw or storyboard," says Miller, "but Conrad is one of those exceptions. He can do both." Asbury concurs, adding, "Conrad was instrumental in both movies in creating some of the funniest, most pithy sequences."

Like other story artists, Vernon was given a brief summation of the sequence from the outline, to wit: *The King hires Puss In Boots to kill Shrek. Puss In Boots confronts Shrek. Shrek beats Puss In Boots. They become friends.*

That's it. The rest was up to the story artist.

"I have been called a highly developed creation ... at least that is what the female felines think."

— Puss In Boots

Vernon started by trying to dredge up every funny, weird thing he could remember about cats. One peculiar nugget was video footage he had once seen of a man being attacked by a house cat. "It was very funny," recalls Vernon, "and I quickly did sketches of this." Another comedic element that did not ultimately make it into the final film involved Puss giving a rather arrogant oration in the middle of attacking Shrek. Carried away with his feline prowess, Puss prattles on about "you and your little pointy hats and white beards, dancing around under daisies. You are such simpletons! I will take care of you and collect my money." In the middle of this tirade, Shrek quietly informs Puss that the creature Puss is referring to is a *gnome*, not an ogre. And then, of course, there is the debilitating hairball attack.

As various ideas, both visual and verbal, continued to accrue, Vernon wrote out the sequence and then sketched it on storyboards. Ten days later, Vernon was ready to pitch the sequence in front of *Shrek 2*'s first audience: fellow directors, producers, and story artists. The term *pitching* encompasses a number of things. As a story artist, your basic objective is quite simple: to sell your vision of the sequence to your creative peers.

However, pitching involves far more than just a dry description of the storyboard. As Miller puts it, "You are performing the boards in front of everyone," supplying voices and sound effects, hitting the comedic moments just right, and having to be constantly aware of pacing. It is not dissimilar from stand-up comedy, and just as demanding, because *you the creator* are part of the show.

The actual techniques for pitching vary widely. According to Asbury, "It depends on the individual. Some storyboard artists are not as prone to wanting to pitch their work as others. Some are simply more shy, some are beautiful at drawing and are great at conveying their ideas through drawings." Adds Miller, "There are some people who will get up there, and they are literally the most quiet, reserved person, and they'll show their boards just as well as anyone." But in all cases, the one constant ingredient is extreme preparation.

For Miller, the pitch session is "a great moment. Now you're performing it in front of everyone, and it's a great atmosphere. Everyone enjoys it." On the other hand, it can also be quite intimidating. There is always a little voice lurking in the back of every storyboard artist's mind that says, "What if they don't like it?" According to Vernon, "All the storyboard artists who pitch really, really well have a way of thinking about it that calms them down. The way I think about is, 'This is who I am. This is me. If they don't like it, well, that's their problem, not mine. We'll work on it, we'll make it work better, but this is who I am.' That kind of calms me down."

When Vernon pitches, it is an exciting, kinetic experience for both the artist and the audience. Says Vernon, "I have to give it my all, doing the sound effects, the explosions, especially with Puss In Boots where I'm doing the cat sounds, Shrek screaming and yelling. You really have to sell all that stuff because it's action, and all you have are single drawings." From Asbury's point of view, watching Conrad pitch is a real pleasure because "he can get up there and literally give you what the sequence is going to be like. He can do the voices, he can act it out. When a storyboard artist has it all, it's the best of all possible worlds."

As the pitch progresses, Vernon describes a level of concentration so intense he's not entirely aware of the audience. Instead, "you're concentrating so much on pitching that if people are cracking up and you stop and crack up with them, you've lost your momentum. So if people are laughing so hard they can't hear you, you wait for a second and then move on. But you're basically just focused on those drawings."

The response to Vernon's pitch was both immediate and enthusiastic. But as successful as this particular pitch was, it was only the very beginning of a long process of adding, subtracting, and refining. "Producers, directors, story artists give you volumes of notes," says Miller, "and you're sent off to apply those notes." After a few days, the story artist comes back with the new boards and the process begins again.

In the second session, Vernon pitched the sequence to someone new: Jeffrey Katzenberg. He too shared in the general approval, but had one comment in particular. According to Vernon, it was this: "I love the part where Puss In Boots attacks Shrek. Push it. Push it further." And so, once again, Vernon retreated to his office.

Vernon recalls thinking, "Okay, how can I push this, because I just had Puss attacking Shrek on the leg." Then, it dawned on him: "Oh, maybe I can have him crawl all over Shrek. Maybe he can go up underneath his shirt and we can do an *Alien* parody . . . and at the very end, when Donkey turns around to kick Puss, and Puss moves, he can hit Shrek right in the groin. That's what it means to push it further, getting you to think at the second and third level."

And so, more pitching, more input, more changes. "Now you get another stack of notes," says Miller, "hopefully smaller, and eventually

Left to right: Kelly Asbury, Andrew Adamson, Aron Warner, David Lipman, and Conrad Vernon

there will be a consensus of 'Okay, now we've arrived and the sequence is where it needs to be. You've accomplished the scene! Congratulations! You're fired! Now get out!'"

But perhaps not quite yet. For in many ways, the development of this sequence had just begun. As the production progressed, Vernon would have to constantly rejuggle his sequence as the surrounding story and scenes changed and improved. Individual sequences serve as both a vessel for incorporating such changes and a springboard for new ideas. This ongoing process, however, can sometimes lead to sequences losing their vitality and humor. The usual remedy, according to Vernon, is to return "pretty much exactly to what you had in the first place, but with the new nugget of information popped in there to get you to the next part of the story."

A sampling of storyboards from the Puss In Boots attack sequence. These drawings clearly depict the action and are used to guide the animators.

Dear Diary

As this collection of detailed illustrations shows, Fiona's childhood bedroom was chock full of pop-music fan posters, trinkets, and toys that playfully mirror the film's characters. Unable to sleep, Shrek explores the room and finds Fiona's old diary, in which the young princess expressed her yearning for a handsome "prince charming."

From here, the boarding process advanced to the editorial department. Storyboard panels were digitized onto an Avid editing machine, and *Shrek 2* editors Mike Andrews, Sim Evan-Jones, and second editor Michelle Belforte, working with the directors and producers, continued to develop and hone the sequence, paying particular attention to the pacing within the scene. "Now we get to see it play like a film," says Miller, "and then it takes on an entirely different look. You think you have the scene cracked, and then you put it on the Avid and it doesn't work. So then you make it work. You keep developing it."

At this stage, sound effects were added, along with a scratch track of dialogue, usually consisting of voices provided by the directors and other creators. Existing songs ("needle-drop music") began to be incorporated, with director Andrew Adamson, producer Aron Warner, and editors Andrews and Evan-Jones playing an important role in both selecting the music and integrating it within the sequence. (For a more in-depth discussion of the music for *Shrek 2,* see Part 5.)

It is an intense, relentless workshopping process with everyone, as Miller puts it, "getting their hands on everything" at least once. Indeed, most sequences ended up being storyboarded more than twenty times. This process of writing and rewriting, on board, on page, and in editorial, was repeated for every single sequence in the movie. All told, there are thirty-two sequences in *Shrek 2.*

"All I know is, Puss is cute, he's got snappy lines, and he purrs."

— Donkey

CONSTRUCTING A 3-D WORLD

Meanwhile, the art department (consisting of a grand total of seven artists) was working intensely with directors and producers to generate the plethora of images needed for the movie. *Shrek 2* production designer Guillaume Aretos comments, "It's a very small department that works like crazy to produce key images, primarily from the storyboards." These germinal paintings, also known as *color keys,* serve two purposes. First, says Aretos, they must convey "the major design options we took during the preproduction phase, and second, give visual information to all the other departments on the lighting, the

mood, the look and feel of the locations." These renderings are used for every transition that involves major lighting and location changes and are essentially a visual road map of the entire movie.

Unlike in live-action movies—where so much of the frame is filled with existing physical objects, settings, and backgrounds (no matter how tightly controlled or designed)—in the world of animation, *everything*, from the loftiest mountain to the tiniest pebble, must be created from scratch. Hence, the pressure on the art department to create images of quantity, quality, and—especially important in CG animation—accuracy. Notes Aretos, "The CG process is so complex, involving so many people, that we just can't say later on, 'Let's add a rock there,' because then we have to have it modeled, then surfaced, then placed by the layout department, and then it has to be lit."

One of *Shrek 2*'s most impressive locations, which consumed much of the art department's time, was the King and Queen's castle. It is here that several pivotal sequences of the movie take place: Shrek, Fiona, and Donkey's arrival; the disastrous first dinner; Fairy Godmother visiting Fiona; and the Royal Ball that is the climax of the movie. The castle would have to convey a fairy-tale majesty and opulence, but at the same time exert a psychological power over Shrek and Fiona. From Shrek's point of view, in particular, it would need to be both impressive and intimidating.

The initial challenge for Aretos was to achieve a balance between authenticity and fairy-tale magic. It would not suit the mood of *Shrek 2* to have a totally realistic, medieval style fortress; the fact that the King and Queen preside over a kingdom as whimsical as Far Far Away demanded something more fanciful. Yet, at the same time, the story also required an imposing rampart surrounding the castle that Giant Gingy would have to breech in the ending.

Cundo Rabaudi created this three-foot model of the castle. Physical representations were essential for giving creators an in-the-round view of crucial sets. Filmmakers would often place a small lipstick camera inside and around the model to study new camera angles.

"They say a man's home is his castle. Only in my case it is quite literally true."

— King Harold

Keeping these diverse requirements in mind, Aretos scoured the French countryside for castles to serve as models, but he could not find exactly what he was looking for. Back at PDI, Aretos continued his research and finally came upon a castle called Challain La Potherie. "It's an unknown castle, even in France," comments Aretos, but its Gothic architectural template was exactly what Aretos had been looking for. The ornamental and sculptural elements of the style seemed particularly appropriate for *Shrek*.

On a psychological level, the angular, highly civilized facade of the castle "sets up the drama with Shrek right away," says *Shrek 2* art director Steve Pilcher, because "it is such a contrast to the curvy, organic nature of Shrek's swamp. Just the sheer scale of the place is a little scary." Careful attention was paid to the interior dimensions as well. Although much of it was cavernous and imposing, Aretos and Pilcher made sure the dining room appeared a bit cramped and uncomfortable, at least for an eight-foot ogre. Eventually, red would be chosen as the room's color. It is a "royal color" in keeping with what one would expect in a castle. However, red also suggests alarm, at least from Shrek's point of view, and creates a sharp contrast with the ogre's green skin.

Once the conceptual basis of the castle was established in a series of paintings, Aretos and others moved on to the next step. In traditional animation, the castle would be created with static, two-dimensional background paintings. But in the world of *Shrek,* the creators needed to work within a three-dimensional "space" inside the computer. A virtual "camera" would be placed inside this space to record the actions of the characters. This meant the castle would have to be virtually "constructed," requiring a highly detailed set of blueprints. The same would be needed for every other set in the movie.

Working with the conceptual paintings, draftsman Paul Westicot carefully evaluated the size of the rooms, the length of the corridors, the height of the towers, and countless other architectural elements, large and small. "He then drafted the set very precisely," says Aretos, "as if it were going to be built, because *it is* going to be built, except that it's inside a virtual world." These blueprints indicate the exact dimensions of the castle to the last inch.

THE CHATTER BOX

The Challenges of 3-D

For the computer-generated actors in the SHREK films, many of whom learned their craft in the world of 2-D cartoons, the new 3-D medium presented its own difficulties.

PUSS IN BOOTS: Toward the end of filming—we were doing the Royal Ball scene, and it was LOCO, with all the props and extras—I got lost in the Castle set and could not find my way out. I felt like I wasted one of my nine lives looking for the right door!

SHREK: I'd done quite a lot of stuff in toons, a couple of the monsters in SCOOBY DOO, body-double stuff for the INCREDIBLE HULK animated series, and some commercial work for a certain frozen vegetables company. But, obviously, SHREK was a real breakout role for me. I was really nervous about messing up in my first scene, especially, as I'd never done CG before. Hitting my marks had never been a problem, but now I had a whole extra dimension to deal with. It didn't help that my first scene was on the rope bridge going to the Dragon's castle . . . that certainly put things into perspective . . . ha, ha, get it? perspective . . . never mind. Anyway, it all went really well until the last take of the day. They called "wrap," and, for some reason, I just thought the set was a good old-fashioned drawn background and stepped straight off the bridge—and into the lava. Luckily, the effects guys hadn't rendered a heat pass yet, but I was finding red goop in my ears for weeks afterward.

DONKEY: 3-D acting is a different art. I mean, once you actually have stuff like teeth and lips and eyelids you want to use 'em. But you don't want to overuse them. It's all about subtlety. I wouldn't like to try some of that eye-poppin', jaw-droppin', tongue-rolling stuff I used to pull out in my early toon days. They might not be able to put me back together again.

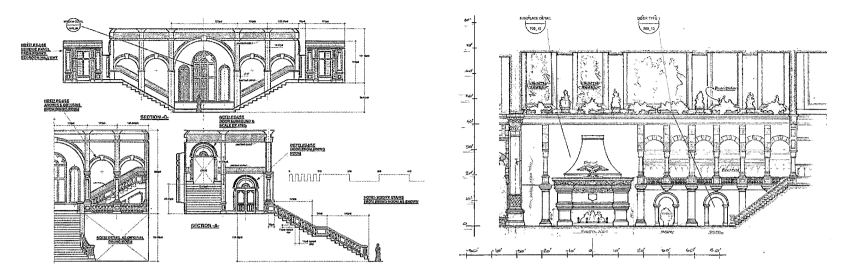

The castle needed to be intimidating to Shrek, and the artists made sure its grandiose scale and massive physical presence stood in stark contrast
to Shrek's comfortable swamp. Here are a few of the many blueprints and architectural drawings needed for the virtual construction of the castle.

Once these blueprints were completed, Westicot worked with the modeling department to start constructing the final set on the computer. Concurrently, the plans were also used by the layout department to create a *rough layout* of the set. This basic 3-D representation exists within the computer and is made up of simple forms that represent complex objects, such as cones for trees and puppetlike forms for characters. Rough layout is used as a visual tool by the creators to precisely locate the virtual camera for each shot and block out the movement of the characters. (See pages 114–15 for a more detailed description of 3-D layout.)

With all the high-tech sophistication of the layout process, it may seem a bit retrograde that physical models were also built, often before any of the virtual construction took place. But, according to Pilcher, there were some very good reasons for doing so: "You can build things extremely quickly, so we get an idea of dimension and size. Sure, we could use a computer but it's awfully time-consuming, and sometimes they need to be doing other things."

And so, using little more than paper, clay, chunks of Styrofoam, and a glue gun, modeler Cundo Rabaudi created a multitude of sets and settings for the film. "I fill in what's missing from the art work," says Rabaudi. "I'm taking a painting and turning it into a 3-D image." Paper is Rabaudi's favorite material because "it's cheap and non-toxic. I prefer to just make things out of stuff you can find in your kitchen." To simulate water Rabaudi used Saran Wrap, for rocks he crushed charcoal briquettes, and for lofty mountain peaks he crumpled up tin foil and slathered it with arm-cast plaster.

For the castle, Rabaudi made three versions, the largest measuring more than three feet. It was finished before the virtual castle was even started, in order to give directors and producers a fast but accurate visual representation for approval. The model provided a crucial eye-level perspective; once a small digital camera was placed within the castle, the creators obtained a cornucopia of angles and perspectives. In all, Rabaudi created thirty models for *Shrek 2*. Their detail, accuracy, and artistry were so great the art department often used them as references for paintings, and a number of them were photographed and used as a guide for matte paintings in the backgrounds.

PROPS

Of course, the visual world of *Shrek 2* consists of far more than just sets. Countless objects exist within these sets, including *props*. As far as the art department is concerned, props are pretty much anything from furniture to lipstick to a glass of water. Maybe a book, a teacup, an acorn—anything that is separate from the main model or set and that a character may (or may not) control or manipulate.

Working from the conceptual key paintings for each scene, the artists extrapolate *prop sheets*, which are detailed renderings of props that are organized according to each item's basic function or classification. These sheets have to convey as many details as possible, including texture and color. Often included on the sheet are photographic references that indicate a visual source for the prop and more clearly illustrate the intended surface texture. (Such references will later be used by the surfacing department to complete the prop.)

Props add enormously to the mood, meaning, and humor of a scene. Every shot in Shrek and Fiona's arrival in Far Far Away is bursting with outrageous props, including a newspaper vending machine featuring a local rag, *The Inquisitor* (detailed right down to the blaring headline "Goldilocks Behind Bars"); a trashy Fairy God-mother billboard that serves to subtly foreshadow Shrek's nemesis; gaudy carriages, complete with vanity plates; even a *Lethal Arrow 4* movie poster. This utter profusion of props plays an important role in overcoming visual predictability, which is a perennial problem in animation, and seductively compels the viewer to believe in the reality of *Shrek 2*.

Models for the Honeymoon Cottage, the Prison, the Castle, and Fairy Godmother's Office. Their accuracy was so great that they often served as visual references for background artists.

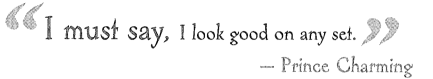

❝I must say, I look good on any set. ❞

— Prince Charming

A number of Steve Pilcher's favorite props can be found in the Poison Apple tavern. In this setting, the mood shifts to something more dark and sinister. Yet, as Pilcher points out, "The props have a sense of humor to them, which is important to *Shrek*. We have things like gnome bowling, a pool table with billiard-ball sculls from what-ever creature, a game of darts with axes. It's a little over the top, but always interesting."

However, it is not just their sheer multitude or artistry or humor that makes for good props. They must also convey the appearance of age in order to achieve the authenticity that the creators of *Shrek 2* are constantly striving for. "It's easy for CG to model a cup and make it look brand new," says Pilcher. "But to give it a sense of age, you have to put some scratches on it, some dust. You have to think about the life of that cup. How many times has it been lifted off a table? How long ago was it washed? There's attention to everything, nothing can be taken for granted. You have to look at it like the whole world is alive."

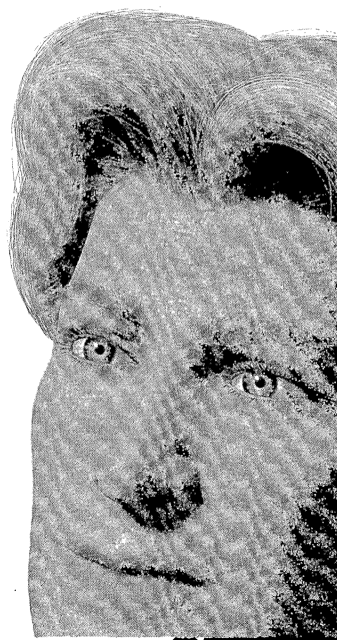

Daddy's Evil Plot

Dragon Wings
pickled eyeballs
crunchy Children Fingers

Unhappy Hour Nightly 5-7pm

The Poison Apple

SOUVENIR SHIRT $10

The Ugly Stepsister is voiced by Larry King.

The seedy Poison Apple tavern features an abundance of outrageous characters and props. The filmmakers had every fairy-tale bad guy to draw from for inspiration.

The Process of 3-D Layout

Before *Shrek 2* could be animated, it first had to be laid out in a rough visual form on the computer. This relatively crude, nondetailed version of characters and sets (basic shapes for objects and puppetlike forms for characters) dramatically reduces the rendering time the computer needs to generate the images, making it a far more practical tool for the constant revisions that would be required. The 3-D layout process is guided by *Shrek 2* layout supervisor Bob Whitehill and his crew, who are the "virtual cinematographers," constructing shots and executing camera movements in the computer.

As they review the 3-D layout together, the directors, producers, and animators can work with the art department to block out the action and refine the sets. For example, a window may need to be lowered so Shrek can peer out of it, or the set may need to be altered for aesthetic reasons. Since sequences are constantly being rewritten, perhaps a character will need more time to play out the scene. Rather than forcing the character to unnaturally alter his pace, a castle hallway can simply be lengthened.

Rough 3-D layout is a particularly important tool for visually complex scenes, such as the sequence where Shrek, Fiona, and Donkey first arrive at the Castle and prepare to meet the King and Queen before

a large crowd of onlookers. For this scene, the 3-D layout helped the creators position the camera as it cut back and forth multiple times between the couple proceeding down the red carpet and the parents at the other end, while also ensuring that the intercut dialogue between the two sets of characters kept pace with the action.

Another challenge was the dinner sequence, where it was important to make sure the characters' sight lines were correct (in other words, that they did not appear to be looking the wrong way when they were talking to each other). Comments *Shrek* 2 director Conrad Vernon, "This was an incredibly difficult scene because people are all sitting around a table. You've got to know who they're looking at, and who to cut to, without making it look like the Queen is just turning into Shrek."

The supreme flexibility of the rough layout also makes it a handy tool for the layout artists in the early stages of set development. When Steve Pilcher and the layout department first built the forest, they could readily move objects such as trees and rocks for more effective composition and blocking, and even change the angle or slope of the ground. These changes would be much more difficult to implement at a later, more visually detailed stage. Pilcher describes the process as "almost like working with clay in a rough fashion. No details—trees can be just tubes at that point. All you're thinking about is composition. If it works there, it's a like a foundation" that will underpin the visual integrity of the sequence through completion of the film.

Part 4
Warts and All

About nine months into production on *Shrek 2*, enough storyboarded sequences had been edited to create a rough story reel. Within this reel there was no final animation, and virtually nothing in the way of backgrounds or special effects. Instead, it was basically an extended, storyboarded version of the film that looked very little like the final, big-screen version.

Shrek 2 director Kelly Asbury refers to this reel as "the blueprint of the movie. It is constantly being built upon, and changed and fixed and edited and redrawn and reshot. It is from this reel that everything springs." Both as a creative compass and an ongoing workshopping tool, the story reel was screened every four or five weeks. Asbury describes it as "a way of stepping back from the canvas and looking at the global picture of the story. It's something all of us have to do."

Initial screenings of the story reel made a number of things clear. First, it is something of a storytelling truism that the more formidable the villain the better, simply because the hero will have to rise to the occasion. Yet, amid the intricate plotting of *Shrek 2*, Fairy Godmother initially lacked some of the necessary evil to be truly intimidating. Her characterization was mostly that of a professional homebody who makes everyone's life beautiful, and although this trait would endure (and grow dramatically in magnitude), the creators felt she needed to go deeper and darker.

For *Shrek 2* director Conrad Vernon, the first step in achieving this was the realization that Fairy Godmother needed a distinctive personality trait—or, more specifically, a compulsion. In short, says Vernon, "There was nothing inside her that was driving her to do the things she needed to do." The creators searched far and wide for this essential element, and, as the narrative simplified with the gradual paring away and refinement of the plot, her character and motivation started to clarify.

A turning point came when the creators were working on the scene where Fairy Godmother takes the King "for a ride" to pressure him to honor their secret deal. Vernon and others had previously toyed with Fairy Godmother having a compulsive eating

Pricilla

disorder, so they decided that here would be the perfect place to exploit it. As she grows more and more annoyed at the King, she and her henchmen take him to Friar's Fat Boy so she can pig out on a Renaissance Wrap.

Although the compulsive-eating-disorder concept would eventually be dropped, Vernon and others kept piling on individual character bits. As the scene was animated, and especially when Jennifer Saunders began to give voice to Fairy Godmother, a distinct, powerful personality took hold. Says Vernon, "Once a character starts to take on a life of its own, and starts performing for you instead of you trying to perform for it," it is clear the characterization is finally starting to click.

The honing of Fairy Godmother's personality traits in turn helped to enlarge and intensify her ultimate goal. Obviously, her most immediate task is to marry off her son. But, like all great villains, she is also obsessed by a grand, demented dream. As Vernon sees it, "A Fairy Godmother has never ruled a kingdom and she is going to be the first, by putting her son on the throne. And she will stop at nothing to get what she wants."

"Compulsive? ME!? Oh goodness gracious, of course not! I AM as a rule rather particular about certain things. But compulsive? Compulsive in what way?. . . Tell me! NOW!"

— Fairy Godmother

The conceptual painting at left depicts Fairy Godmother's base of operations: the oh-so-quaint cottage that serves as her front office and the factory where she manufactures a broad array of powerful (and toxic) magic potions. Before-and-after photos hang on her office wall as testimonials from satisfied customers.

Fairy Godmother's Recipe for Love Potion #9:

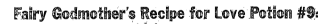

A drop of desire…
A pinch of passion…
And just a hint of…lust!

LUST

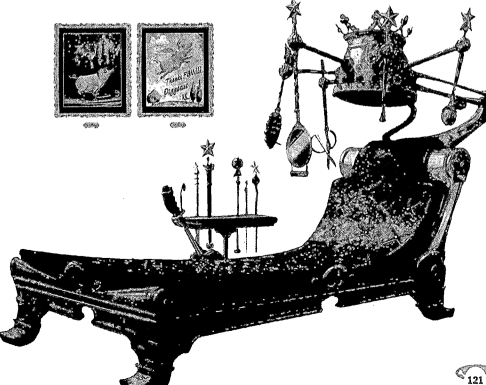

"Believe me, Harold, it's what's best ... not only for your daughter ... but for your kingdom!"

FROM OGRE TO HUNK

But perhaps the most important story element the creators grappled with was the transformation of Shrek himself. *Shrek 2* producer David Lipman emphasizes, "We always have to keep remembering it's Shrek's movie. You don't want Donkey to overpower things, and he does have a tendency to steal the show, as does Puss In Boots." Chris Miller agrees, noting, "You have to make sure the emotional impact of the film is real by making sure it's Shrek's movie. But with all these twists and turns, it's kind of easy to lose your character." Somehow, the creators would have to ensure that Shrek's story remained paramount. Jeffrey Katzenberg is emphatic on this key point: "The story challenge was how to give it heart again, how to keep it emotional. I think one of the things that most surprised people about the first film was how heartfelt it was, and how moved people were in the end by it. And that's a very essential and imperative ingredient in the DNA of Shrek."

The beginnings of a solution came about when story writer Joe Stillman pointed out to Andrew Adamson that Shrek was absent for a brief but very critical period in the third act. Adamson concurred, commenting, "We were kind of losing him from the story." Ultimately, the creators made a slight but significant alteration to the plot. Originally, after Shrek was transformed into a classically handsome hero, he went to Far Far Away to appeal directly to Fiona. Before he could actually make contact, he was arrested and thrown in jail. From there, he had to escape and rush to save Fiona from drinking another potion that would seal her love (and fate) with Prince Charming. The plot line was narratively effective and exciting (and would mostly be preserved), but it never really allowed Shrek a moment of intense, emotional crisis.

The creators achieved this by postponing his arrest and instead

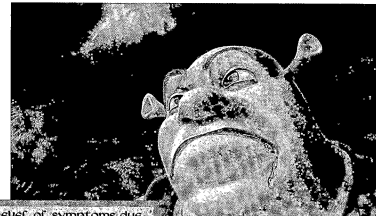

For relief of symptoms due to common unhappiness.

WARNING!

Side effects my include burning, itching, oozing, weeping, not intended for heart patients or those with nervous disorders.

To make the effects of the potion permanent, the drinker must obtain his or hers true loves first kiss by midnight.

inserting a moment where he witnesses what he believes to be Fiona being won over by Prince Charming. Suddenly, all of Shrek's doubts and insecurities crystallize, and he retreats to the Poison Apple tavern to drown his sorrows with Donkey and Puss. As Adamson puts it, "He falls back on his old flaw, which is believing himself to be unlovable." Echoing the crisis of the first *Shrek*, Shrek's most formidable opponent is himself.

Chris Miller, who was the story artist on this sequence (and worked on it for over a year), had to probe Shrek's anguished state of mind. Miller sensed inside Shrek a kind of misguided nobility, born partly out of insecurity and partly out of a genuine and abiding love for Fiona. Miller imagined that Shrek cannot help thinking, "Did I mess things up by rescuing her? Now I see the world she was intended to have, and I don't fit into this world." From this emotional low point, Shrek decides he cannot live without Fiona, and, in Adamson's words, "we build up his character to say, 'Not only am I lovable but I'm going to go to Fiona and tell her I'm willing to do and be whatever she wants me to be if she will just love me.' And that made it a much more emotional ending."

Here, Shrek drinks the magic potion. The effects of the potion are shown on the following spread. The animators made sure that Handsome Shrek had certain key physical traits and mannerisms of Shrek as an ogre.

"*A cute button nose? Thick wavy locks? Taut round buttocks!!*"

THE ACTORS CONTRIBUTE MORE THAN VOICES

One of the most important contributions to story and character development is made by the actors who provide the character voices. Over the course of an animated production, actors are often brought in to record five or six times, or even more. According to Andrew Adamson, "You get a chance to play the movie out several times with the actors and refine it as you go." Because of this crucial input, it was important to involve actors such as Mike Myers, Eddie Murphy, and Cameron Diaz early on.

Having these accomplished actors simply read their lines is an enormous improvement over the existing scratch track. "Scenes that kind of work with the scratch dialogue," says Adamson, "work fantastically with the actors." Yet, their contribution goes much deeper than that.

Mike Myers was instrumental in helping evolve the character of Shrek, as well as in molding key moments such as the Poison Apple sequence. Adamson remembers going into a recording session with Myers, having just rewritten the scene to make it center more on Shrek. "It was still too much about Puss and Donkey," says Adamson, "with Shrek kind of on the edge of the scene. And we tried recording that with Mike, and, of course, he completely busted our chops! He said, 'This isn't working. This is supposed to be a big turnaround for my character and I don't know where I'm turning around to!'" With Myers's input and total commitment to the role of Shrek, Adamson and others managed to find that turnaround.

Mike Myers, Eddie Murphy, and Cameron Diaz give voice to the characters.

"Mike Myers, a man after my own heart! And my own voice, as well!"

— Shrek

128

Myers, as an actor, director, and writer, tends to be analytical in his approach to comedy. Says Adamson, "He likes to take a line and experiment and bounce stuff off us. He was also able to watch our story reels and give us another filmmaker's perspective—but a filmmaker who *is* Shrek. His notes really helped clarify Shrek's story."

Eddie Murphy, on the other hand, tends to be more intuitive. "Eddie is someone who will come in, you'll pitch something to him, he'll read though the script very quietly, he'll smile occasionally, take one pass reading it through to himself, and then he's instantly *on*. He is Donkey," says Adamson. "You'll write a one-line joke, he'll turn it into three. He'll just run with it. You have no idea where it comes from. It's like sometimes *he* has no idea where it comes from. It's just so intuitive."

However, when asked what it was like to work with Andrew Adamson, Eddie Murphy was surprisingly reticent. "Andrew, uh, he's got some issues. This isn't the right place to talk about it. We are supposed to be talking about something that's fun for the kids and the family to come see. A good wholesome entertainment. And don't push my Andrew button. . . ." But Murphy instantly reconsiders: "No, Andrew is a joy to work with. He is a breath of fresh air. He is inventive. He is intelligent.

And he's smart." Moreover, Murphy appreciated the rich comedic possibilities that *Shrek 2* offered. It allowed him room "to stretch out" as a comedian, and since comedians tend to have "vivid imaginations," Murphy believes they can actually "visualize the stuff they're saying."

Cameron Diaz brought a crucial perspective to Fiona, particularly since so many of *Shrek 2*'s writers and directors are men. As far as Adamson is concerned, "While I have a strong feeling about how strong female characters should be, sometimes it's just really impossible to see it from their perspective." In addition, over the span of making both *Shrek* movies, Diaz had taken on many demanding roles and increased her power and range as an actress; says Adamson, "What she brings back to me in these recording sessions is fantastic." Diaz likens the meticulous recording process of animation to building a house, with the actor's voice as the frame. "That's the first thing that goes up," says Diaz, "and then everything else gets built around it. So it's always interesting to see what it becomes."

For the new actors in *Shrek 2,* there was a fairly steep learning curve in trying to understand the new characters, particularly as the writers, directors, and producers were trying to do the same. To help

The PDI/DreamWorks *Shrek 2* crew in Redwood City

define their roles, actors will often start out the in initial sessions by taking their character to extremes. According to Conrad Vernon, an actor's performance may at first be "really over the top, testosterone gallant, and then pulled back to get really soft and sophisticated." Within this wide range lurks the proper tone, intensity, and nuance.

One of the ways Rupert Everett, who plays Prince Charming, hit his character target was by viewing Prince Charming as a very contemporary archetype. "He's just all about image and products and hair and *Entertainment Weekly*," says Everett. "Far Far Away is kind of like Hollywood . . . so he represents all of that. He's living the so-called dream." Vernon admires how Everett "gave a definite sophistication to his character's childishness, so he was believable but just a little tweaked in the head. You know, he has this great voice, and he speaks very regally: 'I will rend his head from his shoulders! Where is this foul ogre!?' And then he puts on a paper crown at Friar's Fat Boy and eats a little Happy Meal. So it's kind of a balance."

Antonio Banderas was also able to explore and expand the character of Puss In Boots. Early on the creators had their eyes set on Banderas, and his performance as Zorro certainly had an effect on how they viewed Puss. But the recording sessions definitely had a further impact. Recalls Adamson, "He brought an element of comedy to the character and a cuteness that I hadn't expected. I was planning initially to keep him a lot more serious all the time, but Antonio does these little moments of cuteness that really come through."

From these initial sessions, the voices were cut into the existing scratch track, and, as Vernon puts it, the effected sequences "leaped up many levels in terms of the life they gave the movie." As the creators continued to add the actors' voices to other sequences, "more layers of the characters came to life," which prompted further creative changes and adjustments.

"Ah, yes! Within Antonio beats the heart of a true gato! "
— Puss In Boots

Largely because of scheduling conflicts, the actors are recorded individually and at different times. This can lead to situations where the performances, as wonderful as they are, do not quite mesh. Says David Lipman, "When you record Cameron, it might put Mike Myers's previous performance off, and so you have to adjust by rerecording Myers. It's this gigantic jigsaw puzzle."

In contrast to the immediacy of live theater or the intense interplay with fellow actors on a movie set, the *Shrek* actors sat alone in a recording booth, with the directors as their only guide. It's a rather peculiar challenge for actors used to playing in front of an audience. "If it's only your voice that you're working with," asks Julie Andrews, who plays the Queen, "are you going too over the top? Are you also being somewhat animated when you should, in fact, be [more] real? It's hard to thread that needle." Yet, in other ways, Andrews found the process rather liberating. "It's slightly freeing up in a way. I mean, anything goes, and I guess you have to just really fly by the seat of your pants and trust your director."

Jennifer Saunders, who plays Fairy Godmother, concurs: "It's terribly freeing in a way, in that it's just your voice. No one's gonna say, 'ooh, she looked a bit rough.'" John Cleese, who plays the King, observes: "Sometimes you're doing a scene and you can't remember what the scene was before, or maybe it's been slightly rewritten. So you have to rely tremendously on [the directors] to explain exactly what the situation is, and exactly what you're feeling. You can't sort of feel it out, like common sense, in the way you would with a script." Cleese once joked in an interview that there were certain sinister connotations in this unusual relationship with the director. Cleese claimed that in playing an animated character he had absolutely no idea of what he was doing. Instead, he theorized, the creators purposely kept him in the dark as a way of controlling him.

Adamson is amused and understanding of this point of view: "It's kind of true because we see the actors every two or three months, give them only two or three scenes, tell them the conflicts of the movie. And so, especially for the first time with the new actors, it's an issue of trust."

The *Shrek 2* crew at the DreamWorks campus in Glendale

"That's mine. Decaf.
Otherwise I'm up all night."

ANIMATION: BREATHING LIFE INTO THE CHARACTERS

Once the sequences were completed in rough layout form and given voice by the actors, they continued along the production pipeline to the animation department. Here, the animators faced the critical task of breathing life into the rough, almost puppetlike forms of the characters. Supervising animators Raman Hui, James Baxter, and Tim Cheung are in charge of a team of forty-nine animators. Hui defines his job primarily as "making sure all the acting, all the performances, all the animation is right for the moment."

Above all, *the moment*. Consider the scene when Shrek observes what he believes to be Prince Charming wooing Fiona. In reality, this seemingly "simple moment" of misunderstanding consists of many smaller moments. The first is when Shrek notices something, the second is when he focuses in on the two of them, the third is confusion, the fourth is a slow realization, the fifth is shock, and so on. Hui and his fellow animators had to infuse *Shrek 2* from beginning to end with these split-second moments of pure emotion.

Animators have a number of resources to draw from in helping achieve this monumental task, including the rough layout, the story reel (and storyboards), highly detailed input from the directors, sophisticated animation tools, and a little bonus from the recording sessions: videotape of the actors reading and acting out their lines. Hui estimates that roughly fifty percent of the scenes with character animation are influenced in one way or another by these valuable performances. As far as he is concerned, "The actors' faces are usually a very inspiring place to start."

When Hui approaches a given scene, he considers himself something of an actor "but in a slow-mo way. A real actor has to do the scene all at once," whereas Hui is able to take all the time he needs to carefully parse the scene into as many individual beats as needed. He starts with basic blocking, in part by creating various positions or *poses* within the given scene. In a ten-second shot there can be anywhere from ten to twenty poses. Then, using proprietary EMO software, the character is manipulated through the individual control of each joint. The power of these proprietary tools is immense. Without them, CG animation, at least on the level of *Shrek 2*, would be virtually impossible. Supervising animator James Baxter comments, "These tools are becoming a lot more artist-friendly. It's so much easier to just click on things and use a few controls on the keyboard. I don't have to actually go in and write code. So really, it's just another tool. It just happens to not be a pencil."

As Hui manipulates the body of the character, almost simultaneously he concentrates on the face. He believes it is important to rough in facial animation early on so as to not "overanimate the body." The process begins with an audio breakdown in which, frame by frame, the characters' voices are pulled apart into individual sounds and syllables. Using his library of twenty-five phonemes, Hui is able to approximate how (and to what degree) the lips form for each syllable. For example, 100 percent of the sound *mmmm* would compress the lips extremely, whereas at fifty percent a softer *mmmm* sound is implied. (For a more detailed description of facial animation, see pages 150–51.)

There are also controls for creating smiles or sneers or frowns. Different sides of the lips or eyebrows can be manipulated to create looks of anger or happiness. Eyes can be locked on a given object when the head moves; they have to blink realistically and expressively. A double blink, for example, may signify flirting or anger depending on the context of the scene.

> **"I can honestly say** Shrek 'double blinked' at me first. And I don't think he was angry! It was definitely flirtatious.**"**
> — Princess Fiona

Later, Hui will do a voice pass where the breathing motions of the character are carefully timed with the dialogue. A breathing motion may involve manipulating lower and upper chest controls, as well as creating a more pronounced exhale motion at the end of a sentence.

Hui has to constantly measure the emotional weight and dimension of each instant: what the given moment means and how it feels from the character's point of view. At the same time, he has to look outside himself, visualizing the moment on the screen. A low-tech tool employed by Hui is a mirror that never leaves his side. With it, he can freeze a certain expression on his face and use it as a guide for the character. (Although all the animators took turns animating all the major characters, Hui's family in Hong Kong claims they can tell which scenes Hui animated himself.)

Furthermore, trademark expressions or gestures often help identify a character. For Shrek, it may be his curiously cocked eyebrow or slightly pained grimace, for Fiona a friendly but skeptical gaze, and

An animator acts before a maze of mirrors to better define a given character motion.

A critical element is capturing a sense of a character's shifting body weight. This not only imparts realism (after all, every living creature is subject to gravity), it also adds another dimension to a character. Similarly, how a character walks is also critical: for Shrek, it is the lumbering stride of a heavy, eight-foot ogre. For Puss, the effortless grace of a swashbuckling feline. And for Donkey?

Hui tends to think of Donkey more like a dog. "In a way, Donkey is like Shrek's puppy," he says. For example, at the dinner-table scene, Donkey races in and leaps onto a chair like an unruly sheepdog (prompting the King to bellow, "Bad Donkey! Down, down!"). Yet, in the midst of this calamitous action, Hui was careful to establish certain limitations to Donkey's movement. This is partly for the sake of believability (when Donkey falls or runs into something, the physical impact looks and feels real), but also to avoid the clash of Donkey's more cartoonish style with that of the realistic human characters.

for Donkey a big toothy smile with bulging cheeks. These signature gestures especially came in handy when Shrek and Donkey were transformed by the magic potion into their "handsome" counterparts. The animators carefully morphed the characters' well-known expressions onto the new characters so that the audience would never question their true identities.

But animation also involves bringing life to the entire body. Hui will often start with the limbs by defining the arc of the movement: How does the arm move, exactly? Does the character lead with the elbow or the hand? Is the movement sharp or languid? Secondary movements involving overlapping motion and follow-through must also be precisely defined: After a character throws an object, for example, how does he regain his balance?

“A dog!!?? I ain't no dog!
And I sure ain't no puppy, neither!
I AM A DONKEY! Got it!!?? ”

— Donkey

The more human the character, the more challenging the animation. Although the Queen is speaking in this development piece, our eyes naturally dart to the King to gauge his reaction. These reactive moments are what animators relish.

Generally speaking, humans such as the King and Queen were the hardest to animate. "Because we watch humans every day," says Hui, "we tend to be more critical when we look at a human character than, say, a cat." Yet, the answer did not involve pure realism either. Jeffrey Katzenberg notes, "when you do photorealistic humans in CG animation they become synthetic. In other words, you can actually get them to look human, but you can't get them to feel human." The answer involved a tricky balance between reality and make-believe. "We ultimately pulled back and stylized our characters more than we originally designed or intended to," explains Katzenberg, "because they were too realistic and therefore less lifelike."

The directors play an essential role in helping the animators to realize these virtual performances. "When we work with the animators," says Kelly Asbury, "we try to convey to them not only the motivations of the characters and the humor, we try and make them think of the characters as *real*. How would they *really act* in this situation." According to Hui, to help convey this, directors will "have a lot of fun in just acting stuff out in front of us, sometimes even sketching out certain expressions they want us to capture."

Andrew Adamson emphasizes that "animators literally are actors, and you have to work with them as actors, to a degree. When you think about what they're doing, they're taking on the characters, how they move and talk and think." And like real actors, animators also have to master the art of subtext, that is, characters saying one thing but thinking or feeling something entirely different.

A key to achieving this subtlety is often through the window to the soul: the eyes. Says Adamson, "People's eyes are constantly in motion. They look away if they're not telling the truth, they look around if they're thinking. The animators have to get all those nuances in there." Usually, after a sequence has been animated, Adamson and the other directors will do an *eye pass*, filling every empty character moment with a specific thought or feeling expressed through the eyes.

Nowhere is this more important than in what Hui regards as the height of the animator's art: a character's reaction. These are the moments animators cherish because there is no dialogue to carry the scene along, just pure, expressive animation. Katzenberg cites a particular moment in the production of *Shrek* when the power of purely reactive animation came alive for him: "Shrek and Fiona are having an argument, and as Fiona moves from the shadow into the light, it's a very beautiful and angelic moment on her face. It was so compelling and so emotional and so revealing of her, that I just remember thinking, 'Okay, there's what we have to achieve for the rest of this movie.'"

It usually takes an animator an entire day to do one second of animation. As a rule of thumb, fifty percent of that initial animation is substantially modified, taking another week to nail down completely. Yet, Hui consoles himself with the fact that "with each layer of animation, it becomes more and more alive."

Adamson relates something that happened once during a recording session: "Mike Myers paid a huge compliment to Raman when he said, 'I'm so thankful to have you looking after my face so well!'" Myers marveled at how Hui, Baxter, Cheung, and the other animators managed to make Shrek move and act the way Myers himself would, if he were physically playing the part. For an animator, that is a very high compliment indeed.

VISUAL EFFECTS: ENRICHING THE CG ENVIRONMENT

While the animators were making painstaking but steady progress, another department was also hard at work. Starting well before production commenced, *Shrek 2* visual effects (VFX) supervisor Ken Bielenberg and *Shrek 2* head of effects Arnauld Lamorlette laid out a plan to design software solutions to drive the complex organic effects that would be required in the film. These effects cover everything from the subtlety of a flickering candle flame to the visually symphonic dynamics of Shrek and Donkey's magic-potion transformation. In a way, their greatest challenge was their own legacy, for *Shrek* had raised the bar of technical and creative excellence so high that any future improvements by definition would be hard to come by. In *Shrek 2*, they would have to generate more effects of even greater complexity, and yet achieve them in less than half the time of the first movie.

A number of factors were stacked in their favor. They were able to draw upon PDI/DreamWorks's extensive repository of experience and proprietary technology. The first *Shrek* had refined a number of tools that could be leveraged for *Shrek 2*. In addition, they were able to take advantage of a precious "time gap" between the two projects, allowing them to advance certain key technologies, particularly those relating to lighting and the refinement of human skin. And, of course, there was always their silent partner, Moore's Law, which posits that the computational power of the microchip doubles every eighteen months.

Still, raw power alone would not do it. While it is true that steadily advancing computers help facilitate the more varied and complex effects that Bielenberg had in mind, he notes rather wryly, "We also keep increasing our demands and continually overwhelm the computer systems. The faster they get, the more we put on them until we reach the breaking point, and then we have to pull back and optimize." And, despite all the technical advances of the last twenty years, time is still money. Bielenberg would always "try to not pull back on what the story needs." Still, practical imperatives would require finding the most efficient means of achieving what the directors and producers wanted.

In this color key, Handsome Shrek, Noble Steed, and Puss In Boots race to the castle to find Fiona.

"Take it from me. Sometimes raw power is all you got!"

— Shrek

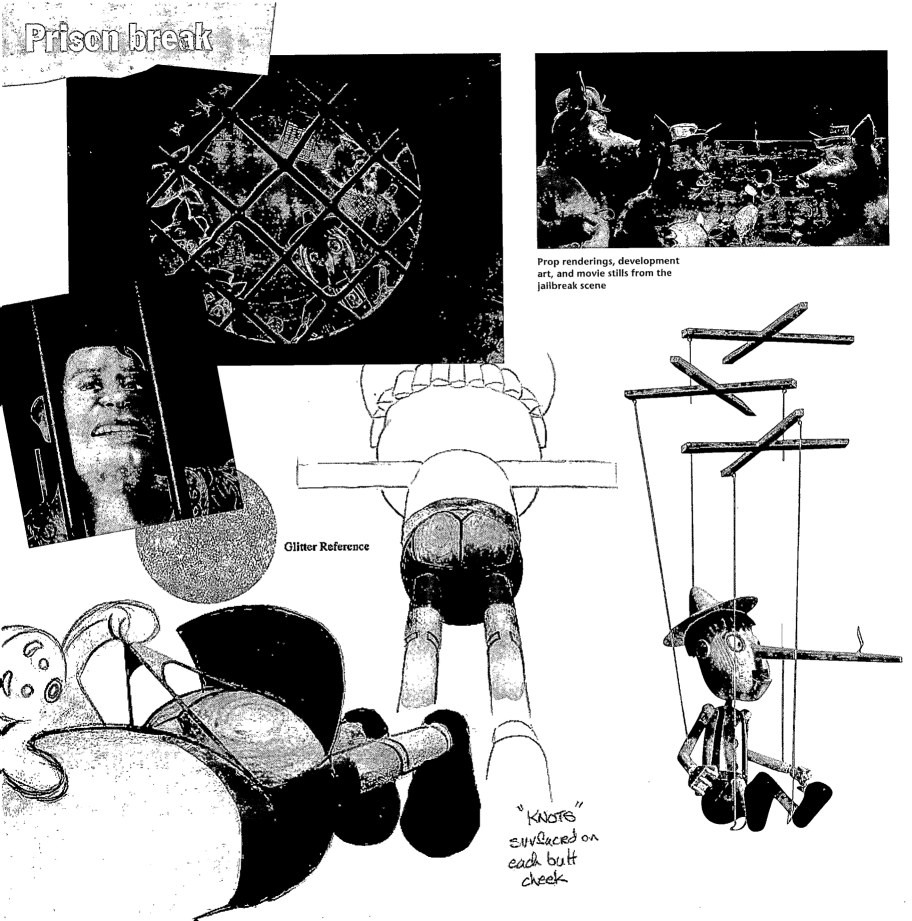

Prop renderings, development art, and movie stills from the jailbreak scene

Glitter Reference

"KNOTS" ensuared on each butt cheek

Perhaps the most important challenge of all, however, was knowing how to harness this power and to what effect. For example, one of the grand obsessions of CG technology is the creation of believable humans. While great strides have been made in the areas of basic movement and facial animation, skin remains a tremendous challenge. As Bielenberg constantly reminds himself, "If you don't do humans quite right, there's always something wrong" in the mind of the audience.

Unlike most inanimate objects, human skin absorbs a good portion of light. Once light penetrates the outside layer, it scatters among the surrounding tissue, creating a soft, translucent glow. One of the reasons CG humans lack believability is that their "skin" is more like a mannequin's; it merely bounces the light. So, PDI/DreamWorks developed and refined a subsurface scattering tool that re-creates this subtle but pervasive phenomenon.

In the course of developing these and other technologies, the animation technology and visual effects departments were not just creating stand-alone effects but also practical production tools that could be employed by other departments, such as animation. Producer David Lipman notes the new crowd systems in *Shrek 2*, as well as complex weather effects, new hair dynamics, and new lighting techniques that enhance the translucency of the skin. "Not only do these new techniques look better," says Lipman, "but they make our lives easier in terms of production." (See pages 152–53 adjoining column for a more detailed description of some of these striking innovations.)

Nowhere was the contribution of these tools more keenly felt than in the next stop along the production pipeline: the surfacing and lighting departments. All objects have a specific surface, be it the skin of an ogre or the bark of a tree. The surfacing department takes fully animated scenes and has to create these surfaces for virtually every solid object within the scene. It is this highly detailed surfacing that gives computer animation much of its striking realism. Over the years, PDI has developed many proprietary tools, including special *shaders* (essentially complex units of code) that are used to surface the characters and objects.

Shrek 2 features improved lighting techniques that enhance the natural translucency of skin.

Working closely with Bielenberg, *Shrek 2*'s surfacing lead, David Doepp, meticulously created the detailed textures that simulate human skin and hair. Surfacing can be as realistic (and complex) as the creators wish. For example, consider Puss In Boots: surfacing animators used flow controls to achieve swirling movements on the character's fur. Says Bielenberg, "The curvature and the direction the hair is grown can be animated so we can get blowing fur." (This type of shader, by the way, was used on everything from Donkey's mane to grass in a field. After all, says Bielenberg, "Grass is just long, green hair.")

But the complexity does not stop there. Puss has variegated tabby markings, and on a real cat these markings originate not just on the surface of the fur but along the entire shaft of each individual strand of hair. Combine this with the fact that characters constantly *deform*, or change shape, and things get even more complicated. And yet, even this does not begin to take into account the actual texture of the fur or the effect of different kinds of light on (and through) the fur. And of course once this fur *gets wet*, an entirely new layer of complexity has to be grappled with. This multitude of variables has to be scrutinized, mastered, and manipulated by the scientists/artists at PDI/DreamWorks.

The fur on Puss In Boots required a battery of software tools to achieve a highly realistic appearance.

LIGHTING

Another key step in the process is lighting. Working in tandem with Bielenberg, Phillippe Gluckman, *Shrek 2*'s co-visual effects supervisor, oversees the lighting and effects in each sequence.

The basic lighting strategy for characters is fairly simple and not too dissimilar from that used in live action. For example, Fiona requires a strong rim light on her hair to delineate her from the background, as well as a flattering key light and soft fill to help enhance her "naturally" attractive face. Shrek, on the other hand, is far more forgiving. Says Bielenberg, "His face has a lot more character to it. It's the difference between a lead actress and a character actor."

> **Soft light!** What are you talking about? I always look this good. It's just my natural bone structure . . . Mummy says I have her cheekbones.
>
> — Prince Charming

Of course, this "lighting" takes place inside a computer, and one of the most exciting lighting innovations used for *Shrek 2* is *global illumination*. Typically, CG animation struggles to achieve a convincing fill light. Global illumination, however, is able to duplicate the phenomenon of light bouncing off of one object and partially illuminating another. Take the dark shadow that often forms under a character's chin: says Bielenberg, "It often gets really dark and black underneath. But with global illumination the computer calculates the bounced light coming off the environment or off their chests and fills in the area under the chin or nose." Thus, instead of having to create a specific fill light (which, in turn, may cause unwanted shadows), global illumination performs this task far more easily and realistically. More than half the shots in *Shrek 2* use this advanced technique.

The journey from story concept to a fully surfaced, effects-laden sequence is a long, complicated road, representing the cumulative efforts of hundreds of technicians, artists, writers, directors, and producers. But as the lights dim in the screening room, and the creators view a freshly finished scene for the first time, the effect is nothing less than magical. Says Kelly Asbury, "A week earlier it was rough animation and generic lighting. Now you get the exact same scene with all this wonderful animation—the fur is on Puss In Boots, the background, the lighting, the dust floating in the air, the light beams—it's just incredible." Conrad Vernon concurs, marveling, "When they ask us what do we think, all we can say is 'Wow!'"

These stills demonstrate the effect of the global illumination technique, which replicates the phenomenon of reflected light.

At the Royal Ball

The Royal Ball is depicted in a series of color keys. A mass of onlookers lines the Red Carpet for the arrival of distinguished guests, while Fairy Godmother lets loose with a solo performance.

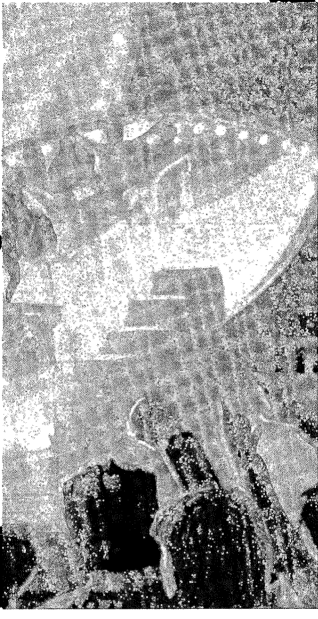

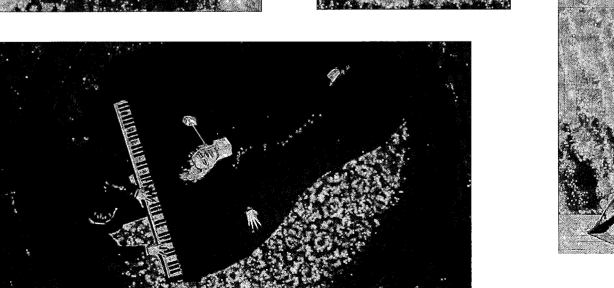

Facial Animation System

A defining element of PDI/DreamWorks's computer animation is its state-of-the-art facial animation system. Typically, CG animation may be able to create human and humanlike creatures, at least initially. But when called upon to express emotion, their photorealistic faces fall short of our expectations. *Antz* marked a significant advance in PDI's attempt to "humanize" CG characters with an early version of the facial animation system. However, it was *Shrek* that finally achieved a truly convincing level of human expressiveness. Quite literally, *Shrek* would not have been possible without this system.

Essentially, the facial animation system re-creates on a computer the highly complex web of muscles that underlie the human face. Says supervising animator Raman Hui, "It's a system that allows you to have total control of all these facial muscles to make the acting come through." More than two hundred facial muscles can be manipulated by the animators; everything from a twitching eye to a broad smile. The system also includes tools such as *lipstick*, which re-creates the phenomenon of lips sticking together before parting.

However, what really distinguishes this system is its everyday practicality. "It's very animator friendly," says Hui. "You're not dealing with physics or math." Instead, the animator is able to completely focus on the character's face and literally "act out the scene. It's like talking to the character's face,

and telling it, 'I want you to smile a little bit more on your left side, and don't smile on your right side. I want you to open your eye wide on the left side, but then close your eye on the right side.' It's a system where you're talking to this character, but using a keyboard to do it." The system even provides *external controls*, allowing Shrek to tug on his lip or rub his chin. (These facial movements can only occur externally, prompted by an object such as a hand.)

As *Shrek 2* was nearing production, the character TDs (technical directors) approached the animators and asked what further improvements could be made. (Quips Hui, "The TDs take very good care of us. We're spoiled!") Notable advances include something called *clinch*, as when someone clinches their teeth and the lower part of their jaw slightly pops out. This

subtle tool proved quite useful when Prince Charming ended a line of dialogue and silently (but effectively) expressed his impatience by clinching his jaw. Another notable addition is the ability to animate swallowing, in part by controlling the Adam's apple.

The end result of this fusion of technology and artistry is a virtual face possessing all the detailed richness of that of an actual human being. At times, according to Hui, the effect "can be spooky," particularly when animated sequences are joined together for the first time. Says Hui, "We look at all the animation everyday, so I know who animated what. But when we put the sequences together, and I lose track, then the characters become alive. And their emotions are so real."

The PDI/DreamWorks Tool Kit

Solutions for achieving the so-called Holy Grails of computer animation such as believable CG humans, fire, flowing liquids, and lighting were a long time in coming. As a pioneer in the art of computer animation, PDI has developed a battery of proprietary software tools and systems that spans almost the entire CG process. This includes software for character setup and animation, cloth simulation, techniques for creating crowds, and the rendering of skin, hair, and fur.

Andy Hendrickson, who heads up technology for PDI/DreamWorks, and Academy Award®–winner Nick Foster, who heads up animation software development, continue to refine and optimize the picture-specific tools to become part of a broader studio tool kit that will ultimately be used across multiple productions. In addition, HP has provided state-of-the-art workstations and servers, which give artists unprecedented interactivity and control at their desktops. This enables the crew to push creative boundaries in bringing *Shrek 2* to life.

These tools are essential in making the world of Shrek possible. Says *Shrek 2* producer David Lipman, "You might notice in the background of a certain scene that the wind is blowing and the leaves in the trees are moving, as are the blades of grass, along with dust floating in the air. We build systems to make these things happen more or less automatically." By "more or less," Lipman means that while the creative component is essential in avoiding effects that look mechanical or lifeless, without a considerable degree of automation, these effects would be impractical if not impossible. He explains: "From a production point of view you go into the movie, saying, 'Okay, this is what we think the story is going to be. We've got crowds, water effects, wind, and so forth. What tools do we need to develop to make this movie?' If it's a single effect for a single scene, we'll make it work, but if it's multiple effects happening many times, let's figure out a way to automate it."

For example, the simulation of water and fluids has always bedeviled CG animators. Among PDI's more notable innovations is the award-winning fluid simulation program FLU, created by Nick Foster. Originally used for *Antz*, this powerful program allows different fluids to be combined in one simulation, such as water and mud. This is quite useful when Shrek

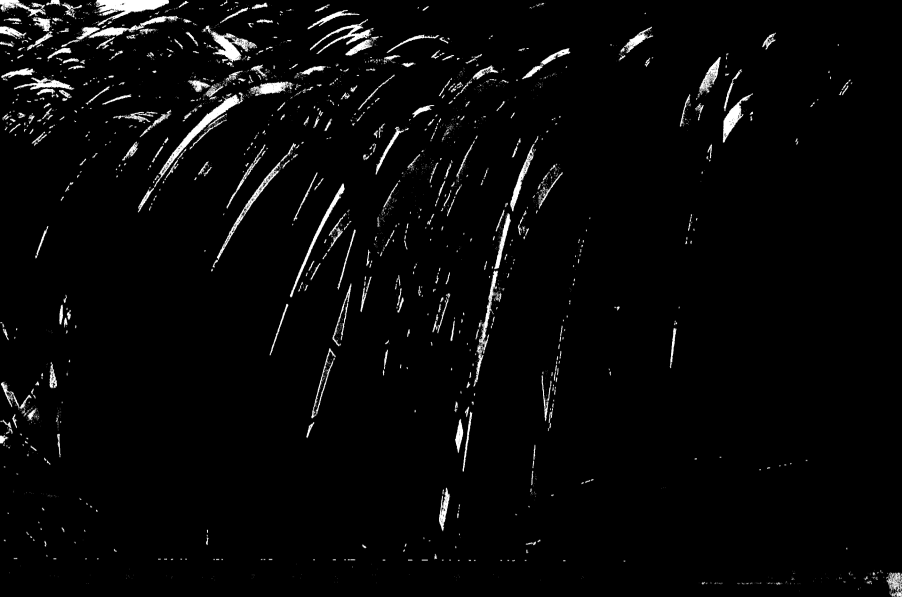

needs to take a mud shower. Explains VFX supervisor Ken Bielenberg, "We have to examine all the different elements that go into making it convincing that someone is taking a mud shower. You have the mud and how it's flowing, how it's sticking to the body, and how it makes the skin wet."

This tool can also be used for totally different elements or materials, such as lava or even blowing leaves. Initial attempts to reproduce the rippling effect of wind on trees using random movements did not look right. The problem is that the multitude of moving leaves did not reflect the hidden swirls and eddies of the blowing wind. By applying a fluid simulation (using FLU software), however, the creators were able to achieve, as Bielenberg calls it, "a coherent movement to the leaves."

Hair is also tricky, and it required a number of innovations. The issue first arose in *Shrek*, with Fiona's hair. The effects team designed a system that was essentially automatic for the animators. For *Shrek 2*, the hair needs of the characters increased significantly. Handsome Shrek and Prince Charming, for example, needed flowing, luxuriant hair, and

the effects team spent over a year working on improving its texture and movement.

In addition to *global illumination* (page 146), another lighting development for *Shrek 2* is called *volume shadows*. As Bielenberg explains, different types of shadows are cast by different objects: for example, Puss In Boots versus a block of wood. Light does not penetrate the surface of the wood, and therefore creates a simple, monochromatic shadow. With Puss however, the light penetrates through many layers of fur, creating shadows that grow progressively darker and gather some of the fur's color. The shadows within the fur add enormously to the realism. Although volume shadows have been achievable in CG animation, *Shrek 2* is one of the first movies to use the effect extensively.

Despite the science, however, there is always an essential artistry at work. It is not exact reality that the creators are striving for but instead, as Bielenberg terms it, "a stylized realism. We start with true physics and then we push it from there. For example, depending on the physical gag, it may become less real for a more comic effect."

Happily Ever After

y fall of 2003, it was apparent to the *Shrek 2* team that the three-year production was finally entering the home stretch. *Shrek 2* producer David Lipman's axiom that "it's never finished until the end, the bitter end" was proving to be quite correct. The blessing (and curse) of being able to constantly develop and refine within the carefully designed production parameters of PDI/DreamWorks ensured this was so. Yet, looking back on it, director Andrew Adamson believes, "The last big hurdle was the third act."

Of course, a huge number of creative details remained. *Shrek 2* director Conrad Vernon believes the key at this stage was to "make sure the animation is completely conveying what the actors and the storyboard artists have given us. We know what we want the emotion to be, but we need to make sure it's crystal clear and powerful."

This final stage of animation is meticulous, time-consuming work, and, according to Vernon, "It gets down to saying, 'Let's add four more frames to that shot because the character needs a little more time to think about what just happened. Is four frames enough? No, lets add another six.' And then the animator takes it, and you're saying to yourself, 'Well, it looks like they're now thinking really hard, but let's have their eyes dart a millimeter to the left, just to give it a little life.' This is definitely the *über*detail work we're doing right now." These adjustments will extend all the way through test screenings. Comments David Lipman, "If people laugh and it drowns out the next joke, we'll have to open up space to allow them to hear the next line. That's one of the many things we discover in test screenings."

MUSIC

Another element that rapidly coalesced in the final stage was the music. Like so much of *Shrek 2,* this was an organic, creative process initiated early on in production. Producer Aron Warner and Adamson experimented with different songs played against various sections of the movie. This meant "going in on weekends with our CD collections," recalls Adamson, "and throwing stuff up against sequences and

PLAYLIST

MERRY MEN
Written by Kirby Tepper,
Andrew Adamson
and Conrad Vernon
Performed by Vincent Cassel

MY BELOVED MONSTER
Written by E
Performed by eels

YOU BELONG TO ME
Written by Pee Wee King,
Redd Stewart and Chilton
Price
Performed by Jason Wade

ALL STAR
Written by Greg Camp
Performed by Smash Mouth

ON THE ROAD AGAIN
Written by Willie Nelson
Performed by Eddie Murphy

FRIENDS
Written by Mark Klingman
and Buzzy Linhart
Performed by Eddie Murphy

WHIPPED CREAM
Written by Naomi Neville
Performed by Herb Albert &
The Tijuana Brass

ESCAPE
(THE PINA COLADA SONG)
Written and Performed by
Rupert Holmes

MEDITATION
Written by Antonio Carlos
Jobim, Norman Gimbel and
Newton Mendonca
Performed by Antonio Carlos
Jobim

WELCOME TO DULOC
Music by Mike Himelstein
Lyrics by Eric Darnell

BAD REPUTATION
Written by Joan Jett, Kenny
Laguna, Ritchie Cordell and
Marty Kupersmith
Performed by Joan Jett

I'M ON MY WAY
Written by Charlie Reid and
Craig Reid
Performed by The
Proclaimers

HALLELUJAH
Written by Leonard Cohen
Performed by John Cale

TRY A LITTLE TENDERNESS
Written by Harry Woods,
Jimmy Campbell and
Reg Connelly
Performed by Eddie Murphy

I'M A BELIEVER
Words and Music by
Neil Diamond
Performed by Smash Mouth
Produced and Mixed by
Eric Valentine
Additional Vocals by
Eddie Murphy

STAY HOME
Written by Matt Mahaffey
Performed by Self
Produced and Mixed by
Eric Valentine

BEST YEARS OF OUR LIVES
Written by David Jaymes and
Geoffrey Deane
Performed by Baha Men
Produced by Michael Mangini
and Steve Greenberg

LIKE WOW!
Written by Jimmy Harry
and Sandra St. Victor
Performed by Leslie Carter

IT IS YOU (I HAVE LOVED)
Music by Harry Gregson-
Williams, John Powell and
Gavin Greenaway
Lyrics by Dana Glover
Performed by Dana Glover
Produced by Gavin Greenaway
and Harry Gregson-Williams

seeing what stuck, and then watching the whole movie and seeing how cohesive it was." For the opening sequence alone they tried more than one hundred songs.

It was partly their backgrounds in live action that inspired Warner, Adamson, and others to think a little differently in terms of how music could work in an animated feature. According to Warner, "Traditionally in animation you either have a soaring, sweeping score to help tell your story or you have individual songs to move the story along." *Shrek* broke new ground in its extensive use of "needle-drop" music (existing

pop songs), along with a more traditional, fully symphonic score. Music supervisors Marylata Jacobs (*Shrek*) and Chris Douritas (*Shrek 2*), along with editor Sim Evan-Jones, played an important role in making this novel approach work, as well as in creating an essential element of the *Shrek* legacy: a hip, hugely popular soundtrack (derived from a family-friendly animated feature no less).

Adamson believes this eclectic approach was essential to *Shrek*, in that "the music should have the same unexpected quality that the movie does—somewhat contradictory. A fairy-tale world, but juxtaposed with more contemporary music." Part of the trick in making this work, says Warner, was finding the right musical "voice" for Shrek: "We had to find singers who you wouldn't feel strange having represent Shrek. We finally figured out that whoever sounded genuine and not overproduced, just a real voice, worked best." Adamson in particular is excited about one of the new voices for *Shrek 2*: Tom Waits. Says Adamson, "You just think of him and he fits into the context of the movie perfectly."

A vivid example of the impact of needle-drop music can be found in *Shrek*, when Shrek and Fiona are sitting by the fire. Fiona is reticent about going back to Lord Farquaad while Shrek tries to build up the courage to ask her what her feelings about him really are. All of this is played against Pee Wee King, Redd Stewart, and Chilton Price's *You Belong to Me* (recorded by Jason Wade), and "When we wrote the dialogue," says Adamson, "we wove it in and out of the lyrics of the song." The effect was intensified in the sound mix when the creators rejected the more traditional approach of keeping the music low so the dialogue stands out. "My point," says Adamson, "was it's okay if the music is a little louder, because what they're saying isn't really that important. You can see by their acting what they're going through. Nearly all that we needed to convey, even though there were words, was said through body language, facial expression, and the music."

This needle-drop approach to music presented composers Harry Gregson-Williams and John Powell with the interesting challenge of weaving a fully symphonic score in and around an existing suite of modern songs. However, like the other Shrek creators, they relished the opportunity to make the world of *Shrek* as real and emotional as possible, and believed firmly that a classically oriented score should be an essential element in achieving this. Gregson-Williams, who is the sole composer on *Shrek 2*, comments, "When you've scored chickens and ants and Winnie the Pooh and Tigger, you learn they all have emotional resonance. It's good fun to do. It's doesn't matter what's in front of the audience. If the story is being told well enough, the emotional payoff is as straightforward a payoff as if the characters were human."

Adamson and others felt that the more traditional symphonic elements should have their own unique Shrekian flavor. "One of the first challenges I gave Harry and John on *Shrek,*" says Adamson, "is I didn't want traditional instrumentation. Shrek is such an eclectic character, such an outsider, that he couldn't be just 'strings and horns.'" Gregson-Williams and Powell responded by using unexpected instruments in unusual combinations, such as double basses and xylophones. The overall effect is at once magical, unique, and timeless.

As is so often the case, scoring the films was a process of discovery and improvisation. During the making of *Shrek,* Adamson recalls, "Harry phoned me up as I was driving home and said, 'Let me play you Shrek's theme.'" Adamson listened, and was very impressed, but could not help feeling that the lilting melody did not quite suit Shrek as a character. Disappointed, the composer went back to work. "He called me three hours later," said Adamson, "and said, 'Let me play you Fiona's theme,' and he played me the same piece of music! And it was, like, 'Why didn't we think of that?' It was perfect for Fiona. So it's all a process of discovery."

A TEAM EFFORT

By the home stretch, the creators were also battling the dangers of being too close to the three-year project and losing perspective. *Shrek 2* director Kelly Asbury points out "that it's very easy in animation to get tunnel vision. To get caught up in the things that seem so funny, or so precious, or so cute. When Mark

Interview from THE GLENDALE TATT-LER, August 12, 2003

GLENDALE TATT-LER: SHREK. A phenomenon none of us saw coming but are glad it did. But the question on the tip of everyone's tongue was—what's next? These . . . oh, what would one call them? One might use the term stars of light that come forth, foisting their wit and love unto the wanting hearts of the adoring public. Well, the adoring public wanted more, and we got it in the form of SHREK 4-D, a thrilling ride through the topsy-turvy world of Shrek in a dimension unlike one that we've ever seen before. I'm here with Lord Faarquad, one-time master and ruler of Duloc, now dead ruler of nothing. Welcome, me-lord.

FARQUAAD: How long is this going to take?

GT: Why, are you in a hurry?

FARQUAAD: I may be dead, but I don't have time to waste on you, so let's get this started.

GT: Yes, of course. Lord Faarquad, why SHREK 4-D?

FARQUAAD: What kind of stupid question is that? I didn't come up with the idea, I just acted in it.

GT: Ah yes, of course. Lord Faarquad . . . why acting?

FARQUAAD: Huh? You mean, why do I act? I like it. I've been doing it since college. I like to think I'm good at it! What does this have to do with SHREK 4-D?!

GT: I apologize. Lord Faarquad, I ask again then, why SHREK 4-D?

FARQUAAD: Look, I told you, I don't understand . . . (sighs audibly) Okay. I found the computer was the best place to stretch my talents as an actor, then, as I became . . .

GT: "Computer"?

FARQUAAD: Yes, a computer, where the film was animated.

GT: I see. And where is this "computer"?

FARQUAAD: Look, I don't know. Like I said, I only acted in the film. I didn't animate it! And stop making the quotation sign every time you say "computer"!

GT: Explain what you meant when you said—oh, what did you call it—anim-mate?

FARQUAAD: Animate! Yes, animation! The technique used to make the film! SHREK and SHREK 4-D! Do you research anything before you show up to an interview?!

GT: Well, I'm sorry, but it's just a little hard for me—and, I'm sure, my readers—to swallow.

FARQUAAD: What?!

GT: The fact that this "comput"—sorry, computer—"animationed" this film.

FARQUAAD: ANIMATED! And it's true!! Animators, human beings with "talent" and obviously more "intelligence" than you, sit at a desk with a computer, a large rectangular object with blinking lights," and move my co-stars and I around frame by frame on a little screen wedged into a white plastic box called a "monitor!" Then an actor comes in and records my voice for me! The pieces are put together, and that's an animated film!

GT: If this is true, then why can't I hear you now?

FARQUAAD: Because this is WRITTEN!!!

GT: Lord Faarquad . . . what are you hiding?

FARQUAAD: That's it! This interview is over! Goodbye!

Twain said you have to be willing to murder your darlings, it never applied more than it does to the animation industry." The directors were constantly screening sequences for people outside the production, trying to keep a clear picture of what was working and what was not. Says Asbury, "It reenergizes you. You know they're laughing at the right parts, and sometimes they're laughing at the parts you didn't expect, and that's even better!"

This practice of "stepping back from the canvas" was critical, especially when "scene fatigue" started to set in. Conrad Vernon describes the phenomenon this way: "Sometimes we've been looking at a scene so many times, over and over and over again, it bores us. The popular way of handling this is to go back in and say, 'Let's just rewrite it, it's just not funny, it's just not working anymore.' And you'll go in and you'll rewrite and rearrange things, and you'll do this for about two or three months. And then, ultimately, most of the time, you end up going back to what you already had, and thinking, 'This works so well.'" Warner echoes this point, and notes something that Adamson had said during the production of *Shrek*: "'If it's funny the first five times you see it, it's still funny. Don't take it out.' I have to rely on Andrew's sensibilities, because I've learned to trust him, and learn to trust when his gut says to him something isn't quite right."

Trust is a word often heard throughout the PDI/DreamWorks organization. Without it, it would be virtually impossible to take three hundred highly creative and opinionated individuals and get them to work as a team. Comments David Lipman, "There is this tremendous trust between the artists, department heads, and crew because you are literally handing over your baby

NOT SO FAR, FAR AWAY....

to someone else to finish. The storyboard artist hands a sequence over to the editor, and the editor interprets it and hands it off to the layout artists, and the layout artists do their work and hand it to the animators, and so on. And along the way, the directors and producers are guiding this process. Ideally it's evolving into a bigger and greater thing, and not," chuckles Lipman, "falling apart."

Yet, paradoxically, the success of the production also hinged on the perspective and guidance of one person: Jeffrey Katzenberg. Aron Warner considers him "one of the most passionate, most supportive people I've ever worked for. He absolutely gets it right away." However, Warner believes these attributes are best utilized when Katzenberg is not too enmeshed in the moment-to-moment details of managing a complex production: "Jeffrey is the final, final word, but we try to use him judiciously so he stays clean about what he's seeing."

This ability to "see" the rapidly evolving, and at times bewildering, production prompts Andrew Adamson to proclaim Katzenberg "the ultimate audience. He has this wonderful ability to see things for the first time very clearly. Much of it is instinctual. If you show him something and he reacts well to it, he'll just go with it. He won't spend a lot of time analyzing it." Yet, as much as Katzenberg appreciates the compliment, it is also with a bit of irony that he comments: "I always go to what's *not* working. It makes it very difficult because rather than enjoying the things that are working, I'm always saying, 'Well, okay, that's good, but . . . .'" And he has words of praise for Adamson: "I think Andrew is an extraordinarily gifted storyteller, in the old-fashioned sense. He's like someone from another era who would be sitting around the fire telling amazing stories. He can paint a picture quite literally and figuratively . . . I consider him to be the gatekeeper to the heart of the movie."

As the May 21, 2004, release date loomed, hope and expectations were running high (tempered, it should be said, with a healthy dose of nervousness). As he ruminates on the making of *Shrek 2*, Warner comments, "It's really, really hard but it's also really, really fun. And it takes a group of people who can strip away all the crap and all their egos and say, '*This* is what I want to do. And I'm going to put my all into it. And I'm going to learn to be a better communicator than I

Jeffrey Katzenberg meeting with members of the creative team

ever have been in my whole life.' And not to get too spiritual on anybody, but there comes a moment in time where everyone gets linked in a really subtle, kind of beautiful way."

Vernon echoes this sentiment: "I'll get to a certain point where I'm really tired, and kind of confused as to where we're going, and wondering how we're going to get all this done. I get to that *point*. . . . And I go into my office, and I have this little computer where I can pull up any of the shots that the technical people are lighting or animating, and it immediately reinspires me. I just look at all their work and I think, 'This is great. This is going to be *so good.*' They blow me away every single day."

In considering these vital, everyday contributions made by the people at PDI/DreamWorks, Katzenberg chooses an interesting analogy. "Making these movies," says Katzenberg, "is in the best sense a team sport. You need so many different skill sets, and these movies are the sum of their parts. Without great production designers, without great artists, without great software writers who make it possible for a dragon to breathe fire, *Shrek* would be impossible. It's an endless cross section of hundreds and hundreds of different talents that come together to pursue a single vision and a single goal. It is a team sport, and they are an all-star team."

When asked about how he was dealing with the pressure of the upcoming release, Andrew Adamson tells the story of an encounter at a roadside restaurant in Poland while preparing another movie. There was a little girl outside, and the Polish location scout asked if she had ever heard of *Shrek*. Her eyes brightened, and the scout pointed at Adamson, saying he was the director. She instantly dashed inside the cafe and told her parents. Upon hearing the news, they looked out the window at Adamson and glared, not believing a word of it.

Adamson chuckles, "Imagine. Somewhere in the middle of Poland, in this little town, a little girl has expectations of what this new movie is going to be like." He shakes his head in amazement, then pauses to reflect. "I guess before the first *Shrek* came out, it was our movie. Now, in a way . . . it's everyone's."

THE CHATTER BOX

The Shrek Movie That Never Was

One of the more fascinating early versions of SHREK 2 involved the rather timely concept of a disputed presidential election. This story centered on Shrek abdicating the throne and calling for a fairy-tale election. Pinocchio ran on the campaign theme of "honesty," while Gingy ran a "smear" campaign. According to director Andrew Adamson, this version was overtly satiric and quite political, and "there were a lot of funny ideas. But it was more intellectual than emotional."

Now that's a thought.
Oh, well, all I can say is . . . I hope she likes it.
— Shrek

SHREK

FIONA

DONKEY

PUSS IN BOOTS

SHREK

 **FAVORITE SONG**

"It's Not Easy Being Green" by Kermit the Frog

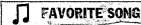 **FAVORITE BOOK**

Books with four-ply pages that don't make me chafe

 FAVORITE FOOD

Swamp Rat au Jus, Soylent Green, anything with a face, feet, and hands

 HOBBIES

Watercolors, gourmet cooking, scaring peasants

★ IDOL

The Hulk, Mean Joe Green, Mr. T, Jolly Green Giant

 MOTTO

Whoever smelt it, dealt it. A house isn't a home without an outhouse.

FIONA

 **ASTROLOGICAL SIGN**

Aries. I'm lovable and creative (but I'll whoop you too).

 **FAVORITE SONG**

Gregorian chants (before they got commercial)

 FAVORITE BOOK

The entire Judy Blume collection

 HOBBIES

Martial arts, needlepoint, sitting alone in my bedroom (I could do that for decades)

★ IDOL

Mother Theresa, The Rock, Bruce Lee

 MOTTO

Never judge an ogre in knight's clothing.

DONKEY

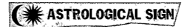 **ASTROLOGICAL SIGN**

The Donkey, right?

 **FAVORITE SONG**

"Sex Machine" by James Brown—which ones did Shrek like?

FAVORITE BOOK

Chicken Soup for the Donkey Soul, Animal Farm

FAVORITE FOOD

Well, you probably expect me to say waffles, but I just go weak in the knees over upside-down coconut soufflé with mango chutney sauce!

HOBBIES

Kickin' it with the "S" man in the swamp, old-school style

WHEN NOT MAKING FILMS, I'D RATHER BE

As close to Shrek as possible

PUSS IN BOOTS

 **ASTROLOGICAL SIGN**

All I know is that all the planets are always in line for me.

FAVORITE SONG

Anything by Cat Stevens

FAVORITE BOOK

Cat on a Hot Tin Roof, To Kill a Mockingbird, Of Mice and Men, Hey Diddle Diddle, the Cat and the Fiddle

FAVORITE FOOD

Sashimi, food I can decapitate

HOBBIES

Napping, scratching furniture, singin', drinkin', dancin', and romancin'

 WHEN NOT MAKING FILMS, I'D RATHER BE

Serenading a saucy Siamese under a cherry moon

 MOTTO

Take the time to smell the catnip, and occasionally chew it.

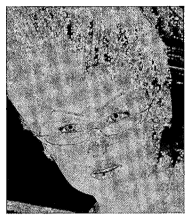

FAIRY GODMOTHER

 ASTROLOGICAL SIGN

All of them, darling. I invented them.

 **FAVORITE SONG**

"Black Magic Woman" by Santana, "Welcome to My Nightmare" by Alice Cooper

 FAVORITE BOOK

My autobiography, *The Joy of Hex*

 FAVORITE FOOD

Anything deep fried and covered in chocolate

 HOBBIES

Scheming, meddling, plotting, and gardening

WHEN NOT MAKING FILMS, I'D RATHER BE

Gently soaring over the countryside destroying the lives of those who don't see things my way

 IDOL

Elizabeth Taylor, Judy Garland, The Wicked Witch of the West

MOTTO

More! More! More!

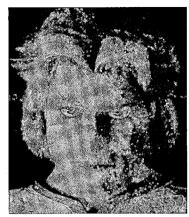

PRINCE CHARMING

 FAVORITE SONG

"You're So Vain" by Carly Simon (funnily enough, this song is actually about me)

 FAVORITE BOOK

Actually, I prefer magazines, especially ones with a lot of pictures.

 HOBBIES

Making out and personal hygiene

WHEN NOT MAKING FILMS, I'D RATHER BE

Getting pampered at a day spa

 IDOL

As a young boy I always idolized myself, since growing up I seem to be the most influenced by me.

 MOTTO

If you are going to wear white after Labor Day, make sure it's leather.

KING HAROLD

 ASTROLOGICAL SIGN

Oh, I don't quite believe in that sort of hocus pocus and . . . Aquarius.

 FAVORITE SONG

"The Rainbow Connection," "Jeremiah Was a Bullfrog (Joy to the World)" by Three Dog Night

 FAVORITE BOOK

The Odyssey, War and Peace, Moby Dick, . . . and *Dilbert*

 FAVORITE FOOD

Chinese, flies (All right, fine! I admit I like flies!)

 HOBBIES

Poleless fly-fishing

 IDOL

Kermit, Old King Cole

 MOTTO

Spare the tower, spoil the child.

QUEEN LILLIAN

 FAVORITE SONG

"Super Freak" by Rick James

 FAVORITE BOOK

The Pottery Barn catalogue

 FAVORITE FOOD

Oh, just a light salad for me, thank you

 HOBBIES

Buying old castles and renovating them

WHEN NOT MAKING FILMS, I'D RATHER BE

Wearing a frock and running through the hills of Switzerland

 IDOL

Queen Victoria (she knew how to keep a secret)

Shrek

DREAMWORKS PICTURES
Presents
A PDI/DREAMWORKS PRODUCTION

CAST
Shrek: Mike Myers
Donkey: Eddie Murphy
Princess Fiona: Cameron Diaz
Lord Farquaad: John Lithgow
Monsieur Hood: Vincent Cassel

ADDITIONAL VOICES
Ogre Hunters: Peter Dennis, Clive Pearse
Captain of Guards: Jim Cummings
Baby Bear: Bobby Block
Geppetto/Magic Mirror: Chris Miller
Pinnochio/Three Pigs: Cody Cameron
Old Woman: Kathleen Freeman
Peter Pan: Michael Galasso
Blind Mice: Christopher Knights, Mike Myers, Simon
    J. Smith
Thelonious: Christopher Knights
Gingerbread Man: Conrad Vernon
Wrestling Fan: Jacquie Barnbrook
Merry Men: Guillaume Aretos, John Bisom, Matthew
    Gender, Calvin Remsberg, Jean-Paul Vignon
Bishop: Val Bettin

FILMMAKERS
Directors: Andrew Adamson, Vicky Jenson
Producers: Aron Warner, John H. Williams, Jeffrey
    Katzenberg
Co-Executive Producer: David Lipman
Executive Producers: Penney Finkelman Cox, Sandra
    Rabins

Andrew Adamson

Based upon the book by: William Steig
Written by: Ted Elliott & Terry Rossio, and Joe
    Stillman, and Roger S. H. Schulman
Co-Producers: Ted Elliott, Terry Rossio
Original Score: Harry Gregson-Williams, John Powell
Editor: Sim Evan-Jones
Production Designer: James Hegedus
Visual Effects Supervisor: Ken Bielenberg
Supervising Animator: Raman Hui
Associate Producer: Jane Hartwell
Production Manager: Triva von Klark
Casting: Leslee Feldman

STORY
Additional Dialogue: Cody Cameron, Chris Miller,
    Conrad Vernon
Co-Heads of Story: Randy Cartwright, David Lowery
Story/Editorial Supervisor: Jenna Grigg Thomas
Story Artists: Kelly Asbury, Francisco Avalos, Rejean
    Bourdages, Ken Harsha, Ken Bruce, Cody
    Cameron, Becky Cassady, Eric Darnell, Rick
    Farmiloe, James Fujii, Edmund Fong, Robert Koo,
    Todd Kurosawa, Robert Lence, Chris Miller,
    Catherine Yuh Rader, Tom Sito, David Soren,
    Robert Souza, John Stevenson, Conrad Vernon
Additional Story Supervision: Jill Ragaway
Production Assistants: Ronald M. Davis, Allier H.
    Zelaya, Jr.

ART DEPARTMENT
Art Directors: Guillaume Aretos, Douglas Rogers
Production Supervisor: Stacey Vandermeer
Character Design: Tom Hester, Raman Hui
CG Visual Development: Wendy Rogers
Set Designer: Craig Edelblut
Additional Set Design: Don Weinger
Costume Designer: Isis Mussenden
Production Illustrators: Mary Locatel, Henrik Tamm,
    James Wood Wilson, Julia Woolf
Head Sculptor: Tom Hester
Sculptor: Dennis Gordon
Model Maker: Facundo Rabaudi
Production Coordinator: Rachael Ellen Miller
Production Assistants: Anthony Byrnes, Fadi Basem
    Kandah

CHARACTER TECHNICAL DIRECTION
Co-Supervisors: Lucia Modesto, Luca Prasso
Lead Character TDs: Beth Hofer, Richard Walsh
Production Supervisor: Michael Garner
Resource Manager: Barbara LaBounta
Character TDs: JJ Blumenkranz, Bart Coughlin,
    Cassidy Curtis, Peter Farson, Milana Huang,
    Nathan Loofbourrow, Kevin Rodgers, Eric Vignola,
    Robert Vogt

Additional Character TD Support: Zsoka Barkacs,
    Stéphane Cros, Irene Decry, Kavita Khosla, Erwan
    Maigret, Alberto Menache, Stephan Osterburg,
    Brian Thompson
Production Coordinator: Andrea Stoops

MODELING AND SURFACING
Modeling Supervisor: Jeff Hayes
Production Supervisor: Patty Kaku
Modelers: Brian Deans-Rowe, Lioudmila Golynskaia,
    Steve McGrath, Matt Paulson, Bill Stahl
Surfacing Lead: David Doepp
Surfacing: Claudia Candia, Edward Deren, Kenneth
    Hébert, Sabrina M. Riegel, Dun Zhao
Additional Surfacing: Kerry Miller
Production Coordinators: Susan Amar, Peter Grassi

LAYOUT
Head of Layout: Simon J. Smith
Production Supervisors: Denise Nolan Cascino,
    Laura Lockwood
Technical Director: Marty Sixkiller
Rough Layout: James Buckhouse, Sue Gleadhill,
    Stephen Moros, Bob Whitehill
CG Set Builder: Sylvain Doreau
Layout: Steve R.J. Bell, John Braunreuther, Brian J.
    Danker, Todd Heapy, Steven Kirchner, Gerald
    McAleece III, David Murphy, Richard Shiba,
    Melissa Tseng, Nick Walker
Production Coordinator: Ilyssa Katz

ANIMATION
Directing Animators: Tim Cheung, Paul Chung, Denis
    Couchon, Donnachada Daly, James Satoru Straus
Additional Animation Supervision: Rex Grignon
Production Supervisor: Jennifer Dahlman
Technical Director: Matt Authement
Animators: Edip Agi, Chung Chan, Raffaella Filipponi,
    Anthony Hodgson, Ethan Hurd, Tim Keon, Ken
    Keys, Boris Kossmehl, Eric Lessard, Noel McGinn,
    Michelle R. Meeker, Fredrik Nilsson, David Rader,
    Jason A. Reisig, Rick Richards, Emmanuel Roth,
    Tom Roth, David Spivack, Don Venhaus
Additional Animation: Kenny Chung, Patricia A.
    Hannaway
Production Coordinator: Gabriel Hernan Villarrubia

David Lipman

LIGHTING AND EFFECTS

Sequence Supervisors: Philippe Gluckman, Susan Hayden, Janet Rentel-Lavin, Apurva Shah, Paul Wang, Mark Wendell
Senior Production Supervisor: Michael Warch
Production Supervisor: Stephen Sobisky
Associate Production Supervisors: Jennifer Freeman, Monty Kimball, Stacy Rentel
Technical Directors: Jeff Beall, Kitt Hodsen, Vanitha Rangaraju, Joe Spampinato
Lead Lighters: Michael Day, Sherry Yun-Shyan Hsieh, Annmarie Koenig, Jin Liou, Joe Palrang, Milton E. Rodriguez-Rios, Frederic Sautai, Pablo Valle
Lighters: Tom Allen, Ken Ball, Chanda Cummings, Christian Cunningham, Philippe Denis, Dado Feigenblatt, Alex Grau, Chad Greene, Laura Grieve, Matthieu Grospiron, Ben Gunsberger, Thane Hawkins, Stephanie Katritos-Sautai, Lee Lanier, Felix J. Mendoza, Barbara A. Meyers, Stephanie Mulqueen, Ronman Yiu Yan Ng, Young Joo Paik-Cheung, Sean Pollack, Bert GJN Poole, Geri Smith, Alessandro Tento, Carlos Vidal, Nathania Vishnevsky
Effects Leads: Jonathan Gibbs, Arnauld Lamorlette, Scott B. Peterson, Bill Seneshen, Scott Singer
Effects: David Allen, Terran Boylan, Karen Schneider Brodine, Juan J. Buhler, Rhett Collier, Alain De Hoe, Grzegorz Duda, Mark Edwards, David Hart, Matt Head, Mirjana Nikolic, Mahesh Ramasubramanian, Erdem Hamsi Taylan, Susan Thayer, Martin Usiak
Cloth Effects: Matt Baer, Randall Hammond, Andrew Harris, Kenneth Ibrahim
Production Coordinators: Audra Koklys, Russell Peavey

MATTE PAINTING

Technical Supervisor: Michael Collery
Technical Directors: Keith Gorham, Michael Wei Mao
Matte Painters: Steven Albert, Joe DiCesare, Thomas Esmeralda, Tony Halawa
Paint Fix: Alicia Bissinger, John "JR" Robeck

PRODUCTION ENGINEERING

Director of Production Engineering: Ed Granlund
Supervising Technical Directors: Mitchell Amino, George Bruder
Lead Technical Director: Gregory A. Dismond
Production Engineers: Dale E. Cieslak, Kevin L. Cureton, Nik Gervae, Mark W. Kirk
PE/Rendering Coordinator: Carrie VanEtten
Animation Technology Coordinator: Marlon Montgomery
Render Assistants: Michael J. Endlich, Colin J. Hodges, Amy Rae Jones, Rob Julien, Vladimir Kanevsky, Michael Macias, Marc Miller, Barry L. Paul, Maria Romero, Steven E. Sorensen, Allen Stetson, Michael C. Walling

EDITORIAL

Second Editor: Michael Andrews
1st Assistant AVID Editor: Michelle Belforte
1st Assistant Film Editor: Christopher Knights
Editorial Apprentice: Paul Monteiro
Add'l Edit. Supervision: Carol Norton
Editorial Coordinator: Nicole Serrano Sewell

FILM ROOM

Production Supervisor: Kathleen Kelly
Technician: John Hanashiro
Film Recordists: Dana Basinger, Cherie Hammond, Alex Zaphiris
Laser Film Coordinator: Kyle Pascucci
Laser Film Recordist: Baron Northrop

R & D STAFF

Animation Software Development
Director of Development: Ken Pearce
Sumit Das, Gilles Dezeustre, Nick Foster, Barry Fowler, Lawrence Kesteloot, Matt Kimball, Joanna Mason, Shawn Neely, Drew Olbrich, Trina M. Roy, Kurt Schaefer, Karl Johann Schmidt, Eric Tabellion, Rahul Chandrakant Thakkar, Deepak Tolani, Daniel Wexler

PRODUCTION

Production Controller: Gary Wohlleben
Production Accountant: Steve Deutsch
Assistant Production Accountant: Susan Beech
Central Production Coordinators: Andre de Oliviera Araujo, Charles G. Baldwin
Assistants to Jeffrey Katzenberg: Cynthia Park, Holly Van Praagh, Marie Walsh
Assistant to Penney Finkelman Cox: Kirstie Field
Assistant to Sandra Rabins: Melissa Wylie
Assistant to the Directors: Matthew Tatom
Assistants to Aron Warner: John Colt, Drew McNeill
Assistant to David Lipman: Katie Intrieri
Assistant to Ted Elliott & Terry Rossio: Shelly Carney
Casting Associates: Sara Getzkin, Christi Soper
Production Assistants: Geoff Koops, Aaron Kruger, PK Livingston Jr., Drew Stewart, Ray Sunglao

ARTISTIC AND TECHNICAL DEVELOPMENT

Director of Training: Rachel Falk
Director of IT: Jennifer Yu
Technical Writers: Nick Thomas, Linda Rae Sande, Jonathan Simonoff
Systems Programmers: Curtis Galloway, Mark Harris, Denise Howard
Coordinators: Yumi Nishiyama, Grazia Ojeda

SYSTEMS ADMINISTRATION

Sr. Systems Administrators: Micheal Cutler, Margaret Myers, Brian Peterson
Systems Administrators: Graham Breeze, Rich Marcos, Bart Feliciano, John O'Sullivan, David Fent, Erik Patton, Rob Toy
I/O Administrators: Frank Richards, Alvin Tenpo
Editorial Technician: Gene Takahashi
Jr. Systems Administrators: Sergio Chaves, Mark Macready, Heather Tensen
Supervising Sound Editors: Wylie Stateman, Lon Bender
Re-recording Mixers: Andy Nelson, Anna Behlmer

Conrad Vernon and Kelly Asbury

Aron Warner

169

POST PRODUCTION

Post Production Executive: James Beshears
Post Production Associate: Andrew Birch
Dialog/ADR Supervisors: Chris Jargo, Hugh Waddell
Sound FX Editors: Scott Gershin, Hector Gika, Tony Lamberti, Wade Wilson
Foley Editors: Valerie Davidson, Jennifer Mann
1st Assistant Sound Editors: Robert Batha, Brandon Spencer
Assistant Sound Editor: David Stanke
Foley Artists: Jimmy Moriana, Jeff Wilhoit
Foley Mixer: Nerses Gezalyan
Foley Recordist: Greg Zimmerman
ADR Recordist: David Lucarelli
ADR Voice Casting: L.A. MadDogs
ADR Group: Ian Abercrombie, Newell Alexander, Rosemary Alexander, Tom Amundsen, Steve Bulen, Mitch Carter, David Cowgill, Ken Danziger, Moosie Drier, Iake Eissinmann, Elisa Gabrielli, Jean Gilpin, Nick Guest, Bridget Hoffman, Richard Horvitz, Sherry Hursey, Rif Hutton, Donna Lynn Leavy, Christina McGregor, Tony Pope, Peter Renaday, Claire Salstrom, Lia Sargent, Bridget Sienna, Claudette Wells, Diz White, Lynnanne Zager
LA Studios Recording Mixer: Carlos Sotolongo
ADR Mixer: Charlene Richards
Color Timer: Terry Claborn
Negative Cutter: Mo Henry
Rostrum Camera: Messy Optics
End Titles: James Williams
Post Production Facilities provided by Twentieth Century Fox Studios
Re-recording Engineer: Denis St. Amand
Recordists: Craig "Pup" Heath, Robert Renga

MUSIC

Music Supervisor: Marylata E. Jacobs
Score Recorded and Mixed by: Nick Wollage
Score Recorded at: Abbey Road Studios
Score Mixed at: Front Page Recorders, Media Ventures
Music Editor: Brian Richards
Additional Recording: Slamm Andrews
Additional Mixing: Alan Meyerson
Assistant Engineers: Chris Clark, Andy Dudman, Craig Nepp

Score Conducted by: Harry Gregson-Williams, Gavin Greenaway
Orchestrations: John Bell, John Coleman, Elizabeth Finch, Bruce L. Fowler, Walter Fowler, Ladd McIntosh, Yvonne S. Moriarty
Music Preparation: Tony Stanton
Orchestral Contractor: Isobel Griffiths
Orchestra Leader: Gavyn Wright
Choir: Metro Voices
Guitars Performed by: Danny Jacob
Music Clearance: Julie Butchko
Music Assistants: Toby Chu, Dave Hecox, Alastair King, Joel Richard
Additional Music by: James McKee Smith

PDI SENIOR MANAGEMENT

VP Special Projects: Richard Chuang
Heads of Production: Jane Hartwell, Denise Minter
VP of Human Resources: Jenene Wilson
Director of Digital Operations: Patty Bonfilio
Head of Marketing: Julie Haddon
Head of Studio Recruitment & Staffing: Marilyn Friedman

Support Staff
Human Resources Manager: Peter Gladysz
Creative Services Specialist: Kelly Brown
Marketing Assistant: Amy Krider
Recruiters: Sonia M. Torigoe-Arroyo, Dana Pettit-Vanhove
Recruiting Coordinator: Christine M. Lingenfelter
Facilities Managers: Earl E. Heinlein Jr., Jan Snyder
Facilities Coordinator: Della Washington
Facilities Maintenance: Caesar Myles
Receptionists: Anthony Correa, Liz Borges-Herzog
Operations Assistants: Jonathan Dooley, Chris Milano

SPECIAL THANKS

Kelly Asbury, Brenda Chapman, Teresa Cheng, Martin Cohen, Bruce Daitch, Ann Daly, Doug Ikeler, Tim Johnson, Michael Kahn, Cecil Kramer, Brad Lewis, Ed Leonard, Alan Myerson, Kristen Niederholzer, Dennis Park, Jennifer Rubin, Asa Tucker, Simon Wells, Lenny Wohl, Hans Zimmer, Barbara Zipperman

LOS ANGELES PRE PRODUCTION

Victoria Alonso, John Garbett, Latifa Ouaou, Alice Alonzo, Bart Gawboy, Bill Perkins, Curtis Augspurger, Carlos Grangel, Mike Ploog, Dale Baer, Timothy Guyer, Amy Rabins, Chris Bailey, Jared Hamaguchi, John Rocco, Michele Barbera, Jay Heit, Paul Shardlow, Anders Beer, Ruben Hickman, Avner Shemi, Toni Blake, Ann Hoyt, Steve Simper, Lisa Brenner Bloomquist, Dale Allen Hoyt, Mike Smithson, Christian Bouyer, Barry Jackson, Mark Solomon, Andrew Bruss, Kelly Kimball, Mike Spokas, Chris Clancy, Sandy Kraft, Mike Stone, Corey Comstock, Ken Larson, Eric Swanborg, Dayla Corcoran, Tim Lawrence, Kate Swanborg, Michelle Cowart, Lori Lewis, Brian Taylor, Luc Desmarchelier, Brian Master, Ron Tippe, Lynn Ezelle, Mike Meckler, Erika Vasquez, Nickson Fong, Christine Norton, Marissa Walker, Crystal Foth, Matt O'Callaghan

PROPELLERHEAD

Jeffrey Abrams, Rob Letterman, Loren Soman, Andy Waisler

Bob Persichetti

Rob Porter

SONGS

ALL STAR
Written by Greg Camp
Performed by Smash Mouth
Courtesy of Interscope Records
Under license from Universal Music Enterprises
Produced and Mixed by Eric Valentine

ON THE ROAD AGAIN
Written by Willie Nelson
Performed by Eddie Murphy

FRIENDS
Written by Mark Klingman
and Buzzy Linhart
Performed by Eddie Murphy

WHIPPED CREAM
Written by Naomi Neville
Performed by Herb Albert & The Tijuana Brass
Courtesy of A&M Records
Under license from Universal Music Enterprises

ESCAPE
(THE PINA COLADA SONG)
Written and Performed by Rupert Holmes
Courtesy of MCA Records
Under license from Universal Music Enterprises

MEDITATION
Written by Antonio Carlos Jobim,
Norman Gimbel and Newton Mendonca
Performed by Antonio Carlos Jobim
Courtesy of Verve Records
Under license from
Universal Music Enterprises

WELCOME TO DULOC
Music by Mike Himelstein
Lyrics by Eric Darnell

BAD REPUTATION
Written by Joan Jett, Kenny Laguna,
Ritchie Cordell and Marty Kupersmith
Performed by Joan Jett
Courtesy of Blackheart Records

I'M ON MY WAY
Written by Charlie Reid and Craig Reid
Performed by The Proclaimers
Courtesy of Chrysalis Records, Ltd.
Under license from EMI-Capitol Music Special
   Markets

MERRY MEN
Written by Kirby Tepper, Andrew Adamson
and Conrad Vernon
Performed by Vincent Cassel

MY BELOVED MONSTER
Written by E
Performed by eels
Courtesy of DreamWorks Records

YOU BELONG TO ME
Written by Pee Wee King,
Redd Stewart and Chilton Price
Performed by Jason Wade
Courtesy of DreamWorks Records

HALLELUJAH
Written by Leonard Cohen
Performed by John Cale
Courtesy of Menhir Music

TRY A LITTLE TENDERNESS
Written by Harry Woods,
Jimmy Campbell and Reg Connelly
Performed by Eddie Murphy

I'M A BELIEVER
Words and Music by Neil Diamond
Performed by Smash Mouth
Courtesy of Interscope Records
Produced and Mixed by Eric Valentine
Additional Vocals by Eddie Murphy

STAY HOME
Written by Matt Mahaffey
Performed by Self
Courtesy of DreamWorks Records
Produced and Mixed by Eric Valentine

BEST YEARS OF OUR LIVES
Written by David Jaymes and Geoffrey Deane
Performed by Baha Men
Courtesy of S-Curve Records
Produced by Michael Mangini
and Steve Greenberg

Steve Gordon

LIKE WOW!
Written by Jimmy Harry
and Sandra St. Victor
Performed by Leslie Carter
Courtesy of DreamWorks Records

IT IS YOU (I HAVE LOVED)
Music by Harry Gregson-Williams,
John Powell and Gavin Greenaway
Lyrics by Dana Glover
Performed by Dana Glover
Courtesy of DreamWorks Records
Produced by Gavin Greenaway
and Harry Gregson-Williams

Prints by
TECHNICOLOR
AVID
KODAK

DISTRIBUTED BY DREAMWORKS DISTRIBUTION LLC

Visit our website at:
www.shrek.com

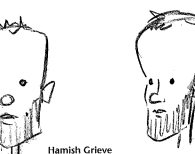

Hamish Grieve

We can launch it today, pitch it this afternoon, shoot it tonight, record scratch tomorrow morning, Mike can cut it tomorrow afternoon, We'll review it tomorrow night, do fixes by Thursday, lock it that night and have it in time for the screening on Friday....

Latifa Ouaou

Shrek 2

Directed by: Andrew Adamson
  Kelly Asbury, Conrad Vernon
Produced by: Aron Warner, David Lipman, John H.
  Williams
Executive Producer: Jeffrey Katzenberg
Based upon the book by: William Steig
Story by: Andrew Adamson
Screenplay by: Andrew Adamson and Joe Stillman
  and J. David Stem & David N. Weiss
Music by: Harry Gregson-Williams
Music Supervisor: Chris Douridas
Editors: Michael Andrews, Sim Evan-Jones
Production Designer: Guillaume Aretos
Visual Effects Supervisor: Ken Bielenberg
Co-Visual Effects Supervisor: Philippe Gluckman
Art Director: Steve Pilcher
Supervising Animators: Raman Hui, Tim Cheung,
  James Baxter
Senior Production Manager: Denise Nolan Cascino
Production Manager: Kristen Chidel
Casting by: Leslee Feldman

CAST
Shrek: Mike Myers
Donkey: Eddie Murphy
Princess Fiona: Cameron Diaz
Queen: Julie Andrews
Puss In Boots: Antonio Banderas
King: John Cleese
Prince Charming: Rupert Everett
Fairy Godmother: Jennifer Saunders

ADDITIONAL VOICES
Wolf: Aron Warner
Page, Elf, Nobleman, Nobleman's son: Kelly Asbury
Pinocchio, Three Pigs: Cody Cameron
Gingerbread Man, Cedric, Announcer, Muffin Man,
  Mongo: Conrad Vernon
Blind Mouse: Christopher Knights
Herald, Man with Box: David P. Smith
Mirror, Dresser: Mark Moseley

Fast Food Clerk: Kelly Cooney
Bar Frog: Wendy Bilansky
Ugly Stepsister: Larry King
Receptionist: Guillaume Aretos
Humphries, Magic Mirror: Chris Miller
Doll, Jill: Latifa Ouaou
Maiden #1, Generic Female #2: Alina Phelan
Maiden #2: Erika Thomas
Joan Rivers: Joan Rivers

STORY
Head of Story: Chris Miller
Story & Editorial Production Supervisor: Latifa Ouaou
Story Artists: Cody Cameron, Walt Dohrn, Steven E.
  Gordon, Hamish Grieve, Mark O'Hare, Bob
  Persichetti, Rob Porter, Catherine Yuh Rader,
  David P. Smith, John Stevenson
Additional Storyboard Artists: Dalton Grant Jr.,
  Raman Hui, David Lux, Rob Koo, Piet Kroon, Jeff
  Snow, Simon Wells, Mike Mitchell
Additional Dialogue: Cody Cameron, Walt Dohrn,
  Chris Miller, David P. Smith, Conrad Vernon
Production Coordinator: Kelly Cooney
Production Assistant: Steve Zegans

ART DEPARTMENT
Character Design: Tom Hester
Costume Designer: Isis Mussenden
Sculptors: Dennis Gordon, Tim Lawrence, Charles
  Rivera
Production Supervisor: Stacey Vandermeer-Hennen
Set Designers: Craig Edelblut, Paul Westacott
Additional Set Design: Douglas Pierce
Production Illustrators: Yuri Bartoli, Kory S. Heinzen,
  Ruben Hickman, Yoriko Ito, Shannon Jeffries,
  Robert MacKenzie, Erwin Madrid, Huy Nguyen,
  Alexandre Puvilland, Christian Schellewald, Henrik
  Tamm, James Wood Wilson, Julia Woolf, Peter
  Zaslav
Model Maker: Facundo Rabaudi
Production Coordinator: Liz Borges-Herzog
Production Assistants: Sarah Maria Goodwin, Travis
  Koller
Additional Production Support: Darci Zalvin

CHARACTER TECHNICAL DIRECTION
Co-Supervisors: Lawrence D. Cutler, Lucia Modesto
Production Supervisor: Claudia South Martin
Department Manager: Patty Kaku
Character TDs: Zsoka Barkacs, Terran Boylan, Gilbert
  Davoud, Daniel Dawson, Peter Farson, Milana
  Huang, Sandy Kao, Quintin King, Shawn Lewis,
  Penny Leyton, Mariette Marinus, Rob O'Neill,
  Stephan Osterburg, Luca Prasso, Nico Scapel,
  Dug Stanat, Todd Taylor, Rob Vogt, Dick Walsh,
  Marc Wilhite, Emre Yilmaz

MODELING
Supervisor: Jeff Hayes
Lead: Bill Stahl
Production Supervisors: Tonia Pizzato, Andrea
  Stoops
Modelers: Brian Deans-Rowe, John Koren Dodelson,
  Pasha Ivanov, Steve McGrath, Charlie Ramos,
  James Stewart, Joshua West, Benjamin Williams
Production Coordinator: Angela Ensele

SURFACING
Lead: David Doepp
Production Supervisor: André de O. Araujo
Surfacers: Claudia A. Candia, Edward Deren, Aaron
  Florez, Sam Gebhardt, Kenneth Hébert, Tomijann
  Nabors, Jennifer Stephenson Newlin, Lance
  Powell, Sabrina M. Riegel, Steffen Sommer, John
  Wake, Gentaro Yamamoto
Technical Director: Mark A. Kauffman
Production Coordinator: Alison Fedrick

LAYOUT
Supervisor: Bob Whitehill
Consultant: Simon J. Smith
Production Supervisor: Carol Norton
Rough Layout: Matt Aspbury, John Braunreuther,
  James Buckhouse, Nol Le Meyer, Gerald McAleece
  III, Nick Walker
Final Layout: Todd Heapy, Amy Rae Jones, Kaishin
  Kam, David Murphy, Brian Newlin, David Nix, David
  Otte, Keith Reicher, Richard Shiba, David Patrick
  Valera, Heather Davis Wang
Technical Director: Marty Sixkiller
Additional Technical Support: Samantha Michel
Rough CG Set Builder: Robert Rossoff
Additional Layout: Jan Carlee
Production Coordinator: Fadi Basem Kandah
Production Assistant: Brad Kane

ANIMATION
Directing Animators: Chung Chan, Paul Chung,
  Donnachada Daly, Anthony Hodgson, Trey Thomas
Production Supervisors: Tony Cosanella, Jennifer
  Dahlman, Philip R. Garrett
Animators: Linda Bel, Jeremy Bernstein, Wolf-Rüdiger
  Bloss, Patrick Bonneau, David Burgess, Darrin
  Butts, Jaime Andrés Castañeda, Kenny Chung,
  Melanie Cordan, Nick Craven, Cassidy Curtis, Lou
  Dellarosa, Robert
  Espanto Domingo,
  Randy Dormans,
  Raffaella Filipponi,
  Emile Ghorayeb,

BACH
CACLE
CACLE

Cody Cameron

Chris Miller

Enrique Navarrete Gil, Antony Gray, Mariko Hoshi, James R. Hull, Ethan Hurd, Manu Ittina, Jeffrey K. Joe, Morgan Kelly, Richard Sang, Uoon Kim, Heather Knight, Kevin Koch, Serguei Kouchnerov, Marek Kochout, Eric Lessard, Sean Mahoney, Sean McLaughlin, Bill E. Miller, Ken Morrissey, Luci Napier, Julie Nelson, Kevin O'Hara, Van Phan, Mark Pudleiner, Pres Romanillos, Carlos Rosas, Trish Schutz-Krause, Kevan Shorey, Jason Spencer-Galsworthy, David Spivack, Sean Springer, Thomas Paul Thesen, Don Venhaus, Dan Wagner, Robert J. Weaver

Technical Directors: Matt Authement, York N. Schueller, Allen Stetson

Production Coordinator: Susan Erokan

Production Assistants: Chris Milano, Aaron Stewart

LIGHTING

Sequence Supervisors: Michael Day, Susan Hayden, Janet Lavin, Jin Chang Liou, Milton E. Rodríguez-Ríos

Production Supervisors: Jennifer Freeman, Stacy F. Rentel, Jenna Grigg Thomas

Lead Lighters: Ken Ball, Chanda Cummings, Philippe Denis, Annmarie Koenig, Barbara Ann Meyers, Stephanie Mulqueen, Ronman Yiu Yan Ng, Young Joo Paik Cheung, Joe Palrang, Vanitha Rangaraju-Ramanan, Geri Smith, Wayne Stables

Lighters: Stephen Bailey, Alan Chen, Adam Chin, Ye Won Cho, Brian Danker, Ben Fischler, Jeff Kasunic, Scott Liedtka, Shanna Chang Lim, Kiki Lippman, Jimmy Maidens, Andrew McPhillips, Marc Miller, Cristian G. Moras, Yuko Okumura, Gabriel Portnof, Ben Radcliffe, Matthew George Rampias, Frank Ritlop, Jung Jin Song, Peter Szewczyk, Nathania Vishnevsky, Craig Welsh, Brian Cordan Young

Additional Lighting: Amy Christensen, Eric Fernandes, Laura Grieve, Sherry Hsieh, Michael J. Manza, Gaku Nakatani, Michael Necci, Marc Toscano, Pablo Valle, Craig Wentworth, Douglas Yoshida

Technical Directors: Steve RJ Bell, Mark A. Decker, Tony Mitzelfelt, Robyn Rindge

Additional Technical Support: Roberto A. Calvo, Michael H. Lee, Christina Yen

Production Coordinators: Kelly M. Jéan, Hannibal P. Odisho, Jenny Wolfe-Binder

EFFECTS

Head of Effects: Arnauld Lamorlette

Production Supervisor: Michael Garner

Effects Leads: David Allen, Juan J. Buhler, Jonathan Gibbs, Seth Lippman, Scott B. Peterson, Scott Singer

Effects: Francois Antoine, Matt Baer, Markus Burki, David Caeiro Cebrian, Alain De Hoe, Rick Glumac, Randall Hammond, David Hart, Greg Hart, Matt Hightower, Lewis Kofsky, Andre LeBlanc, Patricia

Pawlak, Konstantin Promokhov, Marlin Rowley, Martin Usiak, Jason Waltman, Andy Wheeler, Albert Yu

Additional Effects: Antony Field, David Lipton, Mark Manfrey, William Opdyke, Ellen Poon, Mahesh Ramasubramanian, Krzysztof Rost, Joanne Thiel

Technical Directors: Amy McDonald Sandjideh, Taylor Shaw

Production Coordinators: Wendy S. Berry, Jana Spotts

Production Support: Meredith M. Gill

MATTE PAINTING

Technical Supervisor: Michael Collery

Matte Painters: Tony Halawa, Henrik Holmberg, Noah Klocek

Paint Fix/Completion: Hank Grebe, Eli Rod, Hayyim Sanchez, Amber Stewart, Carrie VanEtten

Technical Director: Justin Onstine

CLOTHING & FINALING

Clothing Lead: Bill Seneshen

Finaling Lead: Kevin Rodgers

Production Supervisor: Holly Edwards

Animators: Stephen F. Dobbs, Monika Erande, Oliver Finkelde, Nathan Fok, Lee Graft, Tim Keenan, Kavita Khosla, Robert Kosai, PK Livingston Jr., Damon Riesberg, Kevin Vassey, Sean White, Kalim Winata, Ken Yao

Coordinator: Chris Bunney

EDITORIAL

Second Editor: Michelle Belforte Hauser

Production Supervisors: Laura Lockwood, Julie M. McDonald

1st Assistant Editors: J. John Dorst, Michelle Mendenhall

Assistant Editors: Kaya S. Kim, Christopher Knights

Apprentice Editor: Suvi Salakka Booth

Production Coordinators: Gabrielle Siegel, Virginia Wilson

Production Assistant: Felicia Sanchez

Editorial Technicians: Patrick Danford, Joanna Laurent, Gene Takahashi

TECHNICAL DIRECTION

Lead Technical Director: Jeff Beall

Technical Assistant: Sheryl Aterrado

PRODUCTION

Production Controller: Gary Wohlleben

Assistant Production Accountants: Mary Lou Finn Wingmay, Vivian Liu, Humberto Meza Jr., Debbie A. Rosell

Additional Production Accountants: Steve Deutsch, Cindy LeJeune

Additional Production Management: Triva Von Klark

Central Production Coordinator: Robyn Mesher

Assistants to Jeffrey Katzenberg: Cynthia Park, Tracy Ann Pearson, Michele Lyn Reed

Assistant to the Directors: Alina Phelan

Assistants to the Producers: Barbara A. Crabtree, Kim Romero

Production Assistants: Nick Fumia, Allison L. Mussell Hurd

Technology: Workstations and rendering provided by Hewlett-Packard, DreamWorks' Preferred Technology Provider

ANIMATION TECHNOLOGY

Head of Technology: Andy Hendrickson

Head of Animation Software: Nick Foster

Technology Production Manager: Jerome Solomon

RESEARCH AND DEVELOPMENT

R&D Development Manager: Sanjay Das

Manager: Lisa Marie Lamb

Technology Production Supervisor: John Colt

R&D Staff: Roderick Ang, Steve Baker, Edward A. Bruno, Eduardo Bustillo, Chloe Chao, Gilles Dezeustre, Scott Draves, David Eberle, Barry Fowler, Reid Gershbein, Eric Griswold, Sunil Hadap, Jerry Hébert, Greg Heflin, Neil Le, Nick Long, Erwan Maigret, Pia Miniati, Anna Newman Ghani, Drew Olbrich, Paul Rademacher, Trina M. Roy, Kurt Schaefer, Karl Johann Schmidt, John R. Serene, Eric Tabellion, Kenichiro Tanaka, Kimberly Taylor, Deepak Tolani, Xiaohuan Corina Wang, Feng Xie, Hector Yangli Yee, Daniel Yu

PRODUCTION ENGINEERING

Manager: John Crawbuck

PE Staff: Mitchell Amino, Stewart Birnam, Rob Blau, George Bruder, Fleur Diana Dragan, Corban Gossett, Mark W. Kirk, Jeff Lee, Jim Meyer, Kelly Parker, Kevin Rogers, Michael K. Sanders, Hernan Silberman, Laura Wood, Greg Wuller

Raman Hui

Walt Dohrn

POST TECHNOLOGY
Manager: Barbara Ford
Post Staff: Kristopher Campbel, John M. Hanashiro

SYSTEMS
Manager: Michael Kiernan
Systems Administrators: Alex Bochannek, Greg Bulman, Micheal Cutler, Adam Joseph Czech, John F. Detke, Bart Feliciano, David R. Fent, Scott Kilty, Derek Mann, Richard J. Marco, John Kerry O'Sullivan, Erik J. Patton, Carlos Quinonez, Jr., Daniel Rich, Frank Richards, Christopher S. Stahl, Alvin Tenpo, Tony Huu Tran, John Trappey

STUDIO RESOURCES
Manager: Ed Granlund
Render Wranglers: Pamela Hu, Dan Kirksey, Bryan Gregg LaShelle, Adam Stanley Maino, Drew Perttula, Steven E. Sorensen

COORDINATION
Production Coordinators: Marlon Montgomery, Laura Watts
Administrative Assistants: Kelly Labbe, Ann Dial McMillan, Gina Tosetti

GLENDALE ANIMATION TECHNOLOGY
Ted Burge, Marc Fleury, Emmanuel C. Francisco, Skottie Miller, Andrew Pilgrim, Richard F. Rubio

ARTISTIC & TECHNICAL DEVELOPMENT
Director: Rachel Falk
Training Specialist: Hoyt Lee Ng
Coordinators: Ellen Connell, Sara Peck
Senior Technical Writers: Linda Rae Sande, Jonathan David Simonoff

SOUND DESIGNER
Randy Thom
SUPERVISING SOUND EDITOR
Dennis Leonard

SOUND MIXING
Andy Nelson
Anna Behlmer

POST PRODUCTION
Post Production Executive: James Beshears

Post Production Supervisor: Andrew Birch
Post Production Coordinator: Wayne Hellinger
Post Production Assistant: Chris Hoetger
Videographer: Nelson Lee
Additional Sound Design: David C. Hughes
Sound FX Editors: Andre Fenley, J. R. Grubbs, Scott Guitteau
ADR Editors: Marilyn McCoppen, Ewa Sztompke-Oatfield
Foley Editors: Jonathan Null, E. Larry Oatfield
Assistant Supervising Sound Editor: Stuart McCowan
Assistant Sound Designer: Will Files
Assistant Sound Effects Editor: Coya Elliott
Foley Artists: Ellen Heuer, Dennie Thorpe, Jana Vance
Foley Mixer: Frank Merel
Foley Recordist: Travis Crenshaw
Digital Transfer: Christopher Barron, John Countryman, Jonathan Gerber
Video Services: Ed Dunkley, John Torrijos
Digital Editorial Services: Tim Burby, David Hunter
Client Services: Mike Lane, Gordon Ng, Eva Porter, Megan Thompkins
Editorial Systems Manager: Steven P. Moder
Editorial Systems Engineer: Paul Parmer
Projectionist: Gene Goins
ADR Voice Casting: Mickie McGowan, L.A. MadDogs
ADR Group: Newell Alexander, Tom Amundsen, Steve Apostolina, Bob Bergen, Terry Brannon, Rodger Bumpass, Mitch Carter, Robert Clotworthy, David Cowgill, Jennifer Darling, Debi Derryberry, Paul Eiding, lake Eissinmann, Bill Farmer, Bridget Hoffman, Sherry Lynn, Danny Mann, Mickie McGowan, Edie Mirman, Laraine Newman, Paul Pape, Jan Rabson, Marcelo Tubert, Jim Ward

Post Production Facilities provided by: Twentieth Century Fox Studios

Recordists: Robert Renga, Craig Heath
Re-recording Engineer: Denis St. Amand
ADR Mixer: Charleen Richards-Steeves
ADR Recordist: David Lucarelli
ADR Engineer: Derek Casari
LA Studios Recording Engineers: Carlos Sotolongo, Larry Winer

Post Production Sound Services provided by Skywalker Sound, a Lucasfilm Ltd. Company

Color Timer: Terry Claborn
Negative Cutter: Mo Henry
End Titles: David Morehead

MUSIC
Music Editor: Mark Jan Wlordarkiewicz
Additional Music by: Stephen Barton
Additional Music from Shrek: John Powell
Score Recorded by Nick Wollage at Air Lyndhurst Studios, London

Score Mixed by Alan Meyerson
Orchestra Leader: Gavyn Wright
Choir: Metro Voices
Assistant Engineers: Toby Chu, Meri Gavin
Music Copyist: Tony Stanton
London Musician Contractor: Isobel Griffiths
Music Coordinators: Julie Keel, Cindi Smith
Music Clearances: Julie Butchko

PDI SENIOR MANAGEMENT
Head of Studio: Patti Burke
Head of Production: Teresa Cheng
Special Projects: Richard Chuang
Director of Character Development: Beth Hofer
Studio Recruitment: Marilyn Friedman
Studio Operations: Patty Bonfilio
Production Executives: Paul Hettler, Denise Minter

SUPPORT STAFF
Office Manager: Fu-Ping Irene Taylor
Marketing: Amy Krider
Recruiting Manager: Beth Sasseen
Human Resources Manager: Germaine Yokoyama
Recruiting Coordinator: Trisha Buendia
Recruiters: Dave Barrett, Monty Kimball, Dana Vanhove
Assistant to Head of Recruitment: Nila Le Blanc, Dana Park
Human Resources: Jaclyn T. Yee
Executive Assistant: Laurel Graydon
Finance Clerk: Matthew L. Sanchez
Facility Manager: Earl E. Heinlen, Jr.
Facility Engineer: Jeffrey D. Chandler
Facility Coordinator: Wendy Bilanski
Facilities Clerks: Ilya Neizvestny, Maria Engle

SPECIAL THANKS
Marty Cohen, Bruce Daitch, Bill Damaschke, Jodi DiCenzo, Jane Hartwell, Todd Homme, Andrew Kopperud, Mike Lachance, Ed Leonard, Alison Lima, Kathy Mandato, Dennis Park, Sunny Park, Jennifer Rubin, Lenny Wohl, Lance Young, Hans Zimmer

In Memory of William Steig
1907–2003

*Credits Not Final

John Stevenson

Acknowledgments

Kelly Cooney

Thanks to the following for helping unfold the mystery behind the making of both movies: Andrew Adamson, David Lipman, and Aron Warner.

A special thanks to Amy Krider at PDI/DreamWorks for her tireless work in setting up all the interviews for this book, fielding numerous requests for materials, and answering endless questions.

Thank you also to the following people at DreamWorks: Kristy Cox for providing not only terrific support but also sharp-eyed guidance; Kellie Allred and Fumi Kitahara (who helped with key photos) for supplying much of the useful cast and crew interview material used in this book; Karen Hoffman for diligently shepherding the book through the process; Rhion Magee for her expert art direction; as well as Corinne A. Combs, Ann Daly, Paul Elliott, Anne Globe, and Alison Lima for their invaluable contributions.

I would also like to acknowledge and thank those at PDI/DreamWorks who helped inject authentic Shrekian humor into the book by contributing their splendid comedic writing skills: Andrew Adamson, Kelly Asbury, Walt Dohrn, Hamish Grieve, Chris Miller, Dave Smith, and Conrad Vernon.

At Harry N. Abrams, Inc., a huge thank you to Elisa Urbanelli for her generous, insightful, and always constructive editing, and editor-in-chief Eric Himmel for his creative, clear, and calm perspective. Special thanks to Ellen Nygaard Ford, the visual "author" of this book's beautiful and bold design. Walter de la Vega, Justine Keefe, and Samantha Topol also contributed greatly to the making of the book.

And finally, thanks to my wife Lucinda Lewis, for her good humor and patience as I lay awake in bed, thinking, "What in the name of God have I gotten myself into?"

– John Hopkins

Joe Stillman

Mark O'Hare

For Harry N. Abrams, Inc.:
Editor: Elisa Urbanelli
Designer: Ellen Nygaard Ford
Production Manager: Justine Keefe

For DreamWorks:
Art Director: Rhion Magee
Project Manager: Karen Hoffman

Library of Congress Cataloging-in-Publication Data

Hopkins, John, 1957–
  Shrek : from the swamp to the screen / John Hopkins.
    p. cm.
Includes bibliographical references and index.
  ISBN 0–8109–4309–3 (hardcover)
1. Shrek (Motion picture) 2. Steig, William, 1907–2003 Shrek! I. Title.

PN1997.2.S48H67 2004
791.43'72—dc22
                           2003024831

Printed and bound in the United States of America

10 9 8 7 6 5 4 3 2 1

Page 11: Jacket design from *Shrek!* by William Steig. Copyright © 1990
by William Steig. Reprinted by permission of Farrar, Straus, and Giroux,
L.L.C.

Page 33: Image of Shrek and Donkey at the Oscars © Academy of
Motion Picture Arts and Sciences

Harry N. Abrams, Inc.
100 Fifth Avenue
New York, N.Y. 10011
www.abramsbooks.com

Abrams is a subsidiary of

LA MARTINIÈRE

Dave Smith

best of the best

the best recipes from the 25 best cookbooks of the year

FOOD&WINE

FOOD & WINE MAGAZINE

EDITOR IN CHIEF Dana Cowin
CREATIVE DIRECTOR Stephen Scoble
MANAGING EDITOR Mary Ellen Ward
EXECUTIVE EDITOR Pamela Kaufman
EXECUTIVE FOOD EDITOR Tina Ujlaki

BEST OF THE BEST Volume 6

EDITOR Kate Heddings
ART DIRECTOR Patricia Sanchez
DESIGNER Liz Quan
PRODUCTION MANAGER Janet Regan
PRODUCTION Ethan Cornell
COPY EDITOR Lisa Leventer
EDITORIAL ASSISTANT Melissa Rubel

SENIOR VICE PRESIDENT, CHIEF MARKETING OFFICER Mark V. Stanich
DIRECTOR, BRANDED SERVICES AND RETAIL Marshall Corey
CORPORATE PRODUCTION MANAGER Stuart Handelman
MARKETING MANAGER Bruce Spanier
OPERATIONS MANAGER Phil Black
BUSINESS MANAGER Doreen Camardi

COVER PHOTOGRAPH BY Wendell Weber

FLAP PHOTOGRAPHS
DANA COWIN PORTRAIT BY Andrew French
KATE HEDDINGS PORTRAIT BY Emily Wilson

AMERICAN EXPRESS PUBLISHING CORPORATION
Copyright 2003 American Express Publishing Corporation

ISBN 0-916103-83-8
ISSN 1524-2862

Published by American Express Publishing Corporation
1120 Avenue of the Americas, New York, New York 10036

Manufactured in the United States of America

best of the best
the best recipes from the 25 best cookbooks of the year

FOOD&WINE
BOOKS

American Express Publishing Corporation, New York

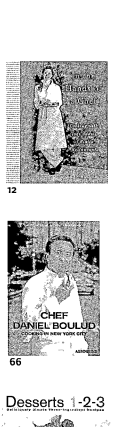

12

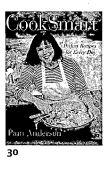

30

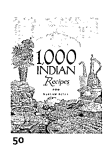

MARIO BATALI
the **BaBBO**
COOKBOOK

40

1000
INDIAN
Recipes

50

SIMPLY BISHOP'S

58

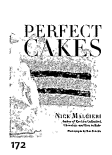

CHEF
DANIEL BOULUD
COOKING IN NEW YORK CITY

66

THE
good cookie
TISH BOYLE

76

MICHAEL CHIARELLO'S
CASUAL COOKING

88

102

INA GARTEN
BAREFOOT
CONTESSA
FAMILY STYLE

112

Desserts 1-2-3

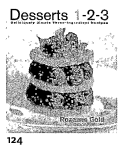

124

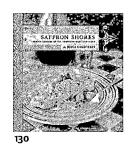

SAFFRON SHORES

130

MEDITERRANEAN
STREET FOOD

144

Ken Hom's Quick Wok

154

The Best Meal of the Day, Any Time of the Day

A Real American
Breakfast

Cheryl Alters Jamison & Bill Jamison

164

PERFECT
CAKES

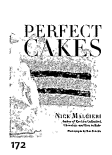

NICK MALGIERI

172

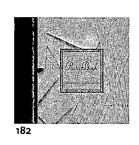

182

MY KITCHEN IN
SPAIN
225 Authentic Regional Recipes

JANET MENDEL

194

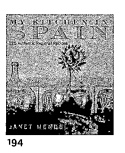

Baking in America

204

Live
Love
Eat
Wolfgang
Puck

218

A Return to Cooking

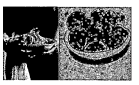

ERIC RIPERT | MICHAEL RUHLMAN

228

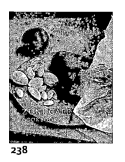

238

charmaine solomon

250

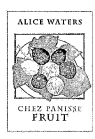

thai food
david thompson

262

ALICE WATERS

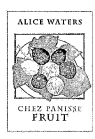

CHEZ PANISSE
FRUIT

270

contents

12 In the Hands of a Chef
BY JODY ADAMS & KEN RIVARD
14 Penne with Shrimp, Artichokes, and Feta
17 Lobster, Corn, and Smoked Fish Chowder
23 Tarte Flambée with Caramelized Onions,
     Smoked Bacon, and Creamy Cheese
28 Panisse with Tomatoes and Black Olives

30 CookSmart
BY PAM ANDERSON
32 Simple, Scrumptious Caesar Salad
     with Quick Garlic Croutons
34 Crab Cakes Worth the Price
36 Chicken and Dumplings with
     Aromatic Vegetables
38 Blue-Ribbon Chili

40 The Babbo Cookbook
BY MARIO BATALI
42 Sweet Pea Flan with Carrot Vinaigrette
45 Escarole with Roasted Shallots
46 Two-Minute Calamari Sicilian
     Lifeguard Style
48 Dry-Rubbed Rib-Eye Steak for Two

50 1,000 Indian Recipes
BY NEELAM BATRA
52 Mushroom Turnovers with Curry Powder
54 Puréed Spinach Soup
55 Pan-Cooked Chile-Chicken Thighs
56 Creamy Mashed Eggplant with Peas

58 Simply Bishop's
BY JOHN BISHOP & DENNIS GREEN
60 Pesto-Crusted Halibut with
     Red Lentil Dahl
63 Potato, Herb and Onion Latkes
64 Roast Duck Breast with Apple Purée

66 Chef Daniel Boulud
BY DANIEL BOULUD & PETER KAMINSKY
68 Tuna Bagnat
70 Stuffed Squid with Piquillo Pepper Coulis
72 Chicken Provençal
74 Rosemary Braised Veal Shank

76 The Good Cookie
BY TISH BOYLE
78 Cookie Shop Chocolate Chip Cookies
81 Raspberry-Filled Shortbread Fingers
83 Lemon Curd Bites
86 Crunchy Peanut Bars

**88 Michael Chiarello's
    Casual Cooking**
BY MICHAEL CHIARELLO WITH
JANET FLETCHER
90 Baby Back Ribs with Espresso BBQ Sauce
93 Linguine with Clams and
     Bagna Cauda Butter
95 Crispy White Beans with Chili Oil
100 Quail with Bacon and Honey

102 Celebrate with Chocolate
BY MARCEL DESAULNIERS
104 Mrs. D's "She Ain't Heavy"
     Chocolate Cake
108 Black Mamba Cookies
110 Cocoa Berry Yogurt Mousse

**112 Barefoot Contessa
    Family Style**
BY INA GARTEN
114 Real Meatballs and Spaghetti
117 Parmesan Roasted Asparagus
118 Scott's Short Ribs
120 Saffron Risotto with Butternut Squash

contents continued

124 **Desserts 1-2-3**
BY ROZANNE GOLD
126 Gianduia Sandwich Cookies
127 Hazelnut Angel Cake
128 Fresh Lime Mousse
129 Pineapple Flan

130 **Saffron Shores**
BY JOYCE GOLDSTEIN
132 Tunisian Fried Pastries with Egg
135 Tuna with Tomatoes
138 Tunisian Fish Ball Tagine
141 Syrian Rice with Vermicelli
142 Cumin-Flavored Meatballs with Onion
Jam and Spicy Tomato Sauce

144 **Mediterranean Street Food**
BY ANISSA HELOU
146 Moroccan Flat Bread
148 Chickpea and Lamb Soup
150 "Red" Rice Croquettes
153 Chickpea Fritters

154 **Ken Hom's Quick Wok**
BY KEN HOM
156 Thai-Style Rice Noodles in Soup
159 Spicy Tuna
160 Stir-Fried Lamb with Garlic and Basil
162 Braised Beef with Beancurd

164 **A Real American Breakfast**
BY CHERYL ALTERS JAMISON &
BILL JAMISON
166 Saturday Summer Strata
168 Blueberry Turnovers
170 Chicago-Style Breakfast Pan Pizza

172 **Perfect Cakes**
BY NICK MALGIERI
174 Zuccotto alla Ricotta
177 Chocolate Chiffon Cake
180 High-Ratio Lemon-Buttermilk
Pound Cake

182 **The Il Fornaio Pasta Book**
BY MAURIZIO MAZZON
184 Beet-Flavored Pasta Stuffed with a
Ricotta-Beet Filling Topped with Brown
Butter and Poppy Seeds
188 Pasta Ribbons with Pesto, Green
Beans, and Potatoes
190 Roasted Peppers and Clams with
Pasta Strands

194 **My Kitchen in Spain**
BY JANET MENDEL
196 Deviled Eggs with Shrimp and Olives
197 Home-Style Pork Chops in
Lemon Marinade
198 Fish Soup with Sour Orange
200 Maria's Roast Chicken with Meat and
Olive Stuffing
202 Flamenco Potato Salad with
Lemon Dressing

204 Baking in America

BY GREG PATENT

206 Nectarine-Raspberry Crisp
209 Rhubarb-Strawberry Pie
214 Gingerbread Little Cakes
216 Cranberry Muffins from Nantucket

218 Live, Love, Eat!

BY WOLFGANG PUCK

220 Hot Spinach-Artichoke Dip
222 Grilled Chicken Breasts with
     Garlic and Parsley
224 Turkey Mushroom Burgers with Chunky
     Tomato Salsa Compote

228 A Return to Cooking

BY ERIC RIPERT & MICHAEL RUHLMAN

230 Cod with Local Wax Beans, Chorizo,
     and Soy-Sherry Sauce
233 Arugula Salad with Goat's Milk
     Yogurt Dressing
234 Shrimp with Fresh Coconut Milk,
     Calabaza, and Avocado
237 Mussels with Spicy Italian Sausage

238 The Zuni Café Cookbook

BY JUDY RODGERS

240 Shrimp Cooked in Romesco with
     Wilted Spinach
245 Lamb's Lettuce with Raw Asparagus,
     Pistachios, and Parmigiano-Reggiano
246 Pasta alla Carbonara
248 Quail and Sausage Braised with Grapes

**250 Complete Vegetarian
Cookbook**

BY CHARMAINE SOLOMON

252 Rice with Fresh Cheese, Nuts and
     Vegetables, Moghul Style
255 Eggplant Lasagne
257 Lentil, Sesame and Sunflower Burgers
260 Peanut Wafers

262 Thai Food

BY DAVID THOMPSON

264 Trout Braised with Caramel, Celery
     and Fish Sauce
267 Cucumber and Pork Stir-Fried with Egg
268 Stir-Fried Minced Beef with Chillies
     and Holy Basil

270 Chez Panisse Fruit

BY ALICE WATERS

272 Green Mango Salad with Shrimp
     and Avocado
274 Sicilian-Style Swordfish Stuffed with
     Currants and Pine Nuts
276 Grilled Salmon with Citrus Sauce
277 Poulet à la Normande

280 Index

recipes by course

breakfast and brunch

23   Tarte Flambée with Caramelized Onions, Smoked Bacon, and Creamy Cheese
166   Saturday Summer Strata
168   Blueberry Turnovers
170   Chicago-Style Breakfast Pan Pizza
216   Cranberry Muffins from Nantucket

hors d'oeuvres

52   Mushroom Turnovers with Curry Powder
95   Crispy White Beans with Chili Oil
146   Moroccan Flat Bread
153   Chickpea Fritters
196   Deviled Eggs with Shrimp and Olives
220   Hot Spinach-Artichoke Dip
260   Peanut Wafers

first courses

17   Lobster, Corn, and Smoked Fish Chowder
32   Simple, Scrumptious Caesar Salad with Quick Garlic Croutons
42   Sweet Pea Flan with Carrot Vinaigrette
54   Puréed Spinach Soup
132   Tunisian Fried Pastries with Egg
148   Chickpea and Lamb Soup
150   "Red" Rice Croquettes
156   Thai-Style Rice Noodles in Soup
233   Arugula Salad with Goat's Milk Yogurt Dressing
234   Shrimp with Fresh Coconut Milk, Calabaza, and Avocado
245   Lamb's Lettuce with Raw Asparagus, Pistachios, and Parmigiano-Reggiano
272   Green Mango Salad with Shrimp and Avocado

pasta

14   Penne with Shrimp, Artichokes, and Feta
93   Linguine with Clams and *Bagna Cauda* Butter
114   Real Meatballs and Spaghetti
120   Saffron Risotto with Butternut Squash
184   Beet-Flavored Pasta Stuffed with a Ricotta-Beet Filling Topped with Brown Butter and Poppy Seeds
188   Pasta Ribbons with Pesto, Green Beans, and Potatoes
191   Roasted Peppers and Clams with Pasta Strands
246   Pasta alla Carbonara
255   Eggplant Lasagne

fish and shellfish

34   Crab Cakes Worth the Price
46   Two-Minute Calamari Sicilian Lifeguard Style
60   Pesto-Crusted Halibut with Red Lentil Dahl
68   Tuna Bagnat
70   Stuffed Squid with Piquillo Pepper Coulis
135   Tuna with Tomatoes
138   Tunisian Fish Ball Tagine
159   Spicy Tuna
198   Fish Soup with Sour Orange
230   Cod with Local Wax Beans, Chorizo, and Soy-Sherry Sauce
237   Mussels with Spicy Italian Sausage
240   Shrimp Cooked in Romesco with Wilted Spinach
264   Trout Braised with Caramel, Celery and Fish Sauce
274   Sicilian-Style Swordfish Stuffed with Currants and Pine Nuts
276   Grilled Salmon with Citrus Sauce

poultry

36 Chicken and Dumplings with Aromatic Vegetables
55 Pan-Cooked Chile-Chicken Thighs
64 Roast Duck Breast with Apple Purée
72 Chicken Provençal
100 Quail with Bacon and Honey
200 Maria's Roast Chicken with Meat and Olive Stuffing
222 Grilled Chicken Breasts with Garlic and Parsley
224 Turkey Mushroom Burgers with Chunky Tomato Salsa Compote
248 Quail and Sausage Braised with Grapes
277 Poulet à la Normande

meat

38 Blue-Ribbon Chili
48 Dry-Rubbed Rib-Eye Steak for Two
74 Rosemary Braised Veal Shank
90 Baby Back Ribs with Espresso BBQ Sauce
118 Scott's Short Ribs
142 Cumin-Flavored Meatballs with Onion Jam and Spicy Tomato Sauce
160 Stir-Fried Lamb with Garlic and Basil
162 Braised Beef with Beancurd
197 Home-Style Pork Chops in Lemon Marinade
267 Cucumber and Pork Stir-Fried with Egg
268 Stir-Fried Minced Beef with Chillies and Holy Basil

vegetables and sides

28 Panisse with Tomatoes and Black Olives
45 Escarole with Roasted Shallots
56 Creamy Mashed Eggplant with Peas
63 Potato, Herb and Onion Latkes
117 Parmesan Roasted Asparagus
141 Syrian Rice with Vermicelli
202 Flamenco Potato Salad with Lemon Dressing
252 Rice with Fresh Cheese, Nuts and Vegetables, Moghul Style
257 Lentil, Sesame and Sunflower Burgers

desserts

79 Cookie Shop Chocolate Chip Cookies
81 Raspberry-Filled Shortbread Fingers
83 Lemon Curd Bites
86 Crunchy Peanut Bars
104 Mrs. D's "She Ain't Heavy" Chocolate Cake
108 Black Mamba Cookies
110 Cocoa Berry Yogurt Mousse
126 Gianduia Sandwich Cookies
127 Hazelnut Angel Cake
128 Fresh Lime Mousse
129 Pineapple Flan
174 Zuccotto alla Ricotta
177 Chocolate Chiffon Cake
180 High-Ratio Lemon-Buttermilk Pound Cake
206 Nectarine-Raspberry Crisp
209 Rhubarb-Strawberry Pie
214 Gingerbread Little Cakes

foreword

This is our sixth edition of *Best of the Best*, yet every time we tackle the book we're surprised at what an extensive project it turns out to be. To find the 25 most outstanding cookbooks of the past year we had to evaluate more than 125. We pored over each, scouring it for recipes that sounded original and appealing and that were doable for home cooks. After months of testing and tasting, we are very proud of our final selection. The recipes in this volume make us want to rush into the kitchen—from Cod with Local Wax Beans, Chorizo and Soy-Sherry Sauce (from Eric Ripert's *A Return to Cooking*) to Pan-Cooked Chile-Chicken Thighs (from Neelam Batra's *1,000 Indian Recipes*) to Linguine with Clams and *Bagna-Cauda* Butter (from *Michael Chiarello's Casual Cooking*).

As in past editions, the recipes here appear as they were first published. But this year we've added some exciting new features: an author Q&A at the beginning of each chapter; a reading list (including everything from the original *Joy of Cooking* to *The French Laundry Cookbook*); and dozens of cooking tips that came out of the testing process.

These 25 cookbooks are a remarkable and varied selection, from authors all around the world. And because the FOOD & WINE Test Kitchen has given each recipe its stamp of approval, you can feel confident they will all work flawlessly. We hope they will inspire you to rush into the kitchen.

Editor in Chief
FOOD & WINE MAGAZINE

Editor
FOOD & WINE COOKBOOK

in the hands of a chef

JODY ADAMS & KEN RIVARD

about adams
Jody Adams is the chef and owner of Rialto, a four-star restaurant in Cambridge, Massachusetts. In addition, she's a partner in the Sapphire Restaurant Group, which manages and operates Rialto as well as Noir and blu, both in Boston. *In the Hands of a Chef* is her first cookbook.

Adams has a knack for reshaping familiar dishes into something special, by adding smoked trout to chowder, say, or anchovy butter to seared sirloin. With some help from her husband, Ken, (a competent but inexperienced home cook), she finds the middle ground between convenience and excitement. Expect to spend some time with these recipes and to be rewarded in the end.

FOOD & WINE How did *In the Hands of a Chef* come to exist?

JODY ADAMS Some people go out and collect recipes for a book, almost as if they're finding them and putting them into a basket; but for me, it was more a process of having all these recipes in my head and needing to find a basket for them. My husband, Ken, and I literally had all the recipes spread out on the dining room table, and we kept shifting them around until finally they fit. It's a lot of work; you have to be critical and self-critical, and you have to listen to everyone—when your editor, your agent, your friends or your children say something is terrible, you have to listen to them. But the short answer is: I had gotten pressure for years from customers, cooking-school students—everyone, really, to do a book. Ken and I talked about it for

1½ years, and finally we got tired of talking and just decided to go ahead.

F&W How would you describe the recipes in the book?

JA Over the years I've taken regional and home recipes and inverted them—twisted and turned them to create white-tablecloth-restaurant recipes. This book takes those recipes and brings them back home. In fact, a working title for the book was *Bringing it Back Home*. The process was interesting; Ken is a good home cook but not highly experienced, and he and a neighbor, another home cook, tested all the recipes. That's why the book provides a level of detail that otherwise wouldn't be there. But ironically, in the five years it's taken to write this book, Ken has become a great cook!

F&W How were you able to translate restaurant food for the home cook?

>> | FEATURED RECIPES

1 | PENNE WITH SHRIMP, ARTICHOKES, AND FETA

2 | LOBSTER, CORN, AND SMOKED FISH CHOWDER

3 | TARTE FLAMBÉE WITH CARAMELIZED ONIONS, SMOKED BACON, AND CREAMY CHEESE

4 | PANISSE WITH TOMATOES AND BLACK OLIVES

JA A dish at Rialto can encompass four or five subrecipes, so I had to distill from the dish what was important while maintaining its integrity. The really complex recipes are in the back of the book, in the section "A Mile in a Chef's Shoes." You can't make those dishes quickly, but I don't see anything wrong with spending time in the kitchen; it's a wonderful place to be.

F&W How do you teach people how to follow their instincts when they're cooking, as chefs do?

JA I think it's really important not to get locked into a recipe and feel like you have to get the proportions exactly right. The title of the book, *In the Hands of a Chef*, refers to my hands, but I want to teach you how to trust your own hands, how to do it all for yourself. And the most important part of that is to start in a comfortable place. Everybody has some kind of culinary history in their lives, so starting with the things you know is really important; I explain how to do that in the "Kitchen in My Head" section of the book's introduction. People do carry a kitchen in their heads, really.

F&W What's the very best piece of information or the most useful cooking technique in your book?

JA I feel like the book is full of useful information—how to shell fava beans, how to work with artichokes. That's all thanks to Ken, who is an absolute stickler for details. This isn't really a book about cooking technique, but there are really helpful explanatory sidebars throughout.

the specifics

recipes	pages	photos	publisher	price
215	384	16 color photos	William Morrow	$34.95

credits

In the Hands of a Chef: Cooking with Jody Adams of Rialto Restaurant by Jody Adams and Ken Rivard. Copyright © 2002 by Jody Adams and Ken Rivard. Photographs by Ellen Silverman. Reprinted by permission of HarperCollins Publishers Inc., William Morrow.

Penne with Shrimp, Artichokes, and Feta

MAKES 4 ENTRÉE SERVINGS

At a conference of women chefs in Mexico City, I tasted a perfect shrimp dish prepared by Monique Andrée Barbeau, the chef of Fullers in Seattle. The shrimp were saturated with flavor, but still mysteriously tender. The trick, she explained, was to first simmer aromatic ingredients in oil, then to cook the shrimp over low heat, all the while keeping them completely submerged in the flavored oil. In this recipe, fennel, hot red pepper flakes, oregano, garlic, and lemon zest create the first level of flavor, followed by a long simmer of artichoke quarters. Only then do the shrimp enter the pan for their own slow cooking.

2   cups extra virgin olive oil

1   teaspoon coriander seeds

1   teaspoon fennel seeds

1   teaspoon dried oregano

½   teaspoon hot red pepper flakes

4   garlic cloves, chopped

1   medium onion, chopped into ½-inch dice

Grated zest of 1 lemon

Kosher salt

3   large artichokes, trimmed, cut into quarters,
    chokes removed, and rubbed with a lemon half

1   pound medium shrimp (20 to 25), peeled and deveined

2   tablespoons freshly squeezed lemon juice

½   pound penne

3   tablespoons chopped fresh mint, plus 4 sprigs for garnish

3   tablespoons chopped fresh oregano

6   ounces feta, crumbled into large pieces

To trim an artichoke, use a sharp, serrated knife to cut off the top third and the stem. Snap off the outer leaves and trim the tough green skin from around the artichoke. Scoop out the hairy choke with a spoon and cut the heart into quarters as directed in this recipe.

1. Combine the olive oil, coriander seeds, fennel seeds, oregano, red pepper flakes, garlic, onion, and lemon zest in a large sauté pan. Season generously with salt. Bring to a simmer and cook for 10 minutes, so the seasonings flavor the oil.

2. Add the artichokes, lower the heat if necessary (the oil should be barely bubbling), and cook until tender, 20 to 30 minutes. Use a slotted spoon to transfer the artichokes to a bowl.

3. Add the shrimp to the oil and cook at the same low simmer, turning once, until done, about 10 minutes.

4. Remove the shrimp from the oil and let cool on a plate. Pour off 1 cup of the oil from the pan, strain, and refrigerate for another use. (The oil is delicious and can be used in vinaigrettes or for sautéing another dish.) Leave the pan over low heat.

5. As soon as they're cool enough to handle, remove the leaves from the artichokes and save for another use. Chop the artichoke hearts and stems into 1-inch pieces and return to the bowl. Add the shrimp and toss with the lemon juice.

6. Meanwhile, bring a large pot of water to a boil and season with salt. Add the penne and stir constantly until the water returns to a boil. Cook until the pasta is tender but still offers some resistance when you bite into it, about 10 minutes. Before draining the pasta, use a measuring cup to scoop out ¼ cup of the pasta water; reserve. Drain the pasta in a colander and add to the sauté pan with the oil.

7. Add the artichokes, shrimp, herbs, and feta and toss until heated through. Taste for seasoning. Depending on the saltiness of the feta, it may not be necessary to add additional salt. If the pasta seems too dry, add some of the reserved pasta water as needed.

8. Divide among four warm bowls. Garnish each portion with a sprig of mint and serve.

Lobster, Corn, and Smoked Fish Chowder

MAKES 4 SERVINGS

Every home cook needs the first-course equivalent of a little black dress—convenient and provocative at the same time. This is a rich, astonishingly quick appetizer soup that leaves you wanting more. The classic chowder trio of seafood, salt pork, and milk metamorphoses into chunks of lobster and corn kernels suspended in an aromatic base of smoked trout and cream. Using homemade lobster or fish stock gives it a depth of flavor unusual in a soup that cooks so briefly. The ingredients shouldn't come together until the last moment, when they're heated for just a few minutes, so don't assemble the chowder until you're ready to serve it.

Kosher salt

One 1-pound lobster (or ¼ pound freshly cooked lobster meat)

1   tablespoon unsalted butter

2   ears corn, husked and kernels stripped off with a sharp knife
(about 1½ cups)

2   shallots, finely diced

1   garlic clove, minced

2   cups light cream

2   cups Lobster Stock or Fish Stock (recipes follow) or
1 cup clam juice plus 1 cup water

2   ounces smoked trout, skin and any bones removed, broken into small pieces

Freshly ground black pepper

2   tablespoons chopped fresh chives for garnish

"Over the years I've taken regional and home recipes and inverted them— twisted and turned them to create white-tablecloth- restaurant recipes. This book takes those recipes and brings them back home."

1. If you're using a live lobster, set a steaming rack in a large pot big enough to hold the lobster. The rack should sit at least 2 inches off the bottom of the pot (support it on ramekins if necessary). Add 1 inch of salted water to the pot and bring to a boil. Set the lobster on the rack, cover, and steam for 10 minutes. Let cool.

2. When the lobster is cool enough to handle, crack open the shell and remove the meat from the tail and claws. Cut the meat into ½-inch pieces. Cover and refrigerate.

3. Melt the butter in a medium saucepan over medium-low heat. Add the corn and cook until it starts to soften, about 2 minutes. Add the shallots and garlic and cook for 3 more minutes until aromatic. Add the cream and lobster stock and heat through. Add the lobster and smoked trout and heat until warmed through. Season with salt and pepper.

4. Ladle the chowder into warm bowls, sprinkle with the chopped chives, and serve.

Lobster Stock

MAKES 3 QUARTS

Every year, my extended family manages to get together for one weekend in Barnstable, on Cape Cod, and one night is dedicated to fixing a lobster dinner. I save the lobster bodies to make stock. After allowing it to cool, I pour the finished stock into ice cube trays and freeze it. The next day, I empty the cubes into freezer bags. Then, for the next six months, I have cubes of lobster stock I can add to soups or use to make quick butter sauces for sautéed seafood.

Homemade lobster stock will keep for 5 days refrigerated; boil refrigerated stock before using it if it is older than a day or two. Refrigerate the stock for several hours before freezing. Frozen stock will keep for up to 6 months; boil before using.

3 sprigs flat-leaf parsley

2 sprigs tarragon

3 bay leaves

1 teaspoon black peppercorns

¼ cup vegetable oil

2 leeks, white part only, trimmed of roots and tough outer leaves, thinly sliced crosswise, and swirled vigorously in a bowl of cold water to remove any grit

1 small onion, thinly sliced

1 medium carrot, thinly sliced crosswise

1 small fennel bulb, trimmed of stalks and tough outer layers, cut in half lengthwise, cored, and thinly sliced crosswise

2 celery stalks, thinly sliced crosswise

5 pounds lobster bodies, rinsed and coarsely chopped

2 tablespoons tomato paste

2 cups dry white wine

½ cup brandy

16 ounces (2 cups) canned whole tomatoes, with their liquid

1. Pile the parsley, tarragon, bay leaves, and peppercorns in the middle of a piece of cheesecloth and tie into a bundle. Set aside.

2. Heat 2 tablespoons of the vegetable oil in a large sauté pan over medium-high heat. Add the vegetables and cook until they brown, about 15 minutes. Transfer the vegetables to a stockpot.

3. Add the remaining 2 tablespoons oil to the sauté pan. Add the lobster bodies and cook until they brown, about 20 minutes, tossing occasionally. If necessary, cook them in a couple of sauté pans or do them in batches.

4. Add the tomato paste to the pan and cook for 3 minutes. Take the pan off the heat and add the wine and brandy. Return the pan to the heat and stir to deglaze. Transfer everything to the stockpot.

5. Add the tomatoes to the stockpot, then add enough water to come ½ inch below the top of the contents of the pot. Add the cheesecloth bundle. Bring to a boil over high heat, then lower the heat to a simmer. Move the pot toward you so it sits 2 inches off the center of the burner. This will cause the fat and impurities to collect at the edge of the pot closest to you, making it easier to skim them off. Simmer for 1 hour.

6. Pour the stock through a fine strainer into another large pot or container. Refrigerate. After the stock has cooled, skim off the fat that has accumulated on the surface. Refrigerate or freeze the stock until ready to use.

Fish Stock

MAKES 3 QUARTS

Fish stock is simple to make, takes far less time than poultry stock, and freezes well. Roasting the bones is actually easier than sautéing them, and it increases the depth of flavor. When the time comes to make a seafood soup or risotto, you'll be glad you invested an hour in this.

Homemade fish stock will keep for 5 days refrigerated; boil refrigerated stock before using it if it is older than a day or two. Refrigerate stock for several hours before freezing. Frozen stock will keep for up to 6 months; boil before using.

5 pounds fish bones, and the heads, from white-fleshed fish such as cod, haddock, or flounder

¼ cup vegetable oil

3 sprigs flat-leaf parsley

2 sprigs thyme

3 bay leaves

1 teaspoon black peppercorns

2 leeks, white part only, trimmed of roots and tough outer leaves, thinly sliced crosswise and swirled in a bowl of cold water to remove any grit

1 small onion, thinly sliced

1 medium carrot, thinly sliced

2 celery stalks, thinly sliced crosswise

1 small fennel bulb, trimmed of stalks and tough outer layers, sliced in half lengthwise, cored, and thinly sliced crosswise

¼ pound mushrooms, cleaned and coarsely chopped

2 cups dry white wine

1. Using kitchen shears, remove the eyeballs and gills from the fish heads. Put the bones in a large pot and rinse under cold running water for at least 30 minutes. Drain.

2. Preheat the oven to 450°F.

3. Spread the fish bones in a large roasting pan and pat dry with paper towels. Drizzle with 2 tablespoons of the vegetable oil and toss well. Roast for 30 minutes, or until all the bones are golden brown.

4. Meanwhile, pile the parsley, thyme, bay leaves, and peppercorns in the middle of a piece of cheesecloth and tie into a bundle. Set aside.

5. Heat the remaining 2 tablespoons vegetable oil in a large stockpot over medium-high heat. Add the leeks, onion, carrot, celery, fennel, and mushrooms. Cook until lightly browned, about 10 minutes.

6. Add the bones to the stockpot, along with the cheesecloth bundle, white wine, and enough water to come ½ inch below the bones. Bring to a boil, then lower the heat to a simmer. Move the pot toward you so it sits 2 inches off the center of the burner. This will cause the fat and impurities to collect at the edge of the pot closest to you, making it easier to skim them off. Simmer for 30 minutes, skimming as necessary.

7. Pour the stock through a fine strainer into another large pot or container. Refrigerate. After the stock has cooled, skim off the fat that has accumulated on the surface. Refrigerate or freeze the stock until ready to use.

Tarte Flambée with Caramelized Onions, Smoked Bacon, and Creamy Cheese

MAKES FOUR 10-INCH TARTS

Contrary to what its name might lead you to expect, this tart isn't flambéed. The "flaming" refers to the burnt edges of this thin Alsatian flatbread, made from pizza dough and strewn with onions and bacon. In the original version, the raw ingredients were tossed over the dough with a little cheese and cooked rapidly in the hot brick oven of the town baker. Somewhere along the line—presumably in more prosperous times—a dollop of rich cheese was thrown into the mixture. Taking the time to caramelize the onions and crisping the bacon beforehand transforms the tart into an even richer, more luxurious dish.

f&w tip
To speed up the process of making the tarts, consider rolling out all of the dough rounds at once and stacking them between sheets of parchment or wax paper to keep them moist.

3 tablespoons plus 1 teaspoon extra virgin olive oil

2 large onions, thinly sliced

Kosher salt and freshly ground black pepper

8 to 12 strips meaty smoked bacon

6 ounces (about ⅔ cup) fromage blanc (or soft cream cheese, if fromage blanc is unavailable)

3 ounces (⅓ cup) mascarpone

3 ounces (⅓ cup) crème fraîche

2 tablespoons unbleached all-purpose flour, plus extra for rolling out the dough

1 recipe Basic Pizza Dough (recipe follows), at room temperature

Cornmeal for dusting

Do ahead Make the dough and caramelize the onions.

1. Heat 2 tablespoons of the oil in a large sauté pan over medium heat. Add the onions, season with salt and pepper, and cook, stirring occasionally, until the onions are translucent, 3 to 5 minutes. Reduce the heat to low and continue cooking, stirring occasionally, until the onions are golden, caramelized, and sweet, 30 to 40 minutes. Do not let them cook too fast, or they'll dry out and burn rather than caramelize; add a little water if they look too dry. Let them cool before using.

2. While the onions are caramelizing, cook the bacon in a second large sauté pan over medium heat just until it starts to become crispy but some of the fat still remains. Transfer to a rack and allow to cool.

3. Cut the bacon crosswise into ½-inch-wide strips. Mix the fromage blanc, mascarpone, crème fraîche, and flour together. Season with salt and pepper.

4. Place a pizza stone on the bottom rack of the oven and preheat the oven to 500°F.

5. Cut the pizza dough into 4 equal pieces and roll into balls. Drape with plastic wrap and let rest for 20 minutes.

6. Using plenty of flour, roll one of the balls of dough into a circle 10 to 11 inches in diameter. Push the crust together to thicken it slightly around the edge for a rim. Transfer the circle to a peel or sheet pan sprinkled with cornmeal. Dimple the dough with your fingertips so it doesn't puff up during baking. Brush 1 teaspoon of the olive oil over the dough or rub it on with your fingertips, leaving a ½-inch border around the edge.

7. Spread one-quarter of the cheese mixture evenly over the dough. Then spread one-quarter of the onions evenly over the cheese. Distribute one-quarter of the bacon over the onions.

8. Slide the tart onto the stone and bake for 12 to 15 minutes, or until the bacon is crispy, the cheese bubbles, and the crust is a deep golden brown. While the first tart is baking, prepare the second.

9. Remove the tart from the oven with the peel, or slide it onto a sheet pan, and transfer to a cutting board. Place the next tart in the oven. Cut the finished tart into 4 slices, place on a plate, and serve immediately. Start working on the third tart, and repeat the process until you've finished all 4 tarts.

on adams's nightstand

Adams has several favorite authors: **Paula Wolfert, Elizabeth David, Julia Child, Irma Rombauer** (Adams prefers the original *Joy of Cooking* rather than the updated one from 1997), **Madeleine Kamman** and **Richard Olney.** A relatively new favorite is **Thomas Keller:** "I love *The French Laundry Cookbook*; I'd recommend that everyone buy it."

Basic Pizza Dough

**MAKES 1 POUND—ENOUGH FOR FOUR
8-INCH OR TWO 12-INCH
THIN-CRUST PIZZAS OR TWO 16-INCH
VERY-THIN-CRUST PIZZAS**

You can make good pizza dough in a few hours. Great dough, one whose crust will make people sit up and wonder if they've been eating cardboard all their lives, requires a little extra time, but almost no extra effort. A memorable pizza crust will almost always have been made from dough that has had the benefit of an extended second rising, usually stretched out over 6 to 8 hours. This second rising allows the gluten fibers greater time to develop, resulting in a chewier crust. The long second rising also eliminates the raw quality that crust made from "quick" dough sometimes seems to have. A good crust tastes mature, like a well-made bread, good enough to stand on its own, instead of just serving as a vehicle for the topping.

¾ cup warm water

½ package yeast (scant 1 teaspoon)

1 tablespoon kosher salt

3 tablespoons extra virgin olive oil

1½ to 1¾ cups unbleached
    all-purpose flour, plus more
    as needed

1. To proof the yeast, put 2 tablespoons of the warm water in a large bowl, stir in the yeast, and let it rest. After a few minutes, bubbles should begin to form, demonstrating that the yeast is alive and active. If nothing happens after 10 or 15 minutes, discard the mixture and start over with fresh yeast.

2. Add the remaining ½ cup plus 2 tablespoons water, the salt, and 2 tablespoons of the olive oil to the yeast mixture and mix well. Use a wooden spoon to stir in 1½ cups flour ½ cup at a time. After incorporating the final ½ cup flour, the dough should be too stiff to stir; if not, gradually add the remaining ¼ cup. Transfer the dough to a clean board and knead until smooth and elastic, about 7 minutes. You can sprinkle the dough with a little flour if it's too sticky to knead, but try to use as little as possible: The more flour you use, the denser the dough will be; the less flour, the lighter the dough, and hence the crisper the crust. Try to work with dough that's still a little tacky.

3. Rub a large bowl with the remaining 1 tablespoon olive oil. Put the dough in the bowl, then flip it so that it's completely coated with oil. Cover with a damp towel and allow to rise until doubled in bulk. Depending on the yeast and flour, this can take anywhere from 1 to 2 hours.

4. *For a quick dough (for use within an hour or so),* punch it down after the first rising, then cut it into 2 or 4 pieces, depending on how many pizzas you intend to make, and roll the pieces into balls. Cover the balls with a towel and let rise again at room temperature until double in bulk, about 45 minutes; as soon as the dough finishes the quick second rising, it's ready to use. *For a slow second rising,* punch the dough down after the first rising, cover with the towel, and refrigerate for 6 to 8 hours.

5. After the second rising, the dough is ready to use. Either proceed with the tart recipe or wrap the dough tightly in plastic wrap and refrigerate. Or, if not using within a day, put the wrapped dough in a plastic bag and freeze it; allow frozen dough to thaw in the refrigerator. All dough should be at room temperature before using.

Panisse with Tomatoes and Black Olives

MAKES 4 ENTRÉE SERVINGS

Tomatoes and olives and basil and anchovies—close your eyes, and the aroma of this dish could fool you into thinking you're in Provence or Liguria, if only you could identify that toasty, cozy part of the smell. The mystery ingredient is chickpea flour, used to make a polenta called *panisse*. Like the familiar cornmeal polenta, panisse recipes often call for letting the cooked mixture firm up, then frying or baking it, perhaps with a topping of mushrooms or tomatoes.

1½ cups chickpea flour

2   cups water

5   tablespoons extra virgin olive oil

Kosher salt and freshly ground black pepper

2   extra-large eggs, separated, yolks lightly beaten

1   medium onion, thinly sliced

4   garlic cloves, finely chopped

1   pint cherry tomatoes

3   anchovy fillets, rinsed and coarsely chopped

½   teaspoon dried oregano

¼   cup chopped fresh basil

½   cup coarsely chopped pitted Niçoise olives

2   tablespoons capers, rinsed

¼   cup freshly grated Parmesan

1. Mix the chickpea flour with the water, 2 tablespoons of the olive oil, 2 teaspoons salt, and 1 teaspoon pepper. Let sit for 1 hour.

2. Preheat the oven to 425°F. Rub an 8 x 12-inch baking dish with 1 tablespoon of the olive oil.

3. Beat the egg yolks into the batter. Whip the egg whites until they hold soft peaks and then fold into the batter. Pour the batter into the prepared pan. Bake until it sets, 12 to 15 minutes. Let cool for 15 minutes.

4. Meanwhile, heat the remaining 2 tablespoons olive oil in a large sauté pan over high heat. Add the onions and cook until they start to brown, about 5 minutes. Be careful not to let them burn. Add the garlic and tomatoes and cook for 3 minutes. Add the anchovies, oregano, basil, olives, and capers, season with pepper, and cook for 2 minutes. Remove from the heat.

5. Preheat the broiler. Spread the onion mixture over the cooled panisse "crust," sprinkle with the cheese, and place under the broiler until the top is brown, about 5 minutes. Serve hot or at room temperature. Let cool for 3 minutes if you want to serve it right away.

f&w tip
Lightly crush the cherry tomatoes with the back of a spoon or fork so they soften a little bit while they cook. You can also halve them.

cooksmart

PAM ANDERSON

about anderson

Pam Anderson is the food columnist for USA WEEKEND magazine and the author of *How to Cook Without a Book* and the best-selling *Perfect Recipe*, winner of an International Association of Culinary Professionals' Julia Child Award. She is the former executive editor of *Cook's Illustrated*.

There aren't a lot of recipes in this book, but each has been so carefully tested that you can count on it to be foolproof. Considering that many other authors don't seem to bother to test their cookbooks at all, that is especially satisfying. Anderson details all her experiences (good and bad) in perfecting each dish, which makes the book a useful teaching tool, and a fun read.

FOOD & WINE Why did you write this book?

PAM ANDERSON I've always had a side of me that wants to break down a dish and put it back together, and then to share that information with other cooks. This book is a sequel to *The Perfect Recipe* [published in 2001] and explores another set of popular dishes that Americans know and love.

F&W Who do you think will get the most out of your book?

PA The recipes are basic, but there's enough solid advice in there for veterans. For example, even an accomplished cook wouldn't necessarily know that boiling shrimp makes them toughen and seize up so they curl up like a little roly-poly. If you steam them over the lowest heat possible, they stay more tender—and they're the perfect shape for shrimp cocktail.

F&W What else did you learn that you found especially useful?

PA I discovered some tips that are useful for more than one recipe. When I made pot roast, I found that I could simulate a pressure cooker in the oven by covering a pot with a concave sheet of heavy-duty aluminum foil. That helped decrease cooking times. In roasting pork tenderloin, I discovered it always needs a glaze or something else sweet to help the outside brown properly before the meat gets done.

F&W Did every trick relate to cooking?

PA No, I found some techniques involving only raw ingredients, like how to make gazpacho cold without chilling the tomatoes. I never refrigerate tomatoes because it makes them spongy and wrecks their flavor. So I refrigerated the other ingredients and the tomato juice, but not the chopped tomatoes.

>> | FEATURED RECIPES

1 | SIMPLE, SCRUMPTIOUS
CAESAR SALAD
WITH QUICK GARLIC
CROUTONS

2 | CRAB CAKES
WORTH THE PRICE

3 | CHICKEN AND
DUMPLINGS WITH
AROMATIC
VEGETABLES

4 | BLUE-RIBBON CHILI

F&W Which recipe went through the most testing?

PA Vegetable lasagna. I had to test every different vegetable and every possible cooking method for each vegetable. I think I did about 70 vegetable tests alone. Raw carrots, steamed carrots, sautéed carrots, blanched carrots—which way is the best? I tested all the vegetables in both a white sauce and a red sauce. And then there were all the noodles.

F&W What was surprisingly difficult to perfect?

PA The chocolate chip cookies. There are so many recipes for chocolate chip cookies out there, and I was trying to make one that was puffy, yet crisp and chewy. Getting that texture just right was really elusive.

F&W Do you have any general tips for beginner cooks?

PA Learn how to handle a knife properly. Make sure you heat the pan up enough. Don't overcrowd the pan or food can steam instead of brown. Be efficient: Don't use three utensils when one is enough. Use the same tongs to stir the pasta and also toss the salad. Finally, follow your instincts more than the recipe, particularly when it comes to cooking times.

F&W What plans do you have for future books or projects?

PA I feel like I've covered weeknight cooking, so I'm working on an entertaining book now. I want to help people with their biggest problem: how to prepare dishes so they all come out at the same time.

the specifics

recipes	pages	photos	publisher	price
38	348	none	Houghton Mifflin Company	$28

credits

From *CookSmart: Perfect Recipes for Every Day.* Copyright © 2002 by Pam Anderson. Illustrations copyright © 2002 by Laura Hartman Maestro. Photographs copyright © 2002 by Melanie Acevado. Reprinted by permission of Houghton Mifflin Company. All rights reserved.

Simple, Scrumptious Caesar Salad with Quick Garlic Croutons

SERVES 4 TO 6

The mayonnaise in this salad does not make the dressing gloppy. It's used as a stand-in for the coddled egg to ensure that the salad is salmonella-free.

Since washing and drying lettuce is time-consuming, try to buy packages of pre-washed romaine hearts. If the idea of serving a whole-leaf lettuce salad that guests eat with their fingers bothers you, simply tear the leaves into bite-size pieces. Slice the bread with a serrated knife. Use heavy-duty kitchen shears to cut the sliced bread into cubes.

Anchovy fans should feel free to garnish the salad with anchovy fillets or to mix in ½ teaspoon anchovy paste along with the mayonnaise and lemon juice.

Garlic croutons

4   garlic cloves

¼   cup olive oil

2   heaping cups ¾-inch bread cubes, cut from a good-quality
    baguette or Italian loaf

Large pinch salt

Salad

3   romaine hearts (remove any dark green outer leaves and
    reserve for another use); about 10 generous cups

2   tablespoons lemon juice

2½ tablespoons mayonnaise

¼   teaspoon Worcestershire sauce

5   tablespoons olive oil

¼   teaspoon salt

Freshly ground black pepper to taste

¼   cup freshly grated Parmesan cheese (preferably Parmigiano-Reggiano),
    plus extra for sprinkling

For croutons

1. Heat a large skillet over low heat. With motor running, drop garlic cloves through feeder tube of a food processor to mince. (A blender works as well.) Scrape down sides of bowl and add oil through feeder tube. Continue to process so that garlic releases its flavor into oil, about 30 seconds. Strain garlic from oil through a fine-mesh strainer; reserve half of garlic for dressing and set aside remaining half for another use. You should have about 3 tablespoons garlic oil.

2. Raise heat under skillet to medium. Place bread cubes in a medium bowl. Drizzle 2 tablespoons garlic oil evenly over bread, along with a big pinch of salt; toss to coat. Add remaining 1 tablespoon oil; toss again.

3. Add bread cubes to hot skillet and toast, turning cubes and shaking pan often, until crisp and golden brown, 5 to 7 minutes. Return croutons to bowl and set aside to cool while preparing salad.

For salad

4. Cut off bottom 1½ to 2 inches of core from each romaine heart. Separate heart into individual leaves. Put leaves in a large bowl.

5. Whisk lemon juice, mayonnaise, Worcestershire, and reserved garlic in a small bowl.

6. Drizzle lettuce with oil, sprinkle with salt and pepper, and toss lightly, carefully, and thoroughly so that lettuce is evenly coated. (Clean hands work well.)

7. Drizzle lemon mixture over lettuce; toss again.

8. Sprinkle ¼ cup Parmesan over greens; toss again.

9. Sprinkle croutons over salad, toss, and serve, sprinkling each portion with a little more Parmesan cheese.

LEAF LOGISTICS To measure whole romaine leaves, lightly pack them in a 2-quart Pyrex measuring cup or a 2-quart (8-cup) bowl. After dumping the 8 cups in the salad bowl, fill the cup or bowl halfway again, equaling the 10 generous cups you need for this salad. (If you make it in the same bowl each time, just remember what 10 cups looks like and you won't have to measure.)

on anderson's nightstand

Pam Anderson develops recipes for home cooks but looks to chefs for inspiration. She likes the *Union Square Cafe Cookbook* by **Danny Meyer** and **Michael Romano;** the recipes are always good, she says, and always appealing. Anderson also loves **Jean-Georges Vongerichten's** *Jean-Georges: Cooking at Home with a Four-Star Chef.* She likes to adapt his recipes, such as the one for crab spring rolls—just crab meat and mayonnaise wrapped in a spring roll wrapper. And **John Ash's** *From the Earth to the Table* may be eight years old, but Anderson still uses it because she likes his way with flavorings.

Crab Cakes Worth the Price

SERVES 8 AS A FIRST COURSE, 4 AS A MAIN COURSE

f&w tip

We loved these traditional crab cakes, which were dense with crab and not a lot of filler. Make sure the crab cakes are tightly packed together or they'll fall apart while they're being fried. We also thought they were equally delicious with an extra pinch of Old Bay seasoning.

If pasteurized jumbo lump is not available or too expensive, this recipe works beautifully with backfin as well. From start to finish, these crab cakes are ready in about 20 minutes. Served with corn on the cob and coleslaw, they make a fast, yet special dinner.

1   **large egg, beaten**

2   **tablespoons mayonnaise**

2   **tablespoons minced scallion greens**

¼   **teaspoon Maryland-style seasoning, such as Old Bay**

¼   **teaspoon hot red pepper sauce, such as Tabasco**

1   **pound pasteurized jumbo lump crabmeat (see note above)**

1   **tablespoon plus 1 teaspoon milk**

Salt and freshly ground black pepper

10   **saltine crackers, crushed (about ½ cup)**

6   **tablespoons olive oil, for frying**

Lemon wedges

1. Mix egg, mayonnaise, scallions, seasoning, and hot red pepper sauce in a small bowl.

2. Very carefully break up crabmeat in a medium bowl and pat with paper towels to remove excess liquid, making sure not to break up lumps (check for shells, but there should not be any). Add milk and season with salt and pepper to taste; toss gently to coat. Add saltines; toss gently to combine. Add egg mixture; gently toss once again to combine. Let stand for about 5 minutes so crackers have a chance to soften.

3. Meanwhile, heat oil in a large (11-to-12-inch) skillet (if using a smaller skillet, you may need to fry in batches) over medium-low heat. Using a standard ⅓-cup measure, scoop up a portion of crab, pressing it into cup to make a compact cake. Shake cake onto a large plate. Repeat process to make a total of 8 cakes.

4. A couple minutes before frying, increase heat to medium. Carefully add crab cakes to skillet. Sauté, turning once, until golden, about 3 minutes per side. Transfer cakes to a paper towel–lined plate. Serve immediately with lemon wedges.

Chicken and Dumplings with Aromatic Vegetables

SERVES 6

A touch of heavy cream gives the dish a more refined look and rich flavor, but for weeknight dinners, you may want to omit it. Flat noodle-style dumplings or round, puffy ones create a more rustic feel, while the cut-out dumplings make a more sophisticated dish.

For flat noodle-like dumplings, roll the dough to a ⅛-inch thickness and cut into approximately 2-by-½-inch strips.

For biscuit-like dumplings, roll the dough to a ½-inch thickness and use a 2-inch biscuit cutter or a round drinking-glass top to cut the dough into rounds.

For round, puffy dumplings, pinch the dough off to form 18 pieces.

1   large roasting chicken, 6–7 pounds

1   large onion, unpeeled, cut into large chunks

2   bay leaves

Salt

3   celery stalks, trimmed and cut into 1-by-½-inch sticks

4   carrots, peeled and cut into 1-by-½-inch sticks

6   boiling onions, peeled and halved

Baking powder dumplings

2   cups all-purpose flour

1   tablespoon baking powder

¾   teaspoon salt

3   tablespoons butter

1   cup milk

4   tablespoons softened butter or skimmed chicken fat

6   tablespoons all-purpose flour

1   teaspoon dried thyme leaves

2   tablespoons dry sherry or vermouth

¼   cup heavy cream (optional)

¾   cup frozen peas, thawed

¼   cup minced fresh parsley leaves

Freshly ground black or white pepper

1. Cut chicken into 2 breast halves, 2 thighs, 2 legs, 2 wings, and back. Cut wings and back into 1-inch pieces.

2. Heat a large Dutch oven over medium-high heat. Add back and wing pieces and onion chunks and sauté until onion softens and chicken loses its raw color, about 5 minutes. Reduce heat to low, cover, and continue to cook until chicken pieces give up most of their liquid, about 20 minutes. Increase heat to medium-high, add 4 cups water, remaining chicken parts, bay leaves, and ¾ teaspoon salt; bring to a simmer. Reduce heat to low and simmer, partially covered, until broth is rich and flavorful and chicken pieces are just cooked through, 20 to 30 minutes longer. Remove chicken pieces with a slotted spoon and set aside to cool. When chicken is cool enough to handle, remove meat from bones in large chunks. Discard bones. Strain broth into a large bowl, discarding backs and wings. Skim and reserve fat from broth for sauce. Rinse out pot.

3. Add ½ inch of water to cleaned pot and fit with a steamer basket; return to medium-high heat. Add celery, carrots, and halved onions, and steam until just tender, about 10 minutes. Remove vegetables and set aside.

For dumplings
4. Mix flour, baking powder, and salt in a medium bowl. Heat butter and milk to a simmer, then add to dry ingredients. Mix with a fork until mixture just comes together. Following illustrations, form dumplings.

5. Heat butter and/or chicken fat in pot over medium-high heat. Whisk in flour and thyme; cook, whisking constantly, until flour turns golden, 1 to 2 minutes. Whisking, gradually add sherry or vermouth, then 4 cups chicken broth (reserving remaining broth for another use); simmer until gravy thickens. Stir in cream, along with the chicken and steamed vegetables; return to a simmer.

6. Add dumplings to simmering chicken; cover and simmer until dumplings are cooked through, about 5 minutes. Stir in peas and parsley. Adjust seasonings, adding a generous amount of pepper. Serve immediately in soup plates, ladling a portion of meat, sauce, vegetables, and dumplings into each dish.

variations
Chicken and Herbed Dumplings with Aromatic Vegetables
Proceed as for Chicken and Dumplings with Aromatic Vegetables, adding a mixture of ¼ cup minced soft fresh herb leaves, such as parsley, chives (or scallion greens), and tarragon, along with milk in dumpling recipe. If other herbs are unavailable, all parsley may be used. Serves 6.

Chicken and Cornmeal Dumplings with Aromatic Vegetables
Proceed as for Chicken and Dumplings with Aromatic Vegetables, adding 1 teaspoon sugar and using 1½ cups flour and ½ cup fine-ground cornmeal in place of 2 cups flour in dumpling recipe. Serves 6.

Blue-Ribbon Chili

SERVES 6 TO 8

> "The biggest mistake home cooks make is not going into the kitchen at all. Cooking is like playing a sport: You have to stay in practice."

Other flavorful pork cuts, especially from the pork shoulder, can be substituted for the country ribs. If using boneless pork for the ribs, you may want to reduce the quantity from 1¼ pounds to 1 pound. Although this chili may take 3½ to 4 hours to make, it requires very little attention. If you prefer to cook your own beans for chili, pour 3 cups boiling water over 1 cup dried kidney or pinto beans that have been rinsed and picked over. Let stand until beans have nearly doubled in volume, about 1 hour. Drain and rinse, then place in a large saucepan with water to cover by 2 inches. Bring to a boil, reduce the heat, and simmer until tender, about 45 minutes, adding salt to taste during the last 15 minutes.

¼ cup vegetable oil

1 flat, boneless chuck roast (2 pounds), patted dry

4 country-style ribs (about 1¼ pounds), patted dry

1 tablespoon plus 2 teaspoons ground cumin

Salt and freshly ground black pepper

9 tablespoons mild chili powder

2 teaspoons dried oregano

2 large onions, cut into medium dice to make about 4 cups

4½ cups (one 28-ounce can, plus an additional scant cup) crushed tomatoes

1 ounce bittersweet or semisweet chocolate

6 garlic cloves, minced

2 cans (15½ ounces each) canned pinto or kidney beans (optional)

Suggested condiments

Tabasco sauce, sliced scallions, minced jalapeño, canned green chiles, sautéed green and yellow bell peppers, minced fresh cilantro, lime slices, sour cream

1. Adjust oven rack to middle position and heat oven to 450 degrees. Set a large Dutch oven or ovenproof pot over medium heat while preparing roast and ribs.

2. Pour 2 tablespoons of the oil into a medium bowl, add roast and ribs, and turn to coat. Generously sprinkle both sides of meats with 1 tablespoon cumin and salt and pepper.

3. A couple of minutes before searing meats, increase heat to strong medium-high. Add chuck roast to pot and cook until a solid brown crust forms on one side, about 5 minutes. Turn roast over, and cook until a crust forms on other side, about 5 minutes longer. Remove from pot. Add ribs; cook until crust forms, 4 to 5 minutes. Turn ribs over and cook until crusty, 4 to 5 minutes longer.

4. Return roast with ribs to pot; add 1¼ cups water (if using a pot that is more than 9½ inches in diameter, increase water to 1½ cups) and turn off heat. Use a potholder or dishtowel to cover pot with a sheet of heavy-duty foil, pressing on foil so that it is concave and touches roast. Seal completely around edges. Place lid on pot. Turn on heat again until you hear juices bubbling. Set pot in oven and cook without checking until roast and ribs are dark brown and very tender, about 1 hour and 20 minutes.

5. Meanwhile, heat chili powder, oregano, and remaining 2 teaspoons cumin in a small, dry skillet over low heat, stirring constantly, until spices are warm, fragrant, and darker in color, being careful not to burn them. Set aside. When roast and ribs are done, remove from pot and set aside until cool enough to handle. Pour meat juices into a measuring cup; add enough water to equal 6 cups. Set pot (which will be very hot from oven) over medium-high heat; add remaining 2 tablespoons oil. Add onions and sauté until soft, 7 to 8 minutes. Add toasted spices, tomatoes, and meat juice—water mixture; stir to combine. When roast and ribs are cool enough to handle, tear meat into shreds and add to chili; discard pork bones.

6. Simmer chili until flavors are deep, rich, and unified, about 1½ hours. Add chocolate and garlic and simmer to blend flavors, about 5 minutes longer. Add beans, if using, and heat through. Chili can be served immediately, but it's better if it is allowed to stand 20 to 30 minutes before serving, and even better if it can be cooled, covered, refrigerated overnight, and reheated before serving. Pass condiments at the table.

the babbo cookbook

MARIO BATALI

No bones about it: This is a chef's cookbook that doesn't hesitate to send you out to buy a squirt bottle to make artful squiggles of sauce. Fortunately, the recipes aren't all terribly complex, and there are many photographs for those who want their dishes to be Babbo restaurant replicas. Since it's virtually impossible to get a reservation at Babbo, buy this cookbook and have a go at it yourself.

FOOD & WINE How long did it take you to write *The Babbo Cookbook?*
MARIO BATALI The beauty of this book is that I never intended to write it, but I had all the recipes and it just took off. I needed just a couple of weeks to do the text, and then a couple of weeks working with Christopher Hirsheimer, the photographer. We took the pictures at Babbo on the second floor under the big, beautiful skylight. So it's really all about Babbo.
F&W What was the biggest challenge of representing Babbo's food in this book? Did you hold back at all to make the recipes simpler for the home cook?
MB The biggest challenge was making sure that we retained the intensity of flavors of Babbo's recipes without making them so laborious that no one would do them. So instead of dumbing down dishes, we just kept out the ones

that couldn't be done in real time, like our rabbit alla cacciatora and our stuffed osso buco. But we did keep some relatively involved recipes in the book. Our signature beef-cheek ravioli, for instance, takes the better part of a day to do—braising the cheeks, making noodles, putting it all together. Some of it is time-consuming, and that is the problem a few people are having with the book. But you know, the good stuff is definitely worth it.
F&W When you're creating a new recipe, do you think it out first and write it down before you head into the kitchen, or is it a spontaneous process that you record afterward?
MB I invent dishes spontaneously. If I know it's going on the menu at the restaurant, someone stands next to me and writes things down while I cook. But look, I'm not reinventing any

>> | FEATURED RECIPES

1 | SWEET PEA FLAN
WITH CARROT
VINAIGRETTE

2 | ESCAROLE WITH
ROASTED SHALLOTS

3 | TWO-MINUTE
CALAMARI SICILIAN
LIFEGUARD STYLE

4 | DRY-RUBBED RIB-EYE
STEAK FOR TWO

wheels; I'm mostly cooking in the style of grandma, not of a technician. The Babbo kitchen is definitely not a lab.

F&W In the book you focus on the concept of Italian hospitality. Is this something anyone should think about when entertaining at home?

MB Definitely. All hospitality means is thinking about the comfort of your guests: lighting, music, whether the wine should be heavy or light. Great food is a given, so you need to go beyond that, say, by inventing your own aperitivo or something like that. The small things are the ones that impress guests. Do you know how many light-bulbs we have at Babbo? So many that every time we get the electric bill my business partners want to kill me, but lighting is key to our success.

F&W If people could come away from reading *The Babbo Cookbook* having learned just one lesson, what would you want it to be?

MB If you feel like an unfamiliar ingredient is just too far out there, then don't feel compelled to track it down: It's okay to substitute something else that you can get at your neighborhood grocery store. In fact, the most important thing is to know the people at your local market, and to make sure they know you. It's important to understand your grocery store. It's really the shopping that makes the meal; 90 percent of your dinner is already decided for you by the time you load up your station wagon with your bags. Shop smart and shop hard, and your work is done.

the specifics

recipes	pages	photos	publisher	price
194	336	168 color and 11 black-and-white photos	Clarkson Potter/Publishers	$40

credits

The Babbo Cookbook by Mario Batali, copyright © 2002 by Mario Batali. Photographs ©2002 by Christopher Hirsheimer. Used by permission of Clarkson Potter/Publishers, a division of Random House, Inc.

Sweet Pea Flan with Carrot Vinaigrette

SERVES 6

This is the Babbo version of peas and carrots. Juice your own carrots if possible, or stop by your local juice bar.

Kosher salt

1   cup fresh mint leaves, packed

¾   pound green peas, fresh or frozen

3   large eggs

¾   cup heavy cream

1   teaspoon fresh lemon juice

Freshly ground black pepper, to taste

1¼ cups carrot juice

1   teaspoon honey

1   tablespoon champagne vinegar

½   cup extra-virgin olive oil

2   cups young pea vines (about ¾ pound)

¼   cup Parsley Oil (recipe follows)

Parmigiano-Reggiano, for shaving

1. Bring about 3 quarts of water to a boil and add 1 tablespoon salt. Set up an ice bath nearby. Blanch the mint leaves and the peas in the boiling water for 1 minute, then drain and immerse them in the ice bath. Drain again and puree them together in the bowl of a food processor until smooth. Pass the mixture through a food mill into a large bowl and combine with the eggs, cream, lemon juice, salt, and pepper.

2. Preheat the oven to 350°F.

3. Coat six 4-ounce ramekins with cooking spray. Divide the pea mixture evenly among the ramekins, filling them two-thirds full. Place the ramekins in a baking dish and fill it with enough hot water to come halfway up the sides of the ramekins. Cover the baking dish with aluminum foil and bake for 25 to 30 minutes, or until

the centers are just set. Remove from the oven, taking care not to splash any water into the ramekins, and allow to cool.

4. Meanwhile, place 1 cup of the carrot juice in a small, heavy-bottomed saucepan and bring to a boil over high heat. Reduce the heat to medium and cook the juice until it is reduced to ¼ cup, taking care not to let it scorch. Remove the juice from the heat and, in a medium bowl, combine it with the honey and champagne vinegar, whisking to blend. Slowly whisk in the olive oil, then stir in the remaining ¼ cup of raw carrot juice. Season with salt and pepper.

5. To assemble the dish, carefully run a knife around the inside edge of each cooled ramekin and unmold one flan onto the center of each of six chilled dinner plates. In a large, nonreactive bowl, toss the pea vines with the carrot vinaigrette and season with salt and pepper if necessary. Divide the pea vines among the six plates, partially covering the flan. Drizzle with carrot vinaigrette and parsley oil, shave a few curls of Parmigiano-Reggiano over each plate, using a vegetable peeler, and serve immediately.

Parsley Oil

MAKES 2 CUPS

1   bunch of flat-leaf parsley, chopped

2   cups extra-virgin olive oil, chilled for 2 hours

1   teaspoon kosher salt

Place all of the ingredients in a blender and puree until nearly smooth and uniformly green. Strain through a fine sieve. The oil can be refrigerated for 24 hours.

Escarole with Roasted Shallots

SERVES 4 AS A SIDE DISH

4   shallots, trimmed and peeled

2   tablespoons plus ¼ cup extra-virgin olive oil

Kosher salt and freshly ground black pepper

1   head of escarole, cored and roughly chopped

1. Preheat the oven to 400°F. Drizzle the shallots with 2 tablespoons of the olive oil, season with salt and pepper, and place in a small roasting pan. Roast until very soft and golden brown, about 25 minutes. Remove from the oven and, when cool enough to handle, cut each shallot in half. Do not worry if the shallots start to come apart a little.

2. In a 12- to 14-inch sauté pan, heat the remaining ¼ cup of olive oil over high heat. Add the escarole and shallots and sauté over high heat until tender, about 7 minutes. Season with salt and pepper and serve immediately.

f&w tips

Be sure to wash the escarole really well as it can be quite sandy and gritty. If you don't have a 12- to 14-inch sauté pan, the escarole can be done in two batches in a smaller pan (use two shallots per batch).

Two-Minute Calamari Sicilian Lifeguard Style

SERVES 4

I have never actually met a Sicilian lifeguard, but if one were to cook up a pot of calamari, this is how he or she might make it. Geographically, Sicily is much closer to Tunisia, Morocco, and the Moorish world than it is to Milano, so the influences on traditional cooking are very Northern African. I love the way currants, caperberries, pine nuts, and chiles combine to create a sweet, hot, and sour Arabic kiss on the delicate tentacles.

Kosher salt

1   cup Israeli couscous

¼   cup extra-virgin olive oil

2   tablespoons pine nuts

2   tablespoons currants

1   tablespoon hot red pepper flakes

¼   cup caperberries

2   cups Basic Tomato Sauce (recipe follows)

1½ pounds cleaned calamari, tubes cut into ¼-inch rounds, tentacles halved

Freshly ground black pepper, to taste

3   scallions, thinly sliced

1. Bring 3 quarts of water to a boil and add 1 tablespoon of salt. Set up an ice bath nearby. Cook the couscous in the boiling water for 2 minutes, then drain and immediately plunge it into the ice bath. Once cooled, remove and set aside to dry on a plate.

2. In a 12- to 14-inch sauté pan, heat the oil until just smoking. Add the pine nuts, currants, and red pepper flakes and sauté until the nuts are just golden brown, about 2 minutes. Add the caperberries, tomato sauce, and couscous and bring to a boil. Add the calamari, stir to mix, and simmer for 2 to 3 minutes, or until the calamari is just cooked and completely opaque. Season with salt and pepper, pour into a large warm bowl, sprinkle with scallions, and serve immediately.

on batali's nightstand

"I use cookbooks all the time; I read them like novels," Batali says. His favorites: anything by **M.F.K. Fisher,** as well as the **Chez Panisse Café Cookbook** by **Alice Waters; River Café Cookbook** by **Ruth Rogers** and **Rose Gray** of the eponymous London restaurant; **La Grande Cuisine Minceur** by **Michel Guerard;** and **White Heat** by **Marco Pierre White.**

Basic Tomato Sauce

MAKES 4 CUPS

¼ cup extra-virgin olive oil

1 Spanish onion, finely diced

4 garlic cloves, peeled and thinly sliced

3 tablespoons chopped fresh thyme, or 1 tablespoon dried

½ medium carrot, finely shredded

2 28-ounce cans peeled whole tomatoes

Kosher salt, to taste

In a 3-quart saucepan, heat the olive oil over medium heat. Add the onion and garlic and cook until soft and light golden brown, 8 to 10 minutes. Add the thyme and carrot and cook for 5 minutes more, or until the carrot is quite soft. With your hands, crush the tomatoes and add them with their juices. Bring to a boil, stirring often, and then lower the heat and simmer for 30 minutes, or until the sauce is as thick as hot cereal. Season with salt and serve. This sauce holds for 1 week in the refrigerator or for up to 6 months in the freezer.

Dry-Rubbed Rib-Eye Steak for Two

SERVES 2

"Look, I'm not reinventing any wheels; I'm mostly cooking in the style of grandma, not of a technician. The Babbo kitchen is definitely not a lab."

We dry-rub a thick-cut, well-marbled steak to help it form a nice crust while cooking. The effect of the sugar and salt on the meat is similar to dry aging, as it causes some of the steak's water weight to dissipate overnight and intensifies the beefy flavor. Serve with roasted potatoes.

2   tablespoons sugar

1   tablespoon kosher salt

5   garlic cloves, finely chopped

1   tablespoon hot red pepper flakes

1   tablespoon freshly ground black pepper

¼   cup dry porcini mushrooms, ground to a fine powder in a spice grinder

¼   cup extra-virgin olive oil

1   28-ounce rib-eye steak, cut 2 inches thick

Best-quality extra-virgin olive oil, for drizzling

Best-quality balsamic vinegar, for drizzling

1. In a small bowl, combine the sugar, salt, garlic, red pepper flakes, pepper, mushroom powder, and olive oil and stir well to form a thick, fairly dry paste. Rub the paste all over the steak, coating it evenly, and refrigerate, wrapped in plastic, for 12 hours or overnight.

2. Preheat the grill or broiler.

3. Remove the steak from the refrigerator and brush off the excess marinade with a paper towel. Cook on the hottest part of the grill for 25 minutes, turning every 6 minutes, or to an internal temperature of 120°F for medium rare.

4. Allow the steak to rest for 10 minutes, then slice against the grain. Drizzle with the olive oil and balsamic vinegar and serve immediately.

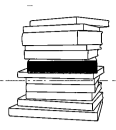

1,000 indian recipes

NEELAM BATRA

about batra
Neelam Batra was born in New Delhi, India, and has been cooking Indian food for three decades. A cooking teacher for more than 20 years, she is also the author of *The Indian Vegetarian* and *Chilis to Chutneys*. She lives in Santa Monica, California.

At first we were overwhelmed by the sheer size of this book. Fortunately, it's well organized and surprisingly easy to use, with helpful notes that explain the origins of different recipes and suggest substitutions. It does an amazing job of making Indian food seem approachable—and irresistible.

FOOD & WINE Are there guiding principles to creating an Indian meal?
NEELAM BATRA First and foremost, each meal should have a balance of sweet, sour, salty, bitter, warm, cool, dry, wet—all sorts of tastes and textures your palate wants so you feel satisfied. You also want a variety of colors so the food looks attractive.
F&W What are the elements of a traditional Indian meal?
NB One wet dish (with a gravy or a sauce in it); one dry dish (such as a cooked vegetable); a yogurt like a raita as a soothing cooler; plus breads, rice or both. For condiments there are pickles; fresh or preserved chutneys with herbs, yogurt or coconut; and chopped salads of tomatoes, cucumbers and daikon radishes—but not lettuce, because we didn't grow up with lettuce in India.

F&W What do you consider to be essential pantry items?
NB I don't think you need too many things to start an Indian kitchen: cinnamon, black pepper, paprika, cumin, coriander and turmeric, plus rice and a lot of different dals [dried beans, peas and lentils] and flours made with whole wheat, say, or chickpeas.
F&W What about key equipment?
NB One can do without any special equipment, but a pressure cooker for steaming and to make dals is a bonus—all Indian kitchens have one. And an Indian (or Chinese) wok is a wonderful piece of equipment that I love for deep-frying samosas or cooking vegetables. An Indian wok is like a Chinese wok except the bottom is round instead of flat. Most Indian kitchens also have a cast-iron griddle called a *tava* to make breads.

>> | **FEATURED RECIPES**

1 | MUSHROOM TURNOVERS WITH CURRY POWDER

2 | PURÉED SPINACH SOUP

3 | PAN-COOKED CHILE-CHICKEN THIGHS

4 | CREAMY MASHED EGGPLANT WITH PEAS

F&W What are some on-line sources you'd recommend for ingredients?

NB I like qualityfoods.com, patelbrothersusa.com and namaste.com.

F&W How do you lighten Indian food?

NB People think Indian food is heavy because they eat restaurant food. The food prepared in Indian homes on an everyday basis is very light. But if you want to further lighten your food, cut back on oil to one or two tablespoons and use it to sauté your spices. Once spices are subjected to heat, they release their inherent flavors. That's all that's needed to make the dish fragrant.

F&W How does Indian food vary from region to region?

NB Generally the food gets spicier as you travel from north to south. North India excels in flat breads and rich, cream-laden foods, with an emphasis on greens. In the south rice-based dishes are very popular, and cooks use a lot of coconut. The coastal areas depend on seafood. In the central part of the country many people are vegetarians; their diet is primarily grains and legumes.

F&W What are some easy Indian desserts to make at home?

NB Most Indian desserts are milk based, like *kulfi* [ice cream], *kheers* [puddings] and *burfee* [milk fudge]. Some easy ones to make are Indian vermicelli pudding prepared with paper-thin vermicelli noodles, boiled milk, sugar, nuts and rose water. Or yogurt mousse, in which you thicken the yogurt by draining it in cheesecloth. Or Indian ice cream made by mixing Cool Whip with evaporated milk, then freezing it.

the specifics

recipes	pages	photos	publisher	price
1,000	704	none	Wiley Publishing, Inc.	$35

credits

Mushroom Turnovers with Curry Powder

Khumbi Pattice

MAKES 24 PIECES

f&w tips
The mushroom turnovers are perfect for making ahead and serving at a party. Once they've been assembled, place them on a tray and wrap them tightly in plastic wrap. Bring them to room temperature before baking them. Also, we suggest tasting the filling and seasoning it before assembling the turnovers.

When I was growing up, there were only three fillings for these turnovers (translated, for some reason, as "patties" in English in India and here): vegetable, chicken, and mutton. And they were found only in special bakeries of British influence. Today, various versions of these are found all over, even in rural villages.

This is a convenient recipe to make, with all ingredients found at the supermarket. If you like, substitute for the mushrooms any dry-cooked filling of your choice. Simply fill, baste with egg wash, and bake.

1½ to 2 teaspoons Basic Curry Powder (recipe follows) or store-bought

2   tablespoons vegetable oil

1   large onion, finely chopped

1   teaspoon minced fresh garlic

1 to 3 green chile peppers, such as serrano, minced with seeds

3   tablespoons all-purpose flour

3   cups finely chopped mushrooms

¼   cup finely chopped fresh cilantro, including soft stems

½   teaspoon salt, or to taste

1   (20-ounce) package frozen puff pastry sheets (2 sheets)

1   large egg white, beaten lightly with 1 tablespoon water

1. Prepare the curry powder. Heat the oil in a large nonstick wok or saucepan over medium-high heat and cook the onion, stirring, until transparent, 2 to 3 minutes. Add the garlic, green chile peppers, curry powder, and flour, and stir over medium-low heat until the garlic and onion are golden, 2 to 3 minutes. Add the mushrooms, cilantro, and salt and cook until the mixture is completely dry, another 3 to 5 minutes. Let cool before using.

2. Divide the filling into two equal parts, one for each pastry sheet. Thaw the pastry sheets at room temperature, until they are slightly softened but still cold to the touch, 15 to 20 minutes.

3. Preheat the oven to 375°F. Lightly grease a baking sheet. On a lightly floured surface, working with each pastry sheet separately, unfold and gently roll it with a rolling pin to make it smooth. Then cut each sheet into 12 squares. Roll each square to make it slightly larger. Baste the edges with water, place 1 tablespoon of filling in the center of each square and fold one corner over the filling to the diagonal corner to form a triangle. Seal the edges by pressing with the back of a fork.

4. Brush the top of each turnover with the beaten egg and then poke a few holes with a fork so the steam can escape. Place the turnovers on the baking sheet and bake until puffed and golden, about 20 minutes. Transfer to cooling racks. Serve hot or at room temperature.

Basic Curry Powder
Kari ka Masala

MAKES ABOUT 1½ CUPS

1	cup ground coriander seeds
⅓	cup ground cumin seeds
2	tablespoons ground turmeric
1	tablespoon ground paprika
1	tablespoon ground cayenne pepper (optional)
1	tablespoon ground dried fenugreek leaves

Put all the spices in a bowl and mix them together with a spoon. Store in an airtight container in a cool, dark place, about 1 month at room temperature or about 1 year in the refrigerator.

Puréed Spinach Soup

Palak ka Soop

MAKES 4 TO 6 SERVINGS

If you or people in your family don't already love spinach, this delicious, simple soup could make you a convert. It may even have people wondering, "Is it really spinach?"

1   small (8- to 10-ounce) bunch fresh spinach, trimmed, washed, and coarsely chopped

1   cup coarsely chopped fresh cilantro, including soft stems

2   tablespoons coarsely chopped fresh mint

1   medium onion, coarsely chopped

4   quarter-size slices peeled fresh ginger

1   large clove fresh garlic, peeled

4   cups water

2   tablespoons vegetable oil

1   tablespoon all-purpose flour

1   cup milk (any kind)

1   teaspoon garam masala

½   cup plain yogurt (any kind), whisked until smooth

1. Place the spinach, cilantro, mint, onion, ginger, and garlic in a large saucepan. Add the water and bring to a boil over high heat. Reduce the heat to medium-low, cover the pan, and simmer, until the onions are soft, about 10 minutes. Let cool, then purée in a blender or food processor until smooth.

2. Heat the oil in separate large nonstick wok or saucepan over medium-high heat; add the flour and cook, stirring, until golden and very fragrant, about 1 minute. Add the milk in a thin stream, stirring constantly to ensure no lumps form. Slowly, while stirring constantly, add the puréed spinach and the garam masala, and mix well. Transfer soup to a serving bowl, add the yogurt, swirl lightly to mix with parts of it visible as a garnish, and serve.

Pan-Cooked Chile-Chicken Thighs

Bhuna Mirchi Murgh

MAKES 4 TO 6 SERVINGS

Called "chile-fry" in southern India, this dish is generally made with a whole chicken. Mine is an easy-to-cook and easy-to-eat version made with cut-up chicken pieces.

2   tablespoons peanut oil

1   teaspoon Asian sesame oil

5 to 7 dried red chile peppers, such as chile de arbol, with stems

2   (1-inch) pieces peeled fresh ginger, cut into thin matchsticks

2   medium onions, finely chopped

1   large clove fresh garlic, minced

½   teaspoon ground paprika

2 to 2½ pounds skinless chicken thighs, cut in half through the bone

1   cup finely chopped fresh cilantro, including soft stems

¼   cup distilled white vinegar

½   cup water

1   teaspoon salt, or to taste

½   teaspoon freshly ground black pepper, or to taste

1. Heat the oils together in a large nonstick pan over medium heat and cook the red chile peppers and ginger, stirring, until lightly browned, about 2 minutes.

2. Add the onions and cook until well-browned, about 10 minutes. Add the garlic, paprika, and chicken and cook, stirring, about 5 minutes.

3. Add the cilantro, vinegar, water, salt, and black pepper. Cook over high heat until it comes to a boil and then over medium heat until the chicken pieces are tender and most of the liquid has evaporated, and the oil separates to the sides, about 20 minutes. Transfer to a serving plate and serve hot.

on batra's nightstand
Neelam Batra loves any of the cookbooks by **Mary Sue Milliken** and **Susan Feniger** because their Mexican-inflected cuisine is some of the best she's tasted, and she thinks **Nancy Silverton** has a fantastic way with breads. **Deborah Madison,** she feels, is great for vegetarian recipes, and she enjoys seeing how Madison interprets vegetables that Batra grew up with. Batra is also a fan of Madison's recipes for dried beans, grains and fresh herbs and spices, some of which are relatively unfamiliar, like chervil and lovage.

Creamy Mashed Eggplant with Peas

Baingan ka Shahi Bhartha

MAKES 4 TO 6 SERVINGS

"If you want to further lighten your food, cut back on oil to one or two tablespoons and use it to sauté your spices. Once spices are subjected to heat, they release their inherent flavors. That's all that's needed to make the dish fragrant."

This dish is often called *shahi bhartha* because the addition of cream and spices gives it a richer status, normally associated with the *rajas* and *maharajas* (kings and emperors). Save it for special occasions, and serve it as part of a larger menu with Grilled Tandoori Chicken, Split Urad Beans and Yellow Split Chickpeas with Spinach, a yogurt *raita*, and oven-grilled *naan* or other flatbreads.

1   large oval-shaped eggplant (about 1 pound)

2   tablespoons melted ghee or vegetable oil

1   large onion, finely chopped

1   large clove fresh garlic, minced

1 to 3 fresh green chile peppers, such as serrano, minced with seeds

1   tablespoon ground coriander

1   teaspoon ground cumin

½   teaspoon garam masala

½   teaspoon cayenne pepper, or to taste

½   teaspoon ground paprika

1   teaspoon salt, or to taste

1   large tomato, finely chopped

1   cup finely chopped fresh cilantro, including soft stems

1   cup frozen peas, thawed

¼   cup heavy or light cream

2   tablespoons finely chopped fresh cilantro

1. Wash, dry, and lightly oil your hands, and rub them over the surface of the eggplant. Then, with the tip of a sharp kitchen knife, puncture the skin in a few places. Place the eggplant, preferably over the hot coals of a grill or over the direct flame of a kitchen stove burner (cover the bottom plate with aluminum foil), and roast, turning with kitchen tongs as the sides blacken, until it is very soft and the skin is completely charred, 5 to 7 minutes. Transfer to a bowl and let cool. Alternatively, lightly oil and puncture the skin in a few places with the tip of a knife and bake in a preheated 400°F oven until the eggplant is tender. You can wrap the eggplant in aluminum foil before baking.

2. When cool enough to handle, peel off the charred skin and discard. Work close to the kitchen sink, because you may need to rinse your fingers as you go along. Do not wash the eggplant. Mash the pulp with your hands or a fork until somewhat smooth but still lumpy. Do not make a completely smooth purée; a little texture is very desirable. Strain and mix in any juices that may have collected in the bowl. (Some people say these are bitter, but I hate to discard good juices.) You can store the mashed eggplant in the refrigerator about 5 days or about 4 months in the freezer.

3. Heat the ghee or oil in a large nonstick wok or saucepan over medium-high heat and cook the onion, stirring occasionally, until golden, about 5 minutes. Add the garlic and green chile peppers, mix in the coriander, cumin, garam masala, cayenne pepper, paprika, and salt, and stir about 1 minute.

4. Add the tomato and cilantro and cook, stirring, until all the tomato juices evaporate, 5 to 7 minutes. Mix in the mashed eggplant and the peas. Reduce the heat to medium-low and cook, stirring occasionally, about 15 minutes. Mix in the cream and cook 1 minute. Transfer to a serving dish, garnish with the chopped cilantro, and serve.

simply bishop's

JOHN BISHOP & DENNIS GREEN

about bishop

John Bishop, a Welshman, opened Bishop's Restaurant in Vancouver in 1985. Since then he has gained renown for his distinctly Pacific Northwestern approach to cooking. He has published two other cookbooks, *Bishop's: The Cookbook* and *Cooking at My House*, and hosted a 2002 documentary, *Deconstructing Supper.*

Bishop's cookbook isn't like those from lots of other chefs: Ingredients lists don't run off the page, subrecipes are few and directions are clear and concise. His m.o. is using the very best fresh ingredients—which is essential, as this determines the success of many of his dishes. His book is not complex, really. And the recipes work beautifully.

FOOD & WINE What inspired you to write this book?

JOHN BISHOP It came out of five years of cooking classes that we've been giving in the restaurant once a month. I wanted to give people a peek behind the scenes. And I wanted to educate them about local ingredients and organic produce.

F&W How would you define your cooking style?

JB It's kind of regional Pacific Northwestern, with a focus on local and seasonal ingredients—strawberries in the summer, game and wild mushrooms in the fall—and organic products. We try to use only wild fish, in season. We serve salmon only in the summer, for instance, when the wild ones can be caught. The flavor is better and the texture is firmer than farmed fish because in the sea, the fish develop more muscle. But serving fish

seasonally confuses people—they don't know many fish are available year-round only because they're farmed.

F&W Why did you make your documentary, *Deconstructing Supper?*

JB I couldn't believe that I'd been a chef for so long and had never inquired into what goes into our food. In the film, I have three meals in three different places. First I cook at an organic farm on Salt Spring Island [British Columbia]. Then I visit a biotech scientist in Saskatchewan, and cook a meal with him in his home, using genetically modified corn. In India I stay in a village trying to get back to traditional farming methods. I see what big companies have done there, patenting basmati rice and trying to sell it back to the farmers. Working on the film really made me more aware of where ingredients come from, who's growing them. Everyone's

SIMPLY BISHOP'S

>> | FEATURED RECIPES

1 | PESTO-CRUSTED HALIBUT WITH RED LENTIL DAHL

2 | POTATO, HERB AND ONION LATKES

3 | ROAST DUCK BREAST WITH APPLE PURÉE

going to have to think about how they feel about genetically modified food at some point.

F&W Did any recipes in the book come out of working on the film?

JB The Pesto-Crusted Halibut with Red Lentil Dahl—well, at least the dahl part. We were in India for two weeks and ate dahl every day. Lentil dahl is a wonderful, quick sauce you can make with ingredients you usually have in your pantry. Often the most difficult part of a meal is the sauce—it's easy to grill or roast a piece of fish or meat, but then what do you serve with it?

F&W Which of the recipes in the book do you cook a lot at home?

JB The slow-cooked pork shoulder, which allows you to go away and forget about it while it's cooking.

I'll also slow-cook a boneless lamb shoulder, perhaps stuffed with garlic cloves and a homemade pesto. And you can put vegetables in the pan, like potatoes, to roast alongside it.

F&W Why do you use shoulder?

JB It's an inexpensive cut of meat you wouldn't normally think to use because it's fatty and full of cartilage. But roasting it renders out the fat and it becomes tender.

F&W What are your future projects?

JB I'm working on a book with our organic farmer whose last name is King, so we're going to call the book *Bishop's and King's*. We sit down with a seed catalog and work out what to grow. It's about our relationship, and includes organic country recipes.

the specifics

recipes	pages	photos	publisher	price
106	176	32 color and 27 black-and-white photos	Douglas & McIntyre	$35

credits

Simply Bishop's: Easy Seasonal Recipes by John Bishop and Dennis Green. Copyright © 2002 by John Bishop and Dennis Green. Photography by John Sherlock. Published by Douglas & McIntyre Ltd, Canada, and distributed in the United States by Publishers Group West as of September 2003. Reprinted by permission of the publisher.

Pesto-Crusted Halibut with Red Lentil Dahl

4 SERVINGS

Recently, I visited India where meals included a lentil dahl, which tasted different each time, depending on who had cooked it. As soon as I arrived back home, I set to making the same kinds of lentil dishes for my family. The garam masala is a spice blend sold in Asian food stores.

Dahl

2 **Tbsp. vegetable oil** (30 mL)

1 **small onion, ¼-inch dice** (6-mm dice)

2 **garlic cloves, crushed**

1 **Tbsp. grated fresh ginger** (15 mL)

1 **cup red lentils** (250 mL)

½ **tsp. garam masala** (2.5 mL)

½ **tsp. cumin** (2.5 mL)

½ **tsp. turmeric** (2.5 mL)

4 **cups water** (1 L)

½ **tsp. sugar** (2.5 mL)

½ **tsp. salt** (2.5 mL)

Freshly ground black pepper

Pesto

½ **lb. fresh basil leaves** (250 g)

4 **garlic cloves**

2 **Tbsp. toasted pine nuts** (30 mL)

Pinch of coarse salt

½ **cup grated Parmesan cheese** (125 mL)

½ **cup extra-virgin olive oil** (125 mL)

f&w tip
Dahl is a traditional Indian
dish made with lentils (or
sometimes beans or peas)
that are simmered in water
and seasoned. It can be spicy
or mild and is most often
served as a sauce or a side
dish, as here. Red lentils are
available at health food
stores and Indian markets or
by mail order from
Kalustyan's (800-352-3451).

Halibut

4   halibut fillets, each 6 oz. (170 g)

Salt and freshly ground black pepper

To make dahl Heat vegetable oil in a large saucepan on medium heat. Sauté
onion, garlic and ginger until onion is soft, 4 to 5 minutes. Add lentils, garam
masala, cumin and turmeric. (If you like your dahl a little spicier, add a dried whole
chili pepper or two, then remove at the end of the cooking process.) Add water
and bring to a simmer on medium-high heat, skimming off any foam that appears
on the surface. Add sugar, salt and pepper. Cover and simmer for 45 minutes.
(Lentil dahl can made ahead and will keep for 1 to 2 days in the refrigerator.)

"Often the most difficult part of a meal is the sauce—it's easy to grill or roast a piece of fish or meat, but then what do you serve with it?"

Pesto Place basil, garlic, pine nuts, coarse salt and Parmesan cheese in a blender or food processor and grind into a paste. Slowly add extra-virgin olive oil until smooth. Refrigerate until needed. (Any extra pesto will keep for a week refrigerated, 3 months frozen.)

Halibut Preheat the oven to 400°F (200°C) and line a baking sheet with parchment paper. Take 1 Tbsp. (15 mL) of pesto for each halibut fillet and rub in, then place fish on the prepared baking sheet. Bake until just cooked through so that flesh is opaque and firm to the touch, about 10 minutes.

To serve, reheat dahl and spoon onto warmed plates. Top each with a piece of halibut.

WINE Australian Semillon

Dennis Green, LEFT, and John Bishop

Potato, Herb and Onion Latkes

4 TO 6 SERVINGS

When it comes to potato latkes, everyone seems to have a special way of making them. This recipe has been well tested over time at Bishop's Restaurant, and we often get requests for them. Most of the time, we serve the latkes with salmon, but they can be served with almost anything, or even by themselves as a light lunch with a dollop of sour cream.

1   **lb. russet or Yukon Gold potatoes** (500 g)

½   **cup onion, 1-inch dice** (125 mL, 2.5-cm dice)

1   **egg**

1   **Tbsp. grainy mustard** (15 mL)

2   **Tbsp. chopped fresh parsley** (30 mL)

1   **lemon, juiced**

1   **tsp. salt** (5 mL)

⅔   **cup flour** (150 mL)

¼   **cup vegetable oil** (60 mL)

To make Peel and quarter potatoes. Place potatoes, onion, egg, mustard, parsley, lemon juice and salt in a food processor and purée. Add flour and mix well.

Heat a small amount of the vegetable oil in a large heavy frying pan. Ladle ¼ cup (60 mL) batter for each latke and fry 2 or 3 at a time until golden brown on both sides, about 3 to 4 minutes per side. Use up the remaining batter, adding oil as necessary. Makes about 12 latkes, 3 inches (7.5 cm) in diameter.

Blot latkes on paper towels and serve hot.

Roast Duck Breast with Apple Purée

4 SERVINGS

f&w tip
It's easiest to score the skin of the duck breast when it's chilled. For the purée we used a Granny Smith apple, which has a tart edge and makes a smooth, delicious sauce.

Duck breasts are almost impossible to buy by themselves, so I buy the birds whole, and then remove the breasts and legs. I freeze the carcasses to make stock from later, and freeze the legs for a duck stew with turnips.

Purée

2   **Tbsp. butter** (30 mL)

1   **apple, peeled, cored and quartered**

2   **shallots, sliced**

½   **cup apple cider vinegar** (125 mL)

2   **Tbsp. maple syrup** (30 mL)

1   **cup chicken stock** (250 mL)

½   **cup chilled butter** (125 mL)

Salt (optional)

Duck

4 duck breast halves

Salt and freshly ground black pepper

To make purée Melt butter in a frying pan on medium heat. Sauté apple and shallots until lightly browned, about 5 minutes. Add apple cider vinegar and maple syrup; simmer, uncovered, until reduced by half, 5 to 7 minutes. Add stock and continue simmering, uncovered, until reduced by half, another 5 to 7 minutes. Allow to cool for a few minutes.

Transfer to a blender or food processor and purée, adding chilled butter 1 Tbsp. (15 mL) at a time. Season to taste with salt (optional). Keep warm in a covered saucepan on low heat.

Duck Preheat the oven to 450°F (230°C).

Score the fat on duck breasts in a cross-hatch pattern ⅛ inch (3 mm) deep to help render the fat while cooking. Season duck with salt and pepper. Heat an ovenproof frying pan on medium heat. Sear duck, skin side down, until lightly browned, about 5 minutes. Turn over and sear lightly on the other side, about 3 minutes.

Turn over again, so duck is skin side down. Place pan in the oven and roast until duck is medium rare, 5 to 8 minutes. Remove from the oven and allow to rest for 5 minutes.

To serve, carve duck into thin slices on a bias. Ladle a pool of apple purée onto each warmed plate and arrange duck slices on top.

WINE RED Pinot Noir   WHITE Riesling

on bishop's nightstand

Bishop has recently been enjoying three books—*The Food and Cooking in 17th-, 18th- and 19th-Century Britain*—from a series published by **English Heritage.** He especially appreciated them when he visited places like Bath, with its rich Georgian history. *Le Répertoire de la Cuisine,* recently revised by **Jacques Pépin,** is another favorite of Bishop's. He owns a beat-up copy from 1957, which he got as a student at hotel school in Wales. The book's an invaluable reference work for French-trained chefs, he says. For fun, he has a 100-year-old edition of *Mrs. Beeton's Cookery and Household Management,* which has information on how to buy a house and deal with staff.

chef daniel boulud

DANIEL BOULUD & PETER KAMINSKY

This is not your typical cookbook: The setup is a day in the life of chef Daniel Boulud, who turns out to have a busy schedule, from a morning meeting (accompanied here by recipes for bread, the first order of business in the kitchen) to a late dinner. We think this is such a creative, refreshing way for a chef to do a cookbook. And we loved taking a peek behind the kitchen door.

FOOD & WINE Why did you decide to do this book?

DANIEL BOULUD I wanted to capture the energy of the people working with me at the restaurant, and the things that affect us. It was like creating a documentary of cooking and shopping. We decided to do a day in the life of the restaurant [Daniel] because we didn't want to get overly elaborate. It had to be a casual read with not too heavy an emphasis on teaching. The photographer came and spent three or four days at the restaurant and we made the book in nine months; normally it takes two years.

F&W Readers may be surprised to see you eating a street vendor hot dog on the cover of your book.

DB Well, I'm famous for my burger with foie gras, but I'm not trying to elevate the hot dog. We were shooting

a portrait of me in the middle of Park Avenue and there was a hot dog stand there, so we took a picture of me with the hot dog. I like all good street food: Asian, Middle Eastern falafel sandwiches, Italian panini.

F&W What do you cook at home?

DB It depends. Last night I made a roasted veal tenderloin with potatoes and leeks *en cocotte*—it took just 25 minutes. Cooking at home shouldn't be as complex as cooking in a restaurant. I keep myself happy doing dishes that are simple. I often do a one-pot meal. I like to use a maximum of four ingredients when I cook at home, with simple but good seasoning. When I cook with my daughter, I like to work on someone else's recipes. That way, we can learn together.

F&W Are there any supermarket products you especially like?

>> | **FEATURED RECIPES**

1 | TUNA BAGNAT

2 | STUFFED SQUID WITH PIQUILLO PEPPER COULIS

3 | CHICKEN PROVENÇAL

4 | ROSEMARY BRAISED VEAL SHANK

DB Tomato sauce, since I think it's hard to make a good tomato sauce at home. And my daughter loves pasta with tomato sauce—we try to test them all. I like Newman's Own and Rao's Homemade.

F&W Do you have any favorite tools or equipment?

DB I like a fine grater for citrus, truffles, wasabi, horseradish. A couple of wooden spoons that my father carved for me. He knows that I'll use them, and they remind me of him when I cook. My copper pans by Mauviel. I have many different knives, but I often choose one by Sabatier.

F&W Are there any dining trends that you've noticed?

DB I think Asian cuisine has great potential for evolution and already seems to be transforming on its own. Spanish tapas are interesting because they fit very well with the American love of variety and little tastes of things.

F&W What will your legacy be?

DB I think I'll be able to answer that question better in 15 years. I still have a lot to do. But I think my legacy will be that I was a great French chef in America, and I understood the role I had to play in this country to inspire others. I hope restaurant Daniel will remain open [long after I'm gone].

F&W If you weren't a chef, what would you be?

DB Maybe a winemaker. It's still in the world of taste and it's creative. Every decision impacts the product—in cooking, it's the same way.

the specifics

recipes	pages	photos	publisher	price
75	240	313 color and 526 black-and-white photos	Assouline Publishing	$34.95

credits

Chef Daniel Boulud: Cooking In New York City by Daniel Boulud and Peter Kaminsky. Copyright ©2002 Assouline Publishing. Photographs by Martin H.M. Schreiber and Hervé Amiard. Front cover photo by Peter Medilek/ClausNY.

Tuna Bagnat

MAKES 4 SERVINGS

2   tablespoons extra-virgin olive oil

½-pound piece sushi-quality tuna (1½ inches thick and 4 inches long)

Coarse sea salt and coarsely ground black pepper

4   cloves garlic (3 unpeeled and lightly crushed, 1 peeled and halved)

4   sprigs thyme

2   sprigs rosemary

One 8-inch round or square focaccia, sliced horizontally in half

Grated zest and juice of 1 lemon

Leaves of Boston or butter lettuce, washed and dried

8   large basil leaves, rinsed and dried

2   large tomatoes, peeled, seeded and cut into quarters

1   ripe avocado, peeled, halved, pitted and cut lengthwise into 8 slices

2   stalks celery, peeled, trimmed and cut into thin diagonal slices

1   small seedless cucumber, peeled, halved, cut into 3-inch segments
and thinly sliced lengthwise

10 kalamata or Provençal olives, pitted and cut in half

4   oil-cured anchovies, cut in half lengthwise

8   quail eggs, hard boiled for 4 minutes, or 2 large eggs,
hard boiled for 10 minutes; peeled

1. Warm 2 tablespoons olive oil in a small sauté pan over medium-high heat.
Season the tuna with salt and pepper. When the oil starts to shimmer, add the tuna,
the 3 unpeeled garlic cloves, the thyme and the rosemary. Cook the tuna for 3 to
4 minutes on each side for rare, or 5 to 7 minutes on each side for medium. Remove
the tuna to a plate to cool slightly. Discard the garlic and herbs.

2. Place the focaccia, cut sides up, on a work surface and brush lightly with olive oil. Rub each side of the focaccia with the cut garlic and sprinkle with salt, pepper, a pinch of the lemon zest and a few drops of lemon juice. Cover each half with the lettuce leaves.

3. Tear the basil leaves into pieces and put on top of the lettuce. Evenly place the tomatoes, avocado, celery and cucumber on each focaccia half. Season with pepper, olive oil, lemon zest and juice and distribute the olives and anchovies on top. Season the sandwich well with more pepper, olive oil and lemon zest and juice.

4. Slice the tuna lengthwise into ⅛-inch-thick strips and place in rows over the vegetables on both sandwich halves. Season with more olive oil, remaining lemon zest and juice and salt and pepper. Carefully put the sandwich halves together, press firmly and wrap tightly in plastic wrap. Weigh the sandwich with a 2-pound weight and refrigerate for 3 hours. Turn the sandwich over every hour, making sure to keep the sandwich weighted.

To serve Cut the sandwich into 4 wedges and serve with the hardboiled quail eggs, a bowl of olive oil and a dish of sea salt. Dip the eggs into the oil and salt and eat between bites of the sandwich.

WINE Napa Valley Rosé (U.S.) Joseph Phelps "Vin de Mistral" 2000
A blend of Grenache and Syrah, this refreshing rosé is round, juicy and light enough so as to not overwhelm this classic summer preparation.

"I have a good feeling for common food. I enjoy twisting classics and giving them another presentation, like my burger with foie gras. I had always wanted to do a very complex burger and db was the perfect place to serve it. Or I buy tomato sauce in the supermarket, since I think it's hard to make a good tomato sauce at home. And my daughter loves pasta with tomato sauce—we try to test them all. I like Newman's Own and Rao's Homemade."

Stuffed Squid with Piquillo Pepper Coulis

MAKES 4 SERVINGS

For the piquillo pepper coulis

2 tablespoons extra-virgin olive oil

1 tablespoon chopped onion

1 clove garlic, peeled and chopped

6 piquillo peppers, seeds removed

2 tablespoons unsalted chicken stock or store-bought low-sodium chicken broth

½ teaspoon freshly squeezed lemon juice

Warm the olive oil in a sauté pan over medium-high heat. Add the onion and garlic and cook until tender but not colored. Add the peppers and stock and cook an additional 2 minutes. Transfer the mixture to a blender, add the lemon juice and purée until smooth. Set aside and keep warm.

For the stuffed squid

¾ pound Swiss chard, stems and tough center ribs removed, washed and cut into thin strips

10 (approximately 1 pound) small squid, cleaned with the tentacles attached

¼ cup extra-virgin olive oil

2 tablespoons finely chopped onion

2 cloves garlic, peeled and finely chopped

1 tablespoon pine nuts

¼ pound chorizo or Italian sausage, finely chopped

8 piquillo peppers, seeds removed and finely chopped

2 tablespoons finely chopped Italian parsley leaves

3 tablespoons fresh bread crumbs

Salt and freshly ground pepper

1. Bring a pot of salted water to a boil, toss in the chard and blanch for 5 minutes. Drain and squeeze the leaves dry of excess water.

2. Roughly chop two of the squid, including the tentacles. Warm 2 tablespoons of the olive oil in a large sauté pan over medium-high heat. Add the onion, garlic and pine nuts and cook until the onion and garlic are tender but not colored, about 4 minutes. Reduce the heat to medium, add the chopped squid and chorizo and cook for 2 minutes. Add the chard, peppers and parsley and cook for 2 minutes more. Toss in the bread crumbs and season with salt and pepper. Let the mixture cool completely.

3. Using a spoon or a pastry bag fitted with a large, round tip, stuff each remaining squid with the filling and use a toothpick to seal shut the opening of each squid. Season with salt and pepper. Warm the remaining 2 tablespoons of the olive oil in a large sauté pan over medium-low heat. Slip the squid into the pan and cook until golden brown on all sides, approximately 5 to 7 minutes. Serve with the piquillo pepper coulis.

WINE Colline Novaresi (Italy) "I Mimo" Rosé 2001
This slightly dry rosé wine from Piedmont plays on the sweet spiciness of the piquillo peppers while adding a fruity side to the dish.

on boulud's nightstand

Daniel Boulud thinks *The Zuni Café Cookbook* by **Judy Rodgers** really shows off the best of American cuisine. And the grilling book he's planning to bring with him when he goes to France this summer with his family is **Al Roker's *Big Bad Book of Barbecue***. Boulud likes Roker's easy writing style and straightforward approach to recipes. He says the book is a great example of American home-style cooking and shows that recipes do not have to be fussy or complicated to be fun and delicious.

Chicken Provençal

MAKES 4 SERVINGS

f&w tip

This hearty stew was terrific right off the stove, but it was also excellent the next day. Reheat it slowly over a low flame and eat it with plenty of crusty bread to soak up the juices.

One 3- to 4-pound chicken

½ cup extra-virgin olive oil

Salt and freshly ground pepper

2 tablespoons all-purpose flour

8 spring onions, white part with ½ inch of green only

1 red pepper, split, seeded and cut into ½-inch-thick strips

8 small Yukon Gold or 16 Fingerling potatoes, peeled

1 cup dry white wine

3 cups unsalted chicken stock or store-bought low-sodium chicken broth

1 tablespoon tomato paste

4 large tomatoes, peeled, seeded and cut into 2-inch chunks

3 cloves garlic, peeled

1 bay leaf

1 sprig thyme

3 ounces haricots verts, tipped

1 cup fava beans, shelled (about 1 pound in pod)

1 medium eggplant, washed, trimmed and cut into 1-inch chunks

1 medium zucchini, washed, trimmed and cut into 1-inch chunks

⅓ cup black olives, pitted

1. Cut the chicken into 8 parts. First, cut off the legs. Then cut each leg in two, separating the thigh from the drumstick. Next, using poultry shears, detach the backbone all the way to the neck; chop both the backbone and neck into 2 to 3 pieces. Split the pair of breasts down the center and then split each breast crosswise in half.

2. Warm ¼ cup of the olive oil in a Dutch oven or large casserole over medium-high heat. Season the chicken all over with salt and pepper and dust with the flour. When the oil is hot, slip the chicken into the pot and sear on all sides until well browned, about 10 minutes. Add the onions, red pepper and potatoes and stir until the vegetables are coated with oil. Deglaze with the wine and reduce by half. Add the stock, tomato paste, tomatoes, garlic, bay leaf and thyme and season with salt and pepper. Bring the liquid to a boil over high heat, reduce the heat to medium and simmer for 30 minutes.

3. Bring a large pot of salted water to a boil. Prepare an ice-water bath in a small bowl. Plunge the haricots verts into the boiling water and blanch for approximately 5 minutes. Immediately put the fava beans in a colander and plunge the colander into the pot so that the beans are submerged and can boil for 3 minutes. Remove the colander with the fava beans. With a slotted spoon or tongs, transfer the haricots verts to the prepared ice-water bath. Hold the fava beans under cold running water to cool them. When cool, drain the haricots verts well and pop the fava beans out of their shells. Rinse the peeled fava beans under cold water and pat dry. Set the beans and haricots verts aside until needed.

4. Warm the remaining ¼ cup olive oil in a large sauté pan over medium-high heat. Add the eggplant and zucchini and cook until golden brown, approximately 8 minutes. Transfer the eggplant and zucchini to a plate lined with paper towels to drain.

5. Add the haricots verts, fava beans, eggplant and zucchini to the chicken and cook it all together for an additional 10 minutes. Stir in the olives and season with salt and pepper, if needed. Discard the bay leaf and thyme. Serve family-style right from the pot.

WINE Bandol (France) Château de Pibarnon 1998
Medium bodied with dark fruit and Provençal herb overtones, this Mourvèdre-based wine is complex yet rustic enough so as not to overshadow the mixed flavors of the vegetables and herbs, yet stand up to the preparation of the chicken.

Rosemary Braised Veal Shank

MAKES 4 SERVINGS

1   veal shank, about 2 pounds (ask your butcher to trim
    the top and bottom bones)

1   tablespoon salt

½   teaspoon freshly ground black pepper

4   sprigs rosemary, cut to the same length as the shank

5   tablespoons extra-virgin olive oil

2   large Spanish onions, peeled, trimmed and cut into ½-inch-thick wedges

6   cloves garlic, peeled and sliced

4   stalks celery, peeled, trimmed and cut on the bias into ½-inch-thick slices

2   large carrots, peeled, trimmed and cut on the bias into ½-inch-thick slices

1   leek, white and light green parts only, sliced and cut
    on the bias into ½-inch-thick slices

1   tablespoon tomato paste

1   tablespoon whole black peppercorns, crushed

2   bay leaves

½   tablespoon all-purpose flour

2   cups dry white wine

8   cups unsalted beef stock or store-bought low-sodium beef broth

1   large tomato, peeled, seeded and cut into ½-inch cubes

1. Center a rack in the oven and preheat the oven to 350°F.

2. Season the shank with the salt and pepper. Use kitchen twine to tie the shank
in 1-inch intervals. Tuck in the rosemary sprigs.

3. Warm 3 tablespoons of the olive oil in a Dutch oven or casserole over high heat.
Slip the meat into the pan and brown it evenly, turning it carefully as needed until
all the surfaces of the meat are a light golden brown. Transfer the shank to a
platter and let rest.

f&w tip
This succulent dish was so good that it wasn't nearly enough to serve four people...but it would be perfect for two. Serve it with roasted potatoes or hearty bread.

4. Warm the remaining 2 tablespoons olive oil in the same pan over medium heat. Add the onions, garlic, celery, carrots and leek and cook until the vegetables are tender but have no color, approximately 8 to 10 minutes. Add the tomato paste, peppercorns and bay leaves and cook for 2 minutes more. Stir in the flour, then add the shank, wine, stock and tomato. Bring the liquid to a boil and cover the pot with a lid. Slide the pot into the oven and braise until the shank is very tender, about 2 hours.

5. Transfer the meat to a heated serving platter. Cut off and discard the kitchen twine and rosemary. Boil the pan liquid until it reduces by three-quarters. Strain the sauce over the meat and serve immediately.

WINE Santa Maria Valley Pinot Noir, California (U.S.) Byron 1998
Light bodied, with cinnamon and red-berry aromas that pair well with the carrots. The vivacious nature of this wine with high acidity enlivens the slowly braised veal shank.

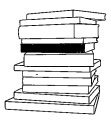

the good cookie

TISH BOYLE

about boyle

Tish Boyle is the food editor and test kitchen director of *Chocolatier* and *Pastry Art & Design* magazines. A graduate of La Varenne École de Cuisine in France, Boyle has been a caterer, pastry chef and food stylist. She is the author of *Diner Desserts* and coauthor of *Chocolate Passion* and the *Grand Finales* series of books.

Tish Boyle begins her book by saying, "Everyone loves cookies." She's right. This book is not groundbreaking, but it's very thorough (there are more than 250 recipes) and extremely well researched and tested. Whether your taste runs to drop cookies, sandwich cookies or "designer" cookies, this book is a great resource.

FOOD & WINE What is the most important thing to remember when baking cookies?

TISH BOYLE Be patient, and follow the directions carefully. That means looking at the ingredients and understanding that you can't make substitutions unless you know they're going to work.

F&W What are the biggest mistakes people make?

TB You'd be amazed at how many people think unsweetened and semisweet chocolate are the same. If you use one instead of the other, chances are the recipe's not going to work. Don't use margarine instead of butter. If it says cake flour, don't use all-purpose. If it says to line the pan with parchment paper, then do it, because otherwise the bottoms of the cookies might burn. A lot of people tend to overbake their cookies, or they're not using an oven thermometer

to make sure the heat isn't too high.

F&W Any other tips for making perfect cookies?

TB Creaming [beating the batter to make it soft] is important, because it breaks down the sharp sugar crystals so they blend with the butter. And make sure not to overwork and overmix the dough, particularly after adding the flour, or you'll get a tough cookie.

F&W What are the most essential pieces of equipment for cookie making?

TB A good quality heavy-gauge aluminum pan that measures 13-by-18 inches (also known as a half sheetpan) and can easily accommodate 16 cookies. A small, spring-loaded cookie scoop is also a great tool for making cookies. It assures perfectly shaped, consistent drop cookies every time.

F&W Where did your recipes come from?

TB Most of them I developed myself from my years as the food editor of

>> | **FEATURED RECIPES**

1 | COOKIE SHOP CHOCOLATE CHIP COOKIES

2 | RASPBERRY-FILLED SHORTBREAD FINGERS

3 | LEMON CURD BITES

4 | CRUNCHY PEANUT BARS

Chocolatier. There are quite a few recipes from colleagues of mine and top pastry chefs as well. Pastry chefs are bound to have a great cookie in their repertoire, even though they're usually focusing on higher-end desserts.

F&W Your book offers a lot of cookie history. What examples did you find particularly interesting?

TB One of my favorite bits involves the brownie. The original 19th-century recipes did not contain any chocolate; the brown color came from molasses. Also, some sources credit a Maine woman named "Brownie" Schrumpf for inventing the brownie. In fact, she didn't invent it; she named herself after it.

F&W What are the differences between American and European cookies?

TB Chefs and cooks in general are more willing to experiment here than in Europe. There are certain classics over there, and pastry chefs don't deviate from the traditional recipes. Here there's a lot of experimentation. Americans throw a bunch of things in a cookie, which is how the chocolate chip cookie evolved.

F&W Why have you chosen to focus on pastry in your professional life?

TB I've always been more focused on details, a requirement for pastry and desserts. There's a lot of science in baking, and while I'm creative, I'm also very interested in food chemistry.

F&W Would you consider *The Good Cookie* to be an encyclopedic resource?

TB No, this book wasn't meant to be a collection of every cookie on the planet. It's just a collection of my favorites.

the specifics

recipes	pages	photos	publisher	price
252 recipes	400	16 color and 98 black-and-white photos	John Wiley & Sons, Inc.	$34.95

credits

The Good Cookie: Over 250 Delicious Recipes, from Simple to Sublime by Tish Boyle. Copyright © 2002 by Tish Boyle. Photographs by John Uher. All rights reserved. Reproduced here by permission of Wiley Publishing, Inc.

Cookie Shop Chocolate Chip Cookies

MAKES ABOUT 60 COOKIES

Adding ground rolled oats to chocolate chip cookies became popular in the 1980's, when chocolate chip cookie stores were all the rage. The oats result in a slightly coarser texture and nuttier flavor than the standard chocolate chip cookie.
This version is buttery, crisp on the outside, and soft on the inside—and loaded with chocolate chips.

2   cups all-purpose flour

1   teaspoon baking soda

1   teaspoon baking powder

1   teaspoon salt

¾   cup old-fashioned rolled oats

2½ cups (15 ounces) semisweet chocolate morsels, divided

1   cup (2 sticks) plus 2 tablespoons unsalted butter, softened

¾   cup granulated sugar

¾   cup firmly packed light brown sugar

2   teaspoons vanilla extract

2   large eggs

1. Position two racks near the center of the oven and preheat the oven to 375°F. Line two baking sheets with parchment paper.

2. Sift together the flour, baking soda, baking powder, and salt into a medium bowl. In the bowl of a food processor, combine the oats and ½ cup of the chocolate morsels and process until finely ground, about 45 seconds. Stir the oat mixture into the flour mixture and set aside.

3. In the bowl of an electric mixer, using the paddle attachment, beat the butter, sugars, and vanilla extract at medium speed until creamy, about 2 minutes. Beat in the eggs one at a time, beating well after each addition and scraping down the sides of the bowl as necessary. At low speed, add the dry ingredients, mixing just until combined. Using a wooden spoon, stir in the remaining 2 cups chocolate morsels.

f&w tip

If you have trouble keeping the parchment paper flat on the baking sheet, lightly butter the baking sheet, then lay down the parchment—it will stick. These cookies store well; they were equally delicious over the next few days.

4. Measure out rounded tablespoonfuls of the dough and, using wet hands, roll each portion into a ball. Arrange the balls 2 inches apart on the prepared baking sheets. Moisten your palm to prevent sticking, and flatten the balls into 1¾-inch disks.

5. Bake the cookies, two sheets at a time, for 11 to 13 minutes, just until golden brown; switch the positions of the baking sheets halfway through baking for even browning. Transfer the cookies to wire racks and cool completely.

Store in an airtight container at room temperature for up to a week.

Raspberry-Filled Shortbread Fingers

MAKES 48 COOKIES

For all its buttery goodness, shortbread is a fairly neutral platform for the succulent sweetness of raspberry. I like to punch up the raspberry flavor with Chambord, though it's not essential. Fresh raspberries combined with raspberry preserves are so refreshing—these are summer cookies, to be enjoyed outdoors, with vanilla ice cream.

Shortbread

2   cups all-purpose flour

½   teaspoon baking powder

Pinch of salt

¾   cup (1½ sticks) unsalted butter, softened

⅔   cup granulated sugar

1   large egg

2   teaspoons vanilla extract

1   teaspoon finely grated lemon zest

Raspberry filling

¾   cup seedless raspberry preserves

1   tablespoon Chambord liqueur (optional)

48 raspberries (about 1½ pints)

Make the shortbread
1. Position a rack in the center of the oven and preheat the oven to 350°F.

2. In a medium bowl, whisk together the flour, baking powder, and salt until well blended; set aside.

3. In the bowl of an electric mixer, using the paddle attachment, beat the butter at medium speed until creamy, about 1 minute. Gradually beat in the sugar and continue to beat until light, about 2 minutes. Add the egg and beat until combined.

"Creaming [beating the batter to make it soft] is important, because it breaks down the sharp sugar crystals so they blend with the butter. And make sure not to overwork and overmix the dough, particularly after adding the flour, or you'll get a tough cookie."

Scrape down the sides of the bowl and beat for another 30 seconds. Beat in the vanilla extract and lemon zest (the mixture will look curdled). At low speed, add the dry ingredients and mix just until blended.

4. Turn the dough out onto a work surface and divide it into four equal parts. Roll each piece into a 12- by ¾-inch log (sprinkle a little flour on the surface if the dough is sticky). Place the logs 2 inches apart on an ungreased baking sheet. Using your palm, flatten the logs slightly. With your index finger, make a trough about ½ inch wide and ¼ inch deep down the length of each log.

Fill and bake the shortbread

5. In a small bowl (or glass measure), stir together the raspberry preserves and Chambord, if using. Spoon about 2 tablespoons of the jam mixture into the depression in each log. Set the remaining jam mixture aside. Bake the logs for 18 to 22 minutes, until golden brown around the edges. Cool the logs on the baking sheet on a wire rack for 10 minutes, then transfer the logs to the rack and cool completely.

6. Transfer the logs to a cutting board. Using a serrated knife, cut each log on the diagonal into twelve ¾-inch cookies. Place a raspberry in the center of each cookie (if the raspberries are large, cut them in half and use just the top half).

7. Heat the remaining jam mixture in the microwave for periods of 7 seconds until it just begins to bubble. Using a pastry brush, lightly coat each raspberry with the jam mixture. Let the jam cool for 10 minutes before serving the cookies.

Store the cookies, without raspberries, for up to 5 days in an airtight container at room temperature; once you add the raspberries, the cookies should be eaten the same day.

Lemon Curd Bites

MAKES 24 MINIATURE TARTS

These miniature tarts, or tassies, are made with a tender cream cheese dough and filled with tangy lemon curd. Very posh, very sophisticated. Lemon curd is popular in England, where it's frequently used as a spread. Its silky texture and bright citrus flavor contrast deliciously with the rich pastry shell.

Cream cheese dough

1¼ cups all-purpose flour

⅓ cup confectioners' sugar

¼ teaspoon baking powder

⅛ teaspoon salt

½ cup (1 stick) cold unsalted butter, cut into tablespoons

One 3-ounce package cream cheese, cut into ½-inch chunks and
    frozen for 30 minutes

1 large egg yolk

1 teaspoon vanilla extract

Lemon curd filling

1 large egg

4 large egg yolks

1 cup plus 2 tablespoons granulated sugar

½ cup freshly squeezed lemon juice

2 teaspoons finely grated lemon zest

Pinch of salt

6 tablespoons (¾ stick) unsalted butter, cut into tablespoons

Garnish

Small fresh spearmint leaves

Special equipment

Two 12-cup miniature muffin pans (1-ounce cups)

Pastry bag fitted with a medium star tip (such as Ateco #5)

variation
Grapefruit Curd Bites
For the filling, substitute grapefruit juice and zest for the lemon juice and zest. Reduce the amount of sugar to 1 cup, and proceed with the recipe as directed.

f&w tip
These little tarts have that "wow" factor. They're tiny and beautiful and packed with sweet, tart flavor. They're really excellent for a party because the tart shells and lemon curd can be made days in advance and assembled a few hours before serving (just keep them chilled).

Make the dough

1. In the bowl of a food processor, combine the flour, confectioners' sugar, baking powder, and salt and process for a few seconds, until blended. Sprinkle the butter and cream cheese pieces over the mixture and pulse about 18 times, until the butter pieces are the size of peas and the mixture resembles coarse meal. In a small bowl, whisk together the egg yolk and vanilla with a fork. Add the mixture to the processor and pulse just until the dough starts to come together (don't let it form a ball around the blade).

2. Turn the dough out onto a work surface and gently press it into a disk. Wrap the dough in plastic wrap and refrigerate for at least 1 hour, until firm (or up to 2 days).

Make the filling

3. Set a fine-mesh sieve over a medium bowl and set aside. In a medium-sized heavy nonreactive saucepan, whisk together the egg, yolks, and sugar until blended. Stir in the lemon juice and zest, salt, and butter and cook over medium

heat, whisking constantly, until the mixture thickens, 7 to 10 minutes (do not let the mixture boil, or it will curdle). Immediately strain the mixture through the sieve, pressing it through with a rubber spatula. Cover the bowl and refrigerate until chilled, about 1 hour.

Bake the crusts
4. Position a rack in the center of the oven and preheat the oven to 400°F. Coat two 12-cup miniature muffin pans with nonstick cooking spray. Cut out twenty-four 2-inch squares of aluminum foil.

5. Remove the dough from the refrigerator and divide it in half. Divide each half into 12 equal portions. Shape each piece of dough into a ball. Place one ball in each muffin cup and press down into the center of the ball with the knuckle of your index finger to form an indentation, then press the dough up the sides of the cup to its rim. The cups should be completely lined with dough. Prick the bottom of each crust with a fork. Line each crust with one of the foil squares and fill with a few pie weights, dried beans, or rice.

6. Bake the crusts for 10 minutes. Transfer the muffin pans to a wire rack and reduce the oven temperature to 350°F. Remove the foil and weights from the crusts and bake the crusts for another 7 to 9 minutes, until golden brown around the edges. Set the muffin pans on a wire rack and cool the crusts completely.

Assemble the bites
7. Scrape the chilled lemon curd into a pastry bag fitted with a medium star tip. Pipe a generous rosette of lemon curd into each crust. Garnish each with a mint leaf. Serve the bites immediately, or chill until serving time.

Store in an airtight container in the refrigerator for up to 1 day.

COOKIE BITE Lemons and other citrus fruits will yield much more juice if you microwave them on high power until they are warm to the touch (about 20 to 30 seconds) before juicing them.

on boyle's nightstand
"**Maida Heatter's** *Book of Great American Desserts* provides the absolute best versions of every down-home American dessert you can think of," Boyle says. "She takes the guesswork out of her recipes by describing each process in great detail, down to the last pinch of salt." Boyle also likes **Richard Sax's** *Classic Home Desserts:* "Not only does it give wonderful, well-tested recipes, it also provides amusing anecdotes and history."

Crunchy Peanut Bars

MAKES 36 BARS

Have you ever had a PayDay, the candy bar that is a dense cluster of nuts held together with caramel. It capitalizes on the combination of salty and sweet (plus crunchy and slightly greasy) that many people crave. These bars are like a PayDay only better, because they are homemade and because I added some peanut butter flavor to the caramel. These are my husband's desert island food choice: he could live on them.

Brown sugar crust

1¼ cups all-purpose flour

½ teaspoon salt

½ cup (1 stick) unsalted butter, softened

½ cup firmly packed light brown sugar

Peanut topping

4 tablespoons (½ stick) unsalted butter

⅔ cup light corn syrup

1⅔ cups (10 ounces) peanut butter chips

2 teaspoons vanilla extract

2¼ cups (12 ounces) salted peanuts

Make the crust

1. Position a rack in the center of the oven and preheat the oven to 350°F. Grease the bottom and sides of a 9- by 13-inch baking pan.

2. In a medium bowl, stir together the flour and salt; set aside.

3. In the bowl of an electric mixer, using the paddle attachment or beaters, beat the butter with the brown sugar at medium speed until combined, about 1 minute. At low speed, add the flour mixture and mix just until crumbly, 10 to 15 seconds.

4. Pat the dough into the bottom of the prepared pan. Prick the dough well with a fork. Bake the crust for 15 to 18 minutes, until golden brown around the edges. Transfer the pan to a wire rack to cool while you prepare the topping. Leave the oven on.

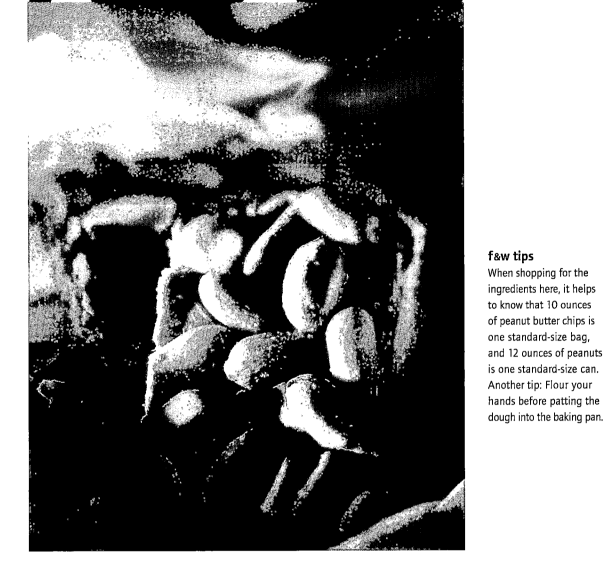

f&w tips

When shopping for the ingredients here, it helps to know that 10 ounces of peanut butter chips is one standard-size bag, and 12 ounces of peanuts is one standard-size can. Another tip: Flour your hands before patting the dough into the baking pan.

Make the topping

5. In a large saucepan, combine the butter, corn syrup, and peanut butter chips and heat over medium heat, stirring constantly, until the chips are melted and the mixture is smooth, about 5 minutes. Remove the pan from the heat and stir in the vanilla extract.

6. Pour the topping over the crust, using a spatula to spread it to the edges of the pan. Sprinkle the peanuts evenly over the topping, and press them lightly into the topping. Bake the bars for 12 to 15 minutes, until the topping is bubbly. Cool the bars completely in the pan on a wire rack.

7. Run a small sharp knife around the edges of the pan to release the bars. Carefully invert the bars onto a baking sheet then reinvert it onto a cutting board. Using a sharp knife, cut into 36 bars.

Store in an airtight container at room temperature for up to 5 days, or freeze for up to a month.

michael chiarello's
casual cooking

MICHAEL CHIARELLO WITH JANET FLETCHER

about chiarello

Michael Chiarello made his name opening Tra Vigne restaurant in St. Helena, California. Host of two PBS series, *Michael Chiarello's Napa* and *Season by Season*, he also sells a line of food products through his Web site (www.napastyle.com). His previous books include *Napa Stories, The Tra Vigne Cookbook, Flavored Vinegars* and *Flavored Oils*.

Michael Chiarello is one of the few chefs who seems truly to understand the way people cook at home. His book is filled with sophisticated recipes that can be made after work, in a style inspired by both Italy and California wine country. It's hard not to want to make everything, as the photographs are so luscious. We'd definitely want this book on our kitchen shelves.

FOOD & WINE What do you mean when you say there's a difference between cooking well and cooking smart?

MICHAEL CHIARELLO Cooking well is comparable to restaurant cooking—spending a lot of money for luxurious ingredients and putting hours of labor into preparing them. Cooking smart is about taking ingredients at the top of their season and preparing them in a way that gets you to the table in 20 minutes. It's about being produce-conscious and doing things in ways that are healthful, quick and affordable. You're a hero when you can pull off smart cooking.

F&W What five ingredients would you never be without?

MC Parmigiano-Reggiano, salt, olive oil, pasta and vacuum-packed free-range chicken broth.

F&W What are some ingredients that you would never scrimp on?

MC You have to have great salt. It's one of the few things you use in absolutely every dish. I only use salt from Brittany, and it's worth it. Olive oil, too, you shouldn't really scrimp on. There are different types of olive oils that are better suited for some things than others. An expensive, unfiltered olive oil may be great for dressing a salad, but if you're poaching a whole halibut, you can use a lighter, later-harvest oil.

F&W Are there ingredients you'd suggest buying premade?

MC I'd never make pizza dough; just go into any pizza joint and buy theirs. I mean, there's so little variation between pizza doughs, you can't go wrong by saving the time and buying it for $5 off the guy around the corner. But I'd never buy premarinated meats—

>> | **FEATURED RECIPES**

1 | BABY BACK RIBS WITH ESPRESSO BBQ SAUCE

2 | LINGUINE WITH CLAMS AND *BAGNA CAUDA* BUTTER

3 | CRISPY WHITE BEANS WITH CHILI OIL

4 | QUAIL WITH BACON AND HONEY

you know they're hiding something.

F&W Any other favorite shortcuts?

MC As a single dad, I realized that casual cooking is about developing time-saving methods. For example, I freeze soups and stocks and have them ready to go.

F&W Your book offers recipes for delicious flavored butters; any tips to make them come out right?

MC Buy the best sweet butter you can find. Don't use a low-calorie substitute. It's better to use whole-fat ingredients sparingly than to try to duplicate the flavor with lesser-quality ingredients.

F&W What are your favorite utensils?

MC I love those flexible cutting boards that you place on top of your regular cutting board and then can just lift and bend to pour food into the pot.

I think everyone needs at least one high-quality 12-by-14-inch sauté pan that can go right into the oven.

F&W A lot of people get stuck in a salad rut; what are your tips for enlivening salads?

MC Make sure not to wash your organic greens. Chances are they're prewashed (double-check with your greenmarket vendor or grocer). Washing them again will only thin them out and cut their flavor in half. [If you do decide to wash your organic greens, make sure to spin them dry; don't beat them up with a paper towel.] Also, consider adding sea salt or crispy prosciutto to your salad: something to add a little punch of flavor, something that will be a surprise when you bite into it.

the specifics

recipes	pages	photos	publisher	price
127	216	111 color and black-and-white photos	Chronicle Books	$35

credits

Michael Chiarello's Casual Cooking: Wine Country Recipes for Family and Friends by Michael Chiarello with Janet Fletcher. Photographs by Deborah Jones. Copyright ©2002 by NapaStyle Inc. Published in the U.S. by Chronicle Books LLC, San Francisco. Used with permission. Visit www.chroniclebooks.com.

Baby Back Ribs with Espresso BBQ Sauce

SERVES 6 GENEROUSLY

These ribs are great party food because they are easy to make in quantity and you can do the preliminary cooking hours ahead. Then when the party gets under way, you can baste the ribs with sauce and grill them in front of your guests. They are unbelievably succulent. Put out lots of napkins.

3   racks baby back ribs, about 6 pounds total

Sea salt, preferably gray salt, and freshly ground black pepper

Barbecue sauce

2   tablespoons extra-virgin olive oil

2   tablespoons minced garlic

1   cup ketchup

1   cup honey

½   cup balsamic vinegar

¼   cup soy sauce

¼   cup brewed espresso

Preheat the oven to 325°F.

Cut each rack of ribs in half crosswise (between 2 ribs). Season with salt and pepper. Cover a baking sheet with heavy-duty aluminum foil. Set 3 of the half-racks side by side on the prepared baking sheet and top each with another slab.

Bake the ribs, rotating the slabs top to bottom every 30 minutes, until tender, about 2½ hours. Remove the ribs from the oven and cover with a foil tent to keep them moist until you are ready to grill them.

Prepare the barbecue sauce Heat the olive oil in a saucepan over moderately low heat. Add the garlic and sauté until it is golden. Remove from the heat and let the garlic cool in the oil. Whisk in the ketchup, honey, vinegar, soy sauce, and espresso. Simmer gently for 15 minutes to blend the flavors. Remove from the heat.

"You have to have great salt. It's one of the few things you use in absolutely every dish. I only use salt from Brittany, and it's worth it."

Prepare a fire in a charcoal grill, preheat a gas grill, or preheat an oven to 425°F. Brush the ribs generously with barbecue sauce. If you are grilling the ribs over charcoal, arrange the hot coals in a ring around the perimeter of the grill so that the ribs can cook in the center over indirect heat; if cooked directly over the coals, they would burn. If you are using a gas grill, adjust the flame so the ribs cook over indirect heat. Grill the ribs in a covered grill with the vents open, or bake them uncovered in the oven. Baste occasionally with additional sauce until the ribs are lightly caramelized. Transfer the rib racks to a cutting board and cut into individual riblets. Serve immediately.

Linguine with Clams and *Bagna Cauda* Butter

SERVES 4

This dish came about because I had *Bagna Cauda* Butter in the freezer. Melted into the pasta and clams at the last minute, the butter delivers subtle notes of anchovy and garlic. I predict this sauce will turn you away from old-fashioned white clam sauce forever.

¾ pound dried linguine

2 tablespoons olive oil

4 pounds clams, scrubbed

1½ cups dry white wine

½ cup *Bagna Cauda* Butter (recipe follows), at room temperature

1 cup coarsely chopped fresh Italian (flat-leaf) parsley

Bring a large pot of salted water to a boil over high heat. Add the pasta.

While the pasta cooks, prepare the clams Heat a large pot over high heat. When very hot, add the olive oil, then add the clams. When the first clams start to open, add the wine and bring to a boil. Boil for a couple of minutes to drive off the alcohol, then cover and cook until the clams open, about 5 minutes. Discard any clams that fail to open.

Drain the pasta when it is 1 minute shy of al dente and transfer it to the pot with the clams. Cook over moderate heat for about 1 minute so the pasta absorbs some of the sauce. Off the heat, add the butter and parsley and toss until the butter melts. Divide among warmed bowls and serve immediately.

MICHAEL'S NOTES If you start the clams in a very hot skillet, they'll open twice as fast.

Bagna Cauda Butter

MAKES ABOUT 1¼ CUPS

In the Piedmont region of Italy, eating *bagna cauda* is a favorite ritual. The diners gather around an earthenware pot filled with hot olive oil, anchovies, and garlic, and they dip raw vegetables or bread into the "hot bath"—a kind of Italian fondue.

I think the same seasonings make an incredible butter for flavoring cauliflower, broccoli, or stuffed baked tomatoes. Let a nugget melt onto a grilled beef steak or fish steak, or toss a generous knob into steamed clams at the last minute. Because the dish is so simple, it's crucial to use extra-virgin olive oil and the best, meatiest anchovies you can find.

¼ cup extra-virgin olive oil

¼ cup chopped garlic

2 tablespoons very finely minced anchovies

1 cup (½ pound) unsalted butter, at room temperature

Sea salt, preferably gray salt

1 tablespoon very finely minced fresh Italian (flat-leaf) parsley

Heat the olive oil in a small saucepan over low heat. When the oil just begins to warm, add the garlic and anchovies and cook slowly, stirring, until the garlic becomes toasty brown and the anchovies dissolve, about 10 minutes. Let cool completely.

Process the butter in a food processor until smooth and creamy. Add the cooled garlic-anchovy mixture and a pinch of salt. Process until well blended. Taste and add more salt if needed. Transfer to a bowl and stir in the parsley.

Refrigerate until firm enough to shape into a log. Put an 18-inch sheet of aluminum foil on your work surface. Spoon the butter down the center of the foil into a log about 1½ inches in diameter. Enclose in foil and twist the ends to make a sealed log, like a Tootsie Roll. Refrigerate for up to 1 week, or freeze for up to 6 months.

MICHAEL'S NOTES Add the garlic just when the oil starts to warm up. If you put the garlic in hot oil, it caramelizes too rapidly and won't flavor the oil as deeply.

Crispy White Beans with Chili Oil

SERVES 4

This dish, now a personal favorite, was a total mistake. One day I was sautéing some white beans, got caught up in something else, and when I looked at the beans again, they were overcooked. I spooned them onto a paper towel and, a few minutes later, popped one into my mouth. To my surprise, I couldn't stop eating them.

I've worked on the recipe a bit to create something that's now intentionally crisp and delicious. You could put these beans out with cocktails as a crunchy nibble, like peanuts, but I typically serve them as a side dish for lobster or shrimp.

f&w tip
We used Great Northern beans for this crispy snack and they were perfect.

Beans

1   cup dried white beans, preferably the largest available

2   fresh sage leaves

1   clove garlic, peeled but left whole

2   teaspoons sea salt, preferably gray salt

Coating

1   cup Arborio Rice Coating (recipe follows)

1½ teaspoons pure California chili powder

¼   teaspoon freshly ground black pepper

¾   cup buttermilk

¾   cup plus 2 tablespoons extra-virgin olive oil

¼   cup Chili Oil (recipe follows)

2   tablespoons thinly sliced garlic

1   tablespoon thinly sliced serrano or jalapeño chili

1½ cups fresh basil leaves

1   tablespoon julienned orange zest

Cook the beans Place the dried beans in a saucepan with cold water to cover by 2 inches. Bring to a boil. Cover, remove from the heat, and let stand for 1 hour. Drain the beans, return to the saucepan, and add cold water to cover by 2 inches, the sage, and the garlic. Slowly bring to a simmer. Simmer gently, uncovered, for about 20 minutes, then add the salt. Continue simmering gently until the beans are tender; the timing will vary depending on the age of the beans. Let cool in the cooking liquid. (The beans may be refrigerated for up to 3 days before continuing.)

Make the coating Combine the rice coating, chili powder, and pepper in a small bowl, stir well, and set aside.

Drain the beans through a sieve and discard the sage and garlic. Place the beans in a bowl, add the buttermilk, and let soak for a few minutes. Drain again in a sieve, then place the sieve with the beans over the bowl.

Heat the ¾ cup olive oil and the Chili Oil in a medium skillet over high heat. While the oil is heating, sprinkle the coating over the beans and shake in the sieve to coat the beans evenly. Repeat with the coating that falls into the bowl. Don't worry if the beans don't absorb all the coating.

When the oil is hot but not smoking, carefully add the beans, spreading them in an even layer. Cook without stirring until they are browned and crisp on the bottom, 6 to 7 minutes. Turn with a spatula and brown on the other side, another 5 to 6 minutes, adjusting the heat so they don't burn. With a slotted spoon, transfer the beans to paper towels to drain.

Pour off the oil from the skillet and wipe it clean with paper towels. Return the skillet to moderately high heat and add the remaining 2 tablespoons oil. When hot, add the sliced garlic and chili and sauté until the garlic begins to color. Add the basil leaves and stand back; they will spatter. Sauté until the leaves turn crisp, about 1 minute. Add the orange zest, then remove from the heat.

Arrange the beans on a serving platter and top with the garlic-chili-basil garnish. Serve hot.

MICHAEL'S NOTES Bringing the beans up to a simmer slowly helps keep the skins from splitting.

Arborio Rice Coating

MAKES ABOUT 5 CUPS

This is by far the best coating I know for nearly anything fried. It gives an especially crisp crust to fried fish fillets, squid, shrimp, eggplant, and veal cutlets. You may as well make a lot because it keeps well in the freezer, and it's hard to grind less than 1 cup of rice in a blender. If you have a spice mill, you can halve the recipe.

1   cup Arborio rice

3   cups unbleached all-purpose flour

1   cup semolina

2   tablespoons table salt

1   teaspoon freshly ground black pepper

Grind the rice in a blender until very fine. Put it in a bowl and add the all-purpose flour, semolina, salt, and pepper. Toss until well blended. Store in a sealed container in the freezer for maximum freshness. It will keep for months.

MICHAEL'S NOTES This is one of the few places I use table salt. Sea salt and kosher salt are too heavy to stay evenly distributed in the coating.

Chili Oil

MAKES ABOUT 1½ CUPS

I like to use a mixture of chilies to get layers of flavor—waves of hot, fruity, roasted, and sweet. Here, I've used the mild California chili; peppery chili flakes; and the lightly smoked, ground Spanish paprika called *pimentón de la Vera.* Dried chipotles, which are smoked jalapeños, are a nice choice, but play around to find the blend you like.

½ cup pure California chili powder

1 tablespoon red pepper flakes

1 tablespoon Spanish *pimentón de la Vera*

2 cups olive oil

Puree the chili powder, red pepper flakes, and *pimentón de la Vera* with the olive oil in a blender until completely smooth. Put the mixture in a saucepan and bring to a simmer over moderate heat. Simmer for 45 seconds, then set aside to infuse for 10 minutes. Pour through a fine-mesh sieve into a bowl. Don't press on the mixture, but you can tap the sieve against your hand to get the oil to drip through faster.

Now strain the oil again through a flat-bottomed paper filter. If the filter clogs, you may need to change the filter partway through. It's okay to pick the filter up and squeeze it gently to force the oil out faster, but take care not to break the filter. Store in an airtight jar in a cool, dark place. It will stay lively for at least 1 month.

MICHAEL'S NOTES Look for California chili powder where Mexican ingredients are sold.

Quail with Bacon and Honey

SERVES 4

I'll never understand why Cornish game hens are so popular. Quail are much more flavorful. Fortunately, they're now more widely available, too, and the semiboneless ones make easy eating. I wrap them in bacon to add smokiness and a richness that they lack on their own, and I brush them with honey and vinegar to create an *agrodolce* (sweet-and-sour) glaze. Don't serve any forks with this dish. It's finger food.

⅓ cup honey

1 tablespoon balsamic vinegar

1 teaspoon finely chopped fresh sage

Sea salt, preferably gray salt, and freshly ground black pepper

8 semiboneless quail with wings and legs attached

8 thin slices bacon

2 tablespoons extra-virgin olive oil

½ cup dry white wine

2 fresh rosemary sprigs, each 6 inches long

1 tablespoon unsalted butter

Preheat the oven to 350°F.

In a small bowl, whisk together the honey, vinegar, sage, and salt and pepper to taste.

Season the quail with salt and pepper, then tuck the wing tips under the body of each quail. Wrap each bird with a slice of bacon. Put 2 quail side by side. (Don't let the quail touch or the bacon won't crisp properly.) Run 2 parallel skewers through both birds. Repeat with the remaining quail. Trim the skewers to fit in a skillet. Generously brush the birds with the honey mixture.

Heat the olive oil over moderately high heat in an ovenproof skillet large enough to hold all the quail. Add the quail, breast-side down, and sauté for 2 minutes. Turn and cook for 2 minutes on the back side. Transfer the skillet to the oven and bake until the quail are firm and nicely caramelized, about 15 minutes.

Transfer the quail to a serving platter and pour off any fat in the skillet. Add the wine and rosemary to the skillet and return to moderately high heat. Simmer, scraping the bottom of the skillet with a wooden spoon, until all the caramelized bits dissolve and the mixture has the consistency of a sauce. Remove from the heat and whisk in the butter. Strain the sauce through a sieve held over the quail and serve immediately.

celebrate with chocolate

MARCEL DESAULNIERS

about desaulniers

Marcel Desaulniers is the co-owner and executive chef of The Trellis restaurant in Williamsburg, Virginia. He is the author of several books, including *Death by Chocolate, Death by Chocolate Cookies* and *Death by Chocolate Cakes.* A graduate of the Culinary Institute of America, Desaulniers has received several awards, most recently the 1999 James Beard Award for Outstanding Pastry Chef.

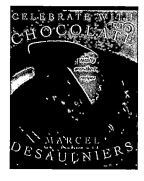

Desaulniers has a vivid imagination, and this book is full of his fanciful recipes—which also happen to be unfailingly reliable. Whether his subject is cakes, cookies, frozen desserts, mousses or candies, he is a meticulous recipe writer who leaves no instruction out. Chocolate lovers will go crazy for his wild creations as well as for his relatively tame ones.

FOOD & WINE What was the inspiration for this book?

MARCEL DESAULNIERS Chocolate has been a passion my whole life. My mom was a single working mother with six kids to raise, but she always found time at night to bake. Almost all of my dessert books have one of her recipes— her caramels, her fudge, her chocolate chip cookies.

F&W What advice would you give someone who's intimidated by baking?

MD I'd say try an easy cookie recipe, like my Black Mamba Cookies, and then build from that. You know, you don't want to start with the recipe for Death by Chocolate.

F&W What's your favorite thing to bake at home?

MD I have a soft spot in my heart for ganache and truffles. They're so simple and you don't need a standing mixer

to make either of them. People ask me what I make on Valentine's Day. I make some ganache and serve it with fresh strawberries, which are just starting to come into season in California in February.

F&W Do you have any equipment tips?

MD I'd buy a mercury-filled oven thermometer. Most home ovens get out of calibration in short order and are 25 degrees hotter or cooler than the dial says, and that can cause major problems. At $10, an oven thermometer is a great investment.

F&W What is the biggest mistake people make with ingredients?

MD I recommend that people who don't bake frequently buy small amounts of ingredients so they're fresh. If you use a can of cocoa powder that you first opened a couple of years ago, you just won't get the right results.

>> | FEATURED RECIPES

1 | MRS. D'S "SHE AIN'T HEAVY" CHOCOLATE CAKE

2 | BLACK MAMBA COOKIES

3 | COCOA BERRY YOGURT MOUSSE

And you have to be disciplined about following recipes. A lot of people will say to me, "I've tried your recipe for years and it worked well and all of a sudden it's not working." It's like pulling teeth to get them to admit that they're not using semisweet chocolate baking bars anymore, they're buying semisweet chocolate chips. People assume both will give you the same result, but they don't.

F&W What about techniques?

MD You have to pay attention. A lot of techniques in baking and making confections demand that the baker constantly monitor the ingredients. You can't step away. After you've added the yeast, you can't take a phone call and chat for 10 or 15 minutes. And people do that routinely.

I don't mean to be condescending, but if you want the right results, you've got to be focused on what you're doing. That's why my recipes tend to be on the long side. It's not because they're complicated; it's because I'm not a baker by training, so I try to give people a lot of information. I think more like the home cook does.

F&W What are the biggest differences between cooking and baking?

MD Measuring is far more important in baking, and people aren't very precise. Measuring seems easy, but it's not. I even have to convince the people who help me test my recipes that it's not *about* that much, it's *exactly* that much. Baking is not like making a pot of soup. Once something is baked, that's it; you have to live with the results.

the specifics

recipes	pages	photos	publisher	price
45	192	20 color photos	William Morrow	$24.95

credits

Celebrate with Chocolate: Totally Over-the-Top Recipes by Marcel Desaulniers. Copyright © 2002 by Marcel Desaulniers. Photographs by Ron Manville. Reprinted by permission of HarperCollins Publishers Inc., William Morrow.

Mrs. D's "She Ain't Heavy" Chocolate Cake

SERVES 12

My mom (Mrs. D.) is an unabashed chocolate lover. Nothing chocolate escapes her appetite, be it M&Ms or, as in this recipe, the most perfect piece of chocolate cake you could possibly imagine passing your lips.

Yes, but if it's a heavy-duty chocolate cake, how come it doesn't contain any chocolate? For hundreds of years a beverage known as chocolate was produced from the fruit of the cocoa tree. But why quibble, Mom knows best, and if she wants to call it chocolate, so be it. For the record, cocoa is derived by pressing out most of the cocoa butter from pure chocolate (known as chocolate liquor), yielding, well after further manipulation, both powdered unsweetened cocoa and baking chocolate.

"She Ain't Heavy" Chocolate Cake

1   tablespoon unsalted butter, melted

2   cups cake flour

¾   cup unsweetened cocoa powder

1¼ teaspoons baking soda

½   teaspoon baking powder

½   teaspoon salt

1¾ cups granulated sugar

¾   pound (3 sticks) unsalted butter, cut into ½-ounce pieces

3   large eggs

1¼ cups whole milk

1   teaspoon pure vanilla extract

"Hasn't Failed Me Yet" Cocoa Icing

1¼ pounds confectioners' sugar

1¼ cups unsweetened cocoa powder

1¼ pounds (5 sticks) unsalted butter, cut into ½-ounce pieces

½   cup whole milk

1   teaspoon pure vanilla extract

on desaulniers's nightstand
Marcel Desaulniers says he turns to *The Cake Bible* by **Rose Levy Beranbaum** for technical information and inspiration. He reads **Amanda Hesser's *The Cook and the Gardener*** when he wants to give his brain a rest and lose himself in the French countryside. **Alice Waters's *Chez Panisse Vegetables*** makes him feel as though he is sitting in her upstairs café enjoying lunch. And he finds *Vegetables from Amaranth to Zucchini* by **Elizabeth Schneider** invaluable when he's writing menus.

Make Mrs. D's "She Ain't Heavy" Chocolate Cake Preheat the oven to 350°F.

Lightly coat the insides of three 9 x 1½-inch cake pans with some of the melted butter. Line the bottoms of the pans with parchment paper (or wax paper), then lightly coat the paper with more melted butter. Set aside.

In a sifter combine the cake flour, cocoa powder, baking soda, baking powder, and salt. Sift onto a large piece of parchment paper (or wax paper) and set aside.

Place the sugar and the ¾ pound butter in the bowl of an electric mixer fitted with a paddle. Mix on low speed for 1 minute, then beat on medium until soft, about 2 minutes. Scrape down the sides of the bowl and the paddle. Continue beating on medium for an additional 2 minutes until very soft. Scrape down the sides of the bowl and the paddle. Add the eggs one at a time, beating on medium for 30 seconds after each addition, and scraping down the sides of the bowl once the eggs have been incorporated. Operate the mixer on low while gradually adding about half of the dry ingredients, followed by about half of the milk. Once these ingredients have been incorporated, about 1½ minutes, gradually add the remaining dry ingredients, followed by the remaining milk; mix until incorporated, about 1½ minutes. Scrape

"I recommend that people who don't bake frequently buy small amounts of ingredients so they're fresh. If you use a can of cocoa powder that you first opened a couple of years ago, you just won't get the right results."

down the sides of the bowl and the paddle. Don't be concerned if the batter looks a bit odd texturally at this point (because of the interaction between the milk and butter); it will come together nicely with the next step.

Add the vanilla extract and mix on low for 5 seconds; beat on medium for 1 minute until thoroughly combined. Remove the bowl from the mixer and use a rubber spatula to finish mixing the ingredients until thoroughly combined. Now the batter looks very thick, a bit like soft-serve ice cream, but please don't taste, because the ingestion of raw yolks may not be salubrious. Immediately divide the cake batter among the prepared pans (about 2¼ cups in each pan), spreading evenly (an offset spatula would work best).

Bake on the top and center racks in the oven until a toothpick inserted in the center of each cake layer comes out clean, about 35 minutes. (Rotate the pans from top to center halfway through the baking time.) Remove the cake layers from the oven and cool in the pans for 15 to 20 minutes at room temperature. Invert the cake layers onto cake circles (or cake plates) wrapped with plastic wrap or lined with parchment paper or wax paper. Carefully peel the paper away from the bottoms of the layers. Refrigerate the cake layers while preparing the icing.

Make Mrs. D's "Hasn't Failed Me Yet" Cocoa Icing In a sifter combine the confectioners' sugar and cocoa powder. Sift onto an extra large (about 12 x 20 inches) piece of parchment paper (or wax paper) and set aside.

Place the butter in the bowl of an electric mixer fitted with a paddle. Mix on low speed for 1 minute; increase the speed to medium and beat for 2 minutes until soft. Use a rubber spatula to scrape down the sides of the bowl and the paddle. Beat on medium for 2 more minutes until very soft. Scrape down the sides of the bowl and paddle. Operate the mixer on the lowest speed (stir) while gradually adding about half the amount of dry ingredients, followed by half the amount of milk. Once these ingredients have been incorporated, about 2 minutes, add the remaining dry ingredients, followed by the remaining milk; mix until incorporated, about 2 minutes.

Scrape down the sides of the bowl and the paddle. Beat on medium for 1 more minute until very soft and fluffy. Add the vanilla extract and mix on low for 5 seconds; increase the speed to medium and beat for 1 minute until very soft and fluffy. Remove the bowl from the mixer and use a rubber spatula to finish mixing the icing until thoroughly combined.

Assemble Mrs. D's "She Ain't Heavy" Chocolate Cake Remove the cake layers from the refrigerator. Turn one of the layers onto a clean cake circle (or cake plate), then peel off the paper. Use a cake spatula to spread 1½ cups of icing evenly and smoothly over the top and to the edges of the cake layer. Turn a second cake layer onto the iced layer, then peel off the paper. Use a cake spatula to spread 1½ cups of icing evenly and smoothly over the top and to the edges of the cake layer. Turn the remaining cake layer onto the second iced layer and gently press the layers into place. Spread the remaining icing over the top and sides of the entire cake. Refrigerate the cake for 1 hour before serving.

To serve Heat the blade of a serrated slicer under hot running water and wipe the blade dry before making each slice. Keep the slices at room temperature for 15 to 20 minutes before serving.

THE CHEF'S TOUCH This cake may be prepared over 2 days.

DAY 1 Bake the "She Ain't Heavy" Chocolate Cake layers Once they're cooled, cover each layer with plastic wrap and refrigerate.

DAY 2 Make the "Hasn't Failed Me Yet" Cocoa Icing Assemble the cake as directed in the recipe. Refrigerate for 1 hour before serving.

After assembly, keep the cake in the refrigerator for 3 to 4 days before serving. To avoid permeating the cake with refrigerator odors, place it in a large, tightly sealed plastic container.

Black Mamba Cookies

MAKES EIGHTEEN 3-INCH COOKIES

Proffering these profoundly chocolate cookies leads to dangerous liaisons. Trellis pastry chef Kelly Bailey says this cookie batter has just enough flour to keep the chocolate and nuts together. Offer a black mamba to one you desire, and it may keep you together forever.

1 pound semisweet baking chocolate, coarsely chopped

3 ounces unsweetened chocolate, coarsely chopped

¼ pound (1 stick) unsalted butter, cut into ½-ounce pieces

½ cup all-purpose flour

¼ cup unsweetened cocoa powder

¼ teaspoon baking powder

¼ teaspoon salt

4 large eggs

1 cup granulated sugar

2 tablespoons instant espresso powder

½ cup semisweet chocolate chips

¼ cup pecans, toasted and coarsely chopped

¼ cup walnuts, toasted and coarsely chopped

1 tablespoon pure vanilla extract

Preheat the oven to 325°F.

Melt the chopped semisweet chocolate, unsweetened chocolate, and butter in the top half of a double boiler or in a medium glass bowl in a microwave oven, and stir until smooth. Set aside.

In a sifter combine the flour, cocoa powder, baking powder, and salt. Sift onto a large piece of parchment paper (or wax paper) and set aside.

Place the eggs, sugar, and espresso powder in the bowl of an electric mixer fitted with a paddle. Beat on medium speed for 4 minutes until the mixture is thickened and slightly frothy. Add the chocolate and butter mixture and mix on medium to combine, about 1 minute. Use a rubber spatula to scrape down the sides of the bowl. Operate the mixer on low while gradually adding the dry ingredients; mix until incorporated, about 45 seconds. Scrape down the insides of the bowl. Add the chocolate chips, pecans, walnuts, and vanilla extract and mix on low to combine, about 10 seconds. Remove the bowl from the mixer and use a rubber spatula to finish mixing the ingredients until thoroughly combined. Note that a yummy batter-like consistency is achieved, rather than dough-like.

Using 3 heaping tablespoons (approximately 2½ ounces) or 1 heaping #20 ice cream scoop of the batter for each cookie, portion 6 cookies, evenly spaced, on each of 3 nonstick baking sheets. Place 1 baking sheet on the top rack and 1 baking sheet on the center rack of the oven and bake for 18 minutes, rotating the sheets from top to center halfway through the baking time (at that time also turn each sheet 180 degrees). The third baking sheet may be placed in another 325°F oven or held at room temperature and then baked after the first 2 sheets are removed from the oven. Remove the cookies from the oven and cool to room temperature on the baking sheets, about 15 minutes. Store the cooled cookies in a tightly sealed plastic container.

THE CHEF'S TOUCH Because of the batter-like rather than dough-like consistency of this cookie mixture you may prefer to prepare it in a large bowl, using a stiff wire whisk or even a rubber spatula rather than a standing electric mixer.

These cookies will stay fresh in a tightly sealed plastic container at room temperature for 2 to 3 days, or in the refrigerator for a week to 10 days (bring the cookies to room temperature before serving). For long-term storage, up to several weeks, the cookies may be frozen in a tightly sealed plastic container to prevent dehydration and freezer odors. Thaw the frozen cookies at room temperature before serving.

f&w tips
The dough for these cookies is so sticky that we found it easier to bake them on parchment paper. Try to resist the urge to eat these cookies hot out of the oven—they get wonderfully chewy as they cool.

Cocoa Berry Yogurt Mousse

SERVES 4

Yogurt brings the tang, strawberries the texture and sweetness, cocoa the raison d'être, and the heavy cream the voluptuousness.

Frosted strawberries

12 large fresh strawberries

¼ cup granulated sugar

Cocoa yogurt mousse

½ cup confectioners' sugar

½ cup unsweetened cocoa powder

1 cup heavy cream

1 cup plain lowfat yogurt

Frost the strawberries Place the strawberries in a colander and spray with lukewarm water. Gently shake the colander to remove excess water. Stem and then cut the berries widthwise into ¼-inch-thick slices. Place the berries in a medium noncorrosive bowl. Sprinkle the sugar over the berries, then toss gently to combine. Equally divide the strawberries among four 8- to 10-ounce glasses, cups, or whatever you desire for presentation (the vessel chosen should be noncorrosive). Set aside at room temperature.

Make the cocoa yogurt mousse In a sifter combine the confectioners' sugar and cocoa powder. Sift onto a large piece of parchment paper (or wax paper) and set aside.

Place the heavy cream in the bowl of an electric mixer fitted with a balloon whip. Operate the mixer on low speed while gradually adding the dry ingredients; mix until incorporated, about 1 minute. Use a rubber spatula to scrape down the sides of the bowl. Now whisk on medium for 5 seconds. Remove the bowl from the mixer. Add the yogurt; fold the ingredients together with a rubber spatula until

f&w tip
If you plan on making this
dessert ahead of time, keep
the strawberries and mousse
separate and assemble
them just before serving.
We found that because
the strawberries are sugared,
when you let them sit they
release a good deal of liquid
that pools in the bottom .
of the dish.

thoroughly combined. Immediately spoon the yogurt mousse onto the strawberries
in each glass (a bit more than ½ cup in each). Serve immediately, or cover the top
of each glass with plastic wrap and refrigerate for up to 24 hours before serving.

THE CHEF'S TOUCH Strawberries are just the tip of an iceberg of possibilities for
this quickie dessert, as many other berries would work well, either fresh or frozen. If
you select frozen fruit, merely thaw it, then portion it along with natural juices into
the serving dish. No need to sprinkle with sugar unless the fruit is fresh.

barefoot contessa
family style

INA GARTEN

about garten

Ina Garten left her job as a budget analyst in the White House 25 years ago to pursue her dream of operating a specialty food store. Since opening Barefoot Contessa in East Hampton, New York, she has written the best-selling *The Barefoot Contessa Cookbook* and *Barefoot Contessa Parties!* She is a frequent contributor to major national magazines, including *Martha Stewart Living* and *O Magazine.* Her new television series on entertaining, *Barefoot Contessa,* can be seen on the Food Network.

This is a great gift for someone who would like to start having more dinner parties but lacks the confidence to do so. Garten knows how to make guests think that she put in a lot more effort than she did, and her many tips here show how she does it. As for her recipes, they're easy, serve a big group and have mass appeal.

FOOD & WINE What's your strategy for easy hors d'oeuvres?

INA GARTEN It's one of my rules not to cook for hors d'oeuvres. I don't want to be running into the kitchen to get the hot spanakopita out of the oven while my friends are having fun in the living room; I think it breaks up the party. So I'll do warm rosemary cashews or smoked salmon with brown bread and herb butter. Or I'll make pan-fried onion dip and serve it with Eli's Homemade Potato Chips—everyone likes an excuse to eat potato chips. Even just a plate of sliced English cucumbers and salami is great.

F&W What about a strategy for main-course foods?

IG I like dishes you can mainly prepare in advance, like Indonesian ginger chicken or turkey meat loaf. Or something easy like fillet of beef with Gorgonzola sauce. I can prepare most

of it in advance, and then right before serving, all I have to do is throw it in the oven for 25 or 30 minutes at a very high heat, and it's just perfect every time. It's the easiest, most elegant meal.

F&W What about that awkward and clunky plates-on-laps thing?

IG Just make sure that whatever you're serving doesn't require a knife. Make a chicken stew with biscuits, something that people can eat with just a fork. You don't want to be balancing a plate plus a knife and a fork.

F&W How do you feel about asking your guests to help you cook and serve?

IG I like parties that get the guests to participate in some way. The more they're involved, the more fun it is for everyone.

F&W How do you get non-cooks or shy guests to join in?

IG I had a New Year's Eve party once and someone asked to bring a teenage

>> | FEATURED RECIPES

1 | REAL MEATBALLS & SPAGHETTI

2 | PARMESAN ROASTED ASPARAGUS

3 | SCOTT'S SHORT RIBS

4 | SAFFRON RISOTTO WITH BUTTERNUT SQUASH

son, and I was thinking, oh, great, what am I gonna do with a teenage boy to get him involved? And then I thought: Empower him. Ask him to serve the wine. And he was fabulous. If you get everyone to participate in some small way, it makes them feel like they're on the A-Team.

F&W How do you foster conversation between guests who don't know each other at all?

IG I generally don't do place cards in advance if I don't know how everybody interacts. While we're having cocktails, I pick the two most talkative people and, if it's a rectangular table, I put them in the middle of the table facing each other. Then I put the least talkative people at the end. That keeps the energy of the party toward the middle. If you put the most talkative people at the ends of the table, then the party tends to break into two parts. Or, if it's a round table, I tend to put them opposite each other. I also avoid seating people boy-girl-boy-girl; instead I seat them boy-boy-girl-girl, so everyone's sitting between a boy and a girl. The boy-girl-boy alternative means that sometimes the guys wind up talking to each other over the girl; we've all had that experience.

F&W What do you bring when you're a guest at someone else's party?

IG Good stories and my sense of humor. Or maybe something I've made, like a lemon cake or a little bag of cookies. Of course, giving a bottle of Champagne is always appreciated.

the specifics

recipes	pages	photos	publisher	price
88	240	145 color photos	Clarkson Potter/Publishers	$35

credits

Barefoot Contessa Family Style: Easy Ideas and Recipes that Make Everyone Feel Like Family by Ina Garten, copyright © 2002 by Ina Garten. Photographs copyright ©2002 by Maura McEvoy. Jacket design by Marysarah Quinn. Used by permission of Clarkson Potter/Publishers, a division of Random House, Inc.

Real Meatballs & Spaghetti

SERVES 6

This is not something my mother made when I was growing up, so I had to do some research about spaghetti and meatballs. The best idea came from the famous New York Italian restaurant called Rao's: they add water to the meatballs, which keeps them moist and delicious. I may not be Italian, but this has definitely become a staple in my house.

f&w tip
Since there were quite a lot of extra meatballs, you can increase the amount of spaghetti or save the extra meatballs for a sub.

For the meatballs

½ pound ground veal

½ pound ground pork

1   pound ground beef

1   cup fresh white bread crumbs (4 slices, crusts removed)

¼ cup seasoned dry bread crumbs

2   tablespoons chopped fresh flat-leaf parsley

½ cup freshly grated Parmesan cheese

2   teaspoons kosher salt

½ teaspoon freshly ground black pepper

¼ teaspoon ground nutmeg

1   extra-large egg, beaten

Vegetable oil

Olive oil

For the sauce

1   tablespoon good olive oil

1   cup chopped yellow onion (1 onion)

1½ teaspoons minced garlic

½ cup good red wine, such as Chianti

1   28-ounce can crushed tomatoes, or plum tomatoes in puree, chopped

1   tablespoon chopped fresh flat-leaf parsley

1½ teaspoons kosher salt

½ teaspoon freshly ground black pepper

For serving

1½ pounds spaghetti, cooked according to package directions

Freshly grated Parmesan cheese

Place the ground meats, both bread crumbs, parsley, Parmesan, salt, pepper, nutmeg, egg, and ¾ cup warm water in a bowl. Combine very lightly with a fork. Using your hands, lightly form the mixture into 2-inch meatballs. You will have 14 to 16 meatballs.

Pour equal amounts of vegetable oil and olive oil into a large (12-inch) skillet to a depth of ¼ inch. Heat the oil. Very carefully, in batches, place the meatballs in the oil and brown them well on all sides over medium-low heat, turning carefully with a spatula or a fork. This should take about 10 minutes for each batch. Don't crowd the meatballs. Remove the meatballs to a plate covered with paper towels. Discard the oil but don't clean the pan.

For the sauce, heat the olive oil in the same pan. Add the onion and sauté over medium heat until translucent, 5 to 10 minutes. Add the garlic and cook for 1 more minute. Add the wine and cook on high heat, scraping up all the brown bits in the pan, until almost all the liquid evaporates, about 3 minutes. Stir in the tomatoes, parsley, salt, and pepper.

Return the meatballs to the sauce, cover, and simmer on the lowest heat for 25 to 30 minutes, until the meatballs are cooked through. Serve hot on cooked spaghetti and pass the grated Parmesan cheese.

NOTES When you cook spaghetti, don't use oil in the water; the sauce will stick better.

When the spaghetti is cooked, drain it in a colander. If you don't use it right away, run hot water over it and it will separate.

I use Pepperidge Farm sandwich white bread for fresh bread crumbs.

Parmesan Roasted Asparagus

SERVES 6

Italians often eat their vegetables as "antipasti," that is, before the main course. This is a very easy first course that I sometimes serve in the classic Italian way, topped with a single fried egg.

2½ pounds fresh asparagus (about 30 large)

2   tablespoons olive oil

½   teaspoon kosher salt

¼   teaspoon freshly ground black pepper

½   cup freshly grated Parmesan cheese

2   lemons cut in wedges, for serving

Preheat the oven to 400 degrees.

If the stalks of the asparagus are thick, peel the bottom half of each. Lay them in a single layer on a sheet pan and drizzle with olive oil. Sprinkle with salt and pepper. Roast for 15 to 20 minutes, until tender. Sprinkle with the Parmesan and return to the oven for another minute. Serve with lemon wedges.

NOTE I prefer thick asparagus to thin ones; they have much more flavor.

f&w tip
Definitely look for thicker spears, as thin ones will overcook easily. Also, instead of popping the asparagus back in the oven to melt the cheese, sprinkle it on as soon as the asparagus are out and it will melt on contact.

Scott's Short Ribs

SERVES 6

Scott Bieber is the wonderful chef at Eli's Manhattan restaurant in New York City. He cooks earthy food that brings out the essence of the ingredients, such as these short ribs. You can make them well in advance and reheat them before dinner.

6   beef short ribs, trimmed of fat

Kosher salt

Freshly ground black pepper

¼   cup good olive oil

1½ cups chopped onion (2 onions)

4   cups large-diced celery (6 large stalks)

2   carrots, peeled and large-diced

1   small fennel, fronds, stems, and core removed, large-diced

1   leek, cleaned and large-diced, white part only

3   garlic cloves, finely chopped

1   750-ml bottle burgundy or other dry red wine (see Note)

Fresh rosemary sprigs

Fresh thyme sprigs

6   cups beef stock

1   tablespoon brown sugar

Preheat the oven to 400 degrees. Place the short ribs on a sheet pan, sprinkle with salt and pepper, and roast for 15 minutes. Reduce the oven temperature to 300 degrees.

Meanwhile, heat the olive oil in a large Dutch oven and add the onion, celery, carrots, fennel, and leek and cook over medium-low heat for 20 minutes, stirring occasionally. Add the garlic and cook for another 2 minutes. Pour the wine over the vegetables, bring to a boil, and cook over high heat until the liquid is reduced

on garten's nightstand

Garten says, "I think specialty food stores often publish the best cookbooks because they've used the recipes over and over again. **Anna Pump,** the owner of Loaves and Fishes in Sagaponack, New York, is one of my favorite authors. I use *Nantucket Open-House Cookbook* and *Cold-Weather Cooking* from **Sarah Leah Chase,** who had a specialty food store in Nantucket. I also like *Cucina Simpatica* by **George Germon** and **Johanne Killeen** from Al Forno restaurant in Providence, and any book by **Patricia Wells.** I just love her sensibility, especially in *Bistro Cooking.*"

by half, about 10 minutes. Add 1 tablespoon salt and 1 teaspoon pepper. Tie the rosemary and thyme together with kitchen twine and add to the pot.

Place the roasted ribs on top of the vegetables in the Dutch oven and add the beef stock and brown sugar. Bring to a simmer over high heat. Cover the Dutch oven and bake for 2 hours or until the meat is very tender.

Carefully remove the short ribs from the pot and set aside. Discard the herbs and skim the excess fat. Cook the vegetables and sauce over medium heat for 20 minutes, until reduced. Put the ribs back into the pot and heat through. Serve with the vegetables and sauce.

NOTE I use a reasonably priced Côtes du Rhône wine.

Saffron Risotto with Butternut Squash

SERVES 4 TO 6

I used to avoid risotto because I thought you had to stand by the stove for hours, stirring—not exactly my style! But, I decided to give it a try and, instead, found a dish that's so delicious and cooks in 30 minutes. Test this first on your family and then when you have a party, you can invite your guests into the kitchen for drinks while everyone takes turns stirring the risotto.

1   butternut squash (2 pounds)

2   tablespoons olive oil

Kosher salt

Freshly ground black pepper

6   cups chicken stock, preferably homemade (recipe follows)

6   tablespoons (¾ stick) unsalted butter

2   ounces pancetta, diced

½   cup minced shallots (2 large)

1½ cups Arborio rice (10 ounces)

½   cup dry white wine

1   teaspoon saffron threads

1   cup freshly grated Parmesan cheese

Preheat the oven to 400 degrees.

Peel the butternut squash, remove the seeds, and cut it into ¾-inch cubes. You should have about 6 cups. Place the squash on a sheet pan and toss it with the olive oil, 1 teaspoon salt, and ½ teaspoon pepper. Roast for 25 to 30 minutes, tossing once, until very tender. Set aside.

Meanwhile, heat the chicken stock in a small covered saucepan. Leave it on low heat to simmer.

"I generally don't do place cards in advance if I don't know how everybody interacts. While we're having cocktails, I pick the two most talkative people and, if it's a rectangular table, I put them in the middle of the table facing each other."

In a heavy-bottomed pot or Dutch oven, melt the butter and sauté the pancetta and shallots on medium-low heat for 10 minutes, until the shallots are translucent but not browned. Add the rice and stir to coat the grains with butter. Add the wine and cook for 2 minutes. Add 2 full ladles of stock to the rice plus the saffron, 1 teaspoon salt, and ½ teaspoon pepper. Stir, and simmer until the stock is absorbed, 5 to 10 minutes. Continue to add the stock, 2 ladles at a time, stirring every few minutes. Each time, cook until the mixture seems a little dry, then add more stock. Continue until the rice is cooked through, but still al dente, about 30 minutes total. Off the heat, add the roasted squash cubes and Parmesan cheese. Mix well and serve.

NOTES Marcella Hazan advises that correct heat is important in making risotto. It should be "lively"; too high heat and the grains don't cook evenly, and too low heat will result in a gluey mess. It should cook in 30 minutes. After the first try, you'll get the idea.

Saffron is collected from the stamens of crocuses, which is why it's so expensive. Use the strands, not the powder.

Pancetta is Italian bacon. If you can't find it, use any good-quality bacon.

Chicken Stock

MAKES 6 QUARTS

3   5-pound roasting chickens

3   large yellow onions, unpeeled, quartered

6   carrots, unpeeled, halved

4   celery stalks with leaves, cut in thirds

4   parsnips, unpeeled, cut in half (optional)

20 sprigs fresh parsley

15 sprigs fresh thyme

20 sprigs fresh dill

1   head garlic, unpeeled, cut in half crosswise

2   tablespoons kosher salt

2   teaspoons whole black peppercorns

Place the chickens, onions, carrots, celery, parsnips, parsley, thyme, dill, garlic, and seasonings in a 16- to 20-quart stockpot. Add 7 quarts of water and bring to a boil. Simmer uncovered for 4 hours. Strain the entire contents of the pot through a colander and discard the solids. Chill the stock overnight. The next day, remove the surface fat. Use immediately or pack in containers and freeze for up to 3 months.

desserts 1-2-3

ROZANNE GOLD

about gold
Rozanne Gold, creator of the wildly successful 1-2-3 series of cookbooks, is a three-time winner of James Beard awards and a recipient of a 2002 International Association of Culinary Professionals' award. Gold is chef-director of the Joseph Baum & Michael Whiteman Company, international restaurant consultants best known for re-creating New York City's magical Rainbow Room and Windows on the World, destroyed on 9/11.

The idea of three-ingredient recipes is compelling, especially when many cookbook recipes seem to have 25 ingredients. Every recipe seems like a test: Can Gold really make a pineapple flan, for instance, with just sugar, eggs and pineapple juice? One of the many satisfactions here is seeing her pass the exam again and again.

FOOD & WINE Where and when did you first get the idea for the 1-2-3 series?
ROZANNE GOLD I had been a professional chef for 25 years, so I was aware of trends. I knew this was the direction cooking was going in. Some magazines weren't using the word "recipes" anymore—they preferred "food ideas."
F&W What are some of the challenges you faced while writing the series?
RG Of course the biggest challenge is that everything has to be made with three ingredients—and not everything should be! I don't cook like this every day, but it's a wonderful way to cut down on prep time, and it certainly cuts down on shopping. It's fun to put three ingredients on the counter and then see the "before" and "after"; sometimes the "after" is quite remarkable. The Gianduia Sandwich Cookies, for instance, were a complete accident: I once made peanut butter cookies with just peanut butter, sugar and an egg. I had some Nutella in the fridge, so I tried substituting Nutella for the peanut butter. When I added the egg to the Nutella it was a sticky mess, so I added some flour and rolled the dough into balls. And when I baked it, the dough kept its shape. These cookies are great because when you eat them, you can't tell what ingredients are in them. And the pineapple flan—I still don't understand why it works. Pineapple has this enzyme that breaks things down. But I added egg yolks and played with the proportions—there's no reason why it should hold together, but it does. And the flavor has tropical intensity.
F&W What challenges did you face specifically with the desserts book?
RG The baking was tricky. In some recipes I eliminated flour and instead

Desserts 1-2-3
Deliciously Simple Three-Ingredient Recipes

Rozanne Gold

>> | FEATURED RECIPES

1 | GIANDUIA SANDWICH COOKIES

2 | HAZELNUT ANGEL CAKE

3 | FRESH LIME MOUSSE

4 | PINEAPPLE FLAN

used ground nuts. And making ice creams that are seductive and luscious with only three ingredients is very hard. It's like a game—you have to think differently. If I have only three ingredients, how can I add an extra flavor dimension? With the strawberry ice cream, I did that by roasting the strawberries first.

F&W You don't include salt, pepper or water as any of your three ingredients. What one other ingredient do you wish you could have included "free" in your dessert recipes?

RG Sugar. And in the savory books it would have been olive oil.

F&W What's the secret to streamlining a ten-ingredient dessert into a three-ingredient one?

RG I don't take a master recipe and reduce it down. Rather, I take a master ingredient and work up. It's about building, not streamlining.

F&W Who has been the biggest influence on your cooking?

RG Jean-Georges Vongerichten. He's the master of restraint and one of the most innovative chefs ever. For a chef at that level he uses relatively few ingredients, but he gets so much with so little. He understands how to extract the maximum from a single note, ingredient or idea.

F&W What kind of culinary training have you had?

RG I was the first chef to New York City mayor Ed Koch when I was 24—that was 25 years ago. Then I became executive chef for all the Lord & Taylor department stores.

the specifics

recipes	pages	photos	publisher	price
131	176	37 color photos	Stewart, Tabori & Chang	$30

credits

Desserts 1-2-3: Deliciously Simple Three-Ingredient Recipes by Rozanne Gold. Text copyright © 2002 Rozanne Gold. Photographs copyright © 2002 Judd Pilossof.

Gianduia Sandwich Cookies

MAKES 18

"I don't take a master recipe and reduce it down. Rather, I take a master ingredient and work up. It's about building, not streamlining."

Be sure to use self-rising cake flour for these delectable sandwich cookies with their European schmear of creamy Nutella, a chocolate-hazelnut spread that also flavors the simple-to-make batter. *Gianduia* is the Italian name of a chocolate-hazelnut confection, and also is the name for that particular flavor combination.

1   cup Nutella

1   extra-large egg

1   cup self-rising cake flour, plus additional for dusting

Preheat oven to 375°F.

In bowl of an electric mixer, put ½ cup Nutella and the egg. Mix well. Slowly add 1 cup flour until a wet dough is formed. Dust a board with a little more flour and transfer dough to board. Knead gently, adding a little more flour if necessary. Dough will be sticky. Roll dough into 18 balls, flouring your hands as you go to make rolling easier, and place on parchment-lined baking sheet, several inches apart.

Bake 12 minutes. Let cool 10 minutes. Using a serrated knife, split cookies in half horizontally. Spread bottom with 1 teaspoon Nutella, then replace top, pressing firmly. Let cool completely. Store in a tightly covered tin.

Hazelnut Angel Cake

SERVES 8

This heavenly cake is made in an angel food cake pan. Finely ground hazelnuts take the place of flour, and the rest is based on simple technique. Using nuts with the skins on, and toasting them before grinding, intensifies their flavor.

7   ounces shelled chopped hazelnuts (about 1 ¾ cups)

1   cup confectioners' sugar

8   extra-large eggs

Preheat oven to 350°F.

Place nuts on a baking sheet and bake 6 to 8 minutes, until nuts are golden and lightly toasted. Shake pan several times to prevent burning. Remove from oven and let cool.

When cool, place nuts in bowl of a food processor with 2 tablespoons confectioners' sugar. Process until very fine and powdery. Set aside.

Separate eggs and place 6 egg yolks in bowl of an electric mixer with 2 tablespoons water. Beat on maximum speed, and after 1 minute add ½ cup confectioners' sugar. Continue to beat 3 to 4 minutes, until mixture is very thick and pale yellow. Gently fold ground nuts into mixture. Transfer to a large bowl.

Thoroughly clean mixing bowl, add 8 egg whites and a pinch of salt, then beat on medium speed. Continue beating and add ¼ cup confectioners' sugar. Beat until whites are glossy and stiff. With a flexible rubber spatula, carefully fold whites into nut mixture. Do not overmix.

Coat a 10-inch angel food cake pan with nonstick vegetable spray. Pour mixture into pan, smoothing top with spatula. Bake 45 minutes. Do not open oven door during baking.

Remove from oven and let cake cool in pan on a rack. When cool, remove cake from pan. Sprinkle with remaining 2 tablespoons confectioners' sugar pushed through a sieve.

Fresh Lime Mousse

SERVES 4

Most desserts lull your senses, but this sassy mousse, with its bracing acidity, actually revs up your tastebuds. I love serving this after a heavy dinner because it gets my guests talking again.

5   **large limes**

6   **extra-large eggs**

½   **cup plus 3 tablespoons sugar**

Grate the rind of enough limes to get 1 tablespoon zest. Cut limes in half and squeeze to get ½ cup juice.

Separate egg yolks from egg whites, saving 2 egg whites. (Reserve remaining whites for another use.) Place yolks in a medium metal bowl and stir in ½ cup sugar. Place over a pot of boiling water to create a "double boiler," making sure the bottom of the bowl does not touch the water. Using a wire whisk, whisk vigorously while cooking eggs and sugar for 1 minute. Slowly add lime juice and 2 teaspoons zest and continue to cook 6 to 8 minutes, whisking constantly, until the mixture is the texture of thick pudding. Remove from heat and let cool 5 minutes, whisking frequently.

Place 2 egg whites in bowl of an electric mixer with 3 tablespoons sugar and a pinch of salt. Beat until very stiff and glossy. Fold beaten whites into lime mixture. Stir gently until smooth.

Spoon mousse into 4 wine glasses. Chill until very cold. Sprinkle with remaining lime zest. Best served the day it is made.

Pineapple Flan

SERVES 5

This is a dessert held together by the commitment of just a few ingredients with no goal other than to soothe and beguile. It is a defiant amalgam of highly acidic pineapple juice, sugar, and eggs that results in a wobbly block of tropical tastes. Also delicious made with mango or guava nectar.

1 cup sugar

8 extra-large eggs

2 cups unsweetened pineapple juice

Preheat oven to 350°F.

In a small nonstick skillet put ½ cup sugar. Cook over medium-high heat, stirring constantly with a wooden spoon, until sugar melts completely into a dark liquid caramel, about 3 minutes. Coat the insides of 5 custard cups or small ramekins with vegetable cooking spray. Immediately divide the caramel among the cups or ramekins to coat the bottom of each.

Separate the yolks and whites of 4 eggs. (Reserve whites for another use. Or make tiny meringues from whites and additional sugar to serve with the flan.) In the bowl of an electric mixer place 4 egg yolks, 4 whole eggs, and ½ cup sugar. Beat for 1 minute, until eggs and sugar are well blended.

Slowly add pineapple juice, little by little, and continue to mix until juice is incorporated. Do not let the mixture become too frothy. With a ladle, divide mixture evenly among the custard cups.

Place custard cups in a large, deep pan. Create a water bath by adding boiling water to the pan so that the water level comes two-thirds up the sides of the cups. Carefully place in the oven. Bake 40 to 45 minutes, until just set. Remove cups from water bath. Let cool and refrigerate until very cold, preferably overnight.

When ready to serve, carefully unmold cups onto flat dessert plates, loosening the sides with a small sharp knife if necessary. Caramel will coat the top and sides of the flan. Serve immediately.

on gold's nightstand
Rozanne Gold thinks the design, photos and food in *The Natural Cuisine of Georges Blanc* have integrity and restraint. *The Dean & DeLuca Cookbook*, by **David Rosengarten** with **Joel Dean** and **Giorgio DeLuca**, is her source for information about an unusual ingredient or dish. And she loves *The Flavor of Italy* and *The Flavor of France*, both by **Narcissa** and **Narcisse Chamberlain**, because she says there are few books that are more evocative of the places they represent.

saffron shores

JOYCE GOLDSTEIN

about goldstein

Joyce Goldstein is a chef, author, teacher and expert on the cooking of the Mediterranean. She has written 18 books, including *Enoteca*, *Sephardic Flavors* and *Cucina Ebraica*. She lives in San Francisco.

As much a history book as a cookbook, *Saffron Shores* conveys on every page Joyce Goldstein's passion for Jewish cooking of the southern Mediterranean. We found the recipes delightful and we loved her menu suggestions for the Jewish holidays. We were also happy to see that, with only a few exceptions, most of the recipes can be prepared using supermarket ingredients.

FOOD & WINE What inspired you to write this book?

JOYCE GOLDSTEIN I grew up in Brooklyn, in a family of Jews who came from Russia and never talked about it again. So I didn't have much of a heritage to connect with. Writing this cookbook was a way to say, "Well, these are my people." Growing up I ate only Ashkenazic food (from the Jews of Eastern and Central Europe), but I discovered that the Sephardic cooking of the Mediterranean Jews is fabulous—better, more interesting and better for you. I've been involved with Mediterranean cooking for a long time, so focusing on the cuisine of the Mediterranean Jews was a natural extension.

F&W What ingredients are the foundation of Mediterranean Jewish cuisine?

JG You'll find basically the same ingredients that you'd find all over the Mediterranean—eggplants, peppers, various grains, greens, olives. The use of saffron is very interesting to me.

F&W Any spices beyond saffron?

JG That depends on the country. Italian Jewish food uses salt, pepper and nutmeg. It's very mild. You get into Turkey and then there's a little allspice and a little cinnamon and the range of herbs gets broader—you get into dill. By the time you reach North Africa you'll find every spice in the box as well as dates, pomegranates and ingredients like that. The use of nuts to thicken sauces is also very Arabic. But, really, these cuisines all use essentially the same ingredients; the main differences have to do with money. If you're poor you'll season your dishes with turmeric, and if you're

>> FEATURED RECIPES

1 TUNISIAN FRIED PASTRIES WITH EGG

2 TUNA WITH TOMATOES

3 TUNISIAN FISH BALL TAGINE

4 SYRIAN RICE WITH VERMICELLI

5 CUMIN-FLAVORED MEATBALLS WITH ONION JAM AND SPICY TOMATO SAUCE

wealthier you'll use saffron.

F&W How does the Jewish cuisine of these regions differ from the non-Jewish cuisine?

JG In a lot of Sephardic cooking, lemon is the signature ingredient. I mean it's on *everything*—and I have a very tart mouth, so this speaks to me strongly.

F&W What's the best way to stock the Mediterranean Jewish pantry?

JG You should always have olives and olive oil. You should always have a starch—pasta or couscous. Canned tuna and dried beans are good things to have on hand.

F&W What about desserts?

JG This cuisine has a real sweet tooth, from the Arabic influence. You'll find lots of raisins, dried apricots—all kinds of dried fruit. Plus almond-paste-y things and lots of syrups.

F&W Do you need any special equipment to make these recipes?

JG Not at all; you can make everything with what you already have at home. You don't need a tagine to make a stew; you can use a Le Creuset casserole, or even a Crock-Pot. You don't have to have a couscousière to make couscous; you can make it in a baking pan and then steam it on top of a colander.

F&W What parts of *Saffron Shores* do you feel the proudest of?

JG I think the little pastries are marvelous and the vegetable section is immense and mind-boggling. The fish recipes are outstanding. And a lot of the stews are good and practical—you can make one on the weekend and just reheat it during the week.

the specifics

recipes	pages	photos	publisher	price
99	192	36 color photos	Chronicle Books	$35

credits

Saffron Shores: Jewish Cooking of the Southern Mediterranean by Joyce Goldstein. Photographs by Leigh Beisch. Copyright © 2002. Published in the U.S. by Chronicle Books LLC, San Francisco. Used with permission. Visit www.chroniclebooks.com.

Tunisian Fried Pastries with Egg

Briks à l'Oeuf

SERVES 8

The small savory pastry called *bestel* or *briouat* in Morocco is called *brik* in Tunisia. In Algeria, they are called *burak*. *Briks* are made with sheets of *malsouka,* the Tunisian name for *ouarka,* or *feuilles de brik,* and they are deep-fried. To make the *brik,* you can use filo, but egg roll wrappers work like a dream. *Briks* may be filled with cooked meat, poultry, canned tuna, or mashed potatoes, usually with a whole egg nested on top of the filling and the pastry carefully sealed without breaking the egg. The meat version is usually lamb seasoned with onions, cumin, paprika, cayenne pepper, and parsley or cilantro. Other fillings are seasoned mashed potatoes or cooked chicken with cooked potatoes and onions. Egg-filled *briks* must be eaten very carefully if you don't want to drip egg yolk on your shirt.

At an American Institute of Wine and Food dinner I fried one hundred egg-filled *briks,* for Tunisian chef Abderrazak Haouari. In truth, we were not supposed to add the raw eggs because everyone was dressed up, but Haouari insisted that we had to do it the right way. We received no complaints and no dry cleaning bills.

1   tablespoon oil, plus more for deep-frying

1   onion, chopped

12 ounces canned tuna, drained and mashed

2   tablespoons chopped fresh flat-leaf parsley

1 or 2 tablespoons fresh lemon juice

Salt and freshly ground black pepper to taste

Pinch of cayenne pepper or harissa (recipe follows)

2   tablespoons capers, rinsed and chopped

8   sheets square egg roll wrappers or filo dough

8   small eggs

1   egg white, lightly beaten

In a medium sauté pan or skillet, heat the 1 tablespoon oil over medium heat. Sauté the onion until soft, about 10 minutes. Let cool slightly and mix with the tuna. Add the parsley, lemon juice, salt, pepper, and cayenne or harissa and capers.

variations
Moroccan Tuna Filling
(a recipe from *Fleur de safran*) Combine 12 ounces canned tuna with ¼ cup chopped fresh flat-leaf parsley, 3 diced boiled potatoes, 2 chopped hard-cooked eggs, 1 minced clove garlic, salt and pepper to taste, and a pinch of ground mace.

Potato Filling
Boil 2 large and cubed potatoes until soft and mash them. Add 1 finely chopped onion and 3 minced cloves garlic that have been sautéed in 2 tablespoons olive oil until tender. Season with 1 teaspoon salt, ½ teaspoon freshly ground black pepper, ¼ cup chopped fresh flat-leaf parsley, and 2 tablespoons chopped fresh coriander (cilantro). Stir in 1 beaten egg. Capers are an optional addition.

f&w tip

Harissa is classic Tunisian hot sauce that is often served as a condiment with couscous. Since the recipe just calls for a pinch of it, use the leftovers to spice up soups and stews. You can also buy it premade at Middle Eastern markets and some supermarkets.

If using egg roll wrappers, place equal parts of filling on each one, spoon a depression into the filling, and break an egg into each depression. Brush the edges of the wrapper with egg white and fold over to make a ½-inch rim. If using filo, brush each sheet with oil, place the filling in the middle, then fold in half, leaving 1 inch on either side. Brush the edges with egg white. Fold in the left side, then the right, then fold up the bottom third to cover.

In a deep saucepan or a wok, heat 3 inches of oil to 365 degrees F. Deep-fry the *briks* in batches until crisp and golden. Using a slotted spoon or wire skimmer, transfer to paper towels to drain. Serve hot and eat carefully.

Harissa

MAKES ABOUT 1 CUP

Harissa is a hot pepper sauce that can be made with fresh, roasted, or dried peppers. You may purchase it in paste form in small jars or tubes, but it is easy to make. To serve it as a sauce, thin it with olive oil and a little lemon juice. This recipe was given to me by Baroui Karoui, a visiting Tunisian chef who cooked with me at Square One restaurant during a Mediterranean food conference sponsored by the American Institute of Wine and Food.

4 large red bell peppers or pimientos, seeded, deribbed, and cut into pieces

3 large cloves garlic, minced

1 tablespoon ground coriander

1 tablespoon caraway seeds, toasted and ground

1½ to 2 teaspoons cayenne pepper

1 teaspoon salt

Extra-virgin olive oil as needed

In a meat grinder, food processor, or blender, grind or puree the bell peppers or pimientos. Strain, pressing on the solids with the back of a large spoon. You should have about ¾ cup puree. Stir in the garlic, spices, and salt. Add oil for spoonability.

NOTE You can also make this harissa with roasted red bell peppers and roasted fresh hot red peppers.

Tuna with Tomatoes

Thon à la Tomate

SERVES 4

This Moroccan recipe for tuna could also be prepared with cod, snapper, or another firm white fish. Leone Jaffin's Algerian version omits preserved lemon and adds 2 small hot red peppers and a few rinsed capers. She fries the fish briefly to color it, then braises it covered with the sauce and serves the fish with steamed potatoes. Keep in mind that in the Mediterranean, tuna is not served rare; all recipes using this meaty fish cook it until opaque throughout.

4   thick 6-ounce slices tuna or another firm fish

⅓   cup *chermoula* (recipe follows), or salt and fresh lemon juice
    for sprinkling

3   cups canned chopped tomatoes with juice

2   cloves garlic, minced

¼   cup chopped fresh flat-leaf parsley

Peel of 1 preserved lemon (recipe follows), cut into thin slivers

¼   teaspoon cayenne pepper, or to taste

12 oil-cured black olives (optional)

2   tablespoons capers, rinsed (optional)

If you have time, put the fish in a large casserole, coat it with the *chermoula*, cover, and refrigerate for 4 hours. This step may be omitted, but it adds a lot of flavor to the fish. If you are pressed for time, just sprinkle fish with salt and lemon juice and marinate at room temperature for a half hour.

Put the tomatoes in a medium saucepan and cook over medium heat, stirring often, until they have been reduced to a thick puree, adding the garlic during the last few minutes. Stir in the parsley, lemon peel, and cayenne, and olives and capers, if using. Simmer for 5 minutes.

Preheat the oven to 400 degrees F. Remove the fish from the refrigerator. Place fish in an oiled baking dish and cover with tomato sauce. Cover the dish with aluminum foil and bake until the fish is opaque throughout, about 20 minutes. Serve hot or cold.

variation

Dip the slices of tuna in flour and fry quickly in oil until browned. Pour the tomato sauce over, cover, and braise over low heat until the fish is opaque throughout, about 20 minutes.

Chermoula

(from Vivianne and Nina Moryoussef)

"I grew up in Brooklyn, in a family of Jews who came from Russia and never talked about it again. So I didn't have much of a heritage to connect with. Writing this cookbook was a way to say, 'Well, these are my people.'"

Chermoula is the classic Moroccan marinade for fish. Whether you plan to bake, grill, fry, or steam fish, marinating it in *chermoula* will only improve its flavor. There are many versions of *chermoula*.

1 onion, finely chopped or grated

6 cloves garlic, minced

2 teaspoons ground cumin

1 teaspoon sweet paprika

½ teaspoon saffron threads, crushed and mixed with 2 tablespoons hot water

½ cup chopped fresh flat-leaf parsley

½ cup chopped fresh coriander (cilantro)

6 tablespoons olive oil

6 tablespoons fresh lemon juice

Kosher salt and freshly ground black pepper to taste

To make the *chermoula,* in a mixing bowl, combine all the ingredients and mix to blend.

Preserved Lemons

Citrons Confits

While you can use fresh lemons in many North African recipes, preserved lemons add a distinctive note to any dish. Unique in flavor and texture, they are a signature condiment in the North African kitchen. Preserved lemons must be prepared 3 to 4 weeks before using. Keep a constant supply in your pantry and you'll probably find a way to use them even in dishes that are not North African in inspiration. I like them in vinaigrettes and as an addition to many fish recipes and vegetable dishes.

16 lemons (about 4 pounds), scrubbed

Kosher salt as needed

Fresh lemon juice as needed

Put the lemons in a nonaluminum container and cover with cold water. (If you have time, soak them for 3 days, changing the water at least once a day. If not, soak for at least a few hours.) Drain the lemons and dry them well. Cut them into lengthwise quarters with a sharp knife but do not cut through the bottom of the lemon. Spoon 1 heaping tablespoonful salt into the center of each lemon. Put 1 heaping tablespoon salt into the bottom of each of 4 hot, sterilized pint jars and add the salted lemons, packing them in tightly. Cover with fresh lemon juice.

Seal the jars. Store in a dry place for 3 to 4 weeks before using, turning the jars upside down and right-side up periodically the first few days. Do not be alarmed if a white film forms on the lemons; it will wash off. Refrigerate after opening. Unopened jars will keep for up to 1 year.

To use the lemons, rinse well under running water. Squeeze the juice from the lemon, remove the pulp, and discard it. Cut the peel into thin slivers or fine dice.

variation
Alternative Quick Brine
Dissolve ⅓ cup kosher salt in 1 cup boiling water. Put 4 lemons (quartered, as at left) in a hot, sterilized pint jar. Pour the brine over them and seal. Store in the pantry for 2 weeks, turning occasionally.

Tunisian Fish Ball Tagine

Tagine Kefta mn Hoot, or *Boulettes de Poisson*

SERVES 6 TO 8

In Spain, Sephardic fish balls, called *albondigas,* were seasoned simply with parsley and maybe a little cheese, then fried and served with tomato sauce. Tunisian Jewish fish balls are more highly seasoned. To hold the fish together, most cooks use fresh bread crumbs, but Simy Danan uses only dry crumbs and some cooked rice. During Passover, matzoh meal is used. The fish balls may be fried or poached, then simmered in fish broth flavored with tomato puree, and served with couscous. Some recipes use chopped tomatoes and peppers in the broth.

For the fish balls

1½ pounds mild white fish, such as cod, sole, snapper, or bass

2 tablespoons chopped fresh flat-leaf parsley

2 tablespoons chopped fresh coriander (cilantro)

3 cloves garlic, minced

2 onions, finely chopped

1½ teaspoons kosher salt

½ teaspoon harissa (see p. 134)

2 teaspoons ground cumin

4 slices stale bread, crusts removed, soaked in water and squeezed dry, or 1½ cups fresh bread crumbs

1 egg, beaten

Olive oil for frying

For the tomato sauce

3 tablespoons olive oil

2 cloves garlic, minced

6 tablespoons tomato puree, or 4 tomatoes, chopped

2 cups fish broth or water

Salt and freshly ground black pepper to taste

Couscous for serving

Chopped fresh flat-leaf parsley for garnish

variation

Instead of frying the fish balls, Hélène Gans Perez, in her book *Marrakech la rouge,* steams them atop a bed of tomatoes. The fish balls are seasoned with parsley, cinnamon, salt, and pepper, but have no bread filler. To cook them her way, sauté 3 pounds peeled, seeded, and chopped tomatoes in 3 tablespoons peanut oil, sprinkle them with salt, and simmer for 15 minutes. Drain off the excess liquid, as you want the mixture to be fairly thick. Place the fish balls on top of the tomatoes, cover the pan, and simmer for 20 minutes.

**on goldstein's
nightstand**
"I have a library of 4,000
cookbooks, so naming a
favorite isn't easy,"
Goldstein says. "When I was
writing *Saffron Shores*,
**Claudia Roden's *The Book
of Jewish Food*** was
wonderful to look at."
Goldstein was also inspired
by author **Paula Wolfert,**
who has written prolifically
about the cuisines
of the Mediterranean.

To make the fish balls, bone and finely chop the fish. In a food processor or large bowl, combine the fish with all the remaining ingredients except the egg and oil. Mix well. Add the egg and mix until smooth. Dipping a spoon and your fingers in cold water, remove a sample of fish paste and roll into a ball. Fry in a little olive oil and taste and adjust the seasoning. Form the rest of the fish paste into 1-inch balls. Either fry now, or place on a baking sheet lined with parchment paper and refrigerate for up to 3 hours.

In a large sauté pan or skillet, heat ½ inch oil over medium-high heat and fry a few fish balls at a time until lightly browned. Using a slotted spoon, transfer to paper towels to drain.

To make the tomato sauce, in a large saucepan, heat the oil over medium heat. Add all the remaining ingredients and bring to a boil. Reduce heat to a simmer. Add the fish balls and simmer for 15 minutes. Serve over couscous, sprinkled with parsley.

NOTE This dish can be made more elaborate by adding cooked vegetables such as fennel, peppers, carrots, turnips, zucchini, and/or pumpkin.

Syrian Rice with Vermicelli

Roz me Shareeyeh

SERVES 4 TO 6

Rice and noodles are a popular side dish in most of the Arab countries. If serving this at a meat meal, use oil and water or meat or poultry broth. If served at a dairy meal, you may use butter and water or vegetable broth.

1½ cups basmati rice

2   tablespoons unsalted butter or olive oil

½   cup broken fideos or vermicelli noodles (1-inch pieces)

3   cups water or broth

1   teaspoon salt

Rinse and drain the rice in a fine-mesh sieve.

In a medium saucepan, melt the butter or heat the oil over medium heat and sauté the noodles, stirring often, until golden brown. Stir in the rice until all the grains are coated. Add the water or broth and salt. Bring to a boil and cook until the water has been partly absorbed and little holes appear in the top of the rice. Cover, reduce heat to a simmer, and cook until the rice is tender, about 20 minutes.

f&w tip

We loved this simple dish and thought it was a great way to jazz up plain rice. We used half butter and half olive oil and the result was perfect. Be careful to watch the noodles, as they can brown really quickly in the saucepan.

Cumin-Flavored Meatballs with Onion Jam and Spicy Tomato Sauce

Kefta de Viande au Cumin et Confiture d'Oignon et Sauce aux Tomates

SERVES 4

variations

Moroccan Variation

Combine 1 pound ground beef with 1 bunch chopped stemmed fresh coriander, (cilantro), 3 chopped fresh mint leaves, 1 teaspoon *each* ground cumin and sweet paprika, 1½ teaspoons salt, and ½ teaspoon freshly ground black pepper. Knead well, form into balls, and flatten. Grill or fry until golden brown. Serve with harissa (see p. 134).

Syrian Variation

Combine 1 pound ground beef, ½ cup finely chopped onion, 6 tablespoons minced fresh flat-leaf parsley, 4 eggs, ¼ cup dry bread crumbs, 1½ teaspoons salt, 1 teaspoon ground allspice, ½ teaspoon ground cinnamon, and ½ teaspoon freshly ground black pepper. Form into small patties, fry, and serve with pita bread and spicy tomato sauce.

Hélène Gans Perez in *Marrakech la rouge* serves meatballs with onion confiture. In *Saveurs de mon enfance*, a few mint leaves are added to the meat mixture, and a bit less cumin. Meatballs are sometimes called *boundigas*, echoing the Spanish word *albondigas*. *Kefta* can be round or flat in shape. Although there is a temptation to treat them as burgers and serve them rare, in the kosher kitchen these are well cooked. Moroccan *kefta* that are to be grilled do not have bread crumbs as a binder; only those sautéed as meatballs, or *boulettes*, will have such an addition.

1   **pound ground beef**

2 to 3 **tablespoons olive oil**

3   **cloves garlic, minced**

2   **tablespoons chopped fresh flat-leaf parsley**

2   **tablespoons chopped fresh coriander (cilantro)**

1   **tablespoon ground cumin**

¼   **teaspoon cayenne pepper**

1½ **teaspoons salt**

½   **teaspoon freshly ground black pepper**

Onion jam (recipe follows)

Spicy tomato sauce (recipe follows)

Light a fire in a charcoal grill. (You may also use a skillet heated over medium-high heat.)

In a medium bowl, combine all the ingredients except the jam and sauce. Mix well. Form into 16 oval meatballs wrapped around skewers, or into 8 oval patties. Grill or cook in oil on a hot pan until browned on all sides. Serve with onion jam and tomato sauce.

Onion Jam
Confiture d'Oignons

MAKES 2½ TO 3 CUPS

Some onion jams are seasoned
with a mixture of sweet spices such as
ginger, mace, nutmeg, cinnamon,
and cloves, or *ras al hanout,* but this
simpler version is seasoned only with
cinnamon and sugar.

3 tablespoons olive oil

3 pounds onions, cut into
   half-round slices or chopped

1 tablespoon ground cinnamon

¼ cup sugar or honey

1 teaspoon salt

In a large sauté pan or skillet, heat
the oil over medium heat. Add the
onions and cook, stirring often, until
very soft and golden, about 15
minutes. Add the remaining ingredients,
reduce heat to low, and cook and stir
until the onions are dark brown,
aromatic, and the consistency of jam,
35 to 45 minutes. Serve warm. Keeps
in the refrigerator for about 1 week.

Spicy Tomato Sauce
Sauce aux Tomates

MAKES ABOUT 1¾ CUPS

¼ cup raisins, plumped in
   hot water to cover for
   15 minutes, not drained

1½ cups tomato puree

1 to 2 cloves garlic

1 tablespoon olive oil

1 tablespoon fresh lemon juice

½ teaspoon cayenne pepper

Pinch of ground cinnamon

In a blender or food processor, combine
all the ingredients and puree. Transfer
to a small saucepan and simmer for
20 minutes until thickened. Serve warm
or at room temperature. Store, covered,
in the refrigerator for up to 5 days.

mediterranean street food

ANISSA HELOU

about helou

Anissa Helou was born in Lebanon and currently lives in London, where she regularly appears on British television and radio and writes about food for the *Financial Times*. Helou is the author of *Café Morocco* and *Lebanese Cuisine;* the latter was a finalist for Britain's André Simon Award.

Anissa Helou seemingly sampled every tea cart, sandwich stand and street-food stall in the Mediterranean from Athens to Beirut to Marrakesh for this exotic book. We'd recommend it to people who like to cook as a hobby; its recipes are the kind you'll want to experiment with when you have time to explore.

FOOD & WINE What are some of the staple ingredients of Mediterranean street food?

ANISSA HELOU Fresh herbs are essential, as are olive oil, bread (or ingredients for making bread), vegetables, tahini, lemons and fresh fruit for juices.

F&W Are there any safety rules for eating street food?

AH You should look at the vendor's cart to see if it's clean and inspires confidence, and you should really always travel with cutlery and straws. Most of the time I forget and just have to take my chances.

F&W How has Mediterranean street food changed since you were growing up in Lebanon?

AH Things have been modernized, from wooden carts to stainless steel carts. Instead of charcoal, vendors use gas burners. On the other hand, you can still find a very old cart next to a modern

one. Certain aspects of the cultures are still very improvised and primitive.

F&W How does Mediterranean street food differ from American street food? How is it different from home cooking?

AH Mediterranean street food is meant to be eaten immediately. It's fresh and fast and still very healthy. Street food in America is typically very greasy, fatty or starchy. Eating Mediterranean street food won't make you feel like you've done something wrong.

F&W What American ingredients can substitute for traditional ingredients, and what doesn't cut it?

AH The most important thing to consider when you're looking for a substitute is that the taste and the texture should be very close to what you're replacing. Take tahini: You cannot use sesame oil instead. Not only will the taste differ, but the action of the oil will be quite different.

>> | FEATURED RECIPES

1 MOROCCAN FLAT BREAD

2 CHICKPEA AND LAMB SOUP

3 "RED" RICE CROQUETTES

4 CHICKPEA FRITTERS

If you can't find an ingredient, it might be better to forget about it altogether, if possible, than to substitute something that is going to change the dish significantly.

F&W What's your favorite street food?

AH I love sandwiches. In Genoa I once went to every single panini bar in the old town to see which ones were good. I also love fruit juices. I never tire of stopping at different juice bars.

F&W Can you talk about the basic breads from each of the cultures that you focus on?

AH Lebanon, Syria and Israel favor pita; Greece and Turkey have the pita without the pocket, a spongy flat bread that is usually rolled around meat. Bread is thicker in Morocco. People cut it in the middle to make a pocket or just hollow it out. In Italy you have a variety of breads, like focaccia or ciabatta. France has the baguette. Spain doesn't have sandwiches, really, but their bread is like a thicker baguette. In Tunisia you have a very fat French baguette or a flat pancake-type bread.

F&W Who was your inspiration?

AH My mother is an amazing cook. She, my grandmother, my aunt and I were always in the kitchen. If we went to my aunt's house in Syria, she was always baking the bread or milking the cows or making the butter.

F&W Have you ever tried to set up shop on the street?

AH Not yet, but if I did I'd have to indulge my sweet tooth with either a juice stand or omelets or pancakes on the griddle.

the specifics

recipes	pages	photos	publisher	price
134	304	79 black-and-white photos	HarperCollins Publishers	$29.95

credits

Moroccan Flat Bread

R'ghäyef

SERVES 4

> **"I love sandwiches. In Genoa I once went to every single panini bar in the old town to see which ones were good."**

It is not often that you see women cooking on the street in North Africa unless they are making this bread. They stand behind large flat griddles on which they cook the bread, flattening it further with their fingers, not seeming to mind the heat. Some occasionally dip their fingers in a small bowl of oil to drizzle on the bread while it is cooking—this slightly greasier version is definitely better. My Algerian food shop in London has a very similar version to r'ghäyef, which they call m'arek or m'hajjib. Theirs is larger and has a spicier filling. In Tunisia there is another, similar bread, m'lawi, which is left plain.

For the dough

¼ teaspoon active dry yeast

1 cup unbleached all-purpose flour

½ teaspoon salt, plus more for the filling

For the filling

1 medium onion, very finely chopped

¼ cup finely chopped flat-leaf parsley

3 tablespoons unsalted butter, softened, plus more for greasing

½ teaspoon ground cumin

1 teaspoon paprika

⅛ teaspoon crushed red pepper flakes

1. Stir the yeast into a scant ½ cup tepid water and leave for about 5 minutes.

2. Sift the flour into a large mixing bowl. Add the salt and yeast water, gradually working it in, until the dough is slightly wetter than that for bread. Knead with your hands for 10 minutes, or until completely smooth and pliable.

3. Put all the filling ingredients in a mixing bowl, add salt to taste, and mix together well.

4. Smear your work surface and hands with butter and divide the dough into 4 equal portions. Flatten 1 portion with your fingers into a very thin square, stretching it as you finish—be careful not to tear it. Spread a quarter of the filling over one half and fold the plain side over. Fold again to form a square. Flatten as thin as possible with your fingers.

5. Grease a large nonstick frying pan with a little butter and place over medium-high heat. Place the folded dough in the pan and cook for 3–4 minutes on each side, or until lightly golden all over. Remove and place on parchment paper. Repeat the procedure to make the rest of the breads, buttering your hands, work surface, and pan before making each one. Serve hot or warm.

Chickpea and Lamb Soup

Harira

SERVES **6**

There are several places in the world where street food is particularly enticing—among them Singapore, Istanbul, and Marrakesh. The last is one of my favorites, especially at Jame' el Fna, a huge square at the entrance of the medina that every day undergoes a magical change. During the day the place is nearly empty, except for a few juice and nut sellers and Berber ladies wanting to decorate your hands with intricate patterns in henna (a natural dye). However, as the day draws to an end, a horde of people descends on the square. They have come for the evening's entertainment: ambulant cooks who every night set up their trestle tables, benches, and makeshift kitchens in a huge rectangular formation and street entertainers who amuse the crowds with snake charming, storytelling, dancing, magic healing, and other diversions. The cooks are grouped by specialty: the soup stalls at one end, the snail ones at another, and the barbecue and various other food stalls in between.

The soup corner is instantly recognizable by the small plates of dates neatly arranged on the tables. They accompany harira, Morocco's national soup and the first nourishment Moroccans take when they break their fast during Ramadan. Throughout that time, the dates are replaced by chbakkiyah (a sweet pastry). The sweetness of the date or chbakkiyah accompaniment provides a good foil to the slightly tart soup.

⅓ cup dried chickpeas, soaked overnight in plenty of water
  with ½ teaspoon baking soda

7 ounces lean lamb, diced into small cubes (about 1 cup)

1 medium onion, thinly sliced

⅓ cup chopped flat-leaf parsley

Pinch saffron threads

¼ teaspoon ground ginger

¾ teaspoon finely ground black pepper

1 14-ounce can peeled tomatoes, coarsely chopped

2 tablespoons unsalted butter

¼ cup broken vermicelli

⅓ cup chopped cilantro

¾ tablespoon tomato paste

Juice of 1 lemon, or more to taste

3–4 tablespoons unbleached all-purpose flour

Salt

1. Drain and rinse the chickpeas. Spread them on a clean cloth. Cover them with another cloth and, with a rolling pin, crush them lightly to split them in half and loosen their skins. Put them in a bowl of water and stir with your hands until the skins float to the surface. Skim off the skins, add more water, and repeat the process a few times until you have discarded all the skins.

2. Put the drained chickpeas in a large saucepan. Add the lamb, onion, parsley, spices, tomatoes with their juice, and 2 quarts water. Bring to a boil over medium-high heat. Drop in the butter, cover, and let boil for 1 hour.

3. Stir in the vermicelli, cilantro, tomato paste, and lemon juice and reduce the heat to low.

4. Mix the flour with ⅔ cup water and dribble the mixture into the soup, stirring constantly to prevent lumps from forming. The soup should thicken to a velvety consistency. Add salt to taste and simmer for a couple more minutes, or until the vermicelli is cooked. Taste and adjust the seasoning if necessary. Serve very hot.

on helou's nightstand
"*Nevin Halici's Turkish Cookbook* is my guide for anything Turkish," Helou says. "Her recipes are brilliant and her introduction about Turkish food rituals and traditions is incredibly informative." Her other two favorites are in French only. "*Zette Guinaudeau-Franc's Les Secrets des Cuisines en Terre Marocaine* is a bible for anyone interested in Moroccan food and cookery. And *La Bonne Cuisine de Mme. E. Saint-Ange* is my resource for French home cooking. Her recipes are still indispensable, three-quarters of a century after the book was first published."

"Red" Rice Croquettes

Arancini (or Arancine) al Ragù

SERVES 6 TO 8

f&w tip
Make sure to taste the rice for seasoning before you roll the arancini. Once the arancini have been fried, drain them on paper towels to remove some of the excess oil, then serve them hot.

Arancini (or arancine, depending on whether you consider them male or female!) are a common staple of Sicilian bars and fry shops. If you travel to Sicily by ferry across the straits of Messina, arancini will be your first taste of the island—they are a fixture on the ferry's bar menu. Once there, you will see them everywhere: rossi (red), filled with ragù (meat sauce), or bianchi (white) when the filling is simply butter and cheese.

Commercial arancini are shaped bigger than those made at home, and often they are not as good. A friend of mine told me of a recent scandal when an arancini supplier was found to be using pet food instead of ragù. Since I heard that story, I've stayed away from store-bought "red" arancini.

Some people cook the rice like a risotto, while others add all the water in one go and, when the rice is done, mix in the cheese and eggs. I find the latter method easier, and I learned from a friend to add a little saffron, both for color and taste. Arancini keep well for a day but it is better not to refrigerate them unless the weather is very hot. Preheat your oven to 400 degrees just before you want to serve them, and put the arancini in to heat for 15–20 minutes.

For the ragù

2   tablespoons extra-virgin olive oil

1   small onion, very finely chopped

1   celery stalk from the heart, diced very small

1   clove garlic, very finely chopped

5   ounces lean ground beef (about ¾ cup)

1   14-ounce can peeled tomatoes, drained and finely chopped

1   teaspoon estrattu (Sicilian sun-dried tomato paste) or,
    if not available, 2 teaspoons tomato paste

¼   teaspoon crushed red pepper flakes

½   cup frozen petits pois, thawed in boiling water and drained

Salt

Freshly ground black pepper

To make the arancini

2   cups arborio rice

Pinch saffron threads

Salt

Freshly ground black pepper

¾   cup grated Parmesan cheese

5   eggs

½   cup caciocavallo or pecorino cheese, diced into small cubes

1½ cups fine bread crumbs

Vegetable oil for frying

1. To make the ragù, place the oil, onion, celery, and garlic in a saucepan over medium-high heat. Cook until the vegetables are lightly golden. Add the ground beef and cook, mashing the beef with a wooden spoon to break up any lumps, until the meat is no longer pink. Add the tomatoes, estrattu (or tomato paste), and red pepper flakes and simmer for 15–20 minutes. Add the peas, season with salt and pepper to taste, and cook for another 5 minutes, or until the peas are tender. The sauce should be very dry. If it is not, increase the heat to high and boil off any excess liquid, not forgetting to stir regularly so that the meat does not stick to the bottom of the pan. Taste and adjust the seasoning if necessary. Let cool.

2. While the ragù is cooking, prepare the rice. Put the rice in a saucepan and cover with 4 cups water. Add the saffron, season with salt and pepper to taste, and place over medium-high heat. Bring to a boil, lower the heat, cover the pan, and simmer for 13–15 minutes, or until the rice has absorbed all the liquid (check the rice after 10 minutes to make sure it is not sticking; if it is, remove from the heat, wrap the lid with a kitchen towel, and leave to sit for 3–5 minutes). Stir in the Parmesan cheese and 1 beaten egg and turn the rice onto a shallow platter. Spread the rice, cover with a clean kitchen cloth, and leave until it is warm.

3. Now comes the difficult part. Lightly dampen your hands and pinch off a handful of rice. Flatten it on the palm of one hand to just under ½ inch thick, put a full tablespoonful of ragù in the middle, and press 1 or 2 cubes of caciocavallo or pecorino in the middle of the meat. Cup the rice around the meat. If you need to use more rice to cover the filling completely, lightly dampen your hand again and pinch off a little more. Flatten it and cover the meat with it. Cup your free hand around the arancino and form it into a round ball the size of a tangerine— do not roll the ball of rice in between the palms of your hands; it will crack. Make sure that there are no cracks in the rice shell; if there are, seal them with a few grains of rice. Make the rest of the arancini. Then roll each into the beaten egg first, then in the bread crumbs. Repeat one more time to make sure the arancini are completely covered with bread crumbs. Leave to sit for 30 minutes. Gently roll the arancini between your hands to get rid of the excess crumbs.

4. Heat enough vegetable oil to deep-fry the arancini. When the oil is hot—test with the corner of an arancino; if the oil bubbles around it, it is ready—fry as many arancini as will fit comfortably in the pan for about 5–6 minutes, turning them over, or until crisp and golden all over. Serve hot or warm as a snack or accompanied by a green salad for a light meal.

Chickpea Fritters

Panelle

MAKES 20 TO 22

Panelle, panisse, and panissa are all different names for the same concoction, a paste made with chickpea flour, water, and salt that is first boiled, then left to set before being cut into different shapes, depending on where you are, and deep-fried. In Sicily panelle are crescent shaped or rectangular; in Genoa and Nice panissa or panisse are cut into sticks like French fries. In Nice the fritters are also made with cornmeal. The recipes vary only slightly from country to country. The one below is Sicilian. Both the Genoese and French do not use parsley in the mixture; instead, they add 2–3 tablespoons olive oil. The French also cut their panisse into round discs and serve it as a dessert, sprinkled with sugar or dipped in jam.

2 cups chickpea flour

Salt

Finely ground white pepper

A few sprigs flat-leaf parsley, most of the bottom stalk discarded,
    then finely chopped

Vegetable oil for frying

1. Put the chickpea flour in a saucepan and gradually add 3 cups water, stirring continuously. The mixture needs to be very smooth; if necessary, use a whisk. Add salt and pepper to taste and place over medium heat. Cook for about 10–15 minutes, stirring constantly. Stir in the parsley and turn out onto an oiled surface. Quickly spread the mixture with an oiled spatula to a thickness of about ½ inch. Let set, then cut into smallish triangles or rectangles about 2 inches wide and 3½ inches long.

2. Heat enough vegetable oil to deep-fry the panelle, and when it is hot—test by dipping the tip of a panelle in the oil; if it bubbles around the panelle, the oil is ready—fry as many panelle as fit comfortably in the pan until crisp and golden on both sides. Remove with a slotted spoon and drain on several layers of paper towels. Serve hot with more salt on the side.

f&w tip
You'll know the chickpea mixture is finished cooking when it gets thick and sticky (it will stick to the bottom of the saucepan). These fritters are addictive, and they're best right out of the frying pan.

ken hom's quick wok

KEN HOM

about hom
Ken Hom was born in the United States of Chinese parents and studied in Berkeley, California, until moving to Europe in the late 1990s. With *Ken Hom's Chinese Cookery* (which accompanied his first BBC television series, in 1984), *Ken Hom's Hot Wok* and *Ken Hom Travels with a Hot Wok,* he has created a trio of bestsellers that have sold more than two million copies worldwide. In 1999 he published the widely acclaimed *Ken Hom Cooks Thai.* He is the chef-consultant to several Yellow River Cafés in Britain.

This is the ideal book for weeknight dinners, with recipes that are ultrasimple and incredibly appealing. Who knew you could cook tuna steak in a wok? Or use a wok to make soup, deep-fry potatoes and steam custards? Each recipe gives accurate prep and cooking times, so you can trust it to help you get food on the table quickly.

FOOD & WINE Which tools are absolutely essential for wok cooking?

KEN HOM All you need is a good wok, a good cleaver, something with which to turn the food and a good chopping board. If you're not going to buy a wok, sure, a deep pan will do—but a wok is worth the investment. Look for one made of carbon steel. I find cast iron too heavy to use. Aluminum woks are good if coated with a thick nonstick surface.

F&W Which ingredients form the basis of the wok-friendly pantry?

KH Ginger, scallions, chiles, soy sauce, rice wine, sesame oil and garlic are all flavors that work well in the wok. You also need bean sauce, oyster sauce or chile bean sauce.

F&W Are you opposed to buying ready-made sauces?

KH Not at all. Chinese cooking has a long tradition of using ready-made sauces. I like Kikkoman soy sauce and many of the Japanese sesame oils. I also like the Lee Kum Kee brand of sauces—great taste and consistency.

F&W What condiments or seasonings do you suggest wok cooks have on hand to enliven their dishes?

KH Five-spice powder and good salt and pepper are useful seasonings. For braised dishes, it's helpful to have star anise and cinnamon.

F&W What is the most important rule to keep in mind when wok cooking?

KH Get the wok as hot as you can and never panic. And be adventurous!

F&W Which foods might people be surprised to learn cook well in a wok?

KH Did you know that you can steam a cake in a wok? You can cook fruits and all kinds of sweets, too.

F&W What kinds of food do not work well in woks?

KH Foods that are delicate or

>> FEATURED RECIPES

1 THAI-STYLE RICE NOODLES IN SOUP

2 SPICY TUNA

3 STIR-FRIED LAMB WITH GARLIC AND BASIL

4 BRAISED BEEF WITH BEANCURD

particularly fragile, like fish, present a real challenge; they'll just disintegrate in a hot wok.

F&W What kind of oil do you prefer?

KH Peanut oil is the best, because it's odorless and quite delicious and has a high burning point.

F&W Rice is the classic stir-fry accompaniment. How can you make it less sticky?

KH Basically, you should boil it in a pot of water until it absorbs all the liquid, then turn down the heat to the lowest flame for 15 more minutes, keeping the lid on. That will give you perfect rice. Make sure to use long-grain white rice.

F&W As an American-born child of Chinese parents, did you embrace wok cooking from an early age, or were you more concerned with assimilating?

KH I grew up in Chicago's Chinatown and I didn't even speak English until I was six. I started working in my uncle's Chinese restaurant when I was 11, so for me, anything not made in a wok was totally alien. My uncle was a great lover of wok cooking, and he was instrumental in fostering my love for it.

F&W Can you describe the traditional Chinese meal?

KH For family meals, you'd have a large soup made with some kind of meat or fish set in the middle of the table. For a more formal Chinese meal, like a banquet, you'd have a series of courses with many more vegetable than meat dishes, some kind of braised meat dish and a fish dish. You'd have fish at the end of the meal, as a symbol of prosperity.

the specifics

recipes	pages	photos	publisher	price
80	160	118 color photos	Headline Book Publishing	$29.95

credits

Ken Hom's Quick Wok by Ken Hom. Recipes and photographs from *Ken Hom's Quick Wok*. Copyright © 2001 Ken Hom. Photographs by Jeremy Hopley. First distributed in the U.S. in 2002. Reproduced by permission of Headline Book Publishing Limited.

Thai-Style Rice Noodles in Soup

SERVES 2 TO 4

This mouth-watering, satisfying Thai-inspired soup is not only healthy but a meal in itself. Its distinctive, delicious taste will appeal even to inveterate meat eaters. Use vegetarian stock if you want to make this dish completely vegetarian.

175g (6 oz) flat dried rice noodles, rice vermicelli or rice sticks

1.2 litres (2 pints) home-made chicken or vegetarian stock or quality store-bought fresh stock

Salt, to taste

1   tablespoon light soy sauce

1   tablespoon lime juice

2   fresh red chillies, seeded and shredded

2   teaspoons sugar

1   tablespoon groundnut (peanut) oil

3   tablespoons coarsely chopped garlic

Garnish

175g (6 oz) fresh beansprouts

3   tablespoons finely chopped spring onions

Handful fresh coriander sprigs

Preparation time 25 minutes   **Cooking time** 15 minutes

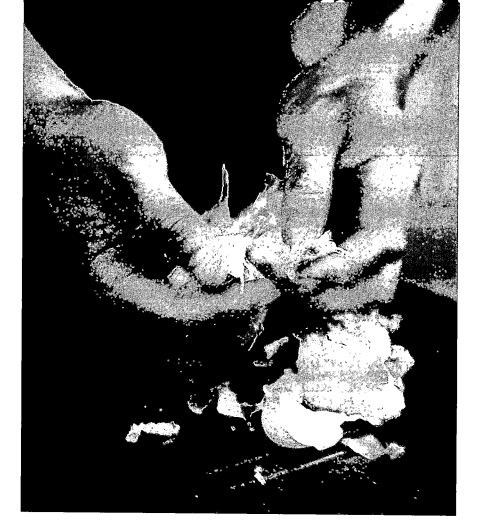

f&w tips

We used flat dried rice noodles that were medium width; they gave great substance to the soup. Try to use a superior quality stock, since most of the soup's flavor relies on that ingredient.

1. Soak the rice noodles in a bowl of hot water for 25 minutes. When soft, drain well in a colander or sieve and set aside. Discard the water.

2. Bring the stock to simmering point in a large saucepan. Add the salt, soy sauce, lime juice, chillies and sugar. Continue to simmer for 10 minutes. Then add the rice noodles and simmer for another 2 minutes.

3. Heat a wok over high heat until it is hot. Add the oil, and when it is moderately hot, add the garlic and stir-fry rapidly until light brown. Remove immediately and drain on kitchen paper.

4. Turn the soup into a tureen or individual bowls. Sprinkle with the fried garlic, garnish with the beansprouts, spring onions and coriander, and serve at once.

Spicy Tuna

SERVES 4

Fresh tuna, simply seared in a hot wok, has become very popular, and it is ideal
for fast cooking. Just remember two things: if overcooked, tuna can quickly dry out,
and it is important to get the highest quality tuna you can afford.

4   fresh tuna steaks, about 100g (4 oz) each, cut thickly

3   tablespoons extra-virgin olive oil

Spice mix

1   teaspoon chilli powder (optional)

1   teaspoon Madras curry powder

1   teaspoon sugar

Salt and freshly ground black pepper, to taste

Garnish

Handful fresh coriander sprigs

Preparation time 5 minutes   **Cooking time** 4 minutes

1. Lay the tuna steaks on a platter. In a small bowl, combine the ingredients
for the spice mix and blend thoroughly. Sprinkle this evenly over both sides of
the tuna steaks.

2. Heat a wok over high heat and when it is hot, add the oil. When the oil is
very hot and slightly smoking, add the tuna steaks and sear them on one side
for 2 minutes.

3. Turn them over and sear the other side for 2 minutes. The tuna should
remain "rare."

4. Turn them onto a warm platter, garnish with the coriander and serve at once.

Stir-Fried Lamb with Garlic and Basil

SERVES 4

Stir-frying is a fast and different way to cook lamb. Here it is combined with two aromatic ingredients—garlic and basil—for an unusual but delicious dish.

450g (1 lb) lean lamb steaks or fillets or boned loin chops

2 tablespoons groundnut (peanut) oil

6 garlic cloves, peeled and thinly sliced

Salt and freshly ground black pepper, to taste

Handful fresh basil leaves

Handful fresh coriander sprigs

Marinade

1 tablespoon Shaoxing rice wine or dry sherry

1 tablespoon light soy sauce

2 teaspoons sesame oil

2 teaspoons cornflour

Preparation time 25 minutes   **Cooking time** 6 minutes

1. Cut the lamb into thin slices. In a medium-sized bowl, combine the ingredients for the marinade. Add the lamb, mix well and marinate for 20 minutes at room temperature. Drain, discarding the marinade.

2. Heat a wok over high heat until it is very hot. Add the oil, and when it is very hot and slightly smoking, add the lamb and stir-fry for 2 minutes.

3. Add the garlic, salt and pepper, and continue to stir-fry for another 3 minutes.

4. Finally toss in the basil and coriander, and continue to stir-fry for 1 further minute or until the herbs have wilted.

5. Turn onto a warm serving platter and serve at once.

"I grew up in Chicago's Chinatown and I didn't even speak English until I was six. I started working in my uncle's Chinese restaurant when I was 11, so for me, anything not made in a wok was totally alien."

Braised Beef with Beancurd

SERVES 4

This is a quick and easy version of a great Chinese favourite that my mother used to make. It is comfort food at its best. Most of the preparation time is for draining the beancurd, to ensure that it is not too wet. An added bonus is that this dish can be cooked ahead of time and then gently reheated.

450g (1 lb) fresh firm beancurd

1½ tablespoons groundnut (peanut) oil

2   tablespoons coarsely chopped garlic

1   tablespoon finely chopped fresh ginger

350g (12 oz) minced beef

3   tablespoons finely chopped spring onions

2   tablespoons oyster sauce

2   teaspoons chilli bean sauce

1   teaspoon sugar

1½ tablespoons Shaoxing rice wine or dry sherry

1   tablespoon light soy sauce

50ml (2 fl oz) home-made chicken stock or
    quality store-bought fresh stock

Garnish

2   tablespoons finely chopped spring onions

Preparation time 25 minutes   **Cooking time** 20 minutes

1. Cut the beancurd into 1 cm (½ in) cubes and put into a sieve to drain for 10 minutes. Then lay on kitchen paper to drain for another 10 minutes.

2. Heat a wok over high heat until it is hot. Add the oil, and when it is very hot and slightly smoking, add the garlic and ginger, and stir-fry for 20 seconds.

3. Add the minced beef and stir-fry for 3 minutes.

4. Now add all the other ingredients except the beancurd, and bring to the boil.

5. Turn the heat down to low, add the beancurd and mix it in well, but gently, taking care not to break up the chunks. Simmer slowly, uncovered, for about 15 minutes. If necessary, add a little more stock. (Can be prepared ahead: Cover and refrigerate for up to 12 hours. Reheat gently in a steamer for 10 minutes.)

6. Turn onto a warm platter, garnish with the spring onions and serve at once.

a real american breakfast

CHERYL ALTERS JAMISON & BILL JAMISON

about the jamisons

Cheryl Alters Jamison and Bill Jamison are the award-winning authors of 14 cookbooks and travel guides, covering topics from American home cooking and barbecue to the food and culture of the Southwest. The Jamisons won James Beard Awards for *Smoke & Spice* and *The Border Cookbook,* and *American Home Cooking* won a James Beard and an IACP award in 2000. They live in Santa Fe, New Mexico.

We put this book on our list of the year's best because of its uniqueness: Very few cookbook authors even bother to acknowledge breakfast, much less devote an entire book to it. The 275 recipes are truly delicious, and we'd be as eager to make them for dinner as for breakfast.

The Best Meal of the Day, Any Time of the Day

A Real American Breakfast

Cheryl Alters Jamison & Bill Jamison

Authors of the award-winning *American Home Cooking* and *Smoke & Spice*

FOOD & WINE Where did you find some of your more unconventional recipes?
CHERYL JAMISON We do research in libraries across the country, looking in old cookbooks and manuscripts.
BILL JAMISON In the 18th and 19th centuries Americans ate just about anything for breakfast: T-bone steak, ham, chops, crawfish, crab cakes, fresh and pickled fish, fried salt pork, corn bread, enchiladas.
F&W What are your favorite breakfasts?
CJ Carolina shrimp and grits. And I love a simple fried egg sandwich with caramelized onions, or warm panela cheese with diablo salsa. Blueberry turnovers were a childhood favorite.
BJ I like red things. Red enchiladas with a fried egg, beet-based red flannel hash.
F&W What are some differences in breakfast preferences across America?
BJ In the Midwest, which was largely settled by Central and Eastern

Europeans who brought the kuchen tradition with them, pastries and breads are still very big. Along the coasts you find different kinds of seafood, like oyster pan roast in New Orleans.
CJ Or Cajun crawfish patties. If you go down to the Florida Keys, there's a fish steamed with aged lime juice. In the Rocky Mountain region there's bacon-fried trout. Salt cod cakes in New England, catfish in Mississippi.
F&W Do you have tips for making fluffy pancakes?
CJ Don't overmix the batter, otherwise the gluten develops and you end up with tougher pancakes. An extra step that's worthwhile is separating the eggs and beating the whites by themselves. It makes a difference in the fluffiness of the pancakes.
F&W What about making perfect poached eggs?
CJ Start with a good-quality fresh egg, because that ensures the white will

>> | FEATURED RECIPES

1 | SATURDAY SUMMER STRATA

2 | BLUEBERRY TURNOVERS

3 | CHICAGO-STYLE BREAKFAST PAN PIZZA

cling very tightly to the yolk, which makes it much easier to poach. Put a little vinegar in the water, bring it to a simmer, then ease the egg into it. Don't overcook it.

F&W What equipment is essential for making a good breakfast?

CJ It's nice to have a good cast-iron griddle or skillet for pancakes, bacon and hash browns. We use our griddle to make toast, too.

F&W Any favorite breakfast spots?

BJ If you've got a sweet tooth, go to Osseo, Wisconsin. A café called the Norske Nook has some of the very best pies on earth. Here in Santa Fe, Cafe Pasqual's is terrific. They serve a delicious polenta with chorizo, corn and red chile sauce.

CJ Chez Zee in Austin, Texas, makes a fantastic baked Crème Brulée French Toast by pouring custard over slices of their house-baked bread. A cafeteria-style joint in New Orleans called Mother's serves up a wonderful "debris" po'boy all day. They slow-roast all these hams and roast beefs, and the "debris" is what falls into the bottom of the pan, so it's moist and crusty.

F&W Beyond Bloody Marys, what are some fun breakfast cocktails?

BJ The mint julep is originally a morning drink, and it's better at breakfast.

CJ To lighten it, you can make the mint julep mixture but substitute sparkling water for the bourbon. Mardi Gras milk punch is fabulous and easy to make. It's milk based and soothing but also has a real kick.

the specifics

recipes	pages	photos	publisher	price
275	464	16 color photos	William Morrow	$34.95

credits

Saturday Summer Strata

SERVES 6 OR MORE

Sheila Lukins and Julee Rosso introduced us to stratas in their popular 1984 *Silver Palate Good Times Cookbook*. We've tinkered ever since then with our version of their Basil Breakfast Strata, which they presented as a front-porch summer brunch dish. This is our current rendition, a big favorite with the Glow Club, Cheryl's Saturday-morning women's running group.

One 1- to 1¼-pound loaf country or sourdough bread, crusts removed if thick

½   **pound cream cheese or St. Andre cheese (rind removed),
     cut into small cubes or bits**

½   **pound fresh or other mozzarella, cut into small pieces or grated**

¾   **cup prepared pesto**

6   **ounces thinly sliced prosciutto**

1   **pound (about 3 medium) red-ripe tomatoes, thinly sliced**

5   **large eggs**

1½ **cups milk or half-and-half**

½   **teaspoon salt**

Freshly milled black pepper to taste

Oil or butter a deep 9- to 10-inch baking dish.

Slice the bread about ½ inch thick. Arrange 2 to 3 equal alternating layers of the bread, cheeses, pesto, prosciutto, and tomatoes in the baking dish. Cut or tear bread slices if needed to make snug layers.

Whisk the eggs with the milk, salt, and pepper. Pour the custard over the bread mixture. Cover and refrigerate the strata for at least 2 hours and up to overnight. Remove the strata from the refrigerator 20 to 30 minutes before you plan to bake it.

Preheat the oven to 350°F. Bake the strata for 50 to 55 minutes, until puffed, golden brown, and lightly set in the center. Serve hot.

Autumn Strata

Eliminate the pesto and tomatoes. Sauté ½ pound sliced mushrooms, 1 or 2 minced garlic cloves, ¼ teaspoon hot red pepper flakes, and ¾ pound fresh spinach, chard, or escarole in 3 tablespoons olive oil until the mushrooms are tender and any liquid has evaporated. Arrange alternating layers of the bread, cheeses, prosciutto, and mushroom mixture and proceed as directed.

Blueberry Turnovers

MAKES 4 LARGE TURNOVERS

f&w tip

These turnovers make an easy and impressive brunch dish. We had a little bit of the blueberry filling left over and thought it would be great on pancakes, waffles or even ice cream, since it can be made ahead of time and refrigerated for a couple of days. We also opted to use only 2 tablespoons of sugar, but the amount you need will depend on the sweetness of the blueberries.

Americans love pastry wrapped fruits, whether in the form of a baked or simmered apple dumpling, fried peach or apricot "hand" pie, or pillowy berry turnover. A particular favorite of Cheryl and her sisters as kids, these turnovers begin with frozen puff pastry to expedite the preparation. The young Cheryl relished everything about them—folding the pastry diamonds around the juicy filling, watching them poof miraculously in the oven, drizzling the glaze over the warm flaky crust, and then finally biting into shattering crust and oozing berries. The resulting blue lips seemed pretty fun too.

Filling

2½ cups fresh blueberries or one 14-ounce bag frozen blueberries

2 to 3 tablespoons sugar

1   teaspoon fresh lemon juice

1   teaspoon instant or granulated tapioca

One ½-pound sheet frozen puff pastry, thawed but chilled

1   large egg

½   cup confectioners' sugar

Preheat the oven to 400°F.

Stir the blueberries, sugar, lemon juice, and tapioca together in a saucepan. Simmer over medium heat long enough for the berries to release their juice and then to get very thick and syrupy, 10 to 15 minutes, depending on the juiciness of the berries. Cool to lukewarm or cover and refrigerate overnight.

Roll the puff pastry out on a floured surface into a 10-inch square. Cut into four 5-inch diamonds, preferably with a floured pizza cutter or pastry wheel. Don't worry about precise measurements, but you want to be in this range. Whisk the egg together with 1 teaspoon water.

Spoon a quarter of the berries onto the center of each pastry square, then brush a bit of the egg around the edge. Fold one half over the other to make a triangle and pinch the edges securely closed using the tines of a fork. Repeat with the remaining pastry and filling. Arrange the turnovers on a baking sheet, leaving at least an inch between them on all sides. Cut 2 small slashes in the top of each turnover, then brush lightly with the egg. Bake for 10 to 12 minutes, until puffed and golden brown.

While the turnovers bake, prepare the glaze. Mix the confectioners' sugar with about 2 teaspoons water. After the turnovers have cooled for about 5 minutes on the baking sheet, drizzle the glaze over them, zigging and zagging it. The sheet will collect your dribbles. Transfer to a baking rack and let cool for at least 10 minutes longer, so that the filling is no longer molten. Eat slightly warm or at room temperature.

Cherry Turnovers
Substitute an equal quantity of pitted sour "pie" cherries for the berries and use 3 to 4 tablespoons sugar. Add just a drop or two of red food coloring if you like.

Lemon Turnovers
Use store-bought lemon curd for the filling, using 2 to 3 tablespoons per turnover. For the glaze, mix the confectioners' sugar with fresh lemon juice instead of water.

Chicago-Style Breakfast Pan Pizza

SERVES 4 TO 6 AS A MAIN DISH, 6 TO 8 AS A SIDE DISH

"In the 18th and 19th centuries Americans ate just about anything for breakfast: T-bone steak, ham, chops, crawfish, crab cakes, fresh and pickled fish, fried salt pork, corn bread, enchiladas."

No Neapolitan would start the day with pizza, but Americans have long taken tremendous liberties with the imported bread. You can start with a pound of frozen bread dough if you like, thawed overnight in the refrigerator, but we describe how to make a better crust from scratch. This pizza is skillet cooked, in the time-honored thick-crusted Chicago style, and makes a full meal on its own. We suggest several tasty toppings, but use your imagination with other family favorites.

Pizza crust

1   envelope active dry yeast

½   teaspoon sugar

About 2 cups bread flour or unbleached all-purpose flour

¼   cup stone-ground cornmeal

1½ teaspoons kosher or other coarse salt

2   tablespoons olive oil

Cheese topping

1½ cups grated mozzarella cheese

6   tablespoons freshly grated Parmesan cheese

3   tablespoons minced fresh basil

1   garlic clove, minced

1   teaspoon hot red pepper flakes or more to taste

¾   teaspoon dried oregano

2   small red-ripe tomatoes, such as plum, thinly sliced

6 to 8 ounces fried bulk sausage

2 to 4 large eggs

Grease a heavy 10-inch skillet, preferably cast iron.

Prepare the crust, first combining the yeast and sugar with ⅔ cup lukewarm water in a small bowl. Let it sit until foamy, about 10 minutes. In a heavy-duty electric mixer with a dough hook or in a food processor, mix the yeast mixture with a scant 2 cups flour and the rest of the dough ingredients for several minutes, until the dough becomes smooth and elastic.

Transfer the dough to a floured work surface and knead for at least 2 more minutes, adding another tablespoon or two of flour if needed to get a mass that is no longer sticky. Dough on the dry side is a bit more challenging to work with but yields a crisper crust. Form the dough into a ball, place it in an oiled bowl, turn to coat it, and cover it. Set the dough in a warm, draft-free spot and let it rise until doubled in size, about 1 hour. Punch the dough down and let it rest for 10 minutes. Roll out the dough to a disk 11 to 12 inches in diameter. Transfer the dough to the skillet and pull or prod the edges with your fingers to make a lip about ½ inch high. The dough is ready to use at this point but can be covered and refrigerated overnight. If you chill it, let the dough skillet sit for about 20 minutes at room temperature before proceeding.

Preheat the oven to 400°F. Combine the cheese topping ingredients in a medium bowl. (This too can be made a day ahead and refrigerated, if you wish.) Arrange tomatoes and sausage over the crust, then sprinkle on the cheese mixture. Bake the pizza for 18 to 20 minutes, until the topping is bubbly and the crust crisp and light brown.

While the pizza bakes, scramble the eggs or fry them sunny side up, as you wish. When the pizza is done, top with the eggs. Slice the pizza into wedges and serve immediately.

Biscuit Breakfast Pizzas

These are quick and tasty little morsels, especially fun for children. You even get to cheat the clock with these by starting from a packaged base. Separate the biscuits in a tube of Pillsbury Corn Grands refrigerated biscuit dough. Roll out each into a ¼-inch-thick round. Top as you like, with grated cheese, a bit of tomato sauce, and anything else compatible. Bake at 400°F for 8 to 10 minutes and serve.

perfect cakes

NICK MALGIERI

about malgieri

Nick Malgieri is the author of *How to Bake, Nick Malgieri's Perfect Pastry, Great Italian Desserts, Chocolate* and *Cookies Unlimited.* He is director of the baking program at the Institute of Culinary Education in New York City and a frequent lecturer on baking and confectionery at cooking schools across the United States.

This books affirms Malgieri's reputation for flawless recipes. He spent years testing cakes from students, friends and family, and the best ones appear here. We like the way he highlights his ingredients lists, which makes them easy to navigate, and had terrific success with both his basic and more complex desserts.

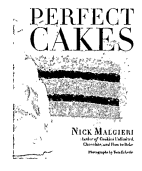

FOOD & WINE Who inspired you to become a pastry chef?

NICK MALGIERI My maternal grandmother lived with us when I was a child, and she was a very good baker.

F&W Did you used to help her out around the kitchen?

NM Well, no, I used to eat.

F&W So what was your direct inspiration for the book?

NM I had always wanted to do a cake book. When I find an interesting article or somebody gives me a recipe, I throw it on the windowsill—that's my filing cabinet—and eventually this all becomes a book.

F&W How do you come up with the ideas for your recipes?

NM Recipes beget recipes.

F&W Do you have any advice for someone who's new to baking?

NM Beginning bakers are always most intrigued by recipes that have 60

steps, but they should really stick to simple things like a pound cake or a coffee cake. People who are accustomed to cooking think baking a cake is like making a meat loaf, but it's not. You can leave the onions out of a meat loaf if you don't feel like putting them in, but you can't leave baking powder or brown sugar out of a cake.

F&W What ingredients do you always have on hand in the kitchen?

NM Baking powder, definitely, but you want to check to make sure it's not past its expiration date. You also want to make sure your spices are fresh— I'm as guilty as anyone about keeping old stuff around. About a month ago I pulled out some ground coriander, smelled it and said to myself, "This smells exactly like an empty jar."

F&W What's the difference between a good cake and a perfect cake?

NM Perfect means everything about it

>> | FEATURED RECIPES

1 | ZUCCOTTO ALLA RICOTTA

2 | CHOCOLATE CHIFFON CAKE

3 | HIGH-RATIO LEMON-BUTTERMILK POUND CAKE

is a step higher. Sometimes a little change in technique or a little addition in an ingredient's quantity can increase quality infinitely. If it's a butter cake your taste buds should be so assaulted with the wonderful sweet taste of butter that you'll never forget it.

F&W What do you think is the easiest technique to master?

NM I think the easiest is getting organized. You really need to discipline yourself and sit down, read the recipe, make a shopping list, do an inventory and make sure you have all of the ingredients. Sometimes I'll open the cupboard and say, "Oh, look, there's brown sugar." Then when I've started making the cake I'll see that there's only one-sixth the amount I need. I also think beginning bakers should measure out all of the ingredients first so that they can proceed to the mixing without interruption.

F&W Do you have a favorite technique?

NM I like using soft or melted butter to grease pans because you get a thicker coating and, as a result, a better release. If I'm going to make a 9-inch cake, I'll cut off about two half-teaspoon pats from a stick of butter and throw them in the pan. When I come back five minutes later, they're perfectly soft so I can use a piece of rumpled-up plastic wrap—not a paper towel, because that will absorb the butter—to spread the butter around inside the pan. And the great thing about the plastic wrap is that you throw it away rather than having a brush to wash.

the specifics

recipes	pages	photos	publisher	price
200	352	44 color photos	HarperCollins Publishers	$37.50

credits

Perfect Cakes by Nick Malgieri. Copyright © 2002 by Nick Malgieri. Reprinted by permission of HarperCollins Publishers Inc. Photographs by Tom Eckerle.

Zuccotto alla Ricotta

MAKES ONE 8- TO 9-INCH CAKE, ABOUT 16 SERVINGS

f&w tips

When finishing the cake, we used more than the ½ cup of chopped pistachios called for in the recipe—it was more like 1½ cups. We also found that lightly toasting the pistachios brought out a little more of their flavor.

This elegant Florentine dessert uses a layer of pan di Spagna to line a bowl which is then filled with a rich ricotta mousse. The chocolate and pistachios add a bit of crunch to the rich filling.

One 9-inch layer Pan di Spagna (recipe follows)

¼ cup white rum for sprinkling

Filling

One 15-ounce container ricotta

1 cup confectioners' sugar

3 tablespoons white rum

1 tablespoon anisette

1 envelope gelatin

3 tablespoons (about 1 ounce) chopped bittersweet chocolate

3 tablespoons (about 1 ounce) chopped pistachios

1 cup heavy whipping cream

For finishing

1 cup heavy whipping cream

2 tablespoons sugar

½ cup chopped pistachios

One 1½-quart bowl, buttered and lined with plastic wrap

1. Cut out a disk the size of the top of your bowl from the pan di Spagna and cut the rest of it into 2 large wedges. Cut the wedges into thin slices and line the bowl with them. Sprinkle with the rum. Reserve the disk to cover the filling.

2. To make the filling, combine the ricotta and confectioners' sugar in the food processor and process until smooth, about 2 minutes. Transfer to a large bowl.

3. Combine the rum and anisette in a small bowl and sprinkle the gelatin over the surface. Allow it to soak until softened, about 5 minutes, then place over a saucepan of simmering water and stir to melt. Whisk the dissolved gelatin into the ricotta mixture, then stir in the chocolate and pistachios. Whip the cream to soft peaks, and fold it in.

4. Pour the filling into the prepared mold and cover with the reserved disk of pan di Spagna. Cover with plastic wrap and chill until set, about 6 hours.

5. Remove the plastic wrap and invert the bowl onto a platter. Remove the bowl and plastic wrap. Whip the cream with the sugar to soft peaks. Cover the Zuccotto with the cream. Sprinkle with the chopped pistachios.

Serving Serve the cake shortly after finishing.

Storage Store the cake without the whipped cream, covered, in the refrigerator for up to 2 days. Finish the cake just prior to serving.

Pan di Spagna

**MAKES ONE 9- OR 10-INCH
ROUND LAYER**

The jury is still out on whether the
name of this Italian sponge cake
means "Spanish bread," which would
be the literal translation, or whether
spagna is really a corruption of
spagna, or sponge. Fortunately it
doesn't matter—the cake is delicious.

4 large eggs, separated

¾ cup sugar

1 teaspoon vanilla extract

Pinch of salt

½ cup all-purpose flour (spoon flour
into dry-measure cup and level off)

½ cup cornstarch

One 2-inch-deep 9- or 10-inch round
cake pan, buttered and bottom
lined with parchment or wax paper

1. Position a rack in the middle of the
oven and preheat to 350 degrees.

2. Whisk together the yolks, 6
tablespoons of the sugar, and the vanilla
in the bowl of a heavy-duty mixer, then
whip with the whisk attachment on
medium speed until very aerated and
pale yellow, about 3 minutes.

3. In a clean, dry mixer bowl, whip the
egg whites and salt with the whisk
attachment on medium speed until the

whites are very white and opaque.
Increase the speed to medium-high,
and whip in the remaining 6
tablespoons sugar in a stream.
Continue to whip the whites until
they hold a firm, dull peak.

4. Use a large rubber spatula to fold
the yolks into the whites.

5. Put the flour and cornstarch in a
strainer or sifter and, in 3 additions,
sift the mixture over the batter and
fold it in. Make sure to keep scraping
the bottom of the bowl with the spatula
to keep the flour from accumulating
there and causing lumps.

6. Scrape the batter into the prepared
pan and smooth the top.

7. Bake the cake for 30 to 40 minutes,
until it is well risen and feels firm
when pressed gently with the palm of
your hand. Immediately run a small
knife or spatula around the inside of
the pan to loosen the cake. Unmold
the layer onto a rack. Leave the paper
on it and turn the layer right side up
onto a rack to cool. Remove the paper
when the cake is cool.

Storage Double-wrap the layer in plastic
and keep it in the refrigerator up to
5 days, or freeze it for longer storage.

Chocolate Chiffon Cake

MAKES ONE 10-INCH TUBE CAKE, ABOUT 16 SERVINGS

I think most chiffon, angel food, and tube-pan sponge cakes are best left unadorned, but this rather lean chocolate chiffon cake turns into something spectacular with a little chocolate ganache frosting. The ganache is easy to make and complements the lightness of the cake perfectly.

Cake batter

½   cup alkalized (Dutch-process) cocoa powder

¾   cup boiling water

1¾ cups cake flour (spoon flour into dry-measure cup and level off)

1   tablespoon baking powder

1¾ cups sugar

½   cup vegetable oil, such as corn or canola

6   large egg yolks

1   teaspoon vanilla extract

1   cup egg whites (from 7 or 8 large eggs)

½   teaspoon salt

Ganache

¾   cup heavy whipping cream

1   tablespoon light corn syrup

2   tablespoons butter

10 ounces semisweet or bittersweet chocolate, cut into ¼-inch pieces

One 10-inch tube pan with removable bottom, ungreased; a narrow-necked
    bottle (such as a wine bottle) to hang the cake on after it is baked

"People who are accustomed to cooking think baking a cake is like making a meat loaf, but it's not. You can leave the onions out of a meat loaf if you don't feel like putting them in, but you can't leave baking powder or brown sugar out of a cake."

1. Set a rack in the middle of the oven and preheat to 350 degrees.

2. Sift the cocoa into a small mixing bowl. Stir in the boiling water until smooth. Set aside to cool.

3. Sift the cake flour into the bowl of a heavy-duty mixer. Add the baking powder and 1¼ cups of the sugar and stir well to mix.

4. In a medium bowl, stir together the oil, egg yolks, and vanilla. Stir the liquid ingredients and the cooled cocoa mixture into the dry ingredients, then beat with the paddle on medium speed for about a minute, or until smooth.

5. In a clean, dry mixer bowl, whip the egg whites and salt with the whisk attachment on medium speed until very white and opaque and beginning to hold a shape. Increase the speed to medium-high, and whisk in the remaining ½ cup sugar in a stream. Continue to whip the egg whites until they hold a firm peak.

6. With a large rubber spatula, fold the yolk mixture into the whipped egg whites, making sure you scrape the bottom of the bowl each time the spatula passes through so the batter is thoroughly mixed. Pour the batter into the prepared pan and smooth the top.

7. Bake for about 55 to 60 minutes, or until the cake is deep gold and firm; a toothpick inserted halfway between the side of the pan and the central tube should emerge clean.

8. While the cake is baking, prepare the ganache. Bring the cream, corn syrup, and butter to a boil in a medium saucepan. Off the heat, add the chocolate and swirl the pan to make sure all the chocolate is submerged. Allow to stand for 3 minutes, then whisk until smooth. Pour into a bowl and refrigerate until the ganache reaches spreading consistency; check it often to make sure it doesn't harden, or it will be impossible to frost the cake.

9. Remove the cake from the oven, invert the central tube onto the neck of the bottle, and let the cake cool completely.

10. To remove the cooled cake from the pan, run a long thin knife around the sides of the pan, scraping against the pan rather than the cake. Remove the pan sides and run the knife around the central tube and under the cake. Invert the cake onto a cardboard cake round or a platter, easing it off the central tube with your fingers.

11. To finish, spread the top and sides of the cake with the cooled ganache, swirling it on with the tip of an offset metal spatula. Chill the cake briefly to set the ganache.

Serving Use a sharp serrated knife to cut the cake.

Storage Keep under a cake dome at room temperature, or wrap loosely and refrigerate; remove from the refrigerator an hour before you serve the cake so that the ganache isn't hard. Or, for longer storage, wrap the unfrosted cake well and freeze; frost the cake after it is defrosted.

High-Ratio Lemon-Buttermilk Pound Cake

MAKES ONE 10-INCH BUNDT CAKE, ABOUT 16 SERVINGS

After you bake this cake, you soak it with a lemon and vanilla syrup that adds just the right note of tartness and moisture. See the variations at the end of the recipe for a sprightly orange or lemon-lime version. Many thanks to my friend Gary Peese of Austin, Texas, for this recipe.

Cake batter

2½ cups bleached all-purpose flour (spoon flour into
    dry-measure cup and level off)

2 cups sugar

2 teaspoons baking powder

½ teaspoon salt

½ pound (2 sticks) unsalted butter, softened

4 large eggs, at room temperature

3 large egg yolks

½ cup buttermilk

1 tablespoon grated lemon zest

1 tablespoon strained fresh lemon juice

1 teaspoon vanilla extract

Lemon syrup

½ cup water

½ cup sugar

⅓ cup fresh lemon juice, strained

2 teaspoons vanilla extract

One 12-cup Bundt pan, buttered and floured

1. Position a rack in the lower third of the oven and preheat to 325 degrees.

2. Place the flour, sugar, baking powder, and salt in the bowl of a heavy-duty mixer fitted with the paddle attachment, add the butter, and beat on the lowest speed for about 2 minutes, or until the ingredients are well combined.

3. Meanwhile, whisk all the remaining batter ingredients together in a mixing bowl until well combined.

4. Increase the mixer speed to medium, add one-third of the liquid and mix for 2 minutes. Stop the mixer and scrape down the bowl and beater. Add another third of the liquid, beat for 2 minutes, and scrape again. Finally, add the remaining liquid and beat and scrape as before.

5. Use a large rubber spatula to give the batter a final vigorous stir, then scrape it into the prepared pan and smooth the top.

6. Bake for about 1 hour, or until a toothpick inserted into the cake halfway between the side of the pan and the central tube emerges clean.

7. Cool the cake in the pan on a rack for 10 minutes, then invert onto the rack to finish cooling.

8. To make the syrup, bring the water and sugar to a boil in a small saucepan. Remove from the heat and stir in the lemon juice and vanilla. Brush the hot syrup evenly all over the cake. Gradually brush until it is all absorbed.

Storage Wrap the cake in plastic wrap and then foil to ensure it doesn't dry out, and serve within a few days. For longer storage, wrap and freeze; defrost loosely covered at room temperature.

variations

Lemon Sour Cream or Yogurt Pound Cake
Substitute sour cream or plain yogurt for the buttermilk.

Orange Buttermilk Pound Cake
Substitute orange zest and juice for the lemon and orange extract for the vanilla extract in the batter. Make the syrup with $\frac{1}{3}$ cup strained fresh orange juice and 2 tablespoons lemon juice. This cake can also be made with sour cream or yogurt as above.

Lemon-Lime Buttermilk Pound Cake
Substitute lime juice for the lemon juice in the batter. Use half lemon and half lime juice for the syrup. This cake can be made with sour cream or yogurt as above.

the il fornaio pasta book

MAURIZIO MAZZON

about mazzon
Maurizio Mazzon, a native of the Veneto region of Italy, developed his extensive knowledge of Italian cuisine in Italy and the United States. He began his career at Il Fornaio as the opening chef of the Palo Alto location of this restaurant group. He was named vice president and executive chef in 1995 and now oversees all of Il Fornaio's chefs, menus and 24 kitchens.

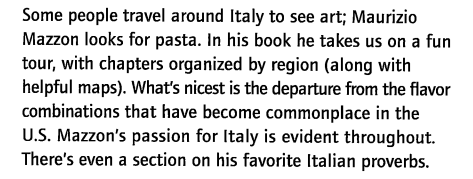

Some people travel around Italy to see art; Maurizio Mazzon looks for pasta. In his book he takes us on a fun tour, with chapters organized by region (along with helpful maps). What's nicest is the departure from the flavor combinations that have become commonplace in the U.S. Mazzon's passion for Italy is evident throughout. There's even a section on his favorite Italian proverbs.

FOOD & WINE Where did the recipes in your book come from?

MAURIZIO MAZZON Most of them were ones I grew up with. I was born and raised in Italy, and I lived there until the age of 26. I spent ten years working in different cities, in restaurants all over Italy. And in our company there are 22 Italian chefs, so I also got feedback from them. Once a year I go on a tour of Italy with other chefs.

F&W What is your favorite region of Italy for pasta?

MM That's like asking the mother of five children which is her favorite. In the Veneto I love pasta with seafood. In Emilia-Romagna, the stuffed pasta, like cappellaci, and in Sicily or Sardinia, pasta with lobster. The best lobsters in the world are there. It doesn't make sense to have lobster pasta in the Veneto; go to Sardinia.

The same with eggplant or sea urchins in Sicily, or sausage in Puglia.

F&W What determines what shape of pasta should go with what sauce?

MM Shell pastas like conchiglie and cavatelli go well with meat ragù because the pasta captures the sauce. Seafood dishes are always better made with long pasta. It's traditional. You can eat penne with clams, but you'll never see that in Italy. If you take your fork and pick up some spaghetti, you can get some clams, but if you stab penne with your fork, you don't get any clams. If you make penne with meat ragù or cream sauce, however, something that clings to the pasta, that's perfect. The ideal is to get pasta and sauce together in one bite.

F&W What are the biggest mistakes American home cooks make when preparing pasta?

>> FEATURED RECIPES

1 BEET-FLAVORED PASTA STUFFED WITH A RICOTTA-BEET FILLING TOPPED WITH BROWN BUTTER AND POPPY SEEDS

2 PASTA RIBBONS WITH PESTO, GREEN BEANS, AND POTATOES

3 ROASTED PEPPERS AND CLAMS WITH PASTA STRANDS

MM They don't take their time, and they prepare too much at once. You should find the right ingredients: the right flour, the right tomatoes. Follow the recipe, and don't make too much.

F&W What's the crucial ingredient for a terrific pasta sauce?

MM Tomatoes. To make a good sauce, all you need are tomatoes, garlic, onion and basil. It's only four ingredients, so you need to choose well. When using canned tomatoes, look for ones without calcium chloride. It's a preservative that makes tomatoes smell like a Jacuzzi. Some canned tomatoes don't have it. Some are organic, but always check that they don't have calcium chloride. In the winter, tomatoes in the can are better than fresh, which are gassed to stay red. I don't want that.

F&W What's the best pasta sauce to make quickly?

MM Get heirloom tomatoes, peel them, cut them in half, squeeze out the seeds, chop them and cook them with some extra-virgin olive oil, two garlic cloves, basil, salt and pepper. And if you like it spicy, add some peperoncini from Italy.

F&W Do you think it's worth the effort to make fresh pasta?

MM Yes, I do. The flavor comes through much better. You taste the simple ingredients: the flour, oil, egg. And fresh pasta takes a minute or less to cook, while dried pasta has to boil for 15 or 20 minutes, so you lose flavor and nutrients in the water. But I don't make fresh pasta every day— only on Sunday, my day off.

the specifics

recipes	pages	photos	publisher	price
74	180	49 color photos	Chronicle Books	$27.50

credits

The Il Fornaio Pasta Book by Maurizio Mazzon. Photographs by Michael Lamotte. Copyright ©2002 by Il Fornaio. Published in the U.S. by Chronicle Books LLC, San Francisco. Used with permission. Visit www.chroniclebooks.com.

Beet-Flavored Pasta Stuffed with a Ricotta-Beet Filling Topped with Brown Butter and Poppy Seeds

Casonsei Ampezzani

SERVES 6

Cortina, the Aspen of Italy, is one of my favorite places to ski. Once, while on a trip with friends, it was suggested that we visit a restaurant renowned for its pasta. We drove for many hours, only to find an old barn in the middle of nowhere. We were pleasantly surprised by the large table in the center of the room, which displayed the most incredible selection of fresh pasta. We selected the pasta we wanted, and the servers carried it to the kitchen to be cooked. That was the first time I tasted this particular dish, and it has since become a favorite.

f&w tip

To cook the beet, cut it in quarters and simmer in water until tender, about 30 minutes. Since this recipe is fairly time-consuming, consider making the pasta dough and the filling a day ahead.

For the pasta

½ cup chopped cooked beet (about ½ of a large beet)

1⅓ cups all-purpose flour

½ teaspoon sea salt

1 large egg at room temperature

For the filling

One 15-ounce container ricotta

⅓ cup finely diced cooked beet

¼ cup toasted bread crumbs

½ teaspoon sea salt

¼ teaspoon freshly ground pepper

¼ teaspoon freshly grated nutmeg

1 egg, beaten

5 teaspoons sea salt

½ cup (1 stick) unsalted butter

½ cup freshly grated Parmigiano-Reggiano

1 tablespoon poppy seeds

To make the pasta Purée the beet in the bowl of a food processor or in a food mill. Combine the flour and salt on a flat work surface or in a wide, shallow bowl and shape into a mound. Make a well in the center and add the egg. Beat the egg with a fork. Add the beet purée to the egg and gradually begin beating in a wider path to incorporate the flour. Continue mixing with the fork until the pasta begins to resemble a dry, crumbly mixture. Transfer to a flat work surface dusted with flour. Begin kneading by hand, rolling the dough sideways across the surface from hand to hand, and applying strong pressure while squeezing the dough. Knead until all of the flour is incorporated, no floury white spots remain, and the pasta begins to soften, about 10 minutes. Shape into a ball, cover with plastic wrap, and let sit 30 minutes. (This allows the flour to continue to absorb moisture from the liquid.)

To make the filling Combine the ricotta, beet, bread crumbs, salt, pepper, and nutmeg in a medium bowl. Mix well. Transfer to a large pastry bag with a 1-inch opening.

Roll out the pasta (see next page). Brush one long half of a pasta sheet with some of the beaten egg. Pipe out (or drop by the spoonful) 9 small mounds (about 1 tablespoon each) of the filling, spacing them about 2½ inches apart on top of the egg-brushed side. Fold the other pasta half over, forming a long rectangle, and gently push the pasta down around each mound to push out any air. Arrange a 2½-inch fluted cookie cutter around the edge of each mound and press down to cut into half-moon shapes. Transfer to a platter dusted with flour. Repeat with the remaining pasta and filling.

Bring 5 quarts of water and the 5 teaspoons of salt to a boil in a large stockpot over high heat. Add the *casonsei* and cook until they rise to the top, about 2 minutes. Transfer to a colander.

Melt 6 tablespoons of the butter in a large sauté pan over medium-high heat. Add the *casonsei.* Cook until crisp, turn, and cook the other side, about 2 minutes per side. Transfer to a platter and sprinkle with the Parmigiano. Melt the remaining 2 tablespoons of butter in the sauté pan over medium-high heat and cook until browned. Spoon over the *casonsei.* Sprinkle with the poppy seeds.

To roll out sheets

1. Adjust the pasta maker to its widest setting. Dust the surface next to the pasta maker with flour.

2. Cut the dough into 2 portions.

3. Working with 1 portion at a time, shape the dough into a flat disk. Flatten 1 edge further to fit between the rollers. Feed the dough into the rollers and begin rolling out the dough, stretching it as you feed it into the pasta maker.

4. Sprinkle lightly with flour, then fold in thirds and roll it through again, pulling the dough taut to stretch it as it goes through the rollers. Repeat 12 to 14 times, each time folding the dough in half before rolling it out.

5. Adjust the pasta maker to the next setting, fold the dough in half, and roll out once. Repeat this procedure on the middle setting, gently stretching the dough as it is fed into the rollers. Dust with flour. The pasta should be the same width as the rollers.

6. Roll out the dough on the next to last setting to form a sheet the same width as the pasta maker, 24 inches long, and ⅛ inch thick. Roll out the second piece of dough in the same manner.

Pasta Ribbons with Pesto, Green Beans, and Potatoes

Trenette con Pesto alla Genovese

SERVES 6

This classic Ligurian dish features pesto, a condiment dating back to Roman times and thought to have originated in Genoa. This particular recipe is from a town called Camogli, where pesto includes a cheese called cagliata, a fresh cow's milk cheese with a spreadable consistency. I've substituted crème fraîche because it tastes similar to cagliata, which is difficult to find in the United States.

50 fresh medium basil leaves, washed and dried thoroughly

3   garlic cloves

¾   cup freshly grated Parmigiano-Reggiano

⅓   cup freshly grated Pecorino Romano

2   tablespoons pine nuts, lightly toasted

½   cup extra-virgin olive oil

5½ teaspoons sea salt

¼   teaspoon freshly ground pepper

1   tablespoon crème fraîche

½   pound Yukon gold potatoes, peeled, quartered, and
     cut into ½-inch-thick slices

¼   pound green beans, cut into 1-inch lengths

1   pound dry trenette

Place the basil in the bowl of a food processor and chop fine. Add the garlic and continue chopping. Add the parmigiano, pecorino, and pine nuts and process until the nuts are chopped fine. Gradually add the olive oil while the motor is running. Add ½ teaspoon of the salt and the pepper and pulse to combine. Add the crème fraîche and pulse to combine. Do not over-process; it should all be blended within 3 to 5 minutes.

"You should find the right ingredients: the right flour, the right tomatoes. Follow the recipe, and don't make too much. In Italy pasta is a first course, just enough to introduce the stomach to the main course."

Bring 5 quarts of water and the remaining 5 teaspoons of salt to a boil. Add the potatoes and return to a boil. Add the beans and pasta and cook until the pasta is al dente.

Heat the pesto in a large sauté pan with 1 to 2 tablespoons of the cooking water from the pasta. Do not boil. Transfer the pasta, beans, and potatoes to a colander to drain, reserving 1 cup of the water. Add the pasta to the pan with the pesto and toss to coat evenly. Add the reserved water, if needed. Toss to mix well. Twist the noodles into a mound on each individual plate.

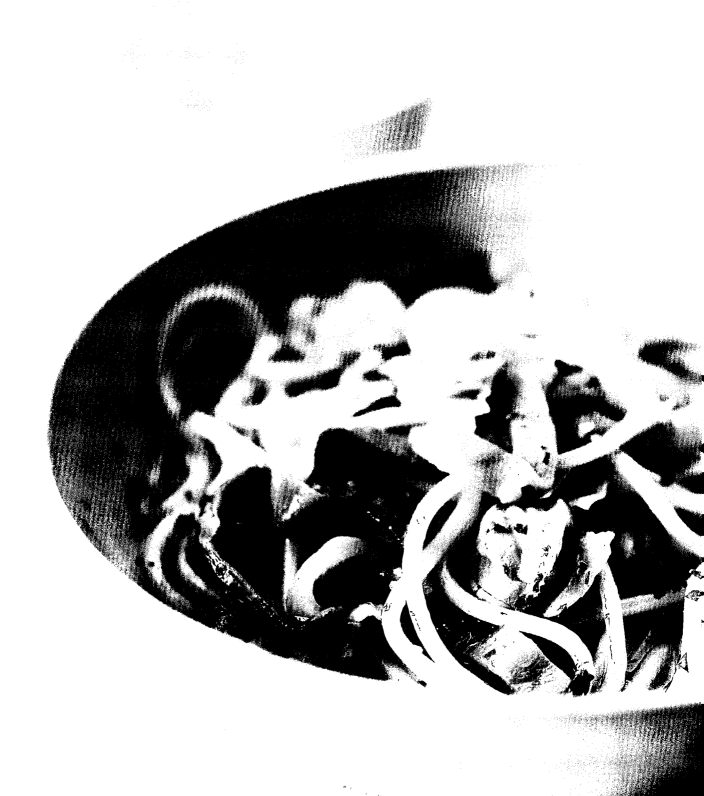

Roasted Peppers and Clams with Pasta Strands

Spaghetti alla Lucana

SERVES 6

This dish reflects the cuisine of Basilicata—once a very impoverished region—which relies heavily on the vegetables grown in the area, including bell peppers. In this recipe, the peppers are roasted to impart a smoky, sweet taste, which complements the salty taste of the clams. Lucana is the original Latin name for Basilicata. The Roman emperor Augustus chose the Latin name in honor of the Lucani, conquerors of the area in the middle of the fifth century B.C.

For the clams

¼   cup olive oil

2½ pounds small, fresh clams, well rinsed (see Note p. 192)

3   garlic cloves, chopped

1   tablespoon chopped fresh Italian parsley

½   lemon

½   cup dry white wine

Freshly ground pepper

5   teaspoons sea salt, plus extra for seasoning

1   medium yellow bell pepper

1   medium red bell pepper

⅓   cup plus 1 tablespoon olive oil

3   garlic cloves, sliced

1½ dried peperoncini, broken into small pieces

2   tablespoons chopped fresh Italian parsley

½   cup dry white wine

1   pound dry spaghetti

2   tablespoons extra-virgin olive oil

Freshly ground pepper

Preheat the broiler.

To prepare the clams Heat the olive oil in a large, high-sided sauté pan over high
heat. Add the clams, garlic, and parsley. Quickly squeeze the lemon over the clams,
then add it to the pan. Add the wine and a pinch of pepper. Cover and bring to a
boil. Cook until the clams begin to open, 1 to 2 minutes. Be careful not to overcook.
Spread on a baking sheet to cool. Strain the liquid into a medium bowl and
reserve. Remove the clams from their shells by gently scraping with a small spoon.
Reserve the empty shells.

Put the shells in a large stockpot. Add 5 quarts of water and the 5 teaspoons of
salt; bring to a boil over high heat. Reduce the heat and simmer 30 minutes.

Brush the bell peppers with 1 tablespoon of the olive oil. Put in an ovenproof skillet
and place under the broiler. Cook until black on all sides, 8 to 10 minutes, turning
frequently; don't overcook. Let cool. Peel the peppers and discard the seeds, stems,
and skin. Cut lengthwise into thin strips.

Heat the remaining ⅓ cup of olive oil in a large sauté pan over medium-high heat.
Add the garlic, peperoncini, and half of the parsley. Cook 2 to 3 minutes. Add the
wine and cook until nearly evaporated, about 5 minutes. Add the roasted peppers,
the clams, and their reserved liquid. Bring to a boil and season with salt.

Remove the clam shells from the water with tongs or a skimmer. Add enough water
so that you have 5 quarts again. Bring to a boil over high heat. Add the pasta
and cook until al dente. Transfer to a colander to drain. Add to the pan with the
clams. Add the remaining parsley. Toss to mix well. Drizzle with the extra-virgin
olive oil and season with pepper.

NOTE ON CLAMS I prefer to use Manila or New Zealand clams because they are
the most readily available on the West Coast. You can use any local fresh clams,
but avoid the larger ones, which can be tough.

my kitchen in spain

JANET MENDEL

about mendel
Janet Mendel is the author of *Cooking in Spain, Tapas and More Great Dishes from Spain* and *Traditional Spanish Cooking,* which won Britain's André Simon Award. She is an American-born journalist who has lived in Andalusia, Spain, for more than 30 years.

This is the rare book that manages to provide doable recipes we haven't seen hundreds of times before, which is why it's now on our permanent gift-giving list. While the ingredients are familiar, the combinations are not. When we fantasize about the expat life in Spain, this is what we dream about: delicious food and wonderful cooks.

FOOD & WINE What ingredients form the foundation of the Spanish pantry?
JANET MENDEL The Mediterranean diet starts with the trinity of wheat, olive oil and wine. You'll also find lots of fresh vegetables, fruits, seafood, nuts and legumes—chickpeas, lentils and different kinds of beans.
F&W What's the difference between Spanish cooking and the cooking of other Mediterranean countries?
JM Spanish cooking is closely related to Italian. And it probably uses more pork, fish and shellfish than any other Mediterranean country, including Italy.
F&W What are the basic principles of Spanish cooking?
JM Often what makes Spanish cooking interesting is the juxtaposition of ingredients, as in a white gazpacho made with almonds, garlic, olive oil, salt and vinegar, with sweet grapes as the garnish. While Spanish cooking

is simple and approachable, there is a real sophistication, a complexity about it that comes from the legacy of the Moorish Arabs.
F&W What are the most common spices?
JM Curiously, the most widely used spice is one most people do not think of as being Spanish: paprika. We call it *pimentón.* It goes into paella, stews and legume dishes. It flavors chorizo and can even be a substitute for saffron. Cumin and saffron are popular. And we use huge amounts of flat-leaf parsley as a main ingredient, not just as a garnish. Thyme goes well with rabbit, and oregano is great for marinades.
F&W What are some of your favorite foods from Spain?
JM I love garlicky, marinated fresh anchovies *(boquerones al natural),* which you can find in the deli section of your supermarket. Spain has the world's best ham, Ibérico. It's like

Serrano ham but even better. (It's still not imported to the U.S.) Torta del Casar is a very creamy cheese from Extremadura in western Spain; Idiazabal is a smoky cheese from the Basque country.

F&W What about Spanish olive oils?

JM They're superb. I like the single-varietal olive oils (Arbequina from Catalonia or Picual from Andalusia are examples). Spain produces more olive oil than any country in the world, but it came late to the marketing game, so close to a third of Spain's olive oil is shipped off to Italy to be packaged and exported. When you're buying olive oil in an American store, it may say "packaged in Italy" or "produced in Italy," but it may very well be Spanish.

F&W What are your favorite on-line sources for Spanish ingredients?

JM Tienda Inc. (www.tienda.com) and The Spanish Table (www.thespanishtable.com).

F&W Are there significant differences between the cooking in different regions of Spain?

JM There's an old cliché that the cooking styles in Spain are like the weather: In the north you stew, in the central plains you roast and in the south you fry. It's a generalization, but there's a bit of truth to it. There are some wonderful stewed dishes in the north; central plains cities like Madrid are known for baby lamb and suckling pigs roasted in big ovens; and in southern Spain, where most of the olive oil in the world is produced, frying is a very old tradition.

>> | **FEATURED RECIPES**

1 | DEVILED EGGS WITH SHRIMP AND OLIVES

2 | HOME-STYLE PORK CHOPS IN LEMON MARINADE

3 | FISH SOUP WITH SOUR ORANGE

4 | MARIA'S ROAST CHICKEN WITH MEAT AND OLIVE STUFFING

5 | FLAMENCO POTATO SALAD WITH LEMON DRESSING

the specifics

recipes	pages	photos	publisher	price
225	368	none	HarperCollins	$34.95

credits

Deviled Eggs with Shrimp and Olives

Huevos Rellenos con Gambas y Aceitunas

SERVES 16

Growing up in the American Midwest, I remember deviled eggs as special for picnics
and parties. This Spanish version, typical of tapa bars, makes an unusual alternative,
with shrimp and olives in the stuffing. Tuna can be substituted for the shrimp
to make this an economical dish, and, if desired, the egg yolks can be eliminated,
to make a low-cholesterol version.

8   eggs, hard-cooked

Lettuce leaves, for serving

½   cup cooked, peeled, and chopped shrimp

3   tablespoons chopped pimiento-stuffed olives

2   teaspoons minced onion

1   tablespoon chopped fresh flat-leaf parsley

1   tablespoon plus 2 teaspoons fresh lemon juice

¼   teaspoon salt

1   tablespoon olive oil

½   cup mayonnaise

1   red bell pepper, roasted, skinned, and cut into strips (or canned pimiento)

Cherry tomatoes, for garnish (optional)

Peel the eggs and cut in half lengthwise. Remove the yolks and set them aside.
Remove a sliver from the bottom of the whites so they will sit flat. Place the lettuce
on a serving platter and set the whites on it.

In a bowl, mash four of the yolks. Add the shrimp, olives, onion, parsley, 2 teaspoons
lemon juice, salt, and olive oil and combine well. Scoop this mixture into the egg
whites so each white is just filled.

Stir the mayonnaise with the remaining 1 tablespoon lemon juice until it reaches
spreading consistency. (If necessary, thin with a little water.) Top each egg with a
cap of mayonnaise. Grate the reserved yolks over the stuffed eggs. Lay a strip of red
pepper on top of each. (The eggs can be prepared and kept chilled for up to 3 hours
before serving.) Garnish the platter with cherry tomatoes.

Home-Style Pork Chops in Lemon Marinade

Chuletas a la Casera, con Aliño

SERVES 4

This is a favorite way to prepare pork chops at home. Tangy lemon juice complements the flavor of fresh pork. A heap of Spanish fries is the perfect accompaniment.

In tapa bars, thin slices of pork loin are marinated in the same manner as these pork chops. They are fried very quickly on both sides and served on a slice of toasted baguette. These open-faced sandwiches are called *montaditos*, which translates roughly as "up in the saddle."

4   center-cut loin pork chops, each ¾ inch thick (about 1½ pounds)

1   teaspoon salt

2   garlic cloves, coarsely chopped

2   tablespoons chopped fresh flat-leaf parsley

Pinch dried thyme

¼   teaspoon pimentón

¼   cup fresh lemon juice

2   tablespoons olive oil

Sprinkle the chops with salt on both sides. Place them in a shallow dish and sprinkle with the garlic, parsley, thyme, pimentón, and lemon juice. Set aside to marinate for 15 minutes. Turn the chops and marinate for another 15 minutes.

In a large skillet, heat the oil over medium heat. Lift the chops out of the marinade and brown them for about 4 minutes on each side. They should be cooked through and slightly pink near the bone.

Pour any remaining marinade into the pan and raise the heat slightly. Cook for another 2 minutes until the chops are slightly glazed. Serve immediately, spooning pan sauce over the chops.

f&w tip
The Spanish fries that Mendel likes to eat with these succulent pork chops are essentially potatoes fried in olive oil, which gives them a Mediterranean flavor. We think steamed or boiled new potatoes would also make a nice accompaniment to these tangy chops.

Fish Soup with Sour Orange

Cachorreñas

SERVES 4

I love this soup, which is unusual and delicious, subtly flavored with the sour juice of the Seville orange. The fruit, with its bitter peel, is the marmalade orange. The trees were brought to Spain by the Moors, long before the arrival of the sweet orange, and are widely planted in courtyards and plazas in Andalusian cities. Nothing is so enchanting as a stroll through the old Santa Cruz district of Seville in the springtime, when the heady scent of orange blossoms perfumes the narrow alleyways. Later when the fruit ripens to glowing orange globes, tourists can't resist picking them. What a shock when they taste that sour juice!

Affectionately called *cachorreñas,* these oranges are used in quite a few Andalusian dishes. Look for bitter oranges at Hispanic markets (December through March). If they are not available, use half orange juice and half lemon juice in this recipe.

I like to make this soup with a whole hake, using the head and trimmings to prepare the broth in which to poach the fillets. I serve it as a main course, possibly preceded by a vegetable dish. However, you can prepare the soup with a lesser quantity of fish and serve it as a first course. Cod, haddock, or whiting could be used instead of hake. The soup is also concocted with *bacalao* (dry salt cod), which has been soaked to remove the salt.

2   pounds whole hake or cod, filleted, heads and trimmings
    reserved, or 1½ pounds fish fillets

2-inch strip orange zest

1   tablespoon salt

Sprig parsley

½   onion, chopped

1   tomato, chopped

1   small green bell pepper, seeds removed and chopped

1   bay leaf

1 cup lightly packed torn pieces of bread (2 ounces)

3 tablespoons olive oil

1 garlic clove

1 teaspoon pimentón

¼ teaspoon ground cumin

½ cup juice from sour oranges (or ¼ cup fresh orange juice
and ¼ cup fresh lemon juice)

Thinly sliced orange, for garnish

Chopped spring onion, for garnish

Combine the fish heads, bones, and trimmings in a soup pot and cover with 6 cups of water. Add the orange zest, salt, parsley, onion, tomato, green pepper, and bay leaf. Bring to a boil and simmer for 30 minutes. (If the heads and trimmings are not available, cook the zest, salt, parsley, onion, tomato, green pepper, and bay leaf in water for 15 minutes.)

Strain the liquid into another pan. Discard the fish heads and bones, parsley, zest, and bay leaf. Remove and discard the tomato core. Combine the tomato, onion, and green pepper in a blender with ½ cup of the reserved liquid, the bread, oil, garlic, pimentón, and cumin. Blend until smooth. (The mixture may be strained, if desired.)

Add the tomato mixture to the soup. Bring to a boil and cook at a slow boil 5 minutes.

Cut the fish fillets into 4 pieces. Add them to the soup and simmer for 5 minutes more. Hake is very delicate, so take care not to break it up. Stir in the orange juice and simmer for 1 minute more.

Serve the soup into four soup bowls, each with a piece of fish, garnished with a thin slice of orange and a sprinkling of chopped spring onion.

on mendel's nightstand

"My copy of **Claudia Roden's *A Book of Middle Eastern Food*** is a tattered Penguin edition from 1970," Mendel says. "The chapters on mezes and salads are great for party planning. I start with stuffed vine leaves and make almost every other dish right through tabbouleh and fattoush. I've even made the brain salad. I also like **Paula Wolfert's *Mediterranean Cooking*** for its range of North African recipes. Wolfert's recipes for preserved lemons and for the hefty soup harira are favorites of mine, but she includes some delectable dishes of France, Italy and Greece as well. With a perfect pistou and pesto, I hardly need another cookbook."

Maria's Roast Chicken with Meat and Olive Stuffing

Pollo Relleno al Horno al Estilo de María

SERVES 6 TO 8

I learned to make this festive dish in Maria's kitchen. Maria did the cooking in the tapa bar where I learned the basics of Spanish cooking. She made this stuffing with olives, pine nuts, chopped ham, and ground pork to fill a Christmas turkey. Use this stuffing mixture for chicken and turkey, as well as for rolled veal breast.

1   (6-pound) roasting chicken or small turkey

1   tablespoon fresh lemon juice

2½ teaspoons salt

1   cup fresh bread crumbs, packed

½   cup sliced pimiento-stuffed olives

¼   cup pine nuts

1   egg, hard-cooked and chopped

2   ounces serrano ham or lean bacon, chopped

¼   cup chopped fresh flat-leaf parsley

1   garlic clove, minced

Freshly ground black pepper

Freshly grated nutmeg

½   pound ground pork or beef

2   tablespoons olive oil

2   tablespoons chopped onions

1   chicken liver, chopped

1¼ cups white wine

Preheat the oven to 350°F.

Clean the chicken thoroughly, wash, and pat dry. Combine the lemon juice and ½ teaspoon of the salt and rub into the cavity.

In a bowl, combine the bread crumbs, olives, pine nuts, egg, ham, parsley, garlic, pepper, nutmeg, ground pork, and the remaining 2 teaspoons salt.

In a small skillet, heat 1 tablespoon of the oil over medium heat and sauté the onions and chopped chicken liver until the liver loses its pink color, about 5 minutes.

Add the liver and onions to the bread crumb mixture with ¼ cup of the wine. Mix well. Stuff the chicken with this mixture. Use a skewer to close the cavity. Place the chicken in a roasting pan. Brush it with the remaining 1 tablespoon oil.

Roast for 45 minutes. Remove the chicken and pour off the excess fat. Brush the chicken with some of the fat, then pour over the remaining 1 cup wine. Roast for 1 hour more, basting occasionally. (The internal temperature of the stuffing should reach 160°F.)

Let the chicken rest for 10 minutes before carving. Skim off the excess fat from the liquid in pan and serve the pan drippings separately.

"While Spanish cooking is simple and approachable, there is a real sophistication, a complexity about it that comes from the legacy of the Moorish Arabs. For example, you find spices and herbs used in subtle ways."

Flamenco Potato Salad with Lemon Dressing
Papas Aliñadas

SERVES 10 TO 12 AS A TAPA; SERVES 6 AS A SIDE DISH

The most exciting *juerga* (flamenco performance) I ever experienced was at a *venta* (country bar) in the province of Cádiz. Wine flowed, spirits rose, and tapas appeared. It was nearly midnight before the music and dancing began. There was no stage. Guitarists, singers, and dancers simply sat on chairs at one end of the room. A few strums, the sound of staccato clapping, a voice rising over the guitar, then a dancer stood, and began moving to the complicated flamenco rhythms. The *juerga* went on until the early hours of the morning, building in intensity, until the whole place seemed to throb with electricity.

This potato salad with its tangy lemon dressing was one of the tapas served at that night of flamenco. While mayonnaise is never mixed into this salad, some bars serve it with a "frosting" of mayonnaise.

2   pounds baking potatoes, such as russets or Idahos
    (5 to 6 medium potatoes)

1   teaspoon salt

4   spring onions or 1 small onion, minced

2   medium tomatoes, diced

¼   cup olive oil

⅓   cup fresh lemon juice

2   tablespoons chopped fresh flat-leaf parsley

2   eggs, hard-cooked and sliced, for garnish

1   (3-ounce) can tuna, drained, for garnish

Strips canned red pimiento, for garnish

12   pitted green olives, for garnish

Lettuce, for serving

In a large saucepan, bring 6 cups water to a boil. Add potatoes and boil in their skins until just tender, 20 to 25 minutes. Drain, then peel and slice the potatoes.

In a large bowl, combine the salt, onions, tomatoes, oil, lemon juice, and parsley. Add the potatoes and combine gently so the potatoes are evenly covered with the dressing. Allow the salad to marinate for at least 2 hours at room temperature before serving. (The potatoes can be prepared up to 1 day in advance and kept, covered and refrigerated, until serving time.)

Spread the potatoes on a platter. Garnish the top with the sliced egg, chunks of tuna, strips of pimiento, and olives. Place a few lettuce leaves around the potatoes.

baking in america

GREG PATENT

about patent

Greg Patent is the author of *A Is for Apple* and *New Frontiers in Western Cooking*. Born in Hong Kong and raised in Shanghai, Patent emigrated to the United States with his family when he was 11. He earned a Ph.D. from the University of California at Berkeley and became a professor of zoology at the University of Montana before leaving to devote himself to cooking. He lives in Missoula, Montana, with his wife, Dorothy.

Buy this book and you can throw out all the flawed and outdated baking books you own. Patent sorted through hundreds of American baking books from the past 200 years, selected the best recipes and adapted them to make sure they work. Perfectly. Instead of scaring you off by sounding overly technical, he'll lure you in.

FOOD & WINE What are some classic American baking recipes, and why did you decide to update them?

GREG PATENT Cheesecake is a 20th-century classic. Boston cream pie, pound cake, layer cake, angel food cake and just about any type of cookie are quintessentially American. I found these recipes in old cookbooks. When I was updating them, I kept in mind that certain ingredients were really different in the past. Flour and sugar weren't as pure white as they are today, for example, and eggs tended to be smaller. Recipes would typically give measurements by weight, and that was my starting point. I would write the recipe out and think, "These proportions aren't going to work today." So I would then tweak the recipe and see how it turned out, but try to stay true to the spirit of the recipe.

F&W How have desserts evolved?

GP In the mid-1800s there was a shift from yeast baking to leavening using baking powder and baking soda. Men began working in factories and offices instead of on the farm, so women had more household responsibilities and less time to bake. We didn't have real layer cakes until the 1880s, when baking powder became a staple.

F&W What are some common mistakes people make when they bake?

GP When combining dry ingredients, they don't stir everything thoroughly with a whisk. I like to sift, and I sift more than once. Another mistake: People don't monitor their oven's temperature. They really need to use an oven thermometer.

F&W How can I make my bread taste like the kind I buy at the bakery?

GP Use a baking stone. I have one oven lined with baking tiles. I spritz

>> | FEATURED RECIPES

1 | NECTARINE-RASPBERRY CRISP

2 | RHUBARB-STRAWBERRY PIE

3 | GINGERBREAD LITTLE CAKES

4 | CRANBERRY MUFFINS FROM NANTUCKET

the walls of the oven with water to create a steam chamber, which gives breads a nice crust.

F&W Do you have ingredient tips?

GP Unbleached and bleached flour are usually interchangeable, but if you're a novice baker making a cake or cookies that call for all-purpose flour, you should use bleached flour—a regular supermarket brand like Gold Medal or Pillsbury. It's slightly lower in gluten content, which makes it hard to make a mistake. I prefer to use unbleached all-purpose flour because it's not been subject to chemical processing. I can't taste any difference, but I like the look of it. It has a creamy cast. I also like unsalted butter. Plugrá, a rich European-style butter, is good for pie crusts; for all-purpose baking I like Land O'Lakes. Low-fat cream cheeses, like Kraft's Philadelphia Neufchâtel cheese with one-third less fat, make the best cheesecakes.

F&W How about storing dry ingredients?

GP If you're not using flour very often, keep it in the refrigerator in an airtight container. Use it within four to five months. A new can of baking powder should last four to six months, but you can test it to see if it's good: Mix half a teaspoon of baking powder in half a cup of tepid water. If the water gets bubbly, the powder is still active. To keep brown sugar from drying out, break it up into pieces and put it in a container with an apple slice. It should be moist within a couple of days. You can also microwave hard brown sugar to soften it.

the specifics

recipes	pages	photos	publisher	price
250	560	16 color photos	Houghton Mifflin Company	$35

credits

Nectarine-Raspberry Crisp

MAKES 8 TO 10 SERVINGS

Yellow nectarines reach their peak in the market just as our raspberries ripen.
The two are wonderful together, either raw or cooked. Do not use white nectarines
in this dessert. They are too sweet and watery. The topping for this crisp is extra
crunchy and buttery.

Topping

1   cup all-purpose flour

½   cup firmly packed light brown sugar

1   teaspoon freshly grated nutmeg

¼   teaspoon salt

8   tablespoons (1 stick) cold unsalted butter, cut in tablespoon-sized pieces

½   cup old-fashioned or quick-cooking (not instant) rolled oats

Filling

2   tablespoons sugar

½   teaspoon freshly grated nutmeg

Pinch of salt

Finely grated zest of 1 lemon

2½ pounds firm but ripe yellow nectarines (8–9), halved, pitted,
    and sliced into ½-inch wedges

2   cups fresh red or golden raspberries

2   tablespoons fresh lemon juice

f&w tip

This juicy crisp is a great make-ahead dish. We let the crisp stand at room temperature for 6 hours after baking it and ate it at room temperature (though it can also be reheated).

1. Adjust an oven rack to the lower third position and preheat the oven to 400°F. Lightly butter a 2½-quart baking dish, such as a 12-x-8-inch or round 10-x-2-inch pan.

2. For the topping, place the flour, brown sugar, nutmeg, and salt in a food processor. Pulse a few times to combine. Add the butter and pulse until it is in small pieces. Add the oats and process for 1 to 2 seconds, just to combine. Set aside.

3. For the filling, combine the sugar, nutmeg, salt, and lemon zest in a large bowl. Add the nectarines, raspberries, and lemon juice and fold everything together gently with a large rubber spatula. Spread the filling evenly in the baking dish.

4. Sprinkle the crumb mixture on top of the fruit, and spread it evenly with your hands to completely cover the fruit. Pat the filling gently in place, without packing it down.

5. Bake for 1 hour, or until the topping is lightly browned and the juices are thickened and bubbly. Cool on a wire rack, and serve warm or at room temperature. Refrigerate leftovers.

Rhubarb-Strawberry Pie

MAKES ONE 9-INCH PIE, 8 SERVINGS

Strawberries and rhubarb have worked their magic together in sauces, compotes, puddings, crisps, and pies ever since cooks first thought to combine the two. Be sure to make this pie only in the early summer, when rhubarb is tender and strawberries are bursting with flavor. Start the filling 6 to 8 hours ahead or the night before; macerating the rhubarb in the sugar overnight coaxes out the excess juices, which would otherwise make the pie unpredictably runny.

Filling

1½ pounds trimmed rhubarb, cut into ½-inch pieces (6 cups)

1¾ cups sugar

¼ teaspoon ground cloves

¼ teaspoon ground ginger

¼ teaspoon ground allspice

Finely grated zest of 1 orange

3 tablespoons fresh orange juice

¼ cup cornstarch

1 pint ripe strawberries, rinsed, patted dry, hulled, and sliced

2 tablespoons cold unsalted butter, cut into small pieces

1 Flaky Piecrust (recipe follows)

1 tablespoon sugar

1. For the filling, combine the rhubarb, sugar, and spices in a large bowl. Cover and let stand at room temperature for at least 6 to 8 hours, or overnight. Refrigerate if your kitchen is warm.

2. Stir the rhubarb mixture to dissolve any remaining sugar. Set a strainer over a bowl, transfer the rhubarb mixture to it, and let drain for about 1 hour.

3. Measure the juice, and add water if necessary to make 1¼ cups. Put the juice in a medium saucepan and whisk in the orange zest, orange juice, and cornstarch. Cook over medium heat, stirring gently and constantly with a heatproof rubber spatula, until the mixture boils and thickens, then cook, stirring gently, for 2 minutes more. Remove from the heat and let cool to room temperature.

4. Meanwhile, adjust one oven rack to the lowest position and the second in the center of the oven. Set a baking sheet on the lower rack and preheat the oven to 450°F.

5. Roll the larger piece of dough out on a lightly floured surface to a 12-inch circle. Fit it into a 9-inch pie plate, without stretching it. Leave the excess dough hanging over the edges. Refrigerate.

6. Roll out the second piece of pastry on the lightly floured surface to an 11-inch circle.

7. In a large bowl, fold together the rhubarb, cooled cornstarch mixture, and strawberries. Spoon the mixture into the bottom crust, mounding it slightly in the center. Distribute the pieces of butter over the filling. Brush the edges of the overhanging pastry lightly with water and cover the pie with the top crust, pressing the edges to seal. Trim away the excess pastry, leaving ½-inch overhang. Fold the overhang under itself to make a standing rim and flute it. Cut 6 slits in the top crust in a spoke pattern with the tip of a small sharp knife. Brush the pastry lightly with cold water and sprinkle it with the sugar.

8. Place the pie on the baking sheet and bake for 20 minutes. Transfer the pie and the baking sheet to the center shelf and reduce the temperature to 375°F. Continue baking for another 45 to 50 minutes, or until the crust is well browned and you can see thickened juices bubbling through the slits. Cool the pie on a wire rack for several hours before serving (if you cut the pie too soon, the filling may run). This pie is delicious slightly cold; I like to cool it for 2 to 3 hours, then refrigerate it for 2 to 3 hours.

f&w tip
If the edges of the pie crust begin browning before the crust is completely baked, carefully wrap the edges in aluminum foil to prevent them from browning any further.

Flaky Piecrust

"Certain ingredients were really different in the past. Flour and sugar weren't as pure white as they are today, for example, and eggs tended to be smaller."

MAKES ENOUGH FOR A
DOUBLE-CRUSTED 9-INCH PIE OR
TWO 9-INCH PIE SHELLS

This is my favorite basic pastry for all-butter double-crust pies. It is quick to make, easy to roll out, and deliciously tender and flaky. Although the dough is easily mixed by hand, I always use the food processor. The speed with which the metal blade chops the butter into the flour and incorporates the liquid minimizes gluten development. The amount of liquid may be a little bit more than you need, so add it very slowly toward the end of mixing. The dough should be moist enough to just hold together, but not at all wet or sticky.

Double Piecrust

2   cups all-purpose flour

⅔   cup cake flour

½   teaspoon salt

1   cup (2 sticks) cold unsalted butter, cut into tablespoon-sized pieces

½   cup ice water

1   large egg yolk

1   teaspoon cider vinegar

1. *If using a food processor,* pulse the flours and salt together for 5 seconds. Add the butter and pulse 4 times for about 1 second each, just to cut it into smaller pieces. Combine the water, egg yolk, and cider vinegar in a measuring cup. Pulsing rapidly, gradually pour the liquid through the feed tube in a thin stream until the dough forms several large clumps and *almost* gathers into a ball, 20 to 30 pulses. Watch closely. You may not need to add all the liquid.

If making the dough by hand, combine the flours and salt in a large bowl. Add the butter and cut it into the flour with a pastry blender or two knives until the mixture resembles coarse meal. Combine the water, egg yolk, and cider vinegar in a measuring cup. Sprinkle in the liquid gradually, about 1 tablespoon at a time, tossing the mixture with a fork and stirring just until the dough gathers into a ball. You may not need to add all the liquid.

2. Transfer the dough to a sheet of plastic wrap. Press the dough together and divide it into two pieces, one slightly larger than the other. Form each piece into a 1-inch-thick disk. Wrap the dough securely in plastic and refrigerate for at least 1 hour. (The dough can be made up to 2 days ahead.) Proceed with instructions in Step 5 of Rhubarb-Strawberry Pie recipe.

Gingerbread Little Cakes

MAKES ABOUT 24 COOKIES

f&w tip
The little cakes—which are really cookies—puff up a bit once they're baked, so avoid intricate cookie cutter shapes (gingerbread men, for example, don't come out well).

In the old days, many types of cookies were called cakes, and gingerbread was made from a dough, cut into various shapes, and baked. What we call gingerbread—the moist and spicy cake—didn't become popular until the late 1800s, after the development of baking powder and baking soda. These cookies are soft and spicy, with an extra kick from crystallized ginger. They are easily made in a saucepan.

2¼ cups all-purpose flour

½   cup finely chopped crystallized ginger

½   cup firmly packed light or dark brown sugar

½   cup molasses (I use Grandma's)

2   teaspoons ground ginger

1   tablespoon ground cinnamon

1   teaspoon ground cardamom

1½ teaspoons baking soda

8   tablespoons (1 stick) unsalted butter, at room temperature, cut into 8 tablespoon-sized pieces

1   large egg, lightly beaten

1. Combine 1 tablespoon of the flour with the crystallized ginger in a small bowl and toss to coat; set aside.

2. Combine the brown sugar, molasses, ground ginger, cinnamon, and cardamom in a medium heavy saucepan. Bring to a boil over medium heat, stirring occasionally with a wooden spoon. Immediately add the baking soda and stir as the mixture becomes thick and foamy and rises to the top of the pan. Remove from the heat and stir in the butter until melted. Stir in the egg. Gradually stir in the remaining flour in 3 or 4 additions, adding the chopped ginger after the second addition. The dough will be stiff.

3. Scrape the dough onto a sheet of waxed paper and knead it briefly to mix well. Cool to room temperature.

4. Adjust two oven racks to divide the oven into thirds and preheat the oven to 325°F. Line two baking sheets with cooking parchment or silicone liners.

5. Transfer the dough to an unfloured work surface and pat or roll it to a ⅜-inch thickness. Cut into shapes with cookie cutters and transfer to the baking sheets, spacing them about 2 inches apart. Gather the scraps, pat or roll them out again, and cut more cookies.

6. Bake for about 15 minutes, reversing the sheets from top to bottom and front to back once during baking, until the cookies look puffy and feel soft; do not overbake. Let cool on the pans for 5 minutes, then, with a wide metal spatula, carefully transfer them to racks to cool completely. Store airtight. These keep fresh for days.

Cranberry Muffins from Nantucket

MAKES 12 LARGE MUFFINS

These muffins are a specialty of the historic Jared Coffin House, a hotel and restaurant in Nantucket. They are light textured and sweet yet tangy. Chopped cranberries add more color and cook more evenly than whole berries. I adapted the recipe from one given to me many years ago by Sherry Strange, a cook who attended one of my food processor classes.

2   cups unbleached all-purpose flour

2   teaspoons baking powder, preferably nonaluminum

½   teaspoon salt

½   teaspoon freshly grated nutmeg

1½ cups fresh or frozen cranberries (see Note)

1   large egg

1   large egg yolk

¾   cup plus 2 tablespoons sugar

4   tablespoons (½ stick) unsalted butter,
    cut into tablespoon-sized pieces, at room temperature

¼   cup vegetable shortening

1   teaspoon pure vanilla extract

½   cup plus 2 tablespoons milk

1. Adjust an oven rack to the center position and preheat the oven to 350°F. Butter a 12-cup muffin pan, preferably nonstick, and set aside.

2. Combine the flour, baking powder, salt, and nutmeg in a food processor and process for 5 seconds. Transfer to a sheet of waxed paper and set aside.

3. Add the cranberries to the processor and pulse 3 to 5 times, until completely chopped. Remove from the work bowl.

4. Add the egg, egg yolk, and ¾ cup of the sugar to the processor and process for 1 minute. Add the butter, vegetable shortening, and vanilla and process for

1 minute, stopping the machine once to scrape the work bowl. With the machine running, add the milk and process for 5 seconds.

5. Sprinkle the dry ingredients over the mixture in the work bowl. Pulse twice, about 1 second each time. The batter will be thick and some flour will not be incorporated. Scrape most of the batter into a medium bowl. Pulse the processor for 1 second to spin off any batter clinging to the blade. Scrape the remaining batter into the bowl. Add the cranberries, and fold them into the batter with a rubber spatula.

6. Divide the batter evenly among the muffin cups, filling them quite full. Don't level the batter. Sprinkle the 2 remaining tablespoons sugar over the muffins, using about ½ teaspoon for each.

7. Bake for 20 to 25 minutes, until the muffins are light golden and spring back when gently pressed and a toothpick inserted into the center comes out clean. Cool the muffins in their cups for 5 minutes, then carefully remove them to a wire rack. Serve hot, warm, or at room temperature. These are best when very fresh.

NOTE If using frozen cranberries, thaw them just until they can be easily pierced with the tip of a sharp knife before chopping.

on patent's nightstand

"For baking, my favorite cookbook author is **Maida Heatter**," Patent says. "Her recipes have an unusual clarity and specificity, so it's hard to go wrong. When I bought her first book, **Maida Heatter's Book of Great Desserts,** in 1974, I felt compelled to make every single recipe in there. It took me a year and half, and there were some days when I would make five different things. I wrote to her once when I had a question about one of her recipes—I was in Montana and it was an altitude problem—and we became pen pals. Maida became a mentor to me."

live, love, eat!

WOLFGANG PUCK

This is definitely one of the most upbeat books on our list. Puck is serious about his food but he's also lighthearted and playful. He makes cooking seem like a labor of love (hence the title of his book) and not a work project (like many other authors). Some of the recipes are from his restaurants; others are Puck family favorites; all are crowd pleasers.

FOOD & WINE Why did you decide to write *Live, Love, Eat!*

WOLFGANG PUCK I've been writing cookbooks for years, but I always geared them toward people in the restaurant business. This time I wanted to keep things manageable and not create a coffee-table cookbook. So often, to make one recipe you have to make two others. And if it's a fancy four-story food tower and you have to make one for each guest? Forget it! You have to hire three sous-chefs just to serve it. The recipes in this book read well and they work. The chicken with garlic and parsley, for instance, doesn't have 100 ingredients. It's simple and delicious and that's what people want. These recipes are for home cooking; they reflect what I grew up eating—some are my mother's recipes—and my real cooking style.

F&W Are the recipes in the book really your favorites?

WP Yes, they are, but I always have new favorites! My style is always evolving. I'm always coming up with new recipes that become favorites. It's like being a singer. Bruce Springsteen is always coming up with new songs but you always know it's Bruce Springsteen.

F&W In the book you urge people to form a relationship with their ingredients. What's the best way to do that?

WP It's very important that you get to know the ingredients you're working with, much more important than following the recipe. Touch them; taste them when they're raw, at least the vegetables and fruits. Keep tasting them, touching them, smelling them, while they're cooking. When you're

>> | FEATURED RECIPES

1 | HOT SPINACH-
ARTICHOKE DIP

2 | GRILLED CHICKEN
BREASTS WTH GARLIC
AND PARSLEY

3 | TURKEY MUSHROOM
BURGERS WITH
CHUNKY TOMATO
SALSA COMPOTE

constantly checking food, you almost have a relationship with it. After an hour you'll start to really understand the process of cooking. Don't just trust the cooking times given in the recipes; they're usually approximate. Most chefs don't use timers; they trust their senses. And home cooks should, too.

F&W Do you think home cooks should throw away their timers?

WP No, there's nothing wrong with them, and if it helps you feel more comfortable, by all means use one. But keep in mind, there are so many variables in a recipe—the ingredients, equipment, the appliances you're using—that all will affect your recipe and the time it takes to cook. Always trust the sensory cues.

F&W Do you have suggestions for wines to drink with your dishes?

WP You can do endless research on the perfect wine and food pairings, and you can also adapt dishes to fit the wines you have, but for this kind of home cooking I think people should just choose any wine they happen to like and drink that. Of course, keeping in mind the flavors of the food and the wine will make the combination even better.

F&W Do you have any suggestions for cooking chicken breasts?

WP I know that everyone wants to cut down on their fat, but you should always roast chicken breasts with the skin on, especially if they're boneless. It helps seal flavorful juices in. And the cooked skin turns golden brown, which makes the dish look better.

the specifics

recipes	pages	photos	publisher	price
126	272	179 color photos	Random House	$35

credits

Live, Love, Eat! by Wolfgang Puck, copyright © 2002 by Wolfgang Puck Worldwide, Inc. Used by permission of Random House, Inc. Photographs by Matthew Klein, Yoshiharu Koizumi and Steven Rothfeld.

LIVE, LOVE, EAT! I **WOLFGANG PUCK**

Hot Spinach-Artichoke Dip

MAKES 4 TO 6 SERVINGS

In this elegant-yet-easy party dip, spinach and artichoke hearts blend together with Parmesan; tangy goat cheese; the thick and slightly soured Italian-style cream cheese known as mascarpone; and the French soured cream known as crème fraîche. All you need to add is hot, crusty French bread or your favorite chips or crackers. To make preparation even easier, look for commercial bags of baby spinach leaves, which need no washing or stemming; one 10-ounce bag is the equivalent of a 1-pound bunch of spinach with its stems.

3	bunches of spinach, thoroughly washed and stemmed
1	package frozen artichoke hearts, 10 ounces, thawed and drained
1	cup mayonnaise
⅓	cup mascarpone cheese
⅓	cup crème fraîche
½	cup freshly grated Parmesan cheese
2	tablespoons goat cheese
2	tablespoons Roasted Whole Garlic (recipe follows)
1	tablespoon lemon juice
1	teaspoon salt
¼	teaspoon black pepper
2	tablespoons bread crumbs
¼	teaspoon paprika

1. Bring a large pot of water to a boil. On the counter near the pot, place a large mixing bowl filled with ice and water. Put a third of the spinach in a large metal sieve and submerge it in the boiling water for about 1 minute. Transfer the spinach in the sieve to the bowl of iced water and leave to cool for 30 seconds. Remove the sieve from the water and, with the back of a large metal or wooden spoon, press firmly down on the spinach to squeeze out as much water as possible. Set aside in another mixing bowl. Repeat with the remaining spinach.

2. Preheat the oven to 375°F. Put the artichoke hearts in the bowl of a food processor fitted with the metal blade. Pulse the machine until the artichoke hearts are very coarsely chopped, 5 to 7 seconds. Add the mayonnaise, mascarpone cheese, crème fraîche, ¼ cup of the Parmesan cheese, the goat cheese, Roasted Whole Garlic, lemon juice, salt, and pepper. Process just until combined, about 5 seconds more.

3. Add the reserved blanched spinach to the processor and pulse the machine a few times more, just until it is thoroughly blended with the other ingredients. The dip should still have some texture. Spoon into a shallow 3- to 4-cup baking dish.

4. In small bowl, toss together the remaining Parmesan with the bread crumbs and paprika; evenly sprinkle the mixture over the dip. Bake in the preheated oven until the dip is heated through and its topping is golden brown, 15 to 20 minutes. Serve hot with crusty bread or crackers for dipping.

f&w tip
We liked dipping vegetables and sliced pita bread into this addictive dip. Instead of fresh spinach, we substituted a 10-ounce package of thawed frozen spinach (well drained), and it worked beautifully.

Roasted Whole Garlic

MAKES ½ TO ¾ CUP

Roasting garlic develops a sweet, mellow, full flavor without raw garlic's familiar harshness. Store it in the refrigerator, covered, for up to 3 days.

4   whole heads garlic

About ⅓ cup extra-virgin olive oil

1. Preheat the oven to 375°F.

2. Arrange the garlic heads in a small roasting pan and toss them with the olive oil, coating them well.

3. Roast the garlic until very tender, 50 to 60 minutes. Remove from the oven and leave them to cool at room temperature. When the garlic is cool enough to handle, use a serrated knife to cut the heads in half, crosswise. Remove the softened garlic pulp from the skins, either by squeezing each half or by scooping the garlic out with a tiny spoon or small knife.

4. Transfer the puree-soft roasted garlic to a container, cover, and refrigerate. Use as needed.

Grilled Chicken Breasts with Garlic and Parsley

SERVES 4

Grilled boneless chicken halves, simply seasoned with garlic and parsley and topped with garlic-lemon butter, have long been a Spago classic. The recipe becomes even simpler and quicker when you use boneless chicken breasts. Make sure you get the charcoal very hot and coated with gray ash before grilling the chicken. If you use a gas or electric grill, get it very hot, too, then turn down the heat to medium just before you put the chicken breasts on. If you prefer, you could sauté or pan-roast the chicken breasts instead of grilling. Either way, serve them with your favorite vegetables, cooked al dente.

12 garlic cloves, peeled

¼ cup flat-leaf parsley leaves

Salt

Freshly ground white pepper

4 boneless chicken breast halves, skin on

2 tablespoons unsalted butter

Juice of 1 large lemon

1 tablespoon finely chopped parsley

1. Bring a small saucepan of water to a boil. Add the garlic cloves and blanch them for 1 minute, then drain the garlic and, as soon as it is cool enough to handle, slice it thinly. Put the slices in a small bowl, add the parsley leaves and a little salt and white pepper, and toss them together.

2. With a finger, loosen a pocket between the skin and meat of each chicken breast, taking care not to separate the skin completely from the meat. Stuff about 2 teaspoons of the garlic-parsley mixture under the skin of each chicken breast. Place the chicken breasts on a plate, cover with plastic wrap, and chill in the refrigerator until ready to use. Cover the remaining garlic-parsley mixture with plastic wrap and refrigerate it, too.

3. Heat a charcoal or gas grill until moderately hot. Grill the chicken breasts 6 to 8 minutes per side, just until cooked through, taking care not to overcook them.

4. While the chicken is grilling, melt the butter in a sauté pan and gently sauté the remaining garlic-parsley mixture just until it is fragrant. Stir in the lemon juice and chopped parsley and season to taste with salt and pepper.

5. As soon as the chicken breasts are done, place them on 4 large heated dinner plates. Spoon the sautéed garlic and parsley over each breast.

f&w tip
This recipe calls for boneless breasts with the skin on, which can be hard to find. Buy bone-in chicken breasts and remove the meat from the bone yourself. It's much less expensive than buying boneless breasts, and you can use the bones to make a quick chicken stock.

Turkey Mushroom Burgers with Chunky Tomato Salsa Compote

SERVES 8

People love turkey or chicken burgers today because they're so lean. But that lack of fat can also make them dry. I solve that problem by adding a moist puree of cooked mushrooms, which also gives the burgers even more flavor. Because you wouldn't want to eat a poultry burger anything other than well done, it's a good idea to shape them thinner than a beef burger so they'll cook fairly quickly without losing too much moisture. Try the special technique I give below for shaping thin burger patties without risk of them falling apart.

Turkey mushroom burgers

2   tablespoons extra-virgin olive oil

¼   pound (1 stick) unsalted butter

3   garlic cloves, peeled and minced

1   teaspoon minced onion

1   bay leaf

1   pound button mushrooms, finely chopped

1   pound portobello mushrooms, stemmed and cut into ¼-inch dice

Salt

Freshly ground black pepper

¼   cup chopped fresh thyme

¼   cup chopped fresh oregano

2   pounds ground turkey

Chunky tomato salsa compote

1   cup Tomato Concassé (recipe follows)

¼   cup minced red onion

¼   cup minced green onion

¼   cup minced fresh cilantro

3 tablespoons lime juice

2 tablespoons minced jalapeño chili

2 tablespoons vegetable oil

1 tablespoon honey

½ teaspoon salt

2 tablespoons extra-virgin olive oil, for oiling
   the grill rack or heating in a skillet

8 hamburger buns

10 ounces queso fresco (Mexican fresh white cheese)
   or other mild white cheese, crumbled or shredded

Thinly sliced red onion

Romaine lettuce leaves

on puck's nightstand
Puck says, "I still always read *Larousse Gastronomique,* the bible of French cooking, and I also like **Nancy Silverton's** first pastry book, *Desserts.* I think one of the most amazing books is *Maida Heatter's Book of Great Desserts:* The recipes are lengthy but they're well tested, and I love the little stories that she has for each one."

1. Heat a large sauté pan over medium-high heat. Add the olive oil and butter and, when the butter has melted, add the garlic, onion, and bay leaf and sauté until fragrant, 1 minute. Add the mushrooms, season with salt and pepper to taste, and cook, stirring frequently, until most of the liquid released by the mushrooms has evaporated and the mixture looks almost dry, 10 to 15 minutes. Stir in the thyme and oregano. Remove from the heat and let the mixture cool to room temperature. Remove the bay leaf.

2. Put the turkey in a large mixing bowl and add the cooled mushroom mixture. Stir with a wooden spoon, or mix with your hands, until the turkey and mushrooms are thoroughly combined. Mix in salt and pepper to taste.

3. Divide the mixture into 8 equal portions, forming each into a compact, even ball. To form each patty, place a sheet of plastic wrap about 12 inches long on a work surface and brush it with some olive oil. Put a ball of turkey mixture in the center of one half of the sheet and fold the other half over it. With the back of a plate, press down on the ball to flatten it to an even patty about ¾ inch thick. Repeat with the remaining balls. Refrigerate until ready to cook.

"Don't just trust the cooking times given in the recipes; they're usually approximate. Most chefs don't use timers; they trust their senses. And home cooks should, too."

4. **To make the chunky tomato salsa compote** In a small saucepan, combine the Tomato Concassé, red and green onion, cilantro, lime juice, jalapeño, vegetable oil, honey, and salt. Bring to a boil over medium-high heat. Reduce the heat to a simmer and cook, stirring occasionally, until most of the liquid has evaporated, about 10 minutes.

5. Build a fire in a charcoal grill or preheat a gas grill, grill pan, or the broiler. Just before cooking, use the oil to grease the grill's cooking grid, or heat a large skillet over medium-high heat and add the olive oil. Remove the plastic wrap from the turkey burgers and grill, broil, or pan-fry them until cooked through, 4 to 5 minutes per side.

6. With a spatula, transfer the turkey burgers to the bottom halves of the buns. Top each burger with a generous spoonful of the chunky tomato salsa compote, some fresh white cheese, sliced red onion, and a romaine leaf. Serve immediately.

Tomato Concassé

The French verb *concasser* means literally to chop coarsely or to pound. In the kitchen, "concassé" most often refers to tomatoes that have been chopped after peeling and seeding them. Doing this will concentrate the flavor of even raw tomatoes. And when Tomato Concassé is added to a cooked dish, the tomatoes break down, cook, and spread through the dish more evenly.

1. Bring a pot of water to a boil. Fill a large mixing bowl with ice and water. With a small, sharp knife, score a shallow X in the flower end of each tomato.

2. Add the tomatoes to the boiling water and blanch them for about 30 seconds. Drain the tomatoes and immediately plunge them into the bowl of ice water.

3. Drain the tomatoes and, starting at the scored X, peel them, using your fingertips or, if necessary, the knife. Cut out the cores. Cut the tomatoes lengthwise into quarters and, with your fingertip, remove their seeds.

4. Cut the quartered tomatoes lengthwise into uniform slices ½ to ¼ inch wide. Cut across the slices in the same uniform width to make even dice.

a return to cooking

ERIC RIPERT & MICHAEL RUHLMAN

about ripert
Eric Ripert is partner and chef of the New York City restaurant Le Bernardin. Born in Antibes, he was trained in classic French cooking and was mentored by Joël Robuchon in the kitchens of Jamin in Paris and by the late Jean-Louis Palladin at the former Jean-Louis at the Watergate in Washington, D.C. He is coauthor of *Le Bernardin Cookbook: Four-Star Simplicity.*

A Return to Cooking

ERIC RIPERT | MICHAEL RUHLMAN

Having established himself as one of the great chefs of our time, Eric Ripert clearly needed to get back to the heart of his cooking: the home kitchen. Watching him struggle to break away from the restaurant mentality is fascinating, especially because the resulting recipes are uncontrived, delicious and doable.

FOOD & WINE Your book takes such an unusual approach, highlighting four of your favorite U.S. destinations (Puerto Rico, Vermont, Sag Harbor on Long Island and Napa Valley), each in a different season. How did you come up with this premise?

ERIC RIPERT It really came from a need for me to get out of the restaurant kitchen and feel connected to cooking again. I simply went into people's houses and worked with the ingredients at hand. It was all improvisation. The photographer who traveled with me had no plans; the painter who came along brought white canvases.

F&W How did the book evolve?
ER I knew how I wanted to approach the book from the start, but I didn't know there would be so many techniques to include, plus so much information about ingredients, like

chorizo. I add it to a Puerto Rican– inspired cod recipe; chorizo is the twist that makes the dish special.
F&W Is chorizo your new favorite ingredient?
ER Maybe! But maybe my new favorite is sausages in general; they are so flavorful, even a little boosts a dish. I can never forget the smoked ones in Vermont.
F&W What was it like to cook in a home instead of a restaurant?
ER Cooking in a home kitchen wasn't that hard for me because I cook at home in New York all the time. But maybe it was a little more difficult because some of the stoves I borrowed had only four burners.
F&W Any other challenges?
ER Well, certainly coming up with original ideas every day and producing so many recipes was a challenge. None of the dishes in the book come from

Le Bernardin. In fact, the opposite: I put some of the book's dishes on the restaurant menu for a while. The baked potatoes with caviar, which I created in Vermont, were really popular.

F&W Does home cooking have any kind of special meaning for you?

ER Yes, absolutely. My mother is an excellent cook. My Salade Monique— a mixture of potatoes, haricots verts, asparagus and apple inspired by her big rustic salads—is dedicated to her.

F&W What's the best advice you can give the home cook?

ER If you're having guests over for dinner, organize yourself before they arrive. Take 20 minutes in the afternoon to write down all the cooking steps. Prepare your ingredients and place them around the kitchen in containers. That will save time and help you avoid panic.

F&W You know fish so well; do you have advice for shopping for it?

ER I've bought fish my whole life. I don't like to catch it, which makes me a hypocrite; I like to cook it but not to kill it. Here's what I do: I make sure it looks appealing, especially the color. If the fish is gray or dark, that's not a good sign. Dry is not a good sign at all.

F&W Will you do another book?

ER I'm going to do another book, but it makes no sense to do *A Return to Cooking II*. I was thinking about describing my return to Le Bernardin— a different kind of return to cooking. We'll see.

>> FEATURED RECIPES

1 COD WITH LOCAL WAX BEANS, CHORIZO, AND SOY-SHERRY SAUCE

2 ARUGULA SALAD WITH GOAT'S MILK YOGURT DRESSING

3 SHRIMP WITH FRESH COCONUT MILK, CALABAZA, AND AVOCADO

4 MUSSELS WITH SPICY ITALIAN SAUSAGE

the specifics

recipes	pages	photos	publisher	price
143	336	253 color photos plus artwork	Artisan	$50

credits

A Return to Cooking by Eric Ripert and Michael Ruhlman. Excerpted from *A Return to Cooking*. Copyright © 2002 by Eric Ripert. Photographs copyright © 2002 by Tammar and Shimon Rothstein. Paintings copyright © 2002 by Valentino Cortazar. Used by permission of Artisan, a division of Workman Publishing Co., Inc., New York. All rights reserved.

Cod with Local Wax Beans, Chorizo, and Soy-Sherry Sauce

SERVES 6

I think of cod as a "masculine" fish—meaning it has a very firm body and hearty character that you can put very strong flavors with, things like garlic and bacon. Scallops would be "feminine," requiring delicate accompanying flavors such as peas or asparagus. Here, I like spicy robust chorizo with the cod, paired with a soy-vinegar-ginger sauce—and plenty of butter, again because the cod is so hearty. Without even realizing it, I'm cooking Spanish. I love these powerful, vibrant flavors.

¼   **pound wax beans**

2   **tablespoons soy sauce, preferably organic**

2   **tablespoons sherry vinegar**

5   **drops Tabasco sauce**

2   **teaspoons minced ginger**

2   **teaspoons minced shallot**

9   **tablespoons unsalted butter**

Fine sea salt and freshly ground white pepper

2   **tablespoons canola oil**

Twelve 3-ounce cod fillets

¼   **pound chorizo, cut into 3-inch julienne**

2   **teaspoons chopped flat-leaf parsley**

Prep 20 minutes   **Cook** 20 minutes

Snap the ends off the beans and halve them lengthwise. Blanch the beans in boiling salted water for 2 minutes, or until crisp-tender. Drain and shock in an ice-water bath to stop the cooking. Drain and set aside.

For the sauce, bring the soy sauce, sherry vinegar, Tabasco, ginger, and shallot to a boil in a small saucepan. Whisking constantly, add 8 tablespoons of the butter to the pan, a tablespoon at a time, making sure each tablespoon of butter has been absorbed before adding another. Season to taste with salt and pepper. Set aside.

"Cooking in a home kitchen wasn't that hard for me because I cook at home in New York all the time. But maybe it was a little more difficult because some of the stoves I borrowed had only four burners."

Place two large nonstick sauté pans over high heat and add 1 tablespoon of the canola oil to each. Season the cod fillets on both sides with salt and pepper. When the oil is hot, add 6 fillets to each pan. Sauté for 3 to 5 minutes, or until the cod is golden brown on the first side. Turn the fillets over and cook for 30 seconds.

Meanwhile, heat the chorizo and beans in a pan with the remaining 1 tablespoon butter. Season to taste with salt and pepper. Add the parsley and toss to incorporate. Gently reheat the sauce, being careful not to let it boil.

To serve, place a piece of cod browned side down on each plate and top with a little of the chorizo-bean mixture. Top each with another cod fillet, browned side up. Drizzle the sauce around the cod. Serve immediately.

Chorizo Eric began to use chorizo here, and it would be like a theme everywhere we went. A chunk was always in the fridge or in the shopping cart or sliced on a board to snack on as we cooked or, as in this cod dish, in the food itself. In Portugal and in the northwestern region in Spain called Galicia, chorizo is often paired with seafood, especially in seafood stews, and so it is a natural extension of Eric's history that he pairs it with fish here (and later with mussels).

Chorizo, which is now available in many places throughout the United States, is a pork sausage powerfully flavored with paprika and garlic and hot spices. It can be fresh or dry, though Eric works only with dry chorizo—and the dryer the better.

It works double duty as an ingredient—when it cooks, the powerful meaty flavors leak into the dish to act as a seasoning device, and the fat, as it renders, enriches the dish.

Arugula Salad with Goat's Milk Yogurt Dressing

SERVES 6

This easy salad combines two powerful and intriguing flavors—peppery arugula and earthy, acidic goat's milk yogurt, enhanced by garlic, shallots, chives, and pine nuts. Wait to dress it at the last minute if it will be traveling.

½   cup goat's milk yogurt

1   teaspoon minced shallot

¼   teaspoon minced garlic

Fine sea salt and freshly ground white pepper

1½ teaspoons thinly sliced chives

2   large bunches arugula, stems removed and thoroughly washed

¼   cup pine nuts, toasted and coarsely chopped

Prep 10 minutes

In a small bowl, whisk the yogurt, shallot, and garlic to combine. Season with salt and pepper. Whisk in the chives. Cover and refrigerate. *(This can be done early in the day.)*

To serve, place the arugula and pine nuts in a large bowl. Lightly season with salt and pepper. Add enough dressing to lightly coat the arugula (you may not need all of the dressing) and toss. Serve immediately.

Shrimp with Fresh Coconut Milk, Calabaza, and Avocado

SERVES 6

The broth

1   tablespoon unsalted butter

2   shallots, thinly sliced

3   garlic cloves, thinly sliced

1   lemongrass stalk, thinly sliced

One 1-inch piece of ginger, thinly sliced

1   kaffir lime leaf

3   cups chicken stock

¾   cup coconut milk, fresh or canned

4   cilantro sprigs

Fine sea salt and freshly ground white pepper

The shrimp

2   tablespoons chopped cilantro

2   tablespoons chopped scallion

2   tablespoons chopped ginger

2   tablespoons canola oil

36 large shrimp, peeled and deveined

⅛   teaspoon cayenne pepper

1   medium calabaza squash (found in Latino markets;
    you can substitute butternut squash)

1   tablespoon unsalted butter

1   avocado

1   lime, halved

Prep 35 minutes   **Cook** 35 minutes

To make the broth, melt the butter in a small sauté pan over medium heat. Add the shallots, garlic, lemongrass, ginger, and kaffir lime leaf and cook until tender; do not allow them to color. Add the chicken stock and bring to a boil. Lower the heat and simmer for 15 minutes.

Add the coconut milk and cilantro and simmer for 5 minutes. Season to taste with salt and pepper. Strain through a fine-mesh sieve and set aside.

For the shrimp, combine the cilantro, scallion, ginger, and oil in a large bowl. Season the shrimp generously with salt, pepper, and the cayenne pepper and add to the bowl, tossing to coat the shrimp with the cilantro mixture. Place the shrimp on a baking sheet, making sure they are not touching one another, cover with plastic wrap, and refrigerate.

Peel the squash with a chef's knife. Cut the squash into ½-inch cubes; you will need at least 60 cubes.

Combine the butter and ½ cup water in a small saucepan and place over medium heat. When the butter has melted, add the squash dice, season with salt and pepper, and cook at a simmer until the squash is tender, about 10 minutes. Let cool to room temperature.

Divide the squash cubes among six ovenproof soup bowls, leaving space to alternate with the avocado dice (which you will prepare just before serving). Set aside. *(You can cover the bowls with plastic wrap and refrigerate until you are ready to serve the shrimp, up to 3 hours.)*

Preheat the oven to 350°F. Remove the bowls from the refrigerator.

Shortly before serving (to prevent the avocado from browning), halve, pit, and peel the avocado. Cut into ½-inch cubes and place 10 pieces in each of the prepared soup bowls, alternating with the squash.

on ripert's nightstand

Ripert uses cookbooks a lot, "not necessarily to follow the recipes but to get inspired." His favorites are **Paul Bocuse's La Cuisine du Marche, Alain Ducasses's La Mediterranées: Cuisine de l'Essentiel** and **Thomas Keller's The French Laundry Cookbook.**

Place the shrimp in the oven for 4 minutes, or until just barely cooked. During the last minute of cooking, put the prepared soup bowls in the oven to heat.

Meanwhile, reheat the reserved sauce over medium heat.

To serve, place 6 shrimp in each bowl, to form a pinwheel. Spoon about ¼ cup of the sauce over the shrimp and squeeze the lime juice over all the bowls. Serve immediately.

Mussels with Spicy Italian Sausage

SERVES 6

A simple ragout of shellfish and sausage, so easy to prepare it's almost a heat-and-serve dish. Cook the shallots and garlic, then the sausage, add the wine and rosemary, then the mussels, which will release their juices into the pan, and finish with the parsley and bread crumbs—a rustic, spicy, brothy dish to be eaten with good crusty bread.

2   **tablespoons extra virgin olive oil**

2   **shallots, thinly sliced**

2   **garlic cloves, thinly sliced**

Fine sea salt and freshly ground white pepper

2   **links spicy Italian sausage, casings removed and roughly chopped**

1   **cup dry white wine**

1   **rosemary sprig**

3   **pounds small mussels, scrubbed and beards removed**

1   **tablespoon chopped flat-leaf parsley**

2   **tablespoons fresh bread crumbs, toasted**

Prep 15 minutes   **Cook** 15 minutes

Place the olive oil in a large heavy-bottomed pot over medium heat. When the oil is hot, add the shallots and garlic, season with salt and pepper, and cook until the shallots are translucent but still have a bit of crunch, about 3 minutes.

Add the sausage to the pan and cook, stirring to crumble it, for 5 minutes, or until thoroughly cooked. Add the wine and rosemary and bring to a boil. Lower the heat to medium, add the mussels, cover the pan, and steam until the mussels open, 3 to 5 minutes.

Sprinkle the parsley and bread crumbs over all. Divide the mussels among six bowls and ladle the broth and sausage over them. Serve with crusty bread.

the zuni café cookbook

JUDY RODGERS

about rodgers
Judy Rodgers was born and raised in Saint Louis, Missouri. She and her business partner, Vince Calcagno, have run Zuni Café in San Francisco for 16 years. She was awarded Best Chef: California 2000 by the James Beard Foundation.

Judy Rodgers's magnum opus, this book is filled with tips on what to look for, listen for, sniff for and taste for in the kitchen. You glean so much from just reading the recipe headnotes that you don't even need to cook from the book to learn enormously from it. Rodgers is precise with every technique and always original in the way she thinks about food.

FOOD & WINE How long did it take you to write this book?

JUDY RODGERS I've been thinking about it for years and years—15 on top of the five it took to actually do it.

F&W What was the biggest challenge in representing Zuni Café's food here?

JR Making sure the recipes are stupendously delicious even when they're not cooked in the smoke and intense heat of a brick oven. The other big thing was sorting out the mix of recipes. The restaurant is well known for lots of off-the-wall stuff, so I wanted the book to represent the unusual things as well as the more mainstream dishes. I was afraid that I'd be critiqued for having a book that's too obscure—you need the right mix of straight and weird things.

F&W So you're happy with the mix?

JR I fought for all the offbeat stuff—ingredients like pig's feet and *bottarga di tonno* [salted, dried tuna roe]. The reason people don't know about some of these ingredients is because no one asks them to use these foods. You probably had to find a substitute for radicchio 15 years ago. I wanted to expand the repertoire of what people are doing, and to make them dream. But not for every recipe.

F&W If people could learn one thing from this cookbook, what would it be?

JR To taste. You should trust your taste and train it frequently—instead of tasting just once at the end and possibly being disappointed, or tasting once in the beginning and once in the end and not knowing what happened in between. I tell people to take a spoonful of something, like a stew, and then salt it; if you don't like it, you can throw it away. I encourage cooks to go too

>> FEATURED RECIPES

1 SHRIMP COOKED IN ROMESCO WITH WILTED SPINACH

2 LAMB'S LETTUCE WITH RAW ASPARAGUS, PISTACHIOS, AND PARMIGIANO-REGGIANO

3 PASTA ALLA CARBONARA

4 QUAIL AND SAUSAGE BRAISED WITH GRAPES

far with a little bit of something to train their palates to recognize the continuum from, say, undersalted to correctly seasoned to oversalted. It's like driving. You have to encounter all conditions, from rain to sleet to snow, preferably in the same car on the same trip, to be a knowledgeable driver.

F&W Why is salt so important?

JR Salt is about more than taste. I'm really interested in how salt makes things juicy and tender. One day I got quizzed about this, literally, by Michael Bauer [the executive food and wine editor at the *San Francisco Chronicle*], who asked me why my hamburger is so succulent. I went on a mission; without enrolling in a chemistry course, I found out why salting the beef improved the burger so much. Harold McGee, the author of *On Food and Cooking,* was extremely helpful, as was Robert L. Wolke, the author of *What Einstein Told His Cook.* In my book I wanted to inform laymen about this without offending scientists.

F&W Do you have a favorite salt?

JR For seasoning I use sea salt and kosher salt. I really like those hand-harvested artisanal salts, but I don't live and die by them—they're just not economically viable at the restaurant.

F&W What do you hope people take away from your book?

JR The importance of being engaged and involved in the process of cooking. I'll feel really lucky and happy if readers find some of the pleasure I've had from cookbooks—even if they don't make a single recipe from them.

the specifics

recipes	pages	photos	publisher	price
250	552	24 color photos	W.W. Norton & Company	$35

credits

The Zuni Café Cookbook: A Compendium of Recipes & Cooking Lessons from San Francisco's Beloved Restaurant by Judy Rodgers. Copyright © 2002 by Judy Rodgers. Wine notes and selections copyright © 2002 by Gerald Asher. Original photographs copyright © 2002 by Gentl & Hyers. W.W. Norton & Company.

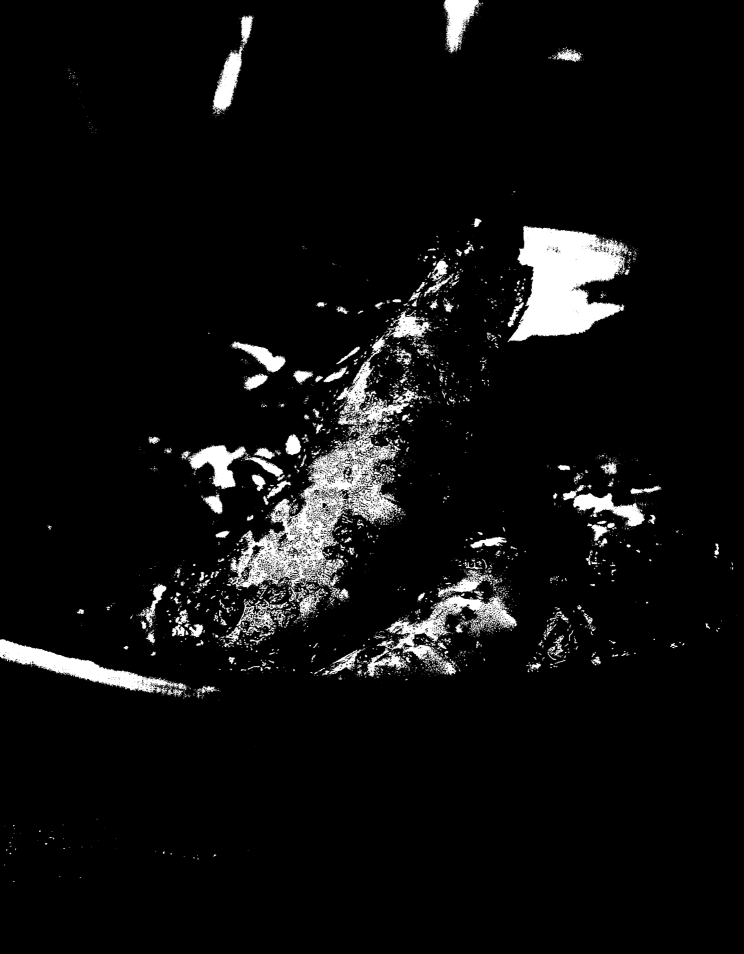

Shrimp Cooked in Romesco with Wilted Spinach

FOR 4 SERVINGS

In Tarragona, on the Catalonian Coast, where romesco is traditional, the word refers to the sauce base, the chili pepper used to make it, and the finished dish it defines, and when there's enough of it, it seems to become a *romescada*.

The romesco sauce base is a bit labor-intensive, but it is versatile, keeps well, and improves as the flavors mingle, so we always make a large amount and use it with different seafood over the course of a week. This shrimp dish is the easiest of our romesco dishes, but it is nearly as easy to steam open and then simmer mussels or clams in romesco. Or you can cook medallions of halibut, monkfish, or salt cod in the sauce. Or make a delicious event of combining a few kinds of fish and shellfish. Regarding ingredients: I encourage you to avoid farmed shrimp. Buy American-caught wild shrimp at specialty fish markets—all of which, by law, ought to be "turtle-safe" (meaning the traps exclude sea turtles). (A similar system that permits shrimpers to avoid destroying massive numbers of juvenile fish has also been mandated by federal law, although its use is not yet well enforced.) Asking for and paying a little more for these sustainably harvested shrimp is a good way to encourage responsible shrimping.

I like to cook the shrimp in their shells, but you can also prepare this dish with peeled and deveined shrimp. (If you are doing the peeling, you may want to turn the shells into a little fumet to flavor the sauce. Allow about an hour to do this.)

As for the sauce, ancho chilis are a good substitute for the romesco pepper, which so far remains elusive on my coast. We use a high-acid, oaky Spanish red wine vinegar from l'Estornel, which imparts a distinct character to the sauce. We also use Spanish paprika, although Hungarian products will do as well—in either case, make sure it is pungent and fresh. Buy all ground spices in quantities that you will exhaust promptly.

"You should trust your taste and train it frequently—instead of tasting just once at the end and possibly being disappointed, or tasting once in the beginning and once in the end and not knowing what happened in between."

For the romesco base (makes 1 generous cup)

½ ounce raw almonds (about 2 tablespoons, or 12 nuts)

1 ounce hazelnuts (¼ cup, or about 32 nuts)

½ cup coarsely chopped drained canned tomatoes or peeled ripe tomatoes

About ¼ cup extra-virgin olive oil

1 ancho chili

About 1 cup mild-tasting olive oil

1½ ounces chewy, white, peasant-style bread (about 1 thick slice)

2 to 3 garlic cloves, peeled

1 teaspoon l'Estornel brand red wine vinegar or other red wine vinegar
   fortified with a few drops of sherry vinegar

1 teaspoon hot paprika

½ teaspoon mild paprika

Salt

To finish the dish

1 cup chicken stock, shellfish fumet, water, or a combination

3 tablespoons dry white wine

½ cup diced yellow onions (2 ounces)

About ¼ cup extra-virgin olive oil

Salt

About 1¼ pounds shrimp in their shells or just over 1 pound peeled shrimp

¾ pound spinach, carefully washed and dried

Making the romesco base (up to a week in advance) Preheat the oven to 325°.

Drop the almonds into a small pot of boiling water and leave for about 10 seconds. Drain, slide off the skins, and rub dry. Set aside.

Roast the hazelnuts on a small baking sheet until the skins darken and start to split, 10 to 15 minutes. While they are still hot, bundle them in a towel beanbag-style, then scrunch and massage them to rub off most of their skins. Pick out the nuts and set aside.

Turn the oven to broil. Spread the tomatoes ½ inch thick in a small, shallow baking dish. Trickle with a little of the olive oil and place under the broiler about 4 inches from the element. Cook until the tomatoes char slightly and bubble, a few minutes. Remove from the broiler.

Reduce the oven temperature to 425°.

Meanwhile, pour a few cups of boiling water over the chili and leave to swell for a few minutes. Drain, then stem and seed the pepper.

Pour mild-tasting olive oil to a depth of ½ inch into an 8- or 10-inch skillet and set over medium-low heat. Test the temperature with the edge of the slice of bread; when it barely sizzles on contact, reduce the heat slightly and add the bread. (You may need to cut the bread into pieces so it fits into the pan in a single layer.) Check the underside at 1 minute; it should just be beginning to color. Fry until it is the color of cornflakes, 2 to 3 minutes per side. Drain and cool on a paper towel.

Thickly slice the garlic, then pound to a paste in a mortar. Scrape into a processor and add the chili, fried bread, almonds, and hazelnuts. Grind to a fine, moist paste, scraping the sides frequently. Scrape in the tomatoes and process to a paste. Add the vinegar, paprika, the remaining extra-virgin oil, and salt to taste. Taste; it should be bursting with flavor, although not overly spicy. The flavor of the paprika will come out over time.

f&w tips
To save time, ask your fishmonger to peel and devein the shrimp for you. Using prewashed baby spinach also saves some time.

Spread the paste in a thick layer in a small shallow baking dish and bake until the surface has turned dark orange with occasional flecks of brown, about 8 minutes.

Finishing the dish Bring the stock, fumet, or water and the white wine to a simmer in a small saucepan. Turn off the heat and stir in the romesco base. Taste for salt. Cover and set aside for about 30 minutes. As this brew cools, the crumbs will begin to swell and soften, which will give the sauce a nice texture.

Place the diced onions in a 3-quart sauté pan with about 2 tablespoons of the olive oil and a few pinches of salt. Cook over medium heat until translucent and tender, about 5 minutes. Add the romesco and warm through. Add the shrimp and turn the heat to medium. Cook gently, turning each one over once in the thickening sauce, until the shrimp are just firm and opaque. This should take no longer than 4 minutes, but depends on the size of the shrimp.

Meanwhile, warm another 2 tablespoons olive oil in a 12-inch skillet over medium heat. Add the spinach and sprinkle with salt. Gently turn and fold leaves until they are uniformly wilted and bright green. Taste for salt and add another trickle of oil if the spinach seems lean.

Divide the spinach among warm plates. Arrange the shrimp on top of the spinach. Taste the sauce, and correct the salt. The romesco should be fluid but thick—reduce briefly or add a splash of water if it seems either watery or pasty. Spoon the sauce over all.

WINE St. Amant Amador Roussanne, 1999

Lamb's Lettuce with Raw Asparagus, Pistachios, and Parmigiano-Reggiano

FOR 4 SERVINGS

Use fleshy jumbo asparagus for this spring salad, the purple variety if you see any in the market. Since it is served raw, it will retain its color. You may be surprised to learn that the stem of any spear of asparagus is sweeter than the tip, especially raw. So trim off the pretty tips and save them for risotto, or pasta. By itself, this spring salad makes a good first course. It is delicious and lovely piled in a small mound on thinly sliced prosciutto.

2   tablespoons raw, shelled pistachios (about ½ ounce)

¼   cup extra-virgin olive oil

1   tablespoon Champagne vinegar or white wine vinegar

Salt

4   spears jumbo asparagus, tips removed and reserved for another use

4 to 5 ounces lamb's lettuce, carefully washed and dried

A small chunk of Parmigiano-Reggiano (about 1 ounce)

Preheat the oven to 350°.

Heat the pistachios in a small pan in the oven until just warm, 2 to 3 minutes. This will heighten their flavor. They should remain bright green.

Coarsely chop the pistachios, culling any shriveled and discolored nuts.

Combine the oil, vinegar, and salt to taste.

Starting at the tip ends, slice the asparagus on a steep angle into ⅛-inch-thick ovals. As you work your way down each stalk, taste an occasional sliver, and stop slicing when the flesh becomes tough. Discard the woody ends.

Toss the lamb's lettuce, asparagus, and pistachios with enough vinaigrette to coat. Taste.

Divide among cold plates, leaving some of the pistachios in the bowl. Use a vegetable peeler to shave tiny curls of the cheese over the salads, then sprinkle the rest of the nuts on top.

Pasta alla Carbonara

FOR 4 TO 5 SERVINGS

This rogue version of carbonara is based on one I had in Rome. It is not very saucy, and the ricotta makes it pleasantly curdy. The bacon should be crispy-tender and aromatic; don't be tempted to cook it in advance—you will sacrifice much of its aroma to convenience, and it will tend to harden. And don't substitute Parmigiano-Reggiano for the aged pecorino.

Serve with a chewy, dried semolina pasta shape that does not grab too much sauce: spaghetti, spaghettini, penne, or bucatini.

5   ounces bacon (4 or 5 thick slices), cut into ¼- to ½-inch segments

5   tablespoons extra-virgin olive oil

4   large or 5 small eggs, at room temperature

½   cup fresh ricotta cheese, at room temperature

1   pound spaghetti, penne, or bucatini

Salt

About ¾ cup shucked sweet English peas or mature sugar snap peas or
    double-peeled favas

About 2 ounces pecorino romano or pecorino sardo, grated
    (1 cup lightly packed)

Freshly cracked black pepper

Warm the bacon in the olive oil in a 12-inch skillet or 3-quart sauté pan (see Note at right) over low heat. It should gradually render a little fat, which will mix with the oil.

Meanwhile, lightly beat the eggs with the ricotta.

Drop the pasta into 6 quarts rapidly boiling water seasoned with a scant
2 tablespoons salt (a little more if using kosher salt). Stir, and cook until al dente.

When the pasta is about 1 minute from being al dente, add the peas to the water, and raise the heat under the bacon. Cook the bacon until it is just crispy on the edges but still tender in the middle. Turn off the heat, slide the pan from the heat, and swirl it a few times to cool it slightly.

Drain the pasta, shake off the excess water, and slide the pasta and peas into the pan of bacon; you'll hear a discreet sizzle. Place back on the burner (the one you used to cook the bacon, which should still be quite warm). Immediately pour the beaten eggs all over the steaming pasta, add most of the pecorino and lots of cracked black pepper, and fold to combine. Work quickly so the heat of the noodles, bacon, and bacon fat slightly cooks the eggs. The eggs and ricotta will coat the pasta and form tiny, soft, golden curds.

Serve in warm bowls and offer the remaining pecorino and black pepper.

NOTE If you prefer the egg cooked further, return the pan to low heat, but use a nonstick pan, or else much of the egg, and some of the pasta, will stick to the pan.

WINE Bodega Norton, Mendoza, Argentina, Malbec Reserve, 1999

on rodgers's nightstand

"I haven't been in a kitchen with a cookbook more than 10 times in my life," Rodgers says. Instead, she uses cookbooks to spark ideas and to look for common themes. She adores anything by **Elizabeth David** and **Ada Boni** and often looks through her "big old assemblage" of books that were already long out of print when she bought them 10 years ago in France, Italy and Spain. "They're not pretty or sexy, but they document the foods of the regions I visited and I consult them all the time."

Quail and Sausage Braised with Grapes

FOR 4 SERVINGS

A fall dish, traditionally made with wine grapes—and without quail—in Umbria. This is a tame interpretation of that dish, *salsiccia all'uva* (sausage with grapes), which is intensely flavored and crunchy with grape seeds. For our version, we use mostly seedless grapes, Black Emerald or Red Flame, in combination with a few seedy ones—wine grapes when we can get them. Choose varieties that are not too sweet, or the result will be cloying. Small grapes with lots of skin in proportion to flesh cook down quickly and produce the best flavor and texture. I don't recommend cooking this dish in advance; the grape sauce quickly loses its bright flavor and the quail and sausages risk drying out. And it's so quick and easy, there is no need to.

Serve with polenta—soft, grilled, or roasted—or grilled bread, and a salad of bitter greens mixed with thinly sliced raw fennel.

4   whole quail (about 6 ounces each) or 4 dressed quail (about 4 ounces each)

Salt

About 6 tablespoons extra-virgin olive oil

A few pinches of fennel seeds, barely crushed

About 2 pounds stemmed, small, red or black grapes (5 to 6 cups),
    at least two-thirds of which are seedless varieties

Balsamic or red wine vinegar, as needed

4   fresh sausages (3 to 4 ounces each), preferably fennel sausage

Seasoning the quail (for the best flavor, do this step 12 to 24 hours in advance)
If using whole quail, first cut off the feet at the knee joint and the head at the base of the neck. (You can double-wrap and freeze these meager trimmings for a future bird stock.) Season the quail evenly all over with salt, cover loosely, and refrigerate.

f&w tip
We suggest a green garnish to liven up the monocromatic plate. A few fresh fennel fronds (to echo the fennel seed in this dish) would make a pretty addition.

Cooking the quail Warm about ¼ cup of the olive oil with the fennel seeds in a 3-quart sauté pan over medium heat. Add the grapes. Stir regularly as the grapes sizzle and release their fruity aroma, until the skins begin to split and the grapes yield their juice. Cook uncovered, stirring occasionally until the grape sauce has a little body, 20 to 30 minutes. You should have about 2 cups. Taste. If the grapes are quite sweet, add a pinch of salt and/or a dribble of vinegar.

Warm about 2 tablespoons olive oil in a 12-inch skillet over medium heat. Wipe the quail and sausages dry, then place in the pan. They should sizzle on contact. Brown the quail and sausages evenly, 3 to 4 minutes on each side. Reduce the heat, tilt the pan, trapping the quail and sausages behind tongs or a strainer, and pour off the excess fat. Add the grapes. They will seethe regally as they bubble up around the quail and sausages—a moment to look forward to when making this dish. Cover and cook over medium-low heat until firm, like a ripe peach, another 12 minutes or so, turning the quail and sausages a few times to ensure even cooking. Uncover and simmer to reduce the sauce to a rich, jammy consistency. Taste and correct with salt or vinegar.

Serve immediately.

WINE Rosso di Montalcino, La Gerla, 1998

complete vegetarian cookbook

CHARMAINE SOLOMON

about solomon
Charmaine Solomon, born in Ceylon (now Sri Lanka), learned to cook as a young wife and mother in Australia. A little more than 25 years ago, she published her first book. Today she is one of Australia's foremost cookbook writers, with more than 30 volumes to her credit.

This is a tome of vegetarian recipes—more than 600 in all. None is the stereotypical anemic kind. Rather, they are fresh and lively, with truly appealing ingredients. You won't feel something is lacking, as with so much vegetarian cooking. We particularly liked the Indian recipes, made with unusual combinations of textures and flavors.

FOOD & WINE Are you a vegetarian?
CHARMAINE SOLOMON Not strictly, but I do prefer vegetarian food.
F&W What ingredients make a vegetarian dish satisfying?
CS Grains such as rice, bulgur and quinoa provide texture contrast and also carry other flavors that are added to them. Miso is a useful ingredient, and it's rich in protein. While tofu is better known, I find it's rather bland, and that I have to spice it up or douse it in teriyaki marinade before it will get my mouth watering.
F&W How do you pick the best produce at the market?
CS By being very sharp eyed. Berries must have a velvety bloom and not leak their juice into the punnet [basket], a sure sign they've been picked too long ago. Okra should be small and tender. How do you know? Press on the end of one, and if it bends, put it back.

It should snap off cleanly.
F&W What are some of your favorite seasonal ingredients?
CS Last summer I grew zucchini, the dark green variety, and found it a perfect base for pancakes—chopped with some green onions and a clove of garlic, then mixed with a beaten egg and a couple of tablespoons of flour, seasoned with salt and pepper and cooked flapjack-style in a nonstick skillet. In winter I combine orange slices with black olives, red onion slices, whitloof leaves [Belgian endive] and a dressing. Cubes of feta cheese make this a complete meal.
F&W Most of your other books have concentrated on Asian foods. What was your inspiration for writing this book?
CS Would you believe it was my nine-year-old son? I took him to an agricultural show where he saw, for the first time, little woolly lambs.

>> FEATURED RECIPES

1 | RICE WITH FRESH CHEESE, NUTS AND VEGETABLES, MOGHUL STYLE

2 | EGGPLANT LASAGNE

3 | LENTIL, SESAME AND SUNFLOWER BURGERS

4 | PEANUT WAFERS

I could almost hear the penny drop. He looked at me and said firmly, "Mummy, no more lamb chops." (Up to that time, he had enjoyed a lamb chop off the barbecue.) "But what will you eat at a barbecue?" I asked. "Will you eat chicken?" Looking at the little fluffy chicks, he said determinedly, "No more chicken!" And so I was plunged willy-nilly into the world of vegetarian food.

F&W Who has inspired you most?

CS Ann Batchelder, a cook and poet who wrote for *Ladies' Home Journal* in the 1930s, '40s and '50s, was my first inspiration.

F&W Where did your passion for Asian cuisines come from?

CS I was born in Sri Lanka, and my family cooked and ate spicy Asian food. My mother and grandmother came from Burma [now Myanmar], and my husband (also born there) has taste buds well attuned to Burmese, Chinese and Indian foods. When we emigrated to Australia, I had to learn to cook the things we liked because there was no one else to do it. My hobby was cooking a great meal for my husband when he got home from work late at night (he's a professional musician).

F&W What are the pitfalls in following a vegetarian diet?

CS People can't imagine that anything can really take the place of meat. Becoming a vegetarian requires a mind-shift, an acceptance that grains, lentils and vegetables can be delicious and nutritious, and that they won't cause you to leave the table hungry.

the specifics

recipes	pages	photos	publisher	price
609	400	110 color photos	Ten Speed Press and HarperCollins, Australia	$39.95

credits

Complete Vegetarian Cookbook by Charmaine Solomon. Copyright © 1990, 2002 Charmaine Solomon. First published in Australia in 1990 and 2002 by HarperCollins Publishers, Sydney, Australia. Photography by Rob Reichenfeld.

Rice with Fresh Cheese, Nuts and Vegetables, Moghul Style

SERVES 6

2½ cups (1 lb) Basmati rice or other long grain rice

250 g (8 oz) Panir (recipe follows) or ricotta cheese

3 tablespoons flour

1 teaspoon ground turmeric

Oil for deep-frying

2 tablespoons ghee (clarified butter)

¼ cup (1 oz) slivered blanched almonds

2 medium onions, thinly sliced

1 teaspoon finely chopped garlic

2 teaspoons finely shredded fresh ginger

5 cardamom pods, bruised

1 small stick cinnamon

3 whole cloves

10 whole peppercorns

1 cup (2½ oz) small cauliflower sprigs

½ cup (2 oz) shelled peas

4 cups (32 fl oz) water

3 teaspoons salt

2 tablespoons chopped pistachios, blanched

¼ cup (1½ oz) sultanas (golden raisins)

on solomon's nightstand

"The Constance Spry Cookery Book, published in 1956, was one of my first books, and from it I learned sauces, patisserie and all kinds of Continental food," Solomon says. "Then I discovered **Julia Child.** I appreciated her down-to-earth instructions and the way she talked me through a recipe; it might have taken four pages, but at the end of it I knew much more about creating a dish than I could have without her help. When it comes to Middle Eastern food, you can't do better than **Claudia Roden.** Her recipes always work. Among vegetarian cooks, I think **Deborah Madison** is superb, and I also love reading **Bert Greene."**

Wash rice well and leave to drain for at least 30 minutes. Cut panir or ricotta cheese into small cubes and leave on absorbent paper to drain if there is any excess moisture. Rub over with flour and turmeric mixed together. In a heavy-based pan, heat enough oil to deep fry the cheese, and add to it 1 tablespoon of the ghee for flavour. Deep fry the cubes of cheese, a few at a time, until golden. Remove from oil with slotted spoon and place on paper towels to drain.

In the same oil, fry the almonds until golden, remove and drain. Pour off all but about 2 tablespoons oil, add the remaining tablespoon of ghee and fry the sliced onions, garlic, ginger, cardamom, cinnamon, cloves and peppercorns. When the onions are golden, add the cauliflower and peas and fry, stirring, for 2 minutes. Add the rice and fry, stirring, for a further 3 minutes. Add water and salt, bring to the boil, then turn heat very low and cook, tightly covered, for 20 minutes without lifting the lid. Remove from heat and pick out whole spices which will have come to the top. Fork the fried cheese, half the almonds, pistachios and sultanas through the rice. Dish up and garnish with remaining nuts and sultanas and small red tomatoes. Serve with two or more accompaniments.

Panir or Fresh Cheese

Bring 4 cups (32 fl oz) milk to the boil, stirring occasionally to prevent a skin forming on the surface. As it rises up in the pan turn off the heat and stir in 3–4 tablespoons of lemon juice. Let it stand for 5 minutes and when firm curds have formed, strain through a fine muslin and let it hang for an hour or so, then press to remove as much moisture as possible. Weight it down and leave in a cool place for an hour or more. Cut into cubes.

Eggplant Lasagne

SERVES 6 TO 8

2   large eggplants (aubergines)

½   cup (4 fl oz) French Dressing (recipe follows)

1   clove garlic, crushed

1   packet instant lasagne noodles

Tomato sauce

3   tablespoons olive oil

2   large onions, finely chopped

2   cloves garlic, crushed

1   large can peeled tomatoes, or 1 kg (2 lb) ripe tomatoes,
    peeled and chopped

1   teaspoon dried oregano

1   teaspoon dried basil

3   tablespoons tomato paste dissolved in ½ cup (4 fl oz) of water

1   tablespoon sugar

1   teaspoon salt

¼   teaspoon pepper

Cheese sauce

2   tablespoons butter

2   tablespoons flour

1¼ cups (10 fl oz) milk

Salt and pepper to taste

2   eggs, separated

250 g (8 oz) tasty (sharp) cheese, finely grated

Wash the eggplants but do not peel them. Cut crossways into slices about 1 cm
(½ in) thick and brush both sides of each slice with French dressing mixed with the
garlic. Preheat griller (broiler), place eggplant slices on a tray lined with foil and grill
until golden brown on one side, then turn over and grill other side.

f&w tips
This light lasagne was pretty
straightforward, but we
came up with a couple of
tips to help ease the
prep and cleanup. For one,
divide the eggplant slices
onto two lined baking sheets
instead of one. Also, make
sure to set the läsagne
on a baking sheet before
cooking it to prevent drips.

To make the tomato sauce, heat oil in a saucepan and cook the onions and garlic over low heat, stirring frequently, until they are soft and golden. Add tomatoes, herbs, the tomato paste dissolved in ½ cup (4 fl oz) of water, sugar and seasonings. Cover and simmer for 30 minutes, or until slightly thickened.

In a well buttered, ovenproof dish (preferably a square or rectangular shape because the lasagne noodles will fit more easily), ladle in just enough tomato sauce to cover the base. Place a layer of lasagne noodles in the sauce. Make a layer of the grilled eggplant slices, cover with tomato sauce, then more lasagne and so on until the dish is three-quarters full. There should always be sufficient sauce on either side of the noodles to moisten them thoroughly. Bake in an oven preheated to 180°C (350°F) for 20 minutes.

Meanwhile, make the cheese sauce for topping lasagne. Melt butter in a saucepan, add flour and stir over low heat for 2 minutes. Whisk in milk and stir constantly until it boils and thickens. Remove from heat, season to taste, then beat in the egg yolks, one at a time. Reserve 3 tablespoons of cheese for topping lasagne and stir in the rest. Whip the egg whites until stiff and fold into the sauce.

Remove lasagne from oven and pour the sauce over the top, taking it right to the edges of the dish. Sprinkle with reserved cheese and return to the oven for a further 25 minutes, or until well puffed and browned. Serve hot, with crusty bread and a green salad.

Basic French Dressing

MAKES ½ CUP (4 FL OZ)

2   tablespoons wine vinegar

½   teaspoon salt

Good grinding of pepper

¼   teaspoon dry mustard

6   tablespoons olive oil

In a small bowl, whisk together the vinegar, salt, pepper and mustard. Gradually add the oil, whisking until thick. Or shake all the ingredients together in a screw-top jar just before using the dressing on the salad.

Lentil, Sesame and Sunflower Burgers

SERVES 6

Barbecue parties are what people feel they miss out on when they eat only vegetarian meals but recipes like this ensure they can still enjoy the outdoor cooking scene. Of course, you can also cook these nutty burgers in a frying pan. Besides being delicious and satisfying, they are rich in protein and calcium.

125 g (4 oz) brown lentils

125 g (4 oz) red lentils

2   cups (16 fl oz) water

1   tablespoon miso or yeast extract

2   tablespoons soy sauce

1   egg, beaten

1   teaspoon dried oregano or marjoram

1   teaspoon curry powder (optional)

1   tablespoon honey

1   clove garlic, crushed

1   large carrot, grated

1   large onion, grated

1   large potato, grated

⅓   cup (1½ oz) sunflower seeds

⅓   cup (1½ oz) sesame seeds

1   cup (3 oz) rolled oats

4   tablespoons wholemeal (whole wheat) flour

f&w tip

We loved these healthy burgers best when we smeared the rolls with a combination of mustard, ketchup and mayonnaise.

Spread the lentils on a tray and pick out any stones. Wash well and drain. Put into a saucepan with the water and bring to the boil, turn off the heat and soak for 2 hours. Add the miso or yeast extract and cook, covered, until all water has been absorbed and the lentils are soft.

Mix the soy sauce, egg, herbs and seasonings together. In a large bowl, combine all the remaining ingredients thoroughly, adding in the egg mixture.

Form the mixture into round patties. Heat the griddle plate of the barbecue, brush with a little oil and cook the burgers over low coals until golden brown. For informal eating, serve in hamburger buns with shredded lettuce and mayonnaise. For a knife and fork meal, serve with thickly sliced tomatoes and salads.

"People can't imagine that anything can really take the place of meat. Becoming a vegetarian requires a mind-shift, an acceptance that grains, lentils and vegetables can be delicious and nutritious, and that they won't cause you to leave the table hungry."

Peanut Wafers

SERVES 6

f&w tip

These crispy wafers were hard to resist. We liked them with the unsalted peanuts, but the recipe worked even better with salted peanuts, which made the wafers perfect as a salty snack with a cocktail.

An accompaniment to rice and curries on festive occasions, these crisp and crunchy wafers are also delicious served by themselves, as a snack or as an accompaniment to drinks. In this case, make them rather small.

½   cup (2 oz) rice flour

2   tablespoons ground rice or plain (all-purpose) flour

1   teaspoon ground coriander

½   teaspoon ground cumin

¼   teaspoon ground turmeric

¾   teaspoon salt

1   cup (8 fl oz) coconut milk

1   clove garlic, crushed

1   small onion, finely chopped

125 g (4 oz) roasted, unsalted peanuts

Oil for frying

Sift all the dry ingredients into a bowl. Add the coconut milk and beat to a smooth thin batter. Crush garlic to a paste then stir to distribute it well through the batter. Stir in onion and peanuts.

Heat enough oil in a frying pan to cover base to a depth of 12 mm (½ in). Oil must be hot, but not to the point of smoking. Drop tablespoons of the batter into the oil. The batter should be thin enough to spread into a lacy wafer. If it holds together and has to be spread with the spoon, it is too thick, and must be thinned by adding a spoonful of coconut milk at a time until the correct consistency is obtained.

Fry until golden brown on the underside, then turn and fry until golden on other side. Drain on absorbent paper over a wire rack to allow air to circulate. This will help wafers retain their crispness for a few hours. Cool and store in an airtight container.

thai food

DAVID THOMPSON

about thompson

David Thompson is one of Australia's foremost chefs and an eloquent ambassador for Thai food and culture. His Sydney restaurants, Darley Street Thai and Sailors Thai, have increased awareness and appreciation of authentic Thai cooking. In July 2001 he opened Nahm in London's Halkin Hotel, which months later was awarded a Michelin star. Currently Thompson is consulting with Suan Dusit College in Bangkok on the preservation of Thai culinary heritage.

David Thompson's ambition here clearly was to create the definitive book on Thai cooking, and this volume probably will be regarded as such for some time. The decision to be rigorous about authenticity means that finding certain ingredients can pose a challenge. Given the number of choices in the book, we had no trouble finding relatively simple dishes made with easy-to-find ingredients, too.

FOOD & WINE What are the guiding principles of Thai food?

DAVID THOMPSON The Thais would emphasize harmony and balance, but if you're a Western cook, you've got to be bold and brave. Food writer Jeffrey Steingarten calls Thai cuisine "the most extreme food." It could walk up to you and slap you across the face.

F&W What are the main flavors?

DT Salty, hot, sweet and sour. Every dish has at least two of those, if not four, all of which must be judiciously balanced. The tastes are so robust and yet—here's the paradox of Thai cooking—they blend together into an elegant, sophisticated finish.

F&W What are the essential pantry items and pieces of equipment?

DT Garlic, chiles, basil, coriander, limes, shrimp paste and fish sauce. A mortar-and-pestle is indispensable.

Parchment paper is also key.

F&W What distinguishes Thai food from other Southeast Asian cuisines?

DT It tastes so bloody good! There's an exuberance to the food that may be due to Thailand's fortunate history. Thailand has been mostly unaffected by traumas of war, invasion or great social dislocation. It's a relatively happy country, a wealthy, fertile place where they grow extraordinary fruit and vegetables. Thais have a culture that lets them enjoy their food. They're not so puritanical as to not relish it.

F&W What's the one key element of a traditional Thai meal?

DT When Thai people eat, they eat rice. Food that accompanies rice is literally called "with rice."

F&W What is the dining etiquette?

DT Never too much at one go. Just have a spoonful of one dish mixed

>> **FEATURED RECIPES**

1 TROUT BRAISED
WITH CARAMEL, CELERY
AND FISH SAUCE

2 CUCUMBER AND
PORK STIR-FRIED
WITH EGG

3 STIR-FRIED MINCED
BEEF WITH CHILLIES
AND HOLY BASIL

with rice (up to two tablespoons of rice mixed with one tablespoon of the dish). Then move on to the next. The Thais don't load up their plate like some unholy wedding buffet pileup. That's treacherously horrid.

F&W What are traditional beverages?

DT Historically, Thais didn't drink during their meal. Soup quenched the thirst. Sometimes they'd drink water infused with jasmine flowers and tea. Then men would drink a rice alcohol. Now they drink anything, including beer. I like to drink wine. Gewürztraminers from Alsace are fantastic with Thai food, and some unwooded Chardonnays are good. I wouldn't recommend heavily wooded or oaked Chardonnays or tight, tannic red wines. A delicate Côtes-du-Rhone can be delicious. You can chill the wine down a few degrees to close it a bit so it can stand up to the sugars and salt in the food. But the tricky thing about pairing wine with Thai food is that if you're eating in the traditional manner, where several dishes arrive at once, it's hard to find a wine that can contend with so many disparate tastes.

F&W What are Thai desserts like?

DT For Thais, it's the pinnacle of their cuisine. There are some extraordinarily delicious desserts, but it's probably the most difficult part of the cuisine to become accustomed to. But there are some familiar tastes, too, like mango and sticky rice. When I go to Thailand, I put on stupid amounts of weight eating desserts that are full of coconut cream and sugar.

the specifics

recipes	pages	photos	publisher	price
381	688	100 color photos	Ten Speed Press	$40

credits

Thai Food by David Thompson. Text copyright © 2002 by David Thompson. Photography copyright © 2002 by Earl Carter.

Trout Braised with Caramel, Celery and Fish Sauce

Dtom Kem Pla Sy Keun Chai

This recipe was included in my first book, *Classic Thai Cuisine*, but it is such a delicious and delicate dish that I must give it again. It is a recipe by Mom Ratchawongse Dteuang Sanitsawongse, whose memorial book has been a steady guide in my unravelling of the complexities of Thai cuisine.

Dtom kem are dishes that can be served either "wet" or "dry": they can be served in a lot of the stock or just a little. I am enamoured by the elegance, the taste and the ease of the *dtom kem* style. Although *kem* means salty, this is not the sole taste, as the garlic and pepper paste imparts a nutty pepperiness and the caramelised palm sugar gives a rich, sweet depth to the dish.

The original recipe calls for *pla chorn*, a pink-fleshed freshwater fish that abounds in Thailand and its cuisine but is unknown outside South East Asia. I think that trout makes an excellent alternative, although any fish, from perch to barramundi, or even prawns and lobster, can be used. Rather than celery, peeled and sliced fresh sugar cane can be used to introduce a rich, raw sweetness to the braise—but then reduce the palm sugar by half.

1   tablespoon oil

3   tablespoons palm sugar

3   tablespoons fish sauce

Stock or water

1   medium trout, brook trout or Murray perch—
    about 250 g (8 oz)—whole or filleted

2   tablespoons chopped Asian celery

2   red shallots, peeled and finely sliced

1   tablespoon coriander leaves

Pinch of ground white pepper

Paste

2   teaspoons scraped and chopped coriander root

Pinch of salt

1   tablespoon chopped garlic

10 white peppercorns

on thompson's nightstand

"I collect old Thai funeral books," Thompson says. "When someone dies, the family commissions a book about the person's life, character and interests. For women, the books include their recipes. These books are a trove of the traditional cooking practices of old Thailand. Sellers who specialize in these books are often based near a monastery. As for more current books, I've been enjoying **Lulu's Provençal Table** by **Richard Olney;** it's a very pleasant read."

"Thais have a culture that lets them enjoy their food. They're not so puritanical as to not relish it."

First, make the paste: using a pestle and mortar, gradually pound the ingredients together until smooth.

Heat oil in a pan then fry the paste until fragrant and golden. Add sugar and when it has begun to caramelise—be careful, it burns very quickly—add fish sauce. Add stock or water to cover and, when it has come to the boil, add fish and celery. Cover with extra boiling liquid and just barely simmer on a very, very low heat until cooked: 2–3 minutes for a fillet, 5–10 minutes for a whole fish. Remove from heat and allow to rest for a few minutes in a warm place. Check seasoning— it should taste salty and sweet—and adjust accordingly. Serve sprinkled with shallots, coriander and pepper.

Cucumber and Pork Stir-Fried with Egg

Kai Pat Dtaeng Gwa Sai Muu

100 g (3 oz) pork belly

2 **tablespoons oil**

2 **cloves garlic, crushed with a pinch of salt**

1 **small cucumber, diagonally cut into chunks about 5 cm x 2 cm (2 in x 1 in)**

2 **eggs**

1 **tablespoon fish sauce**

1 **teaspoon white sugar**

Large pinch of ground white pepper

Handful of coriander leaves

Steam pork belly for 10–15 minutes, allow to cool and then cut into 2 cm (1 in) cubes. Heat oil in a wok and fry garlic until beginning to colour. Add pork and fry for 4 minutes over a high heat. Add cucumber and stir-fry until it begins to turn translucent—about 3 minutes. Add eggs and stir-fry for a further 2 minutes, then season with fish sauce and sugar. Serve sprinkled with pepper and coriander leaves.

Stir-Fried Minced Beef with Chillies and Holy Basil

Neua Pat Bai Grapao

Serve this rustic stir-fry with plenty of steamed rice and a bowl of fish sauce spiked with finely sliced chillies, garlic and a squeeze of lime juice. Often this dish is topped with a fried egg.

3   garlic cloves, peeled

Large pinch of salt

2   long red or green chillies

4   bird's eye chillies (scuds)

1   tablespoon oil or rendered pork fat

100 g (3 oz) minced beef, chicken or pork

3   tablespoons stock or water

Large pinch of white sugar

1   tablespoon light soy sauce

1   tablespoon dark soy sauce

Handful of holy basil leaves

Pound garlic, salt and both kinds of chillies into a paste.

Heat a wok over a very high heat. Add oil or rendered pork fat, then fry the paste for a minute. Add minced meat and continue to stir-fry for a minute. Add stock, sugar and both kinds of soy sauce. Sprinkle over the holy basil and serve.

chez panisse fruit

ALICE WATERS

about waters

Alice Waters opened Chez Panisse restaurant in 1971, introducing the then-radical idea of serving a single fixed-price menu that changed daily. Twenty-five years later she created the Chez Panisse Foundation, which supports programs that demonstrate the transformative power of growing, cooking and sharing food. She has coauthored seven other cookbooks, including the *Chez Panisse Café Cookbook* and *Chez Panisse Vegetables*.

ALICE WATERS

CHEZ PANISSE
FRUIT

This tribute to fruit is from the very best source: America's greenmarket guru. It's full of creative uses for everything from peaches and plums to quinces and mulberries. The book is organized by fruit type, which is fantastic in high season when you face a mountain of gorgeous strawberries or a bucket of blueberries, say, and have run out of ideas for what to do with them.

FOOD & WINE How did you come to write *Chez Panisse Fruit?*

ALICE WATERS I did a book about vegetables seven years ago, and I always thought about doing a companion book on fruit. Unfortunately, Patricia Curtan was so exhausted after doing the illustrations for the vegetable book that she said she couldn't do another one. So I wrote the *Chez Panisse Café Cookbook* while I waited for her to recover.

F&W Why did the subject of fruit appeal to you so much?

AW Fruit is so naturally seductive; people are really brought into a meal when they have a tasty piece of fruit. You remember a beautiful peach all your life. But you can't possibly have a beautiful experience with fruit unless it's ripe and in season. And of course I wanted to teach people all about our organic growers. They're

so important to the taste of the fruit.

F&W Was it difficult to adapt Chez Panisse recipes for the home cook?

AW Not really, because there's a kind of simplicity to the restaurant's food that translates pretty well. The food at Chez Panisse isn't arranged in a complicated way on the plate, there aren't a lot of ingredients, it's not trying to be anything other than what it is. The citrus sauce on the grilled salmon, for instance, doesn't try to disguise the fish at all; it just enhances it.

F&W What pleases you the most about how your book turned out?

AW I like two things about it: the alphabetical order, which makes it easy to find a recipe for a lovely piece of fruit you might see at the market, and Patricia's illustrations, which are very beautiful—they have a fine, delicate, almost alive aspect to them.

>> FEATURED RECIPES

1 GREEN MANGO SALAD WITH SHRIMP AND AVOCADO

2 SICILIAN-STYLE SWORDFISH STUFFED WITH CURRANTS AND PINE NUTS

3 GRILLED SALMON WITH CITRUS SAUCE

4 POULET À LA NORMANDE

F&W Do you have a favorite dish that uses fruit in a savory way?

AW I do like fish with a combination of sweet and sour flavors—swordfish with a papaya-mango salsa, say, or that salmon with citrus sauce from the book. I also like citrus sauce on poultry with a lot of fat in the skin, like duck, because its tanginess cuts through the richness the way a vinegar does.

F&W What's the best way to buy fruit?

AW One must go to the market and buy what's local. I talk with the farmers and ask what has really great taste, what's perfect at that particular moment. It's really important to taste the fruit if you can. Look for fruit that's just been picked, particularly when it comes to buying berries; it's not as important for apples, pears and oranges. And I buy from people who are taking care of the land, so I always ask about their farming methods. Things like strawberries are heavily sprayed in this country, so I always look for growers who don't spray. I want the people who I buy fruit from to care about my good health.

F&W Is there a difference between fruit you might eat uncooked and fruit you would want to cook with?

AW You want to cook with fruit that's really, really ripe, and that might not be the fruit you'd want to serve uncooked. An apricot that's overripe, for instance, would be perfect to use in a recipe—you can make fantastic jams and granitas and amazing sherbets and ice creams—but you wouldn't want that mushy apricot on a plate.

the specifics

recipes	pages	photos	publisher	price
200	352	no photos 48 color illustrations	HarperCollins	$34.95

credits

Chez Panisse Fruit by Alice Waters. Copyright © 2002 by Alice Waters. Illustrations copyright © 2002 by Patricia Curtan. The original illustrations reproduced in this book are color linocut images drawn, cut and printed by the artist. The images were printed as limited editions by hand, one color at a time, on a hundred-year-old letterpress. Reprinted by permission of HarperCollins Publishers Inc.

Green Mango Salad with Shrimp and Avocado

SERVES 4 TO 6

4   small heads romaine lettuce, or 2 hearts of romaine

1   dozen white shrimp, peeled and deveined

Salt and pepper

1   tablespoon olive oil

1   green (underripe) mango

1   firm, ripe avocado

Grated zest and juice of 1 lime

1   shallot, diced fine

2   tablespoons Champagne vinegar

½   teaspoon grated fresh ginger

1   jalapeño chili, seeded and diced fine

½   cup extra-virgin olive oil

1   tablespoon chopped cilantro

Slice the heads of romaine in half lengthwise, remove the root end, and separate the leaves. Wash and dry them carefully.

Cut the shrimp in half lengthwise and season with salt and pepper. In a small skillet, sauté the shrimp in the olive oil over medium-low heat. As soon as they turn opaque, remove them from the pan and set aside to add to the finished salad.

Peel the mango with a vegetable peeler and cut the broad sides into ⅛-inch-thick slices. (The narrow sides tend to be fibrous and difficult to slice.) Cut these slices into ¼-inch-wide strips and set aside.

f&w tip
Even though this recipe calls for an underripe (green) mango, the only one we could find at the market was just beginning to ripen. It was still delicious in this salad. Once you've tossed everything together, use the romaine leaves as a bed for the salad.

Cut the avocado in half lengthwise and remove the pit. Cut into ¼-inch-thick slices, leaving the skin intact. Sprinkle lightly with lime juice.

Put the shallot in a large bowl with the vinegar, remaining lime juice, ginger, and jalapeño. Season with salt and macerate for 15 minutes. Whisk in the extra-virgin olive oil and lime zest. Add the shrimp and mango strips and scoop the avocado slices out of their skin into the bowl. Toss gently and serve sprinkled with chopped cilantro.

Sicilian-Style Swordfish Stuffed with Currants and Pine Nuts

SERVES 6

"Fruit is so naturally seductive; people are really brought into a meal when they have a tasty piece of fruit. You remember a beautiful peach all your life. But you can't possibly have a beautiful experience with fruit unless it's ripe and in season."

The exact dimensions of the swordfish are not so important, but the slices must be very thin in order to be flexible enough to roll up. Your fishmonger may be able to slice the swordfish for you.

This stuffing is also notably delicious rolled up inside boned fresh sardines.

1   cup fresh bread crumbs

Extra-virgin olive oil

1   small onion

1   pinch saffron threads

3   salt-packed anchovies

2   oranges

¼   cup dried currants or sultana raisins

¼   cup pine nuts

3   tablespoons chopped parsley

1   teaspoon chopped oregano

Salt and pepper

2   pounds swordfish, cut into twelve ⅛-inch-thick slices, about 4 by 6 inches

Bay leaves

Preheat the oven to 375°F.

Toss the bread crumbs with 2 tablespoons olive oil, spread them out on a baking sheet, and toast in the oven, stirring occasionally, for 10 to 15 minutes, until golden. Dice the onion and gently sauté with the saffron in 2 tablespoons olive oil until soft, about 12 minutes. Rinse and fillet the anchovies and chop coarsely. Squeeze ¼ cup juice from one of the oranges and pour it over the currants or raisins to plump them. Toast the pine nuts just until golden, about 7 minutes.

In a mixing bowl, stir together the bread crumbs, onion, anchovies, currants (with their orange juice), pine nuts, parsley, and oregano. Season generously with salt and pepper.

Lay out the swordfish slices and season with salt and pepper. Spoon about 2 tablespoons stuffing onto each slice and roll up. Arrange each roll, flap side down, in an oiled baking dish just big enough to hold them all snugly.

Cut the remaining orange in half vertically through the stem and cut each half into ¼-inch-thick half-moon slices. Wedge the orange slices and bay leaves between the swordfish rolls, drizzle olive oil over, and bake for 15 minutes, until the rolls are opaque and just firm to the touch.

Grilled Salmon with Citrus Sauce

SERVES 6

f&w tip

If you buy salmon with the skin on, start by grilling it skin side down so the skin gets extra-crispy. We had quite a bit of leftover zest, which we used to make citrus sugar for tea. To do this, bury the leftover zest in 1 cup of granulated sugar and let it sit for 4 hours.

Our longtime downstairs chef, Jean-Pierre Moullé, came up with this amazing sauce for salmon. It uses the bounty of citrus in the early spring when the first-of-the-season salmon tastes light and delicate. Serve this on a mound of potato purée, with some wilted spinach on the side.

1   tangerine

1   lemon

1   orange

1   lime

1   grapefruit

2   cups fish stock

¼   cup extra-virgin olive oil

Salt and pepper

Six 6-ounce pieces wild salmon

With a sharp vegetable peeler, carefully peel all the zest from the tangerine, lemon, orange, and lime, and half of the grapefruit zest. Be sure to take only the colored peel and none of the bitter white pith. If you do end up with some pith on the strips of zest, remove it with a sharp paring knife. Bring a small pot of water to a boil and parboil the citrus zest for 3 minutes. Drain well and cut the strips into a thin julienne. Squeeze the juice of ½ of each fruit and mix together.

Bring the fish stock to a boil and reduce to ⅓ cup. While the stock is still hot, mix it with ⅓ cup of the fruit juice and whisk in the olive oil. Season with salt and pepper and add 3 tablespoons of the julienned zest. Keep warm but not hot, lest the fruit juices lose their fresh flavor.

Make a fire in the grill and let it burn down to a bed of hot coals. Season the salmon with salt and pepper. Clean the grill well with a wire brush and then oil it with a clean rag and olive oil. Oil the fish well and grill from 3 to 4 minutes on each side, depending on the thickness of the fillets. The salmon should be just set but still a little translucent at its center. Arrange on a plate and spoon the sauce over, distributing the zest evenly around.

Poulet à la Normande

SERVES 4

This simple supper dish from the Norman countryside is one of those French classics that we tried to make over and over in the earliest days of the restaurant. It wasn't until years later that we understood what a great dish it can actually be. What made the difference? The chickens. To be great, dishes like this one have to be made with organically fed, free-ranging, flavorful chickens—like the ones we get from the Hoffman family farm in the Central Valley.

1   chicken (about 3½ pounds)

Salt and pepper

2   onions

2   carrots

2   tablespoons unsalted butter

2   tablespoons pure olive oil

3   sprigs thyme

1   bay leaf

½   cup Calvados

1   cup dry hard cider

1   cup chicken stock

1   cup crème fraîche

Garnish

30 pearl onions

4   tablespoons (½ stick) unsalted butter

Salt and pepper

2 or 3 medium apples

Cut the chicken into 8 pieces. First remove the legs and cut them into thighs and drumsticks. Next cut off the wing tips, leaving the rest of the wings attached to the breast. Then cut the breast off the backbone and divide it in half down the middle of the breastbone. Finally, cut each breast piece in half diagonally, making the piece with the wing a bit smaller than the other. Save the backbone and wing tips for stock. Season the chicken well with salt and pepper. This can be done a day ahead if the chicken is then covered and kept in the refrigerator.

Peel and dice the onions and carrots.

In a heavy-bottomed pot, melt the butter with the olive oil over medium heat. When hot, add the chicken pieces, skin side down, and brown well on all sides. Do this in batches, if necessary. When all the chicken pieces are golden brown, remove them from the pan and set aside.

Pour off most of the fat left in the pan, add the diced carrots and onions and the thyme sprigs and bay leaf, and cook until the onion is translucent, about 5 minutes. Pour in the Calvados and warm before igniting carefully—it will flame up, so stand back while doing this. When the Calvados has finished burning, add the cider, stirring and scraping up any brown bits still sticking to the pan. Bring to a boil and reduce by half. Pour in the chicken stock, return the chicken pieces to the pan, and turn down the heat. Simmer, covered, for 15 minutes. Remove the breast pieces and cook the legs and thighs another 15 minutes. When the chicken pieces are done, remove them to a dish and keep covered in a warm place while you finish the sauce.

While the chicken is cooking, start to prepare the garnish. Soak the pearl onions in warm water for a few minutes before peeling them; their skins will come off much more easily.

Melt 2 tablespoons of the butter in a heavy-bottomed pan and add the peeled onions with a pinch of salt. Cook over low heat, tightly covered, until tender and translucent, about 20 minutes. Shake or stir them now and then and add a touch of water if they are threatening to burn.

Peel and core the apples and slice each one into 8 wedges. Melt the rest of the butter in a sauté pan over medium-high heat. Add the apples, season with salt and pepper, and cook for about 10 minutes, tossing them now and then, until they are golden and tender.

Strain the Calvados sauce, pressing on the vegetables to extract all the liquid, and pour it back in the pan. Skim well and bring to a boil. Pour in the juices that have collected in the dish holding the chicken pieces; stir in the crème fraîche. Reduce the heat and simmer until the sauce is reduced by a third or until it coats the spoon. Taste and adjust the seasoning as needed. Return the chicken to the sauce to warm through.

Serve the chicken in its sauce, garnished with the apples and onions—reheated, if necessary, either together or separately.

on waters's nightstand

Does Alice Waters, whose own cookbooks have inspired a generation of chefs, look to cookbooks herself for inspiration? "All the time, oh, yes," she says. Her favorites are the classics: "I'm crazy about the books of **Elizabeth David** and **Richard Olney,** and for a lot of reasons I love **M.F.K. Fisher.** Those were the first books I read and they continue to inspire me."

index

a

appetizers
Bagna Cauda Butter, 94
Chickpea Fritters, 153
Crab Cakes Worth the Price, 34
Crispy White Beans with
    Chili Oil, 95, **96**
Deviled Eggs with Shrimp
    and Olives, 196
Hot Spinach-Artichoke Dip, 220
Moroccan Flat Bread, 146
Mushroom Turnovers with
    Curry Powder, 52
Parmesan Roasted Asparagus, 117
Peanut Wafers, 260, **261**
"Red" Rice Croquettes, 150
Sweet Pea Flan with Carrot
    Vinaigrette, **42,** 43
Tarte Flambée with Caramelized
    Onions, Smoked Bacon,
    and Creamy Cheese, 23, **24**
Tunisian Fried Pastries with
    Egg, **132,** 133
apples
Poulet à la Normande, 277
Roast Duck Breast with
    Apple Purée, 64
artichokes
Hot Spinach-Artichoke Dip, 220
Penne with Shrimp, Artichokes,
    and Feta, **14,** 15
trimming, tip for, 16
Arugula Salad with Goat's Milk
    Yogurt Dressing, 233

asparagus
Lamb's Lettuce with Raw
    Asparagus, Pistachios, and
    Parmigiano-Reggiano, 245
Parmesan Roasted Asparagus, 117
avocados
Green Mango Salad with Shrimp
    and Avocado, 272
Shrimp with Fresh Coconut Milk,
    Calabaza, and Avocado, 234

b

bacon
Pasta alla Carbonara, 246, **247**
Quail with Bacon and Honey, 100
Tarte Flambée with Caramelized
    Onions, Smoked Bacon,
    and Creamy Cheese, 23, **24**
basil
Pasta Ribbons with Pesto, Green
    Beans, and Potatoes, 188, **189**
Pesto-Crusted Halibut with
    Red Lentil Dahl, 60, **61**
Stir-Fried Lamb with Garlic
    and Basil, **160,** 161
Beancurd, Braised Beef with, 162
beans
Blue-Ribbon Chili, 38
Chicken Provençal, 72
Chickpea and Lamb Soup, 148
Cod with Local Wax Beans, Chorizo,
    and Soy-Sherry Sauce, 230, **231**

Crispy White Beans with
    Chili Oil, 95, **96**
Lentil, Sesame and Sunflower
    Burgers, 257, **258**
Pasta Ribbons with Pesto, Green
    Beans, and Potatoes, 188, **189**
Pesto-Crusted Halibut with
    Red Lentil Dahl, 60, **61**
red lentils, buying, 61
beef
Blue-Ribbon Chili, 38
Braised Beef with Beancurd, 162
Cumin-Flavored Meatballs
    with Onion Jam and Spicy
    Tomato Sauce, 142
Dry-Rubbed Rib-Eye Steak
    for Two, 48, **49**
Maria's Roast Chicken with Meat
    and Olive Stuffing, 200
Real Meatballs and
    Spaghetti, **114,** 115
"Red" Rice Croquettes, 150
Rosemary Braised Veal
    Shank, 74, **75**
Scott's Short Ribs, 118
Stir-Fried Minced Beef with Chillies
    and Holy Basil, 268
beets
Beet-Flavored Pasta Stuffed with
    a Ricotta-Beet Filling Topped
    with Brown Butter and
    Poppy Seeds, 185
tip for cooking beets, 185
Biscuit Breakfast Pizzas (var.), 171
Blueberry Turnovers, 168, **169**

bread puddings
    Autumn Strata (var.), 167
    Saturday Summer Strata, 166, **167**
breads
    Cranberry Muffins from
        Nantucket, 216, **217**
    Moroccan Flat Bread, 146
    Quick Garlic Croutons, 32
burgers
    Lentil, Sesame and Sunflower
        Burgers, 257, **258**
    Turkey Mushroom Burgers
        with Chunky Tomato Salsa
        Compote, 224
Butter, *Bagna Cauda*, 94
Butternut Squash, Saffron
    Risotto with, **120**, 121

C

Caesar Salad, Simple, Scrumptious,
    with Quick Garlic Croutons, 32
cakes
    Chocolate Chiffon Cake, 177
    Hazelnut Angel Cake, 127
    High-Ratio Lemon-Buttermilk
        Pound Cake, 180
    Lemon-Lime Buttermilk Pound
        Cake (var.), 181
    Lemon Sour Cream or Yogurt
        Pound Cake (var.), 181
    Mrs. D's "She Ain't Heavy"
        Chocolate Cake, 104, **105**
    Orange Buttermilk Pound
        Cake (var.), 181
    Pan di Spagna, 176
    Zuccotto alla Ricotta, 174, **175**
Calamari, Two-Minute, Sicilian
    Lifeguard Style, 46, **47**
Carrot Vinaigrette, Sweet Pea
    Flan with, **42**, 43

cheese
    Autumn Strata (var.), 167
    Beet-Flavored Pasta Stuffed with
        a Ricotta-Beet Filling Topped
        with Brown Butter and
        Poppy Seeds, **184**, 185
    Biscuit Breakfast Pizzas (var.), 171
    Chicago-Style Breakfast
        Pan Pizza, 170
    Eggplant Lasagne, 255
    Hot Spinach-Artichoke Dip, 220
    Lamb's Lettuce with
        Raw Asparagus, Pistachios, and
        Parmigiano-Reggiano, 245
    Panir or Fresh Cheese, 254
    Parmesan Roasted Asparagus, 117
    Pasta alla Carbonara, 246, **247**
    Penne with Shrimp, Artichokes,
        and Feta, **14**, 15
    queso fresco, about, 225
    "Red" Rice Croquettes, 150
    Rice with Fresh Cheese,
        Nuts and Vegetables, Moghul
        Style, **252**, 253
    Saffron Risotto with Butternut
        Squash, **120**, 121
    Saturday Summer Strata, 166, **167**
    Tarte Flambée with Caramelized
        Onions, Smoked Bacon,
        and Creamy Cheese, 23, **24**
    Zuccotto alla Ricotta, 174, **175**
Chermoula, 136
Cherry Turnovers (var.), 169
chicken
    breasts, buying, 223
    Chicken and Cornmeal
        Dumplings with Aromatic
        Vegetables (var.), 37
    Chicken and Dumplings with
        Aromatic Vegetables, 36
    Chicken and Herbed
        Dumplings with Aromatic
        Vegetables (var.), 37
    Chicken Provençal, 72
    Chicken Stock, 123

    Grilled Chicken Breasts with Garlic
        and Parsley, 222
    Maria's Roast Chicken with Meat
        and Olive Stuffing, 200
    Pan-Cooked Chile-Chicken
        Thighs, 55
    Poulet à la Normande, 277
chickpeas
    Chickpea and Lamb Soup, 148
    Chickpea Fritters, 153
chiles
    Chili Oil, 99
    Pan-Cooked Chile-Chicken
        Thighs, 55
    Stir-Fried Minced Beef with Chillies
        and Holy Basil, 268
    Stuffed Squid with Piquillo
        Pepper Coulis, 70
Chili, Blue-Ribbon, 38
Chili powder, California, buying, 99
chocolate
    Black Mamba Cookies, 108
    Chocolate Chiffon Cake, 177
    Cocoa Berry Yogurt
        Mousse, 110, **111**
    Cookie Shop Chocolate Chip
        Cookies, **78**, 79
    Gianduia Sandwich Cookies, 126
    "Hasn't Failed Me Yet" Cocoa
        Icing, 104
    Mrs. D's "She Ain't Heavy"
        Chocolate Cake, 104, **105**
chorizo
    about, 232
    Cod with Local Wax Beans, Chorizo,
        and Soy-Sherry Sauce, 230, **231**
Chowder, Lobster, Corn, and
    Smoked Fish, 17
Citrus Sauce, Grilled Salmon
    with, 276
clams
    buying, tip for, 192
    Linguine with Clams and *Bagna
        Cauda* Butter, 93

Roasted Peppers and Clams with
    Pasta Strands, **190,** 191
Cocoa Berry Yogurt
    Mousse, 110, **111**
Cod with Local Wax Beans, Chorizo,
    and Soy-Sherry Sauce, 230, **231**
condiments
    Bagna Cauda Butter, 94
    Basic Curry Powder, 53
    Chermoula, 136
    Chili Oil, 99
    Chunky Tomato Salsa
        Compote, 224
    Harissa, 134
    Onion Jam, 143
    Parsley Oil, 44
    Preserved Lemons, 137
    Roasted Whole Garlic, 221
cookies and bars
    Black Mamba Cookies, 108
    Cookie Shop Chocolate Chip
        Cookies, **78,** 79
    Crunchy Peanut Bars, 86, **87**
    Gianduia Sandwich Cookies, 126
    Gingerbread Little Cakes, 214
    Raspberry-Filled
        Shortbread Fingers, 81
Corn, Lobster, and Smoked
    Fish Chowder, 17
Crab Cakes Worth the Price, 34
cranberries
    Cranberry Muffins from
        Nantucket, 216, **217**
    frozen, chopping, 217
Croquettes, "Red" Rice, 150
Croutons, Quick Garlic, 32
Cucumber and Pork Stir-Fried
    with Egg, 267
Cumin-Flavored Meatballs
    with Onion Jam and Spicy
    Tomato Sauce, 142
Currants and Pine Nuts, Sicilian-Style
    Swordfish Stuffed with, 274
Curry Powder, Basic, 53

d

dahl
    Pesto-Crusted Halibut with
        Red Lentil Dahl, 60, **61**
    preparing and serving, 61
desserts
    Black Mamba Cookies, 108
    Blueberry Turnovers, 168, **169**
    Cherry Turnovers (var.), 169
    Chocolate Chiffon Cake, 177
    Cocoa Berry Yogurt
        Mousse, 110, **111**
    Cookie Shop Chocolate Chip
        Cookies, **78,** 79
    Crunchy Peanut Bars, 86, **87**
    Fresh Lime Mousse, 128
    Gianduia Sandwich Cookies, 126
    Gingerbread Little Cakes, 214
    Grapefruit Curd Bites (var.), 83
    Hazelnut Angel Cake, 127
    High-Ratio Lemon-Buttermilk
        Pound Cake, 180
    Lemon Curd Bites, 83, **84**
    Lemon-Lime Buttermilk Pound
        Cake (var.), 181
    Lemon Sour Cream or Yogurt
        Pound Cake (var.), 181
    Lemon Turnovers (var.), 169
    Mrs. D's "She Ain't Heavy"
        Chocolate Cake, 104, **105**
    Nectarine-Raspberry
        Crisp, **206,** 207
    Orange Buttermilk
        Pound Cake (var.), 181
    Pineapple Flan, 129
    Raspberry-Filled Shortbread
        Fingers, 81
    Rhubarb-Strawberry Pie, 209, **210**
    Zuccotto alla Ricotta, 174, **175**
dips
    Bagna Cauda Butter, 94
    Hot Spinach-Artichoke Dip, 220

dough
    Basic Pizza Dough, 26
    Flaky Piecrust, 212
    Pizza Crust, 170
Dressing, Basic French, 256
duck
    breasts, scoring skin of, 64
    Roast Duck Breast with
        Apple Purée, 64

e

eggplant
    Chicken Provençal, 72
    Creamy Mashed Eggplant
        with Peas, 56
    Eggplant Lasagne, 255
eggs
    Chicago-Style Breakfast
        Pan Pizza, 170
    Cucumber and Pork Stir-Fried
        with Egg, 267
    Deviled Eggs with Shrimp and
        Olives, 196
    Pasta alla Carbonara, 246, **247**
    Tuna Bagnat, 68, **69**
    Tunisian Fried Pastries with
        Egg, **132,** 133
escarole
    Autumn Strata (var.), 167
    Escarole with Roasted Shallots, 45
    washing, 45

f

fish
    Cod with Local Wax Beans, Chorizo,
        and Soy-Sherry Sauce, 230, **231**
    Fish Soup with Sour Orange, 198
    Fish Stock, 21
    Grilled Salmon with Citrus
        Sauce, 276

Lobster, Corn, and Smoked Fish
    Chowder, 17
Pesto-Crusted Halibut with Red
    Lentil Dahl, 60, **61**
Sicilian-Style Swordfish Stuffed with
    Currants and Pine Nuts, 274
Spicy Tuna, 159
Trout Braised with Caramel, Celery
    and Fish Sauce, **264,** 265
Tuna Bagnat, 68, **69**
Tuna with Tomatoes, 135
Tunisian Fish Ball Tagine, **138,** 139
Tunisian Fried Pastries with
    Egg, **132,** 133
flans
Pineapple Flan, 129
Sweet Pea Flan with Carrot
    Vinaigrette, **42,** 43
Fritters, Chickpea, 153
fruits. *See also specific fruits*
citrus, juicing, tip for, 85
citrus, preparing flavored
    sugar from, 276

g

garlic
Bagna Cauda Butter, 94
Grilled Chicken Breasts with Garlic
    and Parsley, 222
Quick Garlic Croutons, 32
Roasted Whole Garlic, 221
Stir-Fried Lamb with Garlic and
    Basil, **160,** 161
Gingerbread Little Cakes, 214
grapefruit
Grapefruit Curd Bites (var.), 83
Grilled Salmon with Citrus
    Sauce, 276
juicing, tip for, 85
Grapes, Quail and Sausage Braised
    with, 248, **249**

Green Beans, Pesto, and Potatoes,
    Pasta Ribbons with, 188, **189**
greens
Arugula Salad with Goat's Milk
    Yogurt Dressing, 233
Autumn Strata (var.), 167
Escarole with Roasted Shallots, 45
Green Mango Salad with Shrimp
    and Avocado, 272
Hot Spinach-Artichoke Dip, 220
Lamb's Lettuce with Raw
    Asparagus, Pistachios, and
    Parmigiano-Reggiano, 245
Puréed Spinach Soup, 54
romaine, measuring, tip for, 33
Shrimp Cooked in Romesco with
    Wilted Spinach, **240,** 241
Simple, Scrumptious Caesar Salad
    with Quick Garlic Croutons, 32
Stuffed Squid with Piquillo
    Pepper Coulis, 70

h

Halibut, Pesto-Crusted, with
    Red Lentil Dahl, 60, **61**
harissa
about, 134
recipe for, 134
hazelnuts
Gianduia Sandwich Cookies, 126
Hazelnut Angel Cake, 127
Shrimp Cooked in Romesco with
    Wilted Spinach, **240,** 241
herbs *See also* Basil
Chermoula, 136
Parsley Oil, 44
Honey, Quail with Bacon and, 100
hors d'oeuvres *See* Appetizers

I

lamb
Chickpea and Lamb Soup, 148
Stir-Fried Lamb with Garlic and
    Basil, **160,** 161
Lasagne, Eggplant, 255
Latkes, Potato, Herb and Onion, 63
lemons
Flamenco Potato Salad with
    Lemon Dressing, 202
Grilled Salmon with Citrus
    Sauce, 276
High-Ratio Lemon-Buttermilk
    Pound Cake, 180
juicing, tip for, 85
Lemon Curd Bites, 83, **84**
Lemon-Lime Buttermilk Pound
    Cake (var.), 181
Lemon Sour Cream or Yogurt
    Pound Cake (var.), 181
Lemon Turnovers (var.), 169
Preserved Lemons, 137
lentils
Lentil, Sesame and Sunflower
    Burgers, 257, **258**
Pesto-Crusted Halibut with
    Red Lentil Dahl, 60, **61**
red, buying, 61
limes
Fresh Lime Mousse, 128
Grilled Salmon with Citrus
    Sauce, 276
juicing, tip for, 85
Lemon-Lime Buttermilk Pound
    Cake (var.), 181
Linguine with Clams and *Bagna
    Cauda* Butter, 93
lobster
Lobster, Corn, and Smoked
    Fish Chowder, 17
Lobster Stock, 19

m

Mango, Green, Salad with Shrimp and
Avocado, 272

meatballs

Cumin-Flavored Meatballs
with Onion Jam and Spicy
Tomato Sauce, 142

Real Meatballs and
Spaghetti, **114,** 115

meats *See* Beef; Lamb; Pork

mousse

Cocoa Berry Yogurt Mousse,
110, **111**

Fresh Lime Mousse, 128

Muffins, Cranberry, from
Nantucket, 216, **217**

mushrooms

Autumn Strata (var.), 167

Mushroom Turnovers with
Curry Powder, 52

Turkey Mushroom Burgers
with Chunky Tomato Salsa
Compote, 224

Mussels with Spicy Italian
Sausage, 237

n

Nectarine-Raspberry
Crisp, **206,** 207

noodles

Syrian Rice with Vermicelli, 141

Thai-Style Rice Noodles in
Soup, **156,** 157

nuts

Crunchy Peanut Bars, 86, **87**

Gianduia Sandwich Cookies, 126

Hazelnut Angel Cake, 127

Lamb's Lettuce with Raw
Asparagus, Pistachios, and
Parmigiano-Reggiano, 245

Peanut Wafers, 260, **261**

Rice with Fresh Cheese, Nuts
and Vegetables,
Moghul Style, **252,** 253

Sicilian-Style Swordfish Stuffed with
Currants and Pine Nuts, 274

Zuccotto alla Ricotta, 174, **175**

o

oats

Cookie Shop Chocolate Chip
Cookies, **78,** 79

Lentil, Sesame and
Sunflower Burgers, 257, **258**

Nectarine-Raspberry
Crisp, **206,** 207

oils, flavored

Chili Oil, 99

Parsley Oil, 44

olives

Chicken Provençal, 72

Deviled Eggs with Shrimp
and Olives, 196

Maria's Roast Chicken with Meat
and Olive Stuffing, 200

Panisse with Tomatoes and
Black Olives, 28

Tuna Bagnat, 68, **69**

onions

Onion Jam, 143

Tarte Flambée with Caramelized
Onions, Smoked Bacon,
and Creamy Cheese, 23, **24**

oranges

Fish Soup with Sour Orange, 198

Grilled Salmon with Citrus
Sauce, 276

juicing, tip for, 85

Orange Buttermilk Pound
Cake (var.), 181

Sicilian-Style Swordfish Stuffed with
Currants and Pine Nuts, 274

p

Panir or Fresh Cheese, 254

Panisse with Tomatoes and
Black Olives, 28

Parmesan Roasted Asparagus, 117

Parsley Oil, 44

pasta

Beet-Flavored Pasta Stuffed
with a Ricotta-Beet Filling
Topped with Brown Butter and
Poppy Seeds, 185

cooking, tips for, 116

Eggplant Lasagne, 255

Linguine with Clams and *Bagna
Cauda* Butter, 93

Pasta alla Carbonara, 246, **247**

Pasta Ribbons with Pesto, Green
Beans, and Potatoes, 188, **189**

Penne with Shrimp, Artichokes,
and Feta, **14,** 15

Real Meatballs and Spaghetti,
114, 115

Roasted Peppers and Clams with
Pasta Strands, **190,** 191

pastries and turnovers

Blueberry Turnovers, 168, **169**

Cherry Turnovers (var.), 169

Lemon Turnovers (var.), 169

Mushroom Turnovers with
Curry Powder, 52

Tunisian Fried Pastries with
Egg, **132,** 133

peanuts

Crunchy Peanut Bars, 86, **87**

Peanut Wafers, 260, **261**

peas

Creamy Mashed Eggplant
with Peas, 56

Pasta alla Carbonara, 246, **247**

Rice with Fresh Cheese,
Nuts and Vegetables, Moghul
Style, **252,** 253
Sweet Pea Flan with Carrot
Vinaigrette, **42,** 43
Penne with Shrimp, Artichokes,
and Feta, **14,** 15
peppers *See also* Chiles
Harissa, 134
Roasted Peppers and Clams with
Pasta Strands, **190,** 191
pesto
Pasta Ribbons with Pesto, Green
Beans, and Potatoes, 188, **189**
Pesto-Crusted Halibut with Red
Lentil Dahl, 60, **61**
Saturday Summer Strata, 166, **167**
pies, savory
Biscuit Breakfast Pizzas (var.), 171
Chicago-Style Breakfast
Pan Pizza, 170
Tarte Flambée with Caramelized
Onions, Smoked Bacon, and
Creamy Cheese, 23, **24**
pies, sweet
baking, 211
Flaky Piecrust for, 212
Rhubarb-Strawberry Pie, 209, **210**
Pineapple Flan, 129
Pine Nuts, Sicilian-Style Swordfish
Stuffed with Currants and, 274
pistachios
Lamb's Lettuce with Raw
Asparagus, Pistachios, and
Parmigiano-Reggiano, 245
Rice with Fresh Cheese, Nuts
and Vegetables, Moghul
Style, **252,** 253
Zuccotto alla Ricotta, 174, **175**
pizza
Basic Pizza Dough, 26
Biscuit Breakfast Pizzas (var.), 171

Chicago-Style Breakfast
Pan Pizza, 170
Pizza Crust, 170
pork *See also* Bacon; Sausages
Baby Back Ribs with Espresso BBQ
Sauce, **90,** 91
Blue-Ribbon Chili, 38
Cucumber and Pork Stir-Fried
with Egg, 267
Home-Style Pork Chops in
Lemon Marinade, 197
Maria's Roast Chicken with
Meat and Olive Stuffing, 200
Real Meatballs and
Spaghetti, **114,** 115
potatoes
Chicken Provençal, 72
Flamenco Potato Salad with Lemon
Dressing, 202
Pasta Ribbons with Pesto, Green
Beans, and Potatoes, 188, **189**
Potato, Herb and Onion Latkes, 63
recipe variation (for Tunisian Fried
Pastries with Egg) using, 133
poultry *See* Chicken; Duck; Quail; Turkey
prosciutto
Autumn Strata, 167
Saturday Summer Strata, 166, **167**

q

quail
Quail and Sausage Braised with
Grapes, 248, **249**
Quail with Bacon and Honey, 100
Queso fresco, about, 225

r

raspberries
Nectarine-Raspberry
Crisp, **206,** 207
Raspberry-Filled Shortbread
Fingers, 81
Rhubarb-Strawberry Pie, 209, **210**
Ribs, Baby Back, with
Espresso BBQ Sauce, **90,** 91
rice *See also* Risotto
Arborio Rice Coating, 98
"Red" Rice Croquettes, 150
Rice with Fresh Cheese,
Nuts and Vegetables, Moghul
Style, **252,** 253
Syrian Rice with Vermicelli, 141
Rice Noodles in Soup,
Thai-Style, **156,** 157
risotto
Saffron Risotto with Butternut
Squash, **120,** 121
Rosemary Braised Veal
Shank, 74, **75**

s

saffron
about, 122
Saffron Risotto with Butternut
Squash, **120,** 121
salads
Arugula Salad with Goat's Milk
Yogurt Dressing, 233
Flamenco Potato Salad with
Lemon Dressing, 202
Green Mango Salad with Shrimp
and Avocado, 272
Lamb's Lettuce with Raw
Asparagus, Pistachios, and
Parmigiano-Reggiano, 245

Simple, Scrumptious Caesar Salad
    with Quick Garlic Croutons, 32
Salmon, Grilled, with Citrus
    Sauce, 276
sandwiches
    Lentil, Sesame and Sunflower
        Burgers, 257, **258**
    Tuna Bagnat, 68, **69**
    Turkey Mushroom Burgers
        with Chunky Tomato Salsa
        Compote, 224
sauces
    Basic Tomato Sauce, 47
    Spicy Tomato Sauce, 143
sausages
    Chicago-Style Breakfast
        Pan Pizza, 170
    chorizo, about, 232
    Cod with Local Wax Beans, Chorizo,
        and Soy-Sherry Sauce, 230, **231**
    Mussels with Spicy Italian
        Sausage, 237
    Quail and Sausage Braised with
        Grapes, 248, **249**
Sesame, Lentil, and Sunflower
    Burgers, 257, **258**
Shallots, Roasted, Escarole with, 45
shellfish
    Crab Cakes Worth the Price, 34
    Deviled Eggs with Shrimp
        and Olives, 196
    Green Mango Salad with Shrimp
        and Avocado, 272
    Linguine with Clams and *Bagna
        Cauda* Butter, 93
    Lobster, Corn, and Smoked
        Fish Chowder, 17
    Lobster Stock, 19
    Mussels with Spicy Italian
        Sausage, 237
    Penne with Shrimp, Artichokes,
        and Feta, **14,** 15

Roasted Peppers and Clams with
    Pasta Strands, **190,** 191
Shrimp Cooked in Romesco with
    Wilted Spinach, **240,** 241
Shrimp with Fresh Coconut Milk,
    Calabaza, and Avocado, 234
Stuffed Squid with Piquillo
    Pepper Coulis, 70
Two-Minute Calamari Sicilian
    Lifeguard Style, 46, **47**
Shortbread Fingers,
    Raspberry-Filled, 81
shrimp
    Deviled Eggs with Shrimp
        and Olives, 196
    Green Mango Salad with Shrimp
        and Avocado, 272
    Penne with Shrimp, Artichokes,
        and Feta, **14,** 15
    Shrimp Cooked in Romesco with
        Wilted Spinach, **240,** 241
    Shrimp with Fresh Coconut Milk,
        Calabaza, and Avocado, 234
soups
    Chicken Stock, 123
    Chickpea and Lamb Soup, 148
    Fish Soup with Sour Orange, 198
    Fish Stock, 21
    Lobster, Corn, and Smoked
        Fish Chowder, 17
    Lobster Stock, 19
    Puréed Spinach Soup, 54
    Thai-Style Rice Noodles
        in Soup, **156,** 157
spaghetti
    cooking, tips for, 116
    Real Meatballs and
        Spaghetti, **114,** 115
spinach
    Autumn Strata (var.), 167
    Hot Spinach-Artichoke Dip, 220

Puréed Spinach Soup, 54
Shrimp Cooked in Romesco with
    Wilted Spinach, **240,** 241
squash
    Saffron Risotto with Butternut
        Squash, **120,** 121
    Shrimp with Fresh Coconut Milk,
        Calabaza, and Avocado, 234
squid
    Stuffed Squid with Piquillo
        Pepper Coulis, 70
    Two-Minute Calamari Sicilian
        Lifeguard Style, 46, **47**
stews
    Blue-Ribbon Chili, 38
    Chicken and Cornmeal
        Dumplings with Aromatic
        Vegetables (var.), 37
    Chicken and Dumplings with
        Aromatic Vegetables, 36
    Chicken and Herbed
        Dumplings with Aromatic
        Vegetables (var.), 37
    Chicken Provençal, 72
stock
    Chicken Stock, 123
    Fish Stock, 21
    Lobster Stock, 19
stratas
    Autumn Strata (var.), 167
    Saturday Summer Strata, 166, **167**
strawberries
    Cocoa Berry Yogurt Mousse, 110, **111**
    Rhubarb-Strawberry Pie, 209, **210**
Sunflower, Lentil, and Sesame
    Burgers, 257, **258**
swiss chard
    Autumn Strata (var.), 167
    Stuffed Squid with Piquillo
        Pepper Coulis, 70
Swordfish, Sicilian-Style,
    Stuffed with Currants and
    Pine Nuts, 274

t

Tagine, Tunisian Fish Ball, **138,** 139

tarts
Grapefruit Curd Bites (var.), 83
Lemon Curd Bites, 83, **84**
Tarte Flambée with Caramelized
Onions, Smoked Bacon, and
Creamy Cheese, 23, **24**

tofu
Braised Beef with Beancurd, 162

tomatoes
Basic Tomato Sauce, 47
Chicken Provençal, 72
Chunky Tomato Salsa
Compote, 224
Eggplant Lasagne, 255
Panisse with Tomatoes and
Black Olives, 28
Real Meatballs and
Spaghetti, **114,** 115
Saturday Summer Strata, 166, **167**
Shrimp Cooked in Romesco with
Wilted Spinach, **240,** 241
Spicy Tomato Sauce, 143
Tomato Concassé, 227
Tuna with Tomatoes, 135
Tunisian Fish Ball Tagine, **138,** 139
Trout Braised with Caramel, Celery
and Fish Sauce, **264,** 265

tuna
Spicy Tuna, 159
Tuna *Bagnat*, 68, **69**
Tuna with Tomatoes, 135
Tunisian Fried Pastries with
Egg, 132, 133
Turkey Mushroom Burgers
with Chunky Tomato Salsa
Compote, 224
turnovers *See* Pastries and Turnovers

V

veal
Real Meatballs and
Spaghetti, **114,** 115
Rosemary Braised Veal
Shank, 74, **75**
vegetables *See specific vegetables*
Vermicelli, Syrian Rice with, 141

W

Wafers, Peanut, 260, **261**

y

yogurt
Arugula Salad with Goat's Milk
Yogurt Dressing, 233
Cocoa Berry Yogurt
Mousse, 110, **111**
Yogurt Pound Cake (var.), 181

Z

Zuccotto alla Ricotta, 174, **175**